THE PARA
AND SOUTH ROW
BLACKHEATH

A triumph in the 18th century unintentional town planning

BY
NEIL RHIND
MBE FSA

In memoriam

Bill Bonwitt
Michael Burton
Hazel Egan
John Measures

Published by
the Bookshop on the Heath
for the Blackheath Society

2012

By the same author

The consumer wakes up (Pergamon Press), 1968

Make me understand pregnancy and childbirth (with Dr Hazel Egan) (Dickens Press) 1969

The Greenwich Theatre Book (with Hilary Evans) (Greenwich Theatre) 1969

Blackheath Centenary 1871-1971 (Greater London Council) 1971

A Scottish painter and his world: Gordon Gunn (Impulse Publications) 1972

Martin House: a short history of the Blackheath Literary Institution (Blackheath Preservation Trust) 1975

Blackheath Village & Environs: Vol I (Bookshop Blackheath) 1976: revised edition 1993

Blackheath Village & Environs: Vol II (Bookshop Blackheath) 1983

The Heath: a companion volume to the above. (Bookshop Blackheath & Warwick Leadlay Gallery) 1987; revised edition 2002

Royal Blackheath: List of members of the Royal Blackheath Golf Club 1766-1923 (Royal Blackheath Golf Club, Eltham) 1992; since revised by the author in computer form

Blackheath names: an index of the names of Blackheath people & their addresses covering the years 1691-1940. (Published by the author in computer form) 1993; constantly revised.

Blackheath Proprietary School: Alumni and proprietors 1831-1907.(Published by the author in computer form) 1993; since revised.

Blackheath Village Trail & Guide (with Tony Aldous). (Blackheath Society) 2005

Greenwich Park: Walking through history. (Friends of Greenwich Park) 2007.

Wyberton House: the story of a house in Lee Terrace and its residents 1868-2000. (Published by the residents) 2009

The Pagoda & Montagu House (with Philip Cooper) Bookshop on the Heath. 2012

In preparation at March 2012:

Blackheath Village & Environs: Vol III

The Greenwich Strip Drawings of Nicholas Hawksmoor 1705-1707 (with Julian Watson)

© Copyright
Neil Rhind. April 2012

ISBN: 978-0-9565327-2-5

First published in
Great Britain 2012

Designed by Mel May

Copy editing by Jane Birkett

Printed by Oakwood Print
For the Blackheath Society and
the Bookshop on the Heath
No: 74 Tranquil Vale, Blackheath,
London SE3 7BW

Alec Wylie

The Paragon in 2005

South Place, Blackheath.

Blackheath Society

South Row in the about 1902 (Note mistake in caption)

Contents

ACKNOWLEDGEMENTS AND THANKS

This book suffered a prolonged gestation but over the last two decades a large number of people and organisations have made a not insubstantial input towards its completion.

They drew my attention to sources and documents which I may not have discovered by myself and corrected slips and errors. If there is a lack of a name or institution then I trust I will be forgiven and it be accepted that no discourtesy is intended. Any mistakes or omissions are entirely the responsibility of the author. Adjustments will be made to any subsequent edition. My primary thanks must go to those who have been so closely involved in recent years and helped to facilitate publication in no small measure now rather than in many year's time:

Anne Burton
George Greaves
Michael Egan
The Blackheath Society (especially Howard Shields & Frank Smith)
Frank Woodgate & the Paragon Management Co Ltd
Liz Rhind

John Coulter, Julian Watson

The late: Bill Bonwitt, Frank Boswell, Charles Bernard Brown, John Cator, Sir Michael Grieson, Brian Kendall, Louis Leff, David & Amory Leggatt, John Measures, Doris Rhind, Stephen Moreton Prichard, Wilfred (Bunny) Teagle, Jean Wait & Anna Wayte

Tony Aldous, John F Burton, Mr & Mrs Desmond Churcher, Angela Croome, Gideon Franklin, F R Furber, Donovan Hailstone, John Harman, Michael Hook, Ralph Hyde, Ian Langlands, Lionel Lewis, Guy Obbard, Mary Mills, Iain Rhind, Jo Stocks, Frances Ward, David Warren, Anthony B Warrick, Elizabeth Wiggans

Jennie O'Keefe & Jonathan Partington at the Greenwich Heritage Centre
Sally Eaton & Linda Merman at the Lewisham Local History Centre

The Blackheath Preservation Trust Ltd; the staff of the British Library; English Heritage; Find my Past; Google; members of the Greenwich Historical Society and the Lewisham Local History Society; Guildhall Library (City of London); the London Library; the London Metropolitan Archives and Family Record Centre; Morden College; National Archives; National Monuments Record (English Heritage); the Central Reference Library of the City of Westminster

Jane Birkett: copy editor
Mel May: designer
Oakwood Print: printer

PREFACE

The Paragon, a crescent of 14 houses in seven blocks all linked by single-storey colonnades, is one of the finest surviving examples of late 18th century architectural design in London and, arguably, one of the best groups of buildings in the country. Listed Grade I on the English Heritage schedule of buildings of outstanding architectural quality and historic interest, the Paragon can be confidently ranked alongside the Royal Crescent at Bath, Park Crescent at Regent's Park and the Crescent at Buxton. Other building groups will come to mind.

Yet until the late 1960s, little that was accurate was known about the origins of this unique block, and the date was usually given as vaguely '… late 18th century', even in official records. Fortunately, the information which could establish the correct dates and the story of its construction and its subsequent history was to be found in the records and files for those who bothered to look. The first person to take a serious stab at this was German-born William (known to all as Bill) Bonwitt, a retired manufacturing stationer, who lived in one of the flats in the restored Paragon during the late 1960s and 1970s. Bonwitt had long been intrigued by the quality and unusual nature of his home and decided, in 1975, to research its origins.

This volume was started with the intention of publishing a book in 1994 to mark the 200th anniversary of the building of the Paragon and other neighbouring houses on the south-east corner of Blackheath by the architect/surveyor Michael Searles. Like so many well-meant intentions, circumstances overtook reality and publication was pushed later and later. Many became exasperated and the author decided that it was time to take a grip before it was too late.

After all, Bill Bonwitt had published (as long ago as 1976) his pamphlet on the Paragon and Paragon House but since this ground-breaking effort a considerable amount of information, both in primary and secondary sources have been uncovered. Bill died in 1992 so there is no longer the chance to publish a revised edition, even if he intended to in his lifetime.

He had found the exact date for the construction of the Paragon crescent hard to verify, due to the lack of original development records. Much more recently it was discovered in the Greenwich Vestry Minutes (for January 1794) that the parish judged it necessary to erect a boundary stone near a new development called the Paragon, on the south side of Blackheath, which would straddle the parish boundary with Lewisham. There is no doubt that this was an important and reliable record for the existence of the new property. Nevertheless, it still lacked the definition needed. While rate-book records for the parish of Greenwich survive, the seven Paragon houses in that parish were not occupied until 1800. The Lewisham rate records for the period 1790–1805 had been lost.

1

Commercial street and court directories embracing south-east London were not yet published in sufficient detail to be of great use.

However, in 2006 the Times Digital Archive was launched, providing instant access to a huge number of references to the Paragon in that newspaper: sale notices, including one in 1791, and birth, marriage and death notices for many of the early inhabitants.

In 2008 legal documents were unearthed, referring to transactions as early as 1791, which related to the building and occupation of Paragon House, on the corner of South Row and Pond Road, Blackheath. These papers are the primary sources we had hoped to discover to turn assumptions into facts, and provide some necessary corrections. Therefore, it seemed sensible for this study to draw together the different strands of the story of Searles' development in Blackheath in a new book. Much original research was undertaken by Bill Bonwitt and I enthusiastically acknowledge it here. But I have corrected some parts (as he would have done in any event) and I have added a considerable amount of new material, some of which we found together and some revealed more recently.

The only liberty I have taken, about which, I suspect, Bonwitt would not have been one hundred per cent delighted, is the transfer of a lengthy section of his original booklet into an appendix. This is the extraordinary story of the Misses Eliza Robertson and Charlotte Sharp, the swindlers who occupied No 3 The Paragon for a short while in the early 19th century. I have moved it because I decided that it interrupted the narrative flow, giving too much importance to a short, albeit fascinating, episode in the history of the buildings, which developed largely away from it.

Fortunately, the Paragon, and Colonnade House to the west, narrowly survived the dreadful damage of the 1939–45 war. Their full glory was only revealed after a painstaking, almost single-handed effort by the late Charles Bernard Brown (1910–1990), an architect who revelled in the delights of Georgian architecture at a time when it was held in somewhat less regard than from the 1950s. It seemed bizarre to Blackheath residents and visitors from the 1970s that anyone, let alone municipal planners, could have contemplated, twenty-five years earlier, the removal of even the bomb-battered fragments of Searles' masterpiece for post-war municipal housing. After all, were not the Paragon and Colonnade House some of the finest examples of their style in London? And this in a district rich in a wide variety of architectural forms, from the late 18th century to the late 19th century?

Bill Bonwitt's original introduction set the scene. He wrote that the visitor who arrived in Greenwich in the time-honoured way, namely by water, landed within a stone's throw of the Seamen's Hospital, later the Royal Naval College and now the University of Greenwich and Trinity College of Music. The blocks which are the masterpiece of the Wren / Hawksmoor /Vanbrugh period.

Bonwitt continued: 'After admiring the beauty of that famous complex [the visitor] usually ascends the steep escarpment to the Old Royal Observatory and beyond. This can be done in either of two ways: through Greenwich Park or up Crooms Hill. The latter is paradise for lovers of English architecture, for all periods from about 1630 to 1850 is well represented.' As the late Sir Nikolaus Pevsner (1902–1983) commented: 'There are not many streets near London which give so good and sustained an idea of the well-to-do private house from the 17th to the early 19th century.'

The chief glory of Crooms Hill is the collection of many 18th-century (mostly Georgian) houses, and as this book is concerned with a splendid example of the later period of that century, a few short remarks on the Georgian style are appropriate.

Clearly, the style derives its name from the reigns of four successive monarchs called George, who occupied the British throne from 1727 to 1830. George III (reigned 1760–1820) became incapacitated during his later life and when, in 1810, his reason was judged to have failed, his eldest son (George IV [1762–1830]), was appointed Prince Regent, succeeding his father in 1820. In architectural shorthand, buildings designed during the period from the middle of the 18th to the early part of the 19th century are usually termed 'Georgian' although by 1820 the term 'Regency' had been applied. This indicated a gentle drift away from the classically refined proportions of the basic Georgian style into something more frivolous.

The Georgian mode is based on the design philosophy of the Italian architect Andrea Palladio (1508–1580) whose rules of architectural grammar were to delight the English architect Inigo Jones (1573–1652). It is claimed that the first serious building in the Palladian style in Britain was Jones's Queen's House, on the north edge of Greenwich Park, initially constructed for Ann of Denmark, consort to James I (VI).

Palladianism is an arrangement distinguished by its reliance on symmetry and proportion, the architectural ornamentation usually being confined to columns or colonnaded porticos. Bill Bonwitt found the words he wanted in the Penguin Dictionary of Architecture (1966): "Georgian architecture is classical in its major exteriors but on the smaller, domestic scale it still has the sensible plainness of the Queen Anne style". Perhaps it is because of this plainness that the contrast between Georgian architecture and that of Wren is as great as that between Victorian design and the modern movement of the 20th century. The latter is often called 'functional' but the same epithet can be applied to the Georgian style, with the marked contrast that many 20th-century architects (the modernists) sometimes seemed to disregard the very symmetry and proportion which so pleases the eye of other students.

To those who have come to love Georgian design, as expressed in Britain and its colonies, it must be the combination of functionalism, symmetry and proportion that renders the form so attractive and intellectually pleasing. Fortunately, Greenwich and Blackheath provide many examples for the student of the style to admire: among the best are the Circus in Greenwich and some houses on Crooms Hill and the Paragon and Colonnade House in Blackheath.

The history of the Paragon and South Row was summarised by Bonwitt as one of rise, fall and resurrection. The scheme, a crescent of 14 houses, and seven more to the west, enjoyed only a brief period of architectural harmony before alteration and decay set in, leading to a slow, creeping decline towards the end of the 1930s. It then suffered terrible damage in the 1939-45 war. But, thanks to the inspiration of Charles Bernard Brown, it arose from the rubble of the Blitz to take its place among London's – if not Britain's – architectural treasures. Its story is recounted in the following pages.

Neil Rhind
The Lane
Blackheath Park
London
April 2012

South Row in 1966. B Soc.

CHAPTER ONE
ORIGINS

T he land upon which the Paragon and South Row were built was, at least until the Middle Ages, part of the open ground of Blackheath. The Heath then extended northwards to include the land subsequently enclosed for Greenwich Park. To the south, the Heath may have included what is now Montpelier Row and westwards it stretched to the end of the back gardens on the west side of Dartmouth Row. The eastern boundary is probably unchanged from what it was in earliest times.

The early Britons left traces of settlement in the area, so did the Romans, whose remains have been found in Greenwich Park and on the Heath. The shadows of Saxon tumuli can still be seen in Greenwich Park. As now, the Heath was windswept, a treeless plain and, on the south boundaries, sloping towards marshy ground created by the rivulets that flowed down from Shooters Hill along various small valleys. One of these ran along the rear of the Paragon gardens, eventually through Blackheath Village. The presence of clean water dictated, to some extent, the reason why this area of south-east London was to become valuable agricultural land and to be developed for building from the late 18th century onwards.

The Domesday Book, compiled in 1085-6, mentions the Hundred of Grenviz, which was to become the Hundred of Blackheath in 1279, at the time of King Edward 1. Among the various settlements described and assessed in the Hundred of Grenviz was one written Witenemers. It consisted of arable land, meadows and woods, and reference is made to a small population and cottages. It was worth £5. The place name Witenemers has been interpreted as meaning 'the marsh where the Witans [councillors] met'; although the modern view is that it was a corruption of the Saxon word Writtlemarsh or Wriddlemarsh. Certainly, by the 15th century Wricklemarsh was the recorded name for a substantial area of the district, to the south of the Heath and covering what is now called the Cator Estate, parts of Kidbrooke and Lee Green.

During the 16th century the Wricklemarsh estate came into the possession of Edward Blount (1559-1617), of the Middle Temple. Blount (sometimes written Blunt) was remembered through the use of his family name until the early 18th century to identify the heart of Blackheath Village, in its valley, as Blount's Hole. Wricklemarsh was also the family home of his son, Thomas (1580-1655) and then of the latter's second surviving son, also Thomas (1605-1678). This was the noted Colonel Blunt, whose enthusiasm for scientific invention led him to earn a number of mentions in the diaries of both John Evelyn (1620-1706) and Samuel Pepys (1633-1703).

Finally, a new generation of the Blount family (another Thomas and his wife, Anne, née Oldfield) took over the property in 1656. And in 1669 the Blounts sold Wricklemarsh to London merchant John Morden, for £1,950. At the same time Morden bought, for £2,250, other land nearby.

John Morden (1623-1708) was a Turkey merchant, i.e., he traded in the exports of Turkey and the Levant, and was a member of the Turkey Company. He was active in London's social and business life and there is good evidence that he was God-fearing and concerned for the welfare of others less fortunate than himself. For example, he served on the trustee board of the Bishop of Rochester's Bromley College, founded in 1666 for the poor widows of clergymen of the diocese. In 1688 he was knighted by James II but not for any known political reasons.

Morden and his wife Susannah (née Brand) came to live in the old Blount house, at Wricklemarsh. Its location is not exactly known but it seems to have been placed on the ridge of high ground now marked by Cresswell Park, from where the views over the Kid Brook valley towards the Heath to the north and the Kentish hills to the south would have been pleasing.

The Mordens were not blessed with children but knew that they would leave a substantial estate in money and land. Inspired, perhaps, by the example of Bromley College, Sir John built and endowed an institution to provide a refuge for merchants, members of the Church of England, mostly from the Turkey Company (his own) who were down on their luck through no fault of their own: the oft-quoted 'decay'd Turkey Merchants'. The building, set on the south-east corner of Blackheath, is attributed without evidence to Sir Christopher Wren (1632-1723). Building work was started in 1695 and the first pensioners were admitted in June 1700. The administrative history of Morden's College is not part of this volume; full details can be found elsewhere in this series and in books quoted in the Bibliography in Volume II.

Sir John Morden supported his College with the benefits derived from the Wricklemarsh estate, which, by his will, was left to the College, subject to a life interest for his wife, Lady Susannah. Morden died in September 1708. During his lifetime, the College had catered for as many as twelve pensioners at any one time. However, as the income of the College proved insufficient to cover its costs after Morden's death, the num-ber of resident pensioners dwindled, at one stage dropping to just four. This was because the estate had to provide Lady Susannah's pension of £600 a year, with the residue applied to the upkeep of the College and its pensioners. Susannah lived for a further thirteen years and her complex will showed that she was not without money or goods when she died. One clause specified: '£200 to be paid out in buying a velvet pall for the use of the College and for setting up Sir John's and my own effigies in stone over the great door in case the same shall not be done in my lifetime.'

On Lady Susannah's death (June 1721) the College trustees owed her £2,640. The trustees found that they were unable to return this to her estate and resolved to dispose of part of Wricklemarsh and invest the proceeds for the benefit of the College. Consequently, much of the land south and west of Morden College, together with the old Wricklemarsh House, was sold, leaving the College set in an 11-acre field to the south-east of Blackheath. The trustees obtained the necessary private Act of Parliament and advertised their proper-ty in the Daily Courant on Saturday, 19 July 1721.

A large Mansion House, lately inhabited by the Lady Morden, deceased, situate in the Parish of Charlton in Kent, with Coach House, stables, out-houses, yards, gardens, orchards, fishponds, vineyard, with a handsome Avenue, is to be lett with or without grounds. Any person desirous to treat for the same may give notice to or leave proposals with Mr. Nathanial Brand [the Treasurer] at Morden College by Black Heath or at his chambers in Thavies Inn, Holborn.

The house was 'empty, out of repair and will cost much to restore' but the surrounding 250 or so acres was good agricultural land. Unfortunately, there were no takers. A further advertisement, also in the Daily Courant, announced that the property was to be disposed of on a 61-year lease for a premium of £2,500 and an annual rent of £100. Even so, it was not until the end of 1722 that an offer was accepted. This was from Gregory Page, a man of enormous wealth, who lived in a grand house a little past the north-east corner of Greenwich Park.

Gregory Page and John Cator

The offer from Page was substantial: £9,000. This amount represented 32 years' purchase of the annual income of £269, with timber worth about £350. The sale was finalised on 30 August 1723. For his money, Page obtained a considerable acreage in the parishes of Charlton, Lewisham, Eltham and Kidbrooke, including the 'messuage and appurtenances known as the Three Tuns', a public house later to be re-established on its present site in Tranquil Vale (see Volume I [revised 1993] of this series]. This pub was renamed 'O'Neills' in 1994 although the swing sign keeps the old name.

The total spread of Morden's land came to just over 271 acres and its north and east boundaries can be defined today where it ran along the east side of Lee Road, through Blackheath Village and along Montpelier Row and South Row, turning south a little to the edge of the Morden College field at the north-east end of what is now Morden Road.

Gregory Page (1689-1775) succeeded his father, also named Gregory, who died in 1720 when his son was only thirty-one. Both were immensely rich from a brewery in Wapping, much property, and profitable investments in the South Sea and East India companies. Gregory senior was Member of Parliament for New Shoreham, in Kent, for many years. In 1711 and 1712 the Page family invested in South Sea stock, which rose in value so that at the time of Page senior's death it was valued at £550 a share. His executors were anxious to settle his estate and distribute the various legacies. They sold the stock in July or August 1720, at the top of the market when it had raised to £1,000 a share, just over nine times its nominal value, clearing over £200,000. In the following month the bubble burst and South Sea stock crashed to £175.

Having purchased the Wricklemarsh estate, Gregory junior tore down the old house and built a new mansion near the site of today's Church of St Michael and All Angels, in Blackheath Park. North of the house was a circular pond which still existed in the 1950s, when it was filled in by order of Greenwich Borough Council, after completion of the municipal estate in the early 1950s behind the Paragon. Pond Road is named after Sir Gregory's ornamental pond and not after the Prince of Wales pond near its northern end.

The new house is said to have cost its owner between £90,000 and £123,000 – reports vary – and the construction is thought to have taken just under a year. The house was built in an early Georgian classical form inspired, it is said, by Colen Campbell's scheme for Houghton Hall, in Norfolk, built for Sir Robert Walpole (1676-1745). The centre block was linked with two projecting wings housing the stables and other offices. The main entrance was on the south side, with steps to a colonnaded portico, surmounted by a balustrade. The north entrance was also approached by two flights of steps but lacked a portico. To the south was large rectangular water (Lays Pond), fed by one of the streams flowing off Shooters Hill.

A well, just south of the present railway tunnel near Morden Road, supplied Page's house with some of its water, but a further supply was held in the rectangular basin on the Heath, the Prince of Wales pond, now concrete lined and the resort of model-boat enthusiasts.

The architect was John James (1672-1746), one-time Clerk of Works to the Greenwich Hospital (now the University of Greenwich and Trinity College of Music). James had also been responsible for the design and erection of the tower of St Alphege Church, Greenwich, but was best known for St George's, Hanover Square. Locally, he is further credited as the architect for Park Hall, the house at the south-east end of Crooms Hill, built in 1723.

Wricklemarsh House was considered one of the finest houses in Britain. It was sumptuously fitted and furnished, and the walls boasted a fine art collection, consisting of over 118 paintings, among them works by Van Dyck, Rubens, Veronese, Titian, Caravaggio, Brueghel and Wouvermans.

Sir Gregory had married Martha Kennard of Yalding, Kent, in 1721 but, like the Mordens, they had no children. Page died in 1775 at the age of 86, predeceased by Martha in 1767. The house and estate passed to his heir, his great-nephew Sir Gregory Turner of Ambrosden, Oxfordshire (who was to take the additional name of Page). He had no wish to live at Wricklemarsh House and in 1783 the house, with its parks, gardens, effects and paintings, was auctioned by Christie & Ansell. The house and grounds were bought by John Cator (1728-1806), a timber merchant, of Becken-ham.

Cator paid £22,550 – something of a bargain for an estate of over 270 acres six to seven miles from the City of London, and a substantial mansion which had cost over £100,000 to build sixty years earlier. He attempted to let the house, even negotiating with the War Office for its use as an officer cadet school. The negotiations proved abortive and Wricklemarsh House, although in an '... excellent state of repair', was pulled down and the materials sold. The process started in 1787 and was completed over the next few years, although the shell of the main block may have been evident as late as 1808. John Cator realised £14,000 from the sale of the building materials alone. Most of the land, which Page had laid out as a formal park, was leased for farming.

Cator came from Quaker stock. During the Commonwealth, the family was settled in Ross-on-Wye, Herefordshire. John's father subsequently moved to Bromley, Kent, where John was born in 1728. He married Mary, daughter of Peter Collinson, reputedly the first Englishman to introduce North American conifers into the British Isles. John Cator's fortune came from a timber-importing business at Mould Strand Wharf (the site of the old Bankside power station – now Tate Modern). He lived at Southwark until he purchased the Manor of Beckenham in 1773 and moved to a house on Stumps Hill which he called Beckenham Place.

The property was fitted up with 'much taste and elegance', but, some time after 1783, he gilded the lily by adding a huge, out-of-scale portico and columns. These had been salvaged from Wricklemarsh House when Cator sold off its materials. Cator's house survives, albeit in poor condition, and is used, presently, as the headquarters of Beckenham Place Golf Club – a municipal course and reputedly one of the busiest in Europe.

In 1774 John Cator represented Wallingford, Berkshire, in Parliament. He was Sheriff of Kent in 1781 and elected Member of Parliament for Ipswich in the same year. However, he was unseated for bribery in 1784. Notwithstanding this seeming disgrace, Cator was a cultivated and erudite man and owned an extensive library. Samuel Johnson, James Boswell and Fanny d'Arblay (Fanny Burney) were among the friends who visited his mansion.

Fanny Burney (1752-1840) did not always speak well of Cator but Johnson (1709-1784), in one of his letters to Esther Thrale [(Mrs Piozzi) 1739-1821], described him thus: 'Cator has a rough, manly, independent understanding, and does not spoil it by complaisance. He never speaks merely to please and seldom is mistaken in things which he has any right to know. There is much good in his character and much usefulness in his knowledge.' A tribute was paid to his business acumen by learned counsel during a court hearing (see Appendix 1): 'Mr Cator had as good eyes as any man and did not gape and let people steal the teeth out of his mouth.'

This was the man who, after a modest but financially successful career in business and some public service, in his late fifties decided to exploit his Blackheath freehold, part of which remained in the ownership of his descendants until the 1980s. Soon after the greater part of Wricklemarsh House had been demolished, during the late 1780s, John Cator sold development leases on some land on the southern and western boundaries of the estate. The first house to be erected was Park House, in Blackheath Village, which was built in 1787 as the result of a lease to Captain Thomas Larkins (d.1794), of the East India Company. It is a finely proportioned, elegant building, with a columned portico, reached by two flights of steps. The facade was fashioned with stone taken from Wricklemarsh when the mansion was demolished for scrap. Captain Larkins' house is now the Roman Catholic Presbytery in Cresswell Park, Blackheath Village.

At the start of the 1790s Cator embarked on the development of the entire northern boundary of his Blackheath estate, from what is now the northeast end of Wemyss Road through to Morden Road. The result was Montpelier Row, South Row and the Paragon, and most of it survives despite war damage and attempts to redevelop the bulk of it in the post-war years of 1945 to 1960.

The best surviving mid-18th-century map of the Page (later Cator) estate is that of cartographer John Rocque (d.1747), drawn between the years 1741–45. This shows the estate as a landscaped park, with the great house in the centre and the principal carriage drive running north. Beyond the emparked ground is the open waste of Blackheath. On the west side is the central triangle and crossroad of what is now Blackheath Village, marked by a handful of buildings and including the old Three Tuns public house.

Once the property passed to Cator (and perhaps for the few years between Page's death and the sale of 1783) most of the ground was let for agricultural purposes. The principal farmer for the greater part of Wricklemarsh was John Umphleby, who was succeeded by his son, William, in 1792. Most agricultural tenancies were for 12 years; at the end of each span, renewal was usually automatic, but the holding could be reduced, or a condition added which would recover some or all of the land at the landlord's request – usually on six months' notice so that the farmer did not lose a harvest. This is what must have happened in the early 1790s at Wricklemarsh when Cator entered into arrangements with builders for land development.

Most of Cator's estate lay in the parishes of Charlton and Kidbrooke, but much of the northern strip was in Lewisham and not all of it was freehold, having been leased by Page from the Earl of Dartmouth for 1,000 years, subject to paying an annual fine to the parish. These payments were for encroachments on what had been parochial waste (i.e., the fringes of the open space of Blackheath). This was land which, while not common, was entitled to be used by parishioners as though it was common land.

The Lewisham Land Tax returns confirm this: in 1793 John Cator's assessment for 'land on Blackheath' was $20; in 1794 it had doubled to $40. Clearly, something was going on and it is safe to assume that Cator had increased the land value by development. Certainly, it was in January 1794 that there was the first prima facie evidence of building works on the Heath frontage: a note in the Greenwich parish Vestry Minutes says that building was taking place on its boundary with the Lewisham parish and that a stone should be set up to mark the parish division (it is still there).

John Cator was not himself a builder. Cator's landholdings were substantial but were used as a safe bank for his capital – his land had to earn its keep, largely from agricultural use. But with the expansion of London as the business centre of the world and the base for imperial administration, the desire for quality housing was growing rapidly. The demand was largely from an expanding middle class: professional men, tied to Parliament, the City or the docks, military establishments and factories in London or along the Thames. They needed to be close to their businesses but did not enjoy living in the noise and stink of the City. They wanted a rural domestic life, with fresh air and clean water, some land for pleasure grounds and congenial neighbours, but also to be able to reach their counting houses, the Inns of Court or the Exchange on a daily basis. Blackheath was one of the districts that fulfilled such requirements. The residents were the first real commuters in that a regular coach service had been established by the 1780s, picking up passengers at the public houses, in particular the Green Man at the top of Blackheath Hill. It was also easy enough to travel to Greenwich and continue the journey to the City and Westminster by water.

In fact, the process of development in Blackheath was well-established. The building of quality houses in Dartmouth Row from as early as the 1690s, and on Maze Hill and in West Grove and Crooms Hill from the early 18th century had been for that purpose. Sir John Vanbrugh's construction of his mock-medieval village, at the south end of Maze Hill, as well as the subsequent development of that road, had established the district as a desirable one in which to live for those engaged in the professions, manufacturing and commerce.

The trustees of Morden College may have sold Wricklemarsh in 1722, on the death of the founder's widow, but they retained substantial landholdings close by, and continued to acquire more. They granted the lease which saw the development of Grotes Buildings on the south side of the Heath in the 1770s but then there was a lull. The end of the 18th century marked the beginning of a new rush of building in Blackheath that was not to stop until the 1860s as more and more of the grounds attached to large mansions were swallowed up by villas for the professional classes. For example, when John Cator decided to develop his Blackheath land in the mid-1790s, so did the Lord Eliot, with his Heath frontage on what is now Eliot Place and Eliot Vale.

If John Cator had a scheme in mind for his Blackheath estate, then there is no surviving evidence as to what this was. Certainly, it was not the success of exploiting one plot which led to another. The development of part of what is now Blackheath Village – Montpelier Row, South Row and the Paragon – was all of a piece, if looked at on a time scale, in that the buildings went up (or were planned) in the years 1793 to 1798. The lease to Captain Larkins, of the East India Company, was for a large plot but saw only one house erected in what is now Cresswell Park. The other leases, to Searles for the Paragon site and South Row, and to William Dyer for Montpelier Row, were development leases for a number of houses, largely in terrace form. It could be conjectured that Cator intended one architect or builder to design the whole – Michael Searles had, after all, experience in volume building (see below) – but if this was the case, there is nothing to prove it.

The position chosen for the Paragon was probably because of the convenience of established carriageways, and the opportunity to build houses which might face more or less north at the front but would enjoy splendid views over the old Page parkland to the south and west. But it is hard to find a sound reason why the Paragon should have been sited at the very east of the estate, looking north and east and lost within a drop in the ground. Bonwitt thought he could provide a solution: the John Rocque plan of 1741-6 shows two eccentric roads at the north–east corner of Page's estate. The arc runs from near Morden College at the east, almost to the carriageway which became Pond Road, with its centre towards the south.

In the late 17th century, this was the part of Blackheath known as the 'New Common' but the title appears in no other reference than the report on Samuel Travers' Survey of the Royal Manor of East Greenwich, of 1696-7. The problem with acceptance of this theory is that the Rocque map, although remarkable for the period, is not one hundred per cent accurate and that the lines marked were probably little more than cart tracks leading to Morden College. Bonwitt's theory cannot be confirmed by the carefully surveyed War Office plan of Cator's estate drawn in 1783 when the government was considering using Wricklemarsh House as a military academy.

Michael Searles erected his crescent just below the southernmost of these two lines, well within the boundary of the estate, perhaps using one of the crescent-shaped cart tracks as his inspiration for the carriage drive (see Rocque map). The crescent here was the Paragon but at the west end was the straight run of South Row, facing an established roadway to Morden College and a public footpath to the farms at neighbouring Kidbrooke

The name and the arrangement were not unique: the first crescent-shaped terrace called The Paragon of which there is information was in Richmond, constructed in the first quarter of the 18th century. Next came the one in Bath, built in 1768, and in 1789/90 a Paragon in New Kent Road was constructed to the designs of Michael Searles. Further Paragons were built in Margate, Bristol, and Hackney in London. The epithet had originally been employed to describe a diamond of flawless quality but was used as a general term of excellence in the 17th century. During the 18th century it came to embrace a regard for the fine quality of construction and craftsmanship as well as design. This was achieved in the Blackheath Paragon in full measure, the crescent now acknowledged as almost the apotheosis of the architectural form generally described as Georgian.

Cator's incentive for granting development leases on his Blackheath property clearly stemmed from the basic fact that he needed to obtain a return for his investment (albeit modest in both respects). There was an income to be obtained from agricultural lettings of the estate but there was also a demand for housing, particularly at the top end of the market.

Central London in the late 18th century (with a population of about 960,000 in 1801) was dirty and ill-drained. The City was crowded and the streets were dangerous after dark. There was no public health system which could cope with the adequate removal of effluent. The swarms of rats and other vermin, the inadequate control of infections which encouraged the spread of contagious diseases, coupled with the smoke of thousands of chimneys, meant that the City of London was not attractive as a residential base. There had been little progress since the Great Plague of 1664–5, when the Court and Cabinet had had to move from London to avoid infection. Samuel Pepys' Navy Office moved to Greenwich, as his Diaries testify in fascinating detail.

So, where better to offer quality houses for those who could afford them than the semi-rural slopes of Blackheath and Hampstead? Both were sited on well-draining soils and open to fresh air and clean water, but within easy reach of the City. Residents of Blackheath would be south of the Thames but there were sufficient crossings and ferrymen to reduce the inconvenience. Inevitably, there were businessmen anxious to respond to the needs of the time.

John Cator was one of these, but he was a landowner and took little risk: the development leases required the developers to fund the building works, and to find tenants for the houses they erected. The market then, as always, was fickle. Ebbs and flows of business confidence or the interruption of war could upset financial forecasts from year to year. When Cator granted the lease to Michael Searles, the war with France had just commenced and thousands of naval and army personnel were recruited, including many officers who might have been enthusiastic purchasers of smart new houses in Blackheath. When the war ended (albeit temporarily) in 1801 they were equally swiftly reduced to half-pay. Nevertheless, overseas business continued to flourish: total imports and exports for the United Kingdom in the year 1700 were valued at about £13 million. From 1756 onwards there was a boom and by 1790 the figure had risen to £24 million. During the last decade of the 18th century, the value of foreign and colonial trade doubled.

Although the short-lived peace provided an opportunity to revive the lucrative trading patterns with Britain's empire, events did not move fast enough for some, like Michael Searles. His business base foundered, almost certainly because he was overstretched financially. By the time Britain and France resumed hostilities, it was too late for recovery and the construction and fitting of the Paragon and South Row moved painfully slowly, the entire estate not being complete and occupied until 1806: the year after the Battle of Trafalgar.

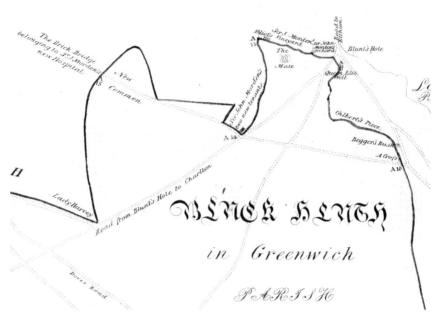

Samuel Travers' Survey of the Royal Manor of East Greenwich, 1695-96. B Soc.

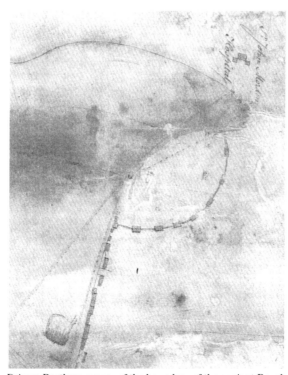

Drivers Brothers survey of the boundary of the ancient Royal
Manor of East Greenwich, 1808. B Soc

CHAPTER two
CONSTRUCTION

John Cator granted a development lease to Michael Searles, an architect and surveyor with considerable experience and expertise locally, almost certainly because he had met him (as early as 1790) and knew of his work. The landowner must have enjoyed some confidence in Searles for it is unlikely that he would have entered into a business relationship without recommendation. Also, to judge by the results, neither Searles nor Cator felt any desire to provide dwellings for the working man, or to cram as many houses as possible on to their development plot – about 30 acres all told. The style was to be generous, with plenty of land for forecourts, gardens and outhouses.

The architect

Michael Searles was well-connected, being the third generation of his family to be engaged as surveyor by the trustees of Morden College, and certainly the most professional and gentlemanly member of the Searle family.

He was born in 1751, the son of Michael Searles Senior (c.1720-1799), and grandson of Leonard Searles, a carpenter. Leonard (c.1690-1776), who worked in Greenwich and had good relations with Morden College, obtained building leases (for plots on the north side of Blackheath Hill) from the College in the 1730s, in addition to acting as its surveyor until about 1756. As well as working for the College – on a freelance basis – he worked for other clients, dabbled a little in property and seems to have lived a busy but blameless life. He was succeeded as College surveyor by his son Michael who held the job until 1773, almost certainly being paid for work as and when required rather than being on a weekly wage. The fact that Searles' father and his son were carpenters by trade should not be understood to mean that they spent their time at the sawyer's bench. It was quite common for men in those days to be apprenticed in a craft but if they enjoyed any extra degree of acumen or business sense, they would hang up their aprons and employ others to undertake the physical jobs. As principals, they found the clients, organised the work and dealt with the business. This same approach applied to brick-layers, plasterers, glaziers, masons and plumbers.

Leonard may well have been mostly engaged in craft work for the College but Michael senior developed a greater interest in the surveying side of his work. Maps of Morden College land and plots, drawn by him, survive in its muniment room to this day. It is, perhaps, from this somewhat 'artistic' endeavour that the family laid down the elements of interest and skill which led Michael junior into the profession of surveyor and architect.

Michael Searles Snr may have designed buildings. As a surveyor he would have had a sound knowledge of building practice and could have instructed local builders to create or alter structures in the relatively simple styles then prevailing. Unfortunately, little detail of local architectural partnerships and practices has survived, and the buildings of that date in Greenwich and Lewisham which stand today cannot be attributed to a particular designer. A good example of a fine building, for which one might assume that it bears the handprints of a professional designing architect, is the block known today as Lydia and Sherwell houses, in Dartmouth Grove. But they were 'designed' by John Groves, a bricklayer, and Thomas Gayfere (1721-1812), a stonemason, albeit a famous one.

There is a faint possibility that Searles senior was responsible for designing and building Grotes Buildings. Dating from about 1773-4, these were a speculation by Andrew Grote, a merchant banker, of Point House in West Grove, on the north side of the Heath. Grote (1710-1788) rented his house from Morden College and may well have met Searles on day-to-day matters concerning repairs, alterations and decorations. It would make sense to employ him for the new buildings if Searles had demonstrated the right technical ability.

It was not until the 19th century that architecture as a profession, separate from surveying and building construction management, established itself outside the sphere of the great monuments, major houses and public works of the day. In fact, Michael Searles Jnr may be the first serious designer-architect who can be identified in Greenwich undertaking modest domestic work at the time. Certainly, the author knows of none but, of course, the records of others may be lost.

Michael junior may have been born in Greenwich, although his birth was registered on10 November at the parish church of St Mary Magdalene in Woolwich. At the tender age of 15 he was apprenticed to his uncle, another Leonard Searles ('the younger') who was a carpenter, goldsmith and citizen of London. This did not mean that Leonard was a practising goldsmith – he had been a carpenter, taught by his father – but the Goldsmiths' Company operated an apprenticeship scheme. Those who completed their articles were able to trade within the City and enjoyed the freedom of London. Michael may have been apprenticed to Leonard Searles but he probably learned the skills of carpentry and the art of surveying from his father. It is possible that he actively assisted him in the preparation of the property plans for Morden College.

Searles was married in October 1771, to one Catherine (her surname has not been discovered), who was to bear him at least twelve children – nine of whom survived into adulthood.

Perhaps because of the City connections, Michael developed his professional interests beyond the parish of Greenwich and its immediate neighbourhood. Once his articles were completed (in 1773) he set up as a surveyor, although resident in the City at the time. Thereafter, his principal professional activity seems to have been in surveying and land measurement. In the late 1780s, Searles was living in what is now the Old Kent Road, in a house belonging to Samuel Driver, surveyor and nurseryman. Driver's sons, Abraham and William, inherited their father's estate, but had been raised in their mother's religious persuasion, as Quakers. They commissioned Searles to survey their property in Bermondsey and, in 1784, employed him to design a development of houses called Surrey Place, fronting on to the Old Kent Road and numbered as 234 to 252 (even). This is the earliest known architectural scheme of Searles and was the precursor of a number of ter-races designed by him.

At the same time Searles was employed by other Bermondsey landowners, among them John Rolls, and John Goad who was a member of the Society of Friends. Through these contacts he was to obtain commissions for single houses and terraces, shops and other work. The period from 1784 until 1793 (when the foundations of the Blackheath Paragon were being laid) was extremely busy. The Quaker connection led to a number of introductions to wealthy men and Searles was not slow in convincing them to employ him in designing their houses, built either for residence or for speculation. Houses and schemes in Deptford, Kennington and elsewhere were produced from his drawing board. His circumstances improved with a legacy and business ventures in partnership with others, two of whom (William Austin and Messrs Pedder, Bates & Co.) engaged in brick-making. Indeed, Searles was a beneficiary of Austin's will as a residuary legatee.

The first scheme which could be said to have been the testing ground for Searles' Blackheath Paragon came as a result of a commission from John Rolls in the late 1780s. This was for the development of a plot in Southwark, on what is now called the New Kent Road. It was for a crescent-shaped terrace and was to be known as The Paragon. The developers were a con-sortium of builders, although Rolls was obliged to provide lessees for the individual houses once completed: 12 were built although 14 were planned.

The Southwark Paragon was a success. It was completed in 1788 and Michael Searles lived at No 2 for a while. John Rolls Jnr lived at No 8 from the start until 1804, and George Gwilt (1746-1807), the architect who worked on Thomas Brandram's house at Belmont Hill, Lee (later called The Cedars), was also a resident.

The technical details and drawings for the Southwark Paragon have been lost but a late 19th-century photograph survives which shows the terrace to consist of three-storey houses, with arched windows on the ground floor. Each house was dressed with a mansard roof with one central small window. Although the entrance porches were to the side, each of the houses was linked at the ground-floor front with four Doric columns in Coade Stone. The photographs show structures above the colonnades but it is likely that the original design did not include these. Also, the terrace suffered the addition of three extra houses, designed in the same style by architect William Chadwick, in 1825. The Southwark Paragon was demolished in 1898 to be replaced by a school, although, according to Bonwitt, one of the Chadwick houses survived until the 1960s.

Searles' next major work was a development in his old parish: Greenwich. This was the Circus – a scheme in which Searles took a personal risk by his investment in the equity along with a consortium of tradesmen and others. The site was once part of garden ground attached to a school which stood at the bottom (north-west) end of Crooms Hill (the building was demolished for the development of Burney Street in 1839). The landowner was the proprietor of the school, since 1781 the Revd Peter James, MA (d.1791). The plan was for a 22-house crescent on the north side of the plot, with an intention to match the design on the south side. As with so many of Searles' schemes, disaster struck early: Peter James died in 1791 and although the drawing for the Circus is captioned 'Built 1790–1791', only 12 houses were completed by 1793; two of the remainder were not ready for occupation until 1810. The plan shows five main blocks – each containing four three-storey dwellings, all linked by porches, which were single storey between the blocks but, somewhat eccentrically, on three storeys within the blocks.

Despite many alterations and war damage, the north side of the Circus (now numbered as 21 to 42 Gloucester Circus) retains much of Searles' original scheme although the harmonious pattern has been destroyed irrevocably. The development of the south side, originally as Gloucester Terrace, was designed by George Gwilt – see above. It was a complex business, not helped by the antagonistic approach to the matter by Peter James's son, Captain Robert Grey James. The unhappy story is carefully examined in Bonwitt's article in the Greenwich and Lewisham Antiquarian Society's *Transactions* (Vol. X, No. 2, 1986).

Meanwhile, Michael Searles kept himself active with commissions for private houses and other works. The volume of business through his office in the period 1785 to 1795 was considerable and he would have employed some assistants in those days without telephones, emails, photocopiers and the other aids common to late-20th-century business administration.

One of the well-connected businessmen Searles met during the course of his professional activities was John Cator, the timber merchant of Southwark and Beckenham. The first evidence of contact came in 1790 when Searles applied for the post of Surveyor to the Court of Commissioners of Sewers of Surrey and Kent, of which Cator (as well as John Rolls) was a committee member. Bonwitt surmises that he was not slow in pressing them to engage him. There was competition for the job and Searles came bottom of the poll. Earlier that year he had successfully tendered to design and build a new workhouse, at Streatham. Unfortunately, the tradesmen engaged on the work (bricklayers and carpenters) proved less than adequate and Searles, having approved payments for their work, was dismissed for incompetence. A court action followed, with Searles suing the Streatham Guardians for administering the poor law, and they engaged in a cross-action against Searles for the recovery of additional expenses and costs. Despite the complexities of the business (fully detailed by Bonwitt in his monograph on Searles) the architect seems not to have lost any status or standing among his clients.

Commissions continued to be obtained and Searles engaged in a number of self-financing speculations, such as the Circus at Greenwich (see above). There was a substantial scheme for the Driver brothers: Surrey Square, now part of SE17, which incorporates a classical structure comprising three houses winged by archetypal three-storey terraces: these were built during 1792 and survive today. Such was the volume of work [at the time] that Searles took on a partner (one Robert Roberts, a surveyor of Bermondsey). He was also engaged in the teaching of apprentices.

Michael Searles produced some of his most inspired work at this time: a house for a John Jeffrey (neither the man nor the location of his house – if built – have been discovered) and a fine villa, Clare House, for timber merchant and paper-mill owner John Larking, at East Malling in Kent. This house also survives and can be accepted as one of Searles' most attractive compositions, incorporating many of the unusual features which he delighted in drawing, even though not all were wholly successful.

Another property, of 1792, was a design for a house for Dr William Mitford (d.1797). Bonwitt and others have misread the caption on the original drawing as 'Dr Metford'. The house stood at the south-east end of what is Vanbrugh Fields. It was known, for many years, as the Manor House, and was distinctive for its half-moon southern wing, enjoying a fine cast-iron curved balcony and covering [see plate no 132, Volume II of this series].The same design element is to be seen on Clare House at East Malling. Unfortunately, the Manor House was demolished in 1957 for the development of the Parkside flats, facing Vanbrugh Park, no one at the time realising both the importance of the building and its architect.

A further local building in which Michael Searles was clearly involved is No 17 West Grove (for many years known as Manna Mead) which was a replacement, in 1793, for a house which the architect's own survey declared to be 'beyond repair'. The style of the replacement – for Captain William Hamilton – bears much similarity to Searles' other work and it would be reasonable to attribute its design to him. Other surviving properties in Blackheath which have been credited to Searles, from time to time but without any written and often little stylistic proof are Heathfield House, No 1 Eliot Place; parts of Montpelier Row; and Nos 20-22 Dartmouth Hill – the latter a trifle altered since its appearance in the early 1780s.

Much earlier, Searles had been involved in the marketing of a patent roofing product which was applied to Montague House, at the south-west end of

Dartmouth Hill. The promotion leaflet is illustrated by an elevation of the house – of late-17th-century origins – and it is clear that the later 18th-century bowed elevation at the west end is the subject of the date stone on the building. This elevation and the fine Doric porch could well be from Searles' drawing board. The variety of known work by Searles at that period included villas (some of quite eccentric design involving hexagonal frontages, colonnades, and round tower-like constructions) for self-made men, some attempts at church repairs at Beckenham and Dartford, and even plans for a gaol at Poole, Dorset.

At this point in the career of Michael Searles, and the historical narrative, we reach the time when he embarked on his most dramatic and lasting exercise in architecture: the design of the estate on John Cator's land at Blackheath.

It seems sensible here to give a brief description of Michael Searles' life and career after 1800 until its conclusion. There is no doubt that the turn of the century also saw the turn of his fortunes and his artistic ability. Colonnade House, in South Row, must have been designed by him and may have been a scheme drawn at the same time, or a little after, the Paragon plans. It is an outstanding creation, perhaps one of his best single houses along with Clare House, at East Malling. But thereafter, little evidence of major work survives and only a handful of drawings; certainly, nothing of any great distinction has been traced to the period after about 1805. Work must have been available and his son, also Michael, joined him in the practice but there is no evidence that the boy was blessed with his father's qualities.

The end came in October 1813. *The Times* newspaper, which had carried advertisements for the Paragon houses so often in the early years, printed the following notice of his death in its issue of Thursday, 22 October 1813:

At Christopher Godmonde's esq, at Lee, Kent, Mr Searles senior, of the Kent Road in consequence of the overturning of his chaise on Saturday last.

Mr Godmonde lived at The Firs, a house in what is now called Old Road. The accident probably happened at a dangerous bend in the road, the position still marked by Boone's Almshouse Chapel, a small but very fine Grade I building and recently [2010] restored for the Blackheath Historic Buildings Preservation Trust by architects Madeleine Adams and Charlie MacKeith.

A bare three years later, in 1816, Mrs Catherine Searles died 'after a long and painful illness', according to *The Times* of 31 October that year.

CHAPTER THREE
BUILDING AND THE BUILDINGS

It **is one of** the difficulties in writing local history that many of the primary documents required for reconstructing the tenancy records of anything but a substantial detached domestic house of the 18th century are usually lost, especially in London. This is certainly the case with the Paragon and South Row. Other than that for Paragon House, the original development leases granted to Searles and the subsequent under-leases to the first occupants of these houses have not survived, or have not been rediscovered to date. A few fragments have been found in archives but not enough for the historian to ignore secondary sources: commercial directories, newspaper advertisements and so on.

The most precise 19th-century primary record, after the parish rate books, is the enumerated census returns but these are only available for the period 1841 to 1891 and then only every tenth year. Nevertheless, these lists do provide important substantial details of householders and their families, and it is possible to construct quite accurate tenancy schedules for the houses.

No 7 The Paragon was in a curious administrative position in that the parish boundary ran through the middle of the property and the unfortunate resident had to pay rates to both parishes. The matter is further complicated in that some Paragon residents (five or six to judge from the parish records of the 1830s) rented extra land to the south, part of which fell in the parish of Charlton. This meant that the owner of No 7 had to pay rates to a third local authority as well at some time; with Nos 1, 3, 5, 6 and 8 all with a similar obligation, although in some cases, it has to be said, very small.. The reform of local government which led to the merging of parishes into London boroughs in 1899 resolved those anomalies: the parishes of Greenwich, Kidbrooke and Charlton were amalgamated administratively as the Greenwich Borough Council. This meant that the entire Paragon and Paragon House (No 1 South Row) were scheduled as part of Greenwich. The remainder of South Row, to the west, stayed part of Lewisham.

The division of the Paragon between Lewisham and Greenwich had an unfortunate consequence. The rate books for Greenwich parish (and later the Borough Council) have survived almost complete from the 1780s to 1930, while those of Lewisham before 1912 have largely gone, with a few exceptions. A Highway Surveyors' book provides much detail for the period 1798 to 1812 (it is less helpful thereafter) but the great bulk of the 19th-century Lewisham parish rate records were scrapped as waste paper in the early 1950s.

Fortunately, the commercial and court directories for the County of Kent (of which Greenwich and Lewisham were considered part until 1889), published by the Post Office or by Kelly & Co. for almost every year since the 1860s, list most residents of middle-class property and are satisfyingly accurate.

It is from these records that the residents of the Paragon and South Row can be discovered. All those found have been listed in full in the second section of this book. It will be seen that most were men of substance, merchants (in the early years), businessmen, army and naval officers, and even clergymen in a surprising number of cases in the mid-19th-century. This situation applied until the start of the Great War in 1914. After the war, from 1919 onwards, there is a marked change. Many of the houses passed into multiple occupation, a number as boarding houses or private hotels.

This was often the fate of buildings coming towards the end of their leases and, effectively, what seemed to be their useful life. Although the Paragon in particular was long considered a block of architectural interest, the Georgian style had not, by the 1920s, been rediscovered by many architectural historians and lacked the popular appeal it was to achieve again in the 1950s and 1960s. The houses were too large for a servantless class, were inconvenient and lacked modern facilities, being difficult to heat adequately and to keep clean, and were expensive to repair and redecorate. Although property was relatively cheap, few bothered to buy their own homes and most houses until the 1930s, particularly on the Blackheath Cator estate, were rented, the landlord being responsible for structural repairs.

Even so, the Paragon and South Row retained a fashionable respectability, if not in quite the same league as Blackheath Park, Dartmouth Row and Eliot Place. It is interesting to speculate what would have been their fate and subsequent history if the 1939–45 war had not intervened in such a dramatic way.

Building the Paragon

The development lease which Michael Searles obtained from John Cator, must have allowed him to build a number of houses on the north-east edge of Cator's Blackheath estate. Searles (or his backers) would have carried the cost of erecting the houses and also been obliged to find people willing to buy them or, put more accurately, to encourage people willing to sign leases with Cator for a specific term of years and for an annual rent. Those same lessees would have paid Searles a premium for the cost of building the houses as well as for the fittings according to taste and need.

This arrangement for the speculative building of houses during the 18th and early 19th centuries followed a custom which was time-honoured from the end of the17th century. Many of the great estates in London were entailed to families or held in trust by private trustees or corporations like livery companies, the Church and other institutions. They could not be sold without a private Act of Parliament which, although usually obtainable, was expensive and time-consuming.

Because of this structure of ownership, land or property was let for terms of anything from 60 to 99 years. Ninety-nine years was considered a reasonable life for the average domestic structure so that, when the lease expired, a new arrangement would be made and a new structure either built or the old one substantially repaired. It is important to remember that, until the middle of the 19th century, basic building materials were recyclable. Bricks, often made from the ground upon which a house was to be built, were joined with lime mortar. The mortar could be tapped off a brick and the brick reused (unlike today where hard sand and cement mortars create a bond so strong that it can damage the bricks it holds together). The main timbers, if not damaged by fire or rot, would be used over and over again, especially those used for the frames, beams and joists. Worked stone was a valuable material and commanded a high second-hand price. Lead for pipes and gutters could be melted down and re-cast. A good example was Page's Wricklemarsh. It was a valuable resource which Cator exploited – Captain Thomas Larkins purchased some of the stone cladding from the mansion to face his house in Cresswell Park in 1787. Parts of the fabric of the house no doubt exist in a good number of buildings in south London to this day.

Thus, when a long lease on a building expired the whole process could begin again, the landlord ensuring a steady return on his land for the next three generations at little cost. And so on, and so on. All this would collapse with the development of private domestic houses on huge estates in the outer suburbs of London (and other cities) in the 1920s and 1930s. By the 1960s, everyman wanted to invest in bricks and mortar and own his property freehold.

But in the late 18th century this was not the case and the Paragon and South Row were developed according to the practices then prevailing. Searles' task was to lay down the infrastructure and find skilled contractors who would build the carcases of the houses: the brick shells. A purchaser would then be found who would not only pay Searles for his part of the work, but also pay for the internal arrangements: the window frames, the staircases, the plastering, the architectural details of the fittings and fixtures. As a result, it is doubtful whether any of the Paragon or South Row houses were the same internally, each being finished according to the new owner's wishes and tastes.

Externally, at least, Michael Searles was able in the Paragon to design a series of houses which proved to be his masterpiece in artistic design and attractive town planning. Whether the landowner, John Cator, influenced the design and was also possessed of a high degree of aesthetic judgement, is hard to establish. It may be that his agent advised him with regard to the saleability of the Paragon and South Row houses. And, more importantly, whether they would still be sufficiently attractive to buyers when the initial leases expired and Mr Cator's descendants would be able to re-sell them.

The crescent scheme prepared by Searles was not unique but did contain elements which he had practised with remarkable skill (but without complete financial success) in his Paragon in Southwark and the Circus in Greenwich. He also employed his experience of designing houses in the terrace form, as he had amply demonstrated on the Rolls estate in Bermondsey and Kennington. All this combined in the Paragon at Blackheath, along with the houses in South Row, to create the distillation of the essence of his genius. His may not have been the most important name among late-Georgian architects but he managed in Blackheath to create something which earned him, with historical hindsight, a place among the best designers of his period.

Evidence for the Paragon designs survives in the Drawings Collection of the Royal Institute of British Architects, presented by Mrs C. E. Ford, a member of the Searles family. These reveal that Searles worked on at least three schemes before going forward with a final design which was built.

The first plan was for a solid block in the centre of which was a massive portico in antis, consisting of four Ionic columns and a large sculptured triangular pediment overall. The building would have been two storeys high throughout, above the colonnaded section. The entire structure was to be surmounted by a parapet wall broken by short balustrades. This may not have pleased John Cator because Searles returned to his drawing board. A further scheme shows an elevation looking substantially as built but with the blocks of houses topped by a pediment incorporating a shell motif, similar to one that Searles placed on houses he designed in Surrey Square.

This plan was also rejected but the final drawing shows the Paragon exactly as it was ultimately built: 14 semi-detached houses forming seven blocks, each block consisting of a basement, ground floor, two upper floors and an attic (see illustrations). The blocks are flanked by one-storey colonnades of plain columns of the Tuscan order, surmounted by a frieze and topped by a balustrade of 84 short pillars. At each end of the terrace was a small house equal in height to the colonnades, with rusticated quoins. The blocks are simple and unadorned except for a horizontal string course in line with the balustrades. The essence of the appeal of this scheme rests entirely on symmetry and proportion. The simplicity of the basic creation, with the minimum of decorative features, demonstrated that the architect had finally got it right. (see illustration in Section B)

As if to underline these qualities, Searles introduced some modest variations in the centre block: i.e., Nos 7 and 8 The Paragon. These houses are deeper by 20 feet and this additional depth is used to provide extra blank windows, giving each floor of the two flanks of the centre block two blind and two glazed windows. The front ground-floor win-dows are deeper and of the same size as the windows under the colonnades. The changes here gave an extra solidity and may have been added to provide an optical strengthening: without the additions, the crescent may have given a false impression of weakness over its considerable length. It is interesting to note that the design for Colonnade House (not built until about 1802-03) was actually improved visually by mid-Victorian additions.

The Southwark and Blackheath Paragons, as well as Colonnade House and, above all, Clare House in East Malling, show considerable originality, especially in the use of circular, oval and square spaces, exceptionally so in Clare House. A crescent of semi-detached houses linked by colonnades, such as made up the two Paragons, seems to have been Searles' own invention. The facades of the main blocks with their horizontal string courses, the four-bay width, the Tuscan columns and balustrades are identical. The sole difference was the length of the colonnade, the Southwark Paragon of 1789 being shorter. It had four columns in each section whereas the Blackheath Paragon has five. (It must be remembered that Searles designed only part of the Southwark schemes, with William Chadwick adding his measure in 1825.)

The rear elevations of the two crescents were also quite similar except that the bays of the New Kent Road Paragon extended to the top floor. Clearly, the Southwark design appealed to John Cator and he considered its appearance and layout suitable for the Blackheath development.

The Blackheath Paragon is noted for the architectural success of its front (north-east) elevation: that is what people see and what draws the student of design and the tourist to make the journey to Blackheath. But the rear (south-west) elevation of the Paragon was also carefully designed, although it looks somewhat different now from its original appearance. The semi-circular bays extended only to the second floor (see illustrations), an arrangement which survives in No 14 The Paragon. The bow windows were smaller; the nibs and piers between each set of the three windows were wider. The original construction of the bay windows can still be seen in houses Nos 4 and 14.

All the original windows were surmounted by brick arches which have survived in houses Nos 4, 13 and 14. Another interesting feature of the bays is that each floor was recessed by about three or four inches. When the bays were rebuilt after the war, this feature was retained (see illustrations).

Nos 13 and 14 The Paragon were not altered externally after the war, having been less affected than some of the houses by bomb damage and blast. It is therefore likely that they remain the closest to Searles' completed designs of all the houses (other than Paragon House) in the group. Also, No 13 did not enjoy a semi-circular bay at the rear.

It is conceivable that Searles was still attached to some elements of the design of the Circus in Greenwich, which he completed only a few months before starting work on the Paragon. In the Circus, two houses each with a bay, alternate with two houses each without a bay. Perhaps Searles wished to introduce a similar scheme in the Paragon but later abandoned the idea. The bay construction on Paragon House was similar to that of No 14 The Paragon, but was raised to the full height of the building.

Unfortunately, no estimates or bills relating to the cost of construction have survived. But a house of similar quality and size to Paragon House (No 6 Eliot Place), built in Blackheath in 1797, was insured immediately for £1,600. Paragon House may have cost about the same to build, whereas the houses in the Paragon, being a little smaller and semi-detached, probably cost less. The rateable (or rent) value put on Nos 2 and Nos 4 to 7 of the Paragon by the Greenwich churchwardens was £64. It is safe to assume that an annual rent at the time was worth anything from 10 to 12 per cent of building value for investment purposes: that is, a value on these houses of about £600 to £640.

Because details of the original Paragon and South Row leases and the rents charged have been lost, it is possible to gain a rough idea of these only from the rateable or rent values attached to the houses by the local authority – the parish. In 1800, No 1 The Paragon was rated at £88, which assessment included the house itself, a stable block and a coach house; as noted above, Nos 2 and 4 were rated at £64 each, and house No 3 at £72. The variation depended on the size of garden, outhouses and a variety of other circumstances. At that time John Julius Angerstein's substantial villa (Woodlands), at Mycenae Road, Westcombe Park, was rated at £74; apart from a handful of houses – those of the Governor of the Royal Naval Hospital, his deputy's house, Montague House and Rangers House (both against the Greenwich Park wall) – no other domestic buildings in the parish of Greenwich were rated quite as high as the Paragon buildings.

The first reliably useful dates for which property values survive for all the Lewisham parish houses in the Paragon (Nos 8 to 14) and the houses in South Row are 1817 and 1818. The values attached to the Lewisham Paragon houses were: No 8 at £94, Nos 9 to 13 at £68, and No 14 at £83 (its garden was very small and this value must have included some outhouses and meadows near the Round Pond, to the south). Paragon House was also rated at £83, the enormous Bryan House (No 2 South Row) at £113, and Nos 3 to 6 South Row all at £38; Colonnade House, with its extensive stable block and ground, was rated at £120.

It is worth noting that the rateable values of the Greenwich Paragon houses were the same in 1817 as in 1800–2, so it would be reasonable to assume that the Lewisham figures of 1817 were much as they had been in 1800, and thus comparable. There are some earlier records – Land Tax returns and the aforementioned Lewisham parish Highway Surveyors' book – but these are fragmentary and less authoritative. Nevertheless, they do not argue a much different position on the house valuations.

The rates moved up (and occasionally down) as the years went by and the surrounding fields were swallowed up by building development: St Germans Place in the 1820s, Shooters Hill Road from the late 1830s, and so on. By the end of the 1860s most of the developed suburb of Blackheath was laid out much as we can recognise it today. More ratepayers meant more services, especially as more and more functions of social welfare and administration were added to the local authority burden.

The materials

The materials used in the construction of the Paragon and South Row were simple: yellow London stock bricks of a colour and pattern in use widely in the area. Many houses of an early period, especially in Crooms Hill and Dartmouth Row, had been built using red bricks but the fashion had moved away from that colour. Also, the brick earth available and the techniques of manufacture had changed. Brickfields were being developed to the south of Lee High Road and along what is now Burnt Ash Road. While the houses in Grotes Buildings may have been made with the earth upon which they were to be built, it is unlikely that the same deal was made for the Paragon. One of Searles' business companions was Robert Killick, a brickmaker, and he was among the principal creditors named in a statement of Michael Searles' financial affairs compiled in 1796 (see below). Perhaps he had provided the bricks for the construction and, like many other contractors, had not been paid.

The roof covering was, and still is, slate – almost certainly Welsh slate but there is no evidence as to its origins. The gutters, drainpipes, hopper heads and other external ironmongery would have been in cast iron and lead but it is doubtful whether any of these items survived the war and the subsequent total restoration.

The dressings are of stone (with some replacements cleverly fashioned in fine cement) but the original columns for the Paragon were artificial: they were made of Coade Stone, a patent material comprising ground stone and powdered glass, enjoying similar properties to cement but more durable. The composition and formula (which have been lost although modern techniques of analysis have now revealed the recipe) had been devised in 1722 by Richard Holt, who was unable to exploit his invention.

In 1769 the business was taken over by his daughter Eleanor (1733–1821), by then Mrs Coade. She was blessed with remarkable business acumen and promoted Holt's invention, but called it by her married name and not that of her father.

Mrs Coade's artificial stone proved a huge success and acceptable to even the most exacting specifiers, being used for decorating important buildings all over London. The lions outside the old Lion Brewery, one of which stood on the South Bank near today's Royal Festival Hall, were made of Coade Stone and so were the four statues by Benjamin West (1738–1820) in the vestibule of the Royal Naval College Chapel in Greenwich.

Perhaps the finest local example is the Nelson Pediment on the King William

Building of what is now the University of Greenwich (the erstwhile Royal Naval College). Coade Stone decorations were used on Buckingham Palace, Westminster Abbey, the Bank of England and the Royal Exchange, in fact on most notable public and private buildings of the period.

It was the clear proof of the use of Coade Stone in Blackheath which finally dispelled the myth that the columns of the Paragon came from Wricklemarsh House. Sir Gregory Page's house was finished late in 1724 or early in 1725 and Coade Stone did not come into popular use until 1769. Besides, the Wricklemarsh columns were about 32 inches in diameter, whereas the Paragon columns have a diameter of 18 inches. The base of a Wricklemarsh column, about two feet in height, survived and was found by Charles Bernard Brown, he said, in the back garden of No 103 Blackheath Park. It had been cut for use as- a mounting block. Brown, during his Paragon restoration contract, placed it on the north lawn of the Paragon opposite houses Nos 7 and 8, where it can be seen today, close by the Victorian watering post.

Those of the Paragon columns which survived World War II are marked *'Coade Lambeth'*, and some are said to bear dates between 1793 and 1796. Painting has obliterated most of these marks but in the garden outside No 8 The Paragon is an unpainted column base, used as a plant container. This,though clearly showing the *Coade Lambeth* inscription, bears no date. The base of the pilaster at No 13 The Paragon is of Coade but only the place and date: *London 1793*, can be seen through the encrustations of paint.

The dates on the columns have misled various writers who thought, understandably, that they corresponded to the year of construction of the Paragon. In fact, Coade items were cast in quantities for stock and they may have needed a lengthy period of weathering. In view of the popularity of the Palladian and Classical styles for London's more expensive houses and public buildings, Mrs Coade's factory produced an enormous range of decorative items. Her catalogue shows the variety of ornamental stoneware produced and stocked at the Coade works in Narrow Wall, Lambeth. It is interesting to note that her will (she died in November 1821) indicates that she held a lease on a property in the Paragon, Blackheath; however, it was not possible to identify the house as No 2 until Times Digital revealed that *The Times* had published a sales notice for the house in November 1822. It could be that Searles failed to pay Mrs Coade's bills and that she took a lease for this house instead, as a payment. There is evidence for similar arrangements elsewhere at the Paragon (see below).

The construction period for the Paragon stretched from 1793 until at least 1804: from first footings and foundations through to final fitting-up. Paragon House and Bryan House were erected in the earlier segment of the ten years, and the two pairs of semi-detached houses (Nos 3–6) and Colonnade House, in South Row, were probably fully complete and fitted as late as 1803.

The site was accessible by the rough roads then leading from London and Greenwich and the Thames, by which routes most of the materials would have been transported. Although it may seem obvious, it has to be remembered that all the work of fetching and carrying on site would have been by hand; the longer-distance motive power would have been by horse and cart. The scaffolding was wooden poles. And there would have been many groups of tradesmen, each under their own foreman or employer, probably paid by the day. At least the building site would have been some way off from neighbouring dwellings (the nearest being Morden College) and the few small houses perhaps on the site of the Princess of Wales public house.

When the first houses were ready – Paragon House, Bryan House and Nos 11 and 12 and Nos 13 and 14 The Paragon – new residents would find themselves living for some years on a major building site, exacerbated by the financial failure of Searles in 1796 and the slow process of completion. It is not surprising that there was a considerable turnover in tenancies in the early years of the development's life.

The Paragon crescent was built sides-to-middle, so to speak. Each house, while externally part of a seamless whole, was markedly different inside and it is doubtful whether one exactly matched its neighbour.

What accommodation did the houses afford when they were built? Not much is known from contemporary sources but the early sale notices give some idea, albeit they would have been compiled by estate agents who employed the same degree of marketing hyperbole as still do their professional descendants. Those discovered are quoted in full in the Registers section of this book in which all the known tenants of the various properties are listed, but some extracts are appropriate here.

An advertisement for No 1 The Paragon, which appeared in *The Times* on 24 October 1801, described the arrangement thus:

... the family apartments consist of two handsome drawing rooms, fitted up with great taste; a spacious eating parlour, a gentleman's room, library and boudoir; and excellent entrance hall, and light staircase; eight family bedchambers; dressing rooms; water closets; and admirable nursery and store rooms complete. The servants' apartments are suitable and the domestic offices of every description with good cellaring and dairy. The out-door offices are [a] laundry, men's room, stabling, coach house, attached farm yard, with every requisite for pleasure and economy. The kitchen garden [is] well stocked and in most excellent heart and the pasture land is immediately supplied with fine water ...

Advertisements for other Paragon houses are similar, with mention made of water closets (a novelty), cow houses and dairies. Nos 7 and 8, being the most commodious houses, enjoyed nine bedrooms, and the lofty drawing rooms opened to offer a huge room of 52 ft by 18 ft, with windows to the floor and 'statuary' chimney-pieces; the kitchens were 25 ft by 18 ft, with a butler's pantry and vaulted cellars. Colonnade House, being perhaps the grandest of them all, was not only substantial but expensively arranged and fitted (see below).

An inventory was taken of No 4 The Paragon in October 1833 (the result of which is listed in Appendix III at the end of this book) which itemised everything found in the rooms. The arrangement was as follows: kitchen, scullery, larder, butler's pantry, kitchen passage, two attic rooms, four bedrooms, three water closets, entrance hall, dining room, drawing room, library, schoolroom, anteroom and garden

It is unlikely that many of the floor plans of the houses changed much before 1862. From that year there survives an accurate 'Particulars and Conditions of Sale' for house No 12 The basement, which had a separate servants' entrance, contained one large, south-facing room with a bow window which served as a breakfast room. The remaining space was taken up by a scullery, pantry and larder, and there were wine, beer and coal cellars under the pavement. The ground floor consisted of an entrance hall, dining room, sitting room and two drawing rooms. On the first and second floors were two bedrooms, each for the use of the family. The attic contained four small servants' bedrooms. The space was adequate for a family of, say, five children and up to four servants.

Of Paragon House, only the original layout of the ground floor is known. This is from a plan preserved among the collection of Michael Searles' drawings in the library of the Royal Institute of British Architects. It shows that there was an entrance hall with a staircase and three rooms, of which the one with the bay window was the smallest. Next to it - facing south - was a large reception room; the rest of the ground floor – nearly half – was given over to one large north room of 40 ft by 24 ft, with three large windows. The upper floors probably contained four rooms each and the residential servants' quarters were, as usual, in the attic. The basement was probably similar to that of the Paragon houses and accommodated the kitchens, scullery and other offices.

Further evidence of the original internal arrangement of a house in the Paragon can be found in documents relating to the Misses Sharpe and Robertson, of No 3. These suggest that the two ladies probably leased a finished shell but had their house completed to their own tastes and needs, employing bricklayers, chimney-piece manufacturers, carpenters, glaziers and painters. These details can be deduced, alas, in schedules of Miss Robertson's debts to local tradesmen because she never paid her bills (see Appendix II).

One useful document to survive is the full-coloured floor and house plan, drawn (from a remarkable memory) by the late Francis Kendall, of No 1 The Paragon (with its attached stable block), which almost certainly indicates the original arrangement. This shows remarkable detail and it is reproduced (by kind permission) in this book. What is particularly useful here is that No 1 was destroyed in World War II and Bernard Brown's reconstruction created a fully modern interior. It is also interesting to see how the stable or lodge house was ordered and the planting plan of the garden is the only one discovered of any date.

At the time when the Paragon was built, Greenwich had no universal public drainage system and all effluent was discharged into cesspits, or removed by what were known as night-soil collectors. Public sewers were not installed on a large scale until the 1850s. A water closet features prominently in an advertisement dated 20 July 1804 for the sale of Colonnade House. As the Paragon houses were erected at roughly the same time, it is most likely that they had the same amenity. In the collection of Searles' drawings at the RIBA are some working plans for the conversion of the Rolls Estate Office, which he had built in 1795. He adapted it in 1800 for use as his own residence and lived there until his death in 1813. On these plans are what appear to be water closets and a sort of bathroom on the first floor. The house is still in existence and is now No 155 Old Kent Road.

The water for the Paragon development must have come from wells sunk beneath each house or in the gardens and, in some cases, may have been drawn from the Kid Brook, flowing to the south. There was a well south of the garden of house No 2 from which some of the inhabitants might have drawn their water. Only one water company existed in the area, the Ravens-bourne Water Company, founded in 1701. The company was sold in 1809 and during the negotiations a map was drawn of its network of pipes, none of which seem to have reached Blackheath. Although water-carts and water-sellers supplied the needs of the less well-off, and there were public wells and pumps, there must have been a more satisfactory arrangement for the residents of the class of dwellings to be found in the Paragon and along South Row.

Mains water did not reach the Paragon until the 1830s and a supply of gas came to the terrace in the late 1820s. It was provided by the Phoenix Gas Company until the 1880s, when the supply was taken over by the South Metropolitan Gas Light and Coke Company, an amalgamation of many local gas companies. The Paragon carriage drive is still lit by gas lamps and the residents have always been proud of this anachronism although the lamps may not be quite as old as some imagine. There are no lamps shown in the photograph of the late 1860s/1870s, reproduced in this book.

Electricity arrived during the years 1899–1901 and the first telephone was installed in Blackheath in 1893. Few private persons had telephones in those days and no Paragon residents seem to have subscribed to the private exchanges before 1900. Generally, the earliest subscribers were commercial and retail groups with, perhaps, doctors and solicitors leading the professionals. There was, after all, no need to install a telephone if there was no one to ring up.

The attached gardens of each house were, surprisingly, of the same depth as now but enclosed by brick walls. Beyond these was a carriage drive roughly in line with today's Fulthorp Road. In addition, houses Nos 1 to 8 had further meadows and pleasure grounds which provided space for horses, cows, and vegetable gardens and, in a few cases, coach houses and stables. The gardens of houses 9 to 14 were progressively smaller because the Paragon House garden extended as far as the dividing wall between houses 9 and 10.

Houses 13 and 14 had no formal rear access but enjoyed footpaths and strips of territory which stretched south towards the round pond, in Pond Road. Residents of many of the Paragon houses and of Nos 3 to 6 South Row who owned coaches and horses had to stable these elsewhere, probably at Stubbs' stables in Pond Road, or the Colonnade House stables, operated by Robert Vice. The gardens of Bryan House and Colonnade House were substantial: in fact, both enjoyed such generous stable accommodation that, quite early in the 19th century, those facilities were hived off from the houses and let commercially. Numbers 3 to 6 South Row had very small gardens but had the visual benefit of the Colonnade House meadows beyond their boundaries.

The front lawn of The Paragon looked much as it does today, including the ha-ha which separated the lawn from the road. Over the years a line of elms grew up which virtually screened the crescent and a thicket of suckers filled the ha-ha so effectively that there was no need to maintain it. Instead, a wooden post and rail fence marked the boundary between the green and the road. Although the loss of the elms, through Dutch elm disease in 1975, altered the view, the elm thicket continued to flourish, as it does to this day.

The restoration of the front green, after the last war, led to a certain amount of acrimony in that not all Blackheath residents (primarily those not living in the Paragon) approved of Charles Bernard Brown's landscaping treatment.

Numbering of houses in the London suburbs was neither necessary nor common until about 1840, when the penny post was introduced and the letter deliverers needed to know who lived where. Until then, a letter addressed to Mr Jones, The Paragon, Blackheath, Kent, would have been sufficient. Nevertheless, the first evidence of numbering for the Paragon has been found in a sales notice of 1801. This was unusual: as late as the 1841 enumerated census return, no house numbers are given for the Paragon, although the houses in the Circus at Greenwich are numbered in that year. Even so, it is not difficult to allocate residents to the Paragon houses as well as to those in South Row. Although the rate collectors' books did not mark house numbers until the mid-19th century, the collector generally followed a set route and it is possible to attach house numbers to the names of all the ratepayers once the pattern has been understood.

The threat of bankruptcy

By 1796 Michael Searles had seriously over-extended himself financially and faced bankruptcy. No doubt the cost of the initial building work on the Paragon, the failure to recover his investment in other properties, like the Circus in Greenwich, and further ventures being less profitable than forecast, led to these circumstances. This was a state of affairs which, it has to be said, faced builders and developers from long before the 18th century, and still does today.

Searles was forced by his creditors to assign his entire property, including leasehold premises, effects and book debts, to a trust composed of his five principal creditors, four of whom were building contractors. This was formalised in a document of 14 April 1796, the Deed of Assignment, which set up the trust on behalf of all the creditors, with powers to administer Michael Searles' properties until the debts were discharged. Among the leasehold pre-mises assigned were houses Nos 12 and 14 The Paragon, along with the agreement with John Cator relating to the Paragon site and 30 acres of land behind.

The Deed states: 'These two houses with ground for two more and 14 other houses are held by way of mortgage for £   by John Cator, Esq.'

The total of 18 houses must refer to the 14 houses in the Paragon, and Paragon House and Bryan House in South Row; and perhaps also to the site of what was to be the semi-detached pairs 3 + 4 and 5 + 6 South Row but may have been originally intended to accommodate rather more superior detached properties like Bryan House. The whole building venture had apparently been abandoned by 1795, not to be restarted until further finance became available. Nevertheless, it is likely that the empty shells of the crescent were sufficiently far forward to remain. The Greenwich Vestry Minutes of January 1794 note that '... a Pile in the form of a Crescent ...' was being erected. This is the first *prima facie* evidence of the building of the Paragon and indicates that the crescent form, at least, was apparent early on. It is likely that Searles' difficulty arose because he funded the creation of the brick carcases but lacked money (or purchasers) to take the scheme any further.

The Greenwich half of the Paragon, for which there is evidence in the entries in the parish rate books, was not to be beneficially occupied until the summer of 1800. The first four houses (Nos 1 to 4) are shown in the October rate books as occupied: this was six years after the Vestry Minute and nearly five years after the Deed of Assignment. Numbers 5 and 6 were ready by 1801 and 1803 respectively. According to records covering Lewisham parish, Nos 7 to 11 were not occupied until the period 1805-6, with No 8 not tenanted until as late as 1808. Numbers 12 and 13 were occupied by 1798. Number 14, one of the first to be finished, may have been Searles' own house from as early as the end of 1794.

Paragon House and Bryan House may have been ready by 1792 – they do not seem to have been included in the Deed of Assignment ('... such interest as the said MS has *if any* in two houses situate upon Blackheath at the entrance to the park late belonging to Sir Gregory Page Turner ...') Unfortunately, there is no record of tenancies of these until 1798; Nos 3 and 4 South Row were occupied in 1800 but Nos 5 and 6 not until 1805. Colonnade House dates from 1803 and, while designed by Michael Searles, was probably erected by the local developer William Dyer.

It is not known at what date the trust was in a position to discharge all Searles' debts and the remaining properties reverted to him, if they ever did. The matter must have been resolved one way or the other before the building lease expired, probably towards the end of the year 1800. In her memoirs, Miss Robertson writes about No 3 The Paragon: 'The one [house] we agreed for was about to fall into the hands of Mr Cator, the landowner, in consequence of a mortgage.' The phrase is an odd one but it could indicate that Cator had recalled his interest in view of Searles' failure.

The leases

If Michael Searles had not fallen into financial difficulty there may have been little problem in deducing the terms on which the houses were let. On the assumption that he lost much of the equity in the property, and that the ground reverted to Cator, the leases would then have been issued by others. Certainly, No 8 was first occupied in 1806 on a lease to Thomas Maryon Wilson from John Cator and William Pitcher of Salisbury Square, one of Searles' creditors: the term was 75 years from 25 December 1804.

Some of the Blackheath properties had been unlet when Searles' business failed so that when the leases were available for disposal the terms were relatively short: No 1 The Paragon was for sale in October 1801 with 78 years of its lease remaining, whereas the lease on the land at the rear expired at Michaelmas 1827. When the purchaser re-let the property in 1804 this was, for some reason, undiscovered, for a term remaining of 17 years – which must have represented an under-lease. In 1803, when No 3 was for sale, it was for a remaining term of 27 years. The details of the head lease covering Nos 5 and 6, sold in March 1804 (along with [other] Searles-related property at the Circus, Greenwich), indicate a term of 90 years at £7.10.0 per annum. Numbers 7 and 8 were offered for sale in 1806 with the benefit of 74 years unexpired.

Thus, it seems that most of the buildings enjoyed leases due to expire in 1880. Bryan House enjoyed a lease of 72 years unexpired when it was offered in June 1807 at £15.12.0 per annum, thus expiring in 1879. If it had been built in 1795 (as may have been the case), and immediately sold on a long lease, the term would have been about 85 years. Colonnade House was offered for 76 years at £40.15.8 per annum in 1804, but this house may not have been subject to the same contract as the remainder of the Paragon and South Row.

Some details of the original leases for buildings in South Row have survived. They were granted for varying terms, but most of them were for 80 years. In the Particulars of Sale of No 12 The Paragon (see above), the lease on offer was for only 21 years from 1859: clearly the remainder of the original 80-year lease offered at the outset in the late 1790s. In 1861, the lease of house No 4 was offered for sale following the bankruptcy of the then lease-holder, Matthew Hutchinson Jnr. The remaining term offered was for just under 19 years.

Some of the Cator leases for houses in South Row must have been for 90 years but in his will, proved in March 1806, John Cator had urged that, after his death, no leases on the Blackheath estate were to be granted for more than 70 years and that 'no consideration or premium should be accepted for granting any such lease'. This is a most curious provision because Cator himself granted leases for longer terms. There may have been a legal or technical reason for it (the beginning of income tax legislation, perhaps) although he did lend Miss Robertson (see Appendix II) £850 and took her lease (probably the under-lease from Searles) as a security.

The leases contained no provisions which would not be found in similar agreements today and were granted to people unlikely to have abused them. The outside of the property was to be painted every four years and the inside every seven years (these provisions still apply [2011]). No occupier was allowed 'to build on a bow window', which is a somewhat ambiguous requirement. It could mean either that nothing must be built above the bay, i.e., on the top floor, or that no bow window was to be added to the building where none existed originally, at the front, for example.

The leases also contained the usual restrictions: nobody was '... to exercise the art mystery trade or business of a school master or mistress, tallow chandler, bagnio [bath] keeper, butcher or fishmonger'. In fact, the list of trades not permitted to be exercised was extremely long and covered every eventuality, although it was unlikely that typical Paragon or South Row residents would have wished to follow any of these callings, at least from their private dwellings. Even so, there were a number of breaches of the prohibition on the use of the houses as schools: the Reverend Jenkins conducted a boys' school at No 2 The Paragon from 1809 to 1820, and Mrs Bryan's girls' school at South Row, from 1798, was nationally famous.

Alas, a full schedule of the initial financial arrangements for the Paragon and South Row has not survived, and what is known has to be derived from sale notices. The first occupier of No 12 The Paragon paid £84 a year. That figure is in line with the rateable value for 1800 which corresponded, more or less, with the actual ground rent paid. Naturally, in later years the rateable value diverged from the ground rent: whereas the latter remained stable, the rate burden increased as improvements to the houses were introduced by the residents, adding to the responsibilities and, therefore, to the cost of local authority administration.

Also, the collapse of Searles' business meant that many of the houses were let and under-let by creditors and investors, each adding their profit margin to the ground-rent level due to Mr Cator and his successors. For example, No 3 was to let in 1803, on a lease of 27 years, at a ground rent of £140 p.a., although it did include four-and-a-half acres of meadow at the back; while the ground rent on Nos 5 and 6 The Paragon was fixed by the Cators at £7.10.0 for the whole term of 90 years. The purchaser of these would have paid a hefty premium relevant to the value of the completed and fitted house. A twelve-and-a-half year remaining term on No 6 in 1812 attracted a ground rent of £92.18.6 for the rest of that lease. No 7 was available at an annual ground rent of £18.8.0 a year for the following 74 years. William Damant paid £1,240 [as Register 1: p.41] for No 8 when, in 1818, he purchased the remainder of the term from the Maryon Wilson estate. In the 1860s, when No 13 was let during the summer holidays, it found ready takers for the house, fully furnished, at £6.6.0 a week. No 4 South Row was let at £60 a quarter when the owner, the Reverend Hawtayne, took a position in Boulogne.

LEWISHAM, BLACKHEATH, SOUTHEND, SYDENHAM,
LEE AND NEIGHBOURHOODS.

LEWISHAM is a most respectable village and parish in the hundred of Blackheath and lathe of Sutton-at-Hone, six miles and a half s.e. from London and about one from Greenwich, situate on the river Ravensbourne; the village extending about a mile along the Tonbridge road. It is inhabited by a great number of opulent merchants and tradesmen, who have selected this pleasant and healthful neighbourhood as a place of retirement from business. The inhabitants are supplied with water from a stream rising at the upper end of the village, and flowing through it. The Surrey canal passes through the parish, and the Ravensbourne propels the machinery of several corn mills. The Earl of Dartmouth is lord of the manor, and holds, by his steward, a manorial court once a year. The county magistrates hold a weekly session here every Monday, and the jurisdiction of the court of requests at Greenwich extends over this parish, the vestry here contributing twelve commissioners. The church, dedicated to St. Mary, was rebuilt in 1774; it is an elegant structure, with a square tower at the western end, and a portico, the latter much admired for its lightness and beauty; the benefice is a vicarage, in the gift of the Earl of Dartmouth, and incumbency of the Hon. and Rev. Henry Legge. There are episcopal chapels at Sydenham and Blackheath, within the parish, and places of worship for independents, Wesleyan methodists and unitarians. Many seminaries, of the highest character, are established in Lewisham and its vicinity. Among its charities are the grammar school, founded by the Rev. Abraham Colfe [see Blackheath]; alms-houses, endowed by the same benevolent divine; and the union workhouse. The entire parish (including a portion of Blackheath and the hamlet of Sydenham) contained a population, in 1831, of 9,659 inhabitants.

Contiguous to Greenwich park, and included in the parishes of Greenwich, Lewisham and Lee, in the hundred of its name and same lathe as Greenwich, is the village of Blackheath; within the last century it was, what its name implies, a bleak heath, with scarcely any habitations; this appearance has, however, for a long period, been completely changed, and it now presents some splendid edifices, and innumerable elegant villas and mansions; amongst these the Paragon, a range of superb residences, stands eminently conspicuous. At South Vale are convenient and well fitted-up baths. A new church, the design and execution of which reflects much credit upon the architect, Mr. G. Smith, has within these few years been erected in Blackheath park by T. Cater, Esq.; there are likewise two episcopal chapels here, and a free grammar school for thirty-one boys of Lewisham and the adjoining parishes, and for the sons of clergymen of the hundred of Blackheath, founded in 1652 by the Rev. Abraham Colfe, with seven exhibitions, of £10. each, to either of the universities; there are also a British school and other smaller schools, efficiently supported by the respectable residents of this district; and a college, called Morden college, founded and endowed, in 1695, by Sir John Morden, Bart., an

319

Pigot's Commercial Directory, 1832. B Soc

CHAPTER FOUR
THE RESIDENTS

The **Paragon and South Row** houses were built for men with money. Blackheath had proved its worth as a residential district for mercantile and professional people as early as the last years of the 17th century with the development of Dartmouth Row and substantial houses at the top (south) end of Crooms Hill. This was sustained with the erection of sizeable houses in West Grove, and later with Grotes Buildings, and on the north-east side of Blackheath Hill. Sir John Vanbrugh's mock-medieval village, at the south end of Maze Hill, comprised large, albeit eccentric, houses built originally for his family but later leased by people of comfortable means.

The attraction of Blackheath was exploited by development of the rim of Heath frontages during the 1780s and 1790s. Montpelier Row and Eliot Place were contemporary with the building of South Row. It is unlikely that Blackheath was ever considered 'fashionable' [cf. p.40] despite the presence for some years of HRH Caroline of Brunswick, Princess of Wales, in Montague House on the south-west corner of Greenwich Park, her principal home from 1799 until about 1811. Most of the new residents were people who were tied to the City or developing industry along the Thames but who could afford to live away from their counting houses and factories. It was the first high ground on the south-east side of London, the soil was gravel and drained well, the air was clear and the prospects were rural. Enterprising carriage proprietors provided a public transport system with horse buses and carriages operating a regular timetable of vehicles from the local public houses, like the Green Man on Blackheath Hill, to Gracechurch Street in central London.

If you could afford it, then Blackheath was a nice place in which to reside. There was space for the family and servants, yet it was close enough to the centre of London for its professional and social benefits to be available. It was handy for the industrial belt along the Thames from London Bridge to Woolwich. Also, for some, it was close to the ship-building yards of Deptford and Blackwall, and the garrison at Woolwich. Then, as now, Blackheath was on the main road leading to the Channel ports. It was, for some of the Scots expatriates involved in ship broking and insurance, the headquarters of the only golf club in England. It was the ideal *rus in urbe*, and Michael Searles, with his Paragon scheme, knew who the likely purchasers would be.

The advent of the railway (to Greenwich in 1838) and the development of steamboats on the Thames improved communications, and although the horse-bus service declined for long-distance travel, the attractions of Blackheath remained powerful. The development of the old Wricklemarsh Park, to the south of South Row, was started in earnest in the mid-1820s, by which time it had passed, by inheritance, to John Cator's nephew, John Barwell Cator (1791–1858). The building of St Germans Place in the mid-1820s and the growth of Blackheath Village between the years 1800 and 1825 were inevitable. Development of the bigger estates on the old meadows and pastures continued until the 1860s – but always for middle-class house-holders.

Any schemes comprising smaller units, like Paragon Mews (now Paragon Place), Bath Place (gone) and Camden Row (in the Village), were largely to provide dwellings for the humbler members of the population: the carriage drivers, chimney-sweeps, laundresses, shoemakers, shopkeepers, and the small army of servants needed to serve those living in the nearby large houses in Blackheath Park, the Paragon and Lee Terrace.

Personal information about the inhabitants of the houses can be gleaned from a variety of sources, the best of which are the enumerated census returns, taken every tenth year from 1841. The census is a confidential record, closed for 100 years so that the details available for public scrutiny (on microfilm) at the time of writing reach only to 1911. These returns list all the people living in a house on a particular night (usually in April) and, from 1851, give other information such as profession, trade or calling and relationship to head of household, place of birth, age and so on. The 1841 census is much simpler, and therefore less helpful; an accurate statement of age was not required so that anomalies occur. This is highlighted when examining the records of a family which may have lived in a house over the span of 1841 and 1851 and so appears in both census returns.

Nevertheless, there are countless other primary and secondary records which help to add detail, and a full schedule of known Paragon and South Row tenants is included as a substantial section in this book: the Registers.

The very earliest tenants may not have been typical, in that Searles' financial upset led to a number of properties being taken by creditors, almost certainly not intending a long occupation. It is not until well into the first decade of the 19th century that there were occupancies of any great length and the beginnings of a stable community.

Nevertheless, advertisements for the houses, on leases of varying length, appeared in the London press, most particularly in *The Times*. Sometimes these houses can be identified from names of the sellers but often the arrangement was anonymous, handled by one of the London surveyors. A good example covers what is, in all probability, the sale of No 5 The Paragon, in May 1841: It seem to have been the largest house in the crescent, with the largest plot – a five acre paddock is included.

The Times, May 1841 (various dates)

Blackheath Paragon. *To be sold, the lease of a convenient, substantial well-built FAMILY RESIDENCE. In the most complete repair; comprising on the third floor, four bedrooms; second floor, two large bedrooms with water laid on; first floor, four bedrooms, dressing room and water closet; ground floor, entrance hall leading to dining room, two excellent drawing rooms communicating by folding doors, library, gentlemen's room with warm and shower bath, water closet; basement, front and back kitchens, larder, manservant's room, store room and excellent and extensive walled kitchen garden and pleasure ditto; paddock about five acres; garden cottage; coach house; three stall stable; hay and corn loft; cow house, piggery, etc. For particulars and card to view apply to Mr Jones, Little Moorfields; or Messrs Wilkinson & Co, Ludgate Hill.*

With the discovery of quite substantial records and information since Bill Bonwitt's book of 1976, much more about the early occupants can be revealed. The predominant group were of the mercantile class – what we would now call import and export agents but then important intermediaries in the developing trade patterns between Britain and the rest of the known, exploitable world, particularly the colonial territories. It was their role to arrange the export of British manufactures and bring in raw materials from across the world.

Only a handful of the first Paragon and South Row residents were local people, so it seems that there was not a large parochial population waiting eagerly for bigger and better houses than those they occupied. Eventually, most came from the City and it can be deduced that the influential men with shipping interests who lived in Dartmouth Row, Grotes Buildings and West Grove may have spread their enthusiasm for Blackheath through social and business circles in the City. Many of them were members of the Blackheath Society of Goffers (later the Royal Blackheath Golf Club) which was also a Masonic lodge. The members met every Saturday in the summer for the game and in the winter as well for its dinners at the Chocolate House (subsequently a school) in West Grove and, from 1789, at the Assembly Room in the Green Man Hotel.

Be that as it may, it was the merchants who came to the Paragon. And they were followed by the professions: mostly the law and the Church. There were also not a few schools in South Row, despite the fact that leases issued by the Cator trustees prohibited tenants from exercising both 'the art and mystery of the school teacher' and the operation of a bagnio, or bathhouse. The growing number of private schools in the area, from as early as 1798, suggests that this calling, at least, was not always proscribed. How many people would have wanted to open a bathhouse in South Row is not known, but they would have been few, if any.

Not surprisingly, the first resident in the Paragon may have been Michael Searles himself. According to a document seen by the late Mr A. R. Martin (1901-1974), a prominent local historian, Michael Searles signed a lease for an unspecified building on 30 December 1794 and in that document he describes himself as Michael Searles 'of Blackheath'. As far as is known, he had not built any other property in Blackheath speculatively and therefore this could well refer to the Paragon. Further evidence comes in a legal document, the Deed of Assignment first mentioned (see page 25), dated 14 April 1796, describing him as 'Michael Searles, late of The Paragon, Blackheath, Kent, but now of Surrey Place in the Kent Road, Surrey'. It could be that at least one of the Paragon houses in Blackheath had been built and was ready for occupation in 1794, but was lived in by Searles for want of a purchaser. If so, this would have been No 14 The Paragon. It was not uncommon for a builder/developer to occupy a newly built house of his own, acting as caretaker until the permanent security of a householder could be found.

No 1 The Paragon was taken by 1800 by William Thompson, an insurance broker, with premises at the Royal Exchange. He was succeeded quite rapidly by Henry Waddington, a merchant, of Bridge Street, Blackfriars. The sale of the contents of his house, on his departure in December 1808, included some dozens of bottles of Madeira and port. The next owner was Edward Spencer Curling, an underwriter for whaling vessels, probably those owned by the Greenwich-based ship owners, the Enderby family. The Curling family were heavily engaged in merchant shipping in all its aspects: Robert Curling, a broker of Torrington Street in the 1790s, was a director of the London Dock Company; there were also a number of Curling companies engaged in shipbuilding at Limehouse and ship and insurance broking from offices at Castle Street, Brick Lane.

Curling was followed at No 1 by Charles Bankes, a sugar refiner, of Upper Thames Street, probably the son of George Bankes who was in the same business. A number of local men were engaged in this trade with the West Indies, including Duncan Campbell, Captain of the Blackheath golfers. Campbell (1741-1803) was Commissioner of Convicts as well as 'fixer' for shipping arrangements to provide the vessels – largely owned by his business friends – for the transport of convicts to Australia. Another man with a West Indies connection was golfer William Innes (1719-1795) of Grotes Buildings, as was Sir Robert Stuart of Paragon House [see No 1 South Row)

No 2 was first leased to Thomas Barnard, a merchant of Jefferies Square, St Mary Axe. No 3, after the disastrous letting to the ladies Sharp and Robertson (see Appendix II), was sold to Henry Smithers, a coal merchant in a substantial way of business, and in turn, to George Elliott, merchant, of South Street, Finsbury. No 4 went to Samuel Wadesdon, an attorney, in partnership as Wadesdon, Barlow & Grosvenor, Austin Friars, from at least 1804 to 1812 but practising by the 1790s. The lease was taken in 1811 by Lancelot Loat (1770-1841), a sand and gravel merchant, of Charlton, who was also a land developer and speculator. He achieved respectability and honorary office in a number of local causes but disgraced himself, in later life, by misusing the considerable funds of the New Cross Turnpike Trust to his own benefit. Thereafter, the occupants were merchants, a block and mast maker, dealers in hemp and flax, clergymen and solicitors.

No 5 may have been rescued from the Searles' debacle by a Cator relative: this was Joseph Sparkes (sometimes written Sparks), son of Joseph who had married Mary, John Cator's sister. Sparkes was here for only two years and the house was taken in 1804 by Thomas Gowland, a merchant then of Muscovy Court, Tower Hill. He was succeeded at No 5 by Henry Alexius Abbott, a Calcutta merchant and navy agent, of Essex Street, the Strand. Three of his sons enjoyed distinction in the Army and one, Major-General Augustus Abbott (1804–1867), died at No 4 The Paragon, but in Cheltenham, not Blackheath. The owner until 1826 was Charles Lewis Muller, an exchange broker of No 10 Great Winchester Street. Muller, whose name is sometimes miswritten as Miller, suffered the confusion of having exactly the same name as his father. Thereafter, No 5 was occupied by only three families from 1827 to 1895: Joseph Lawrence, a stockbroker in partnership with Cazenove, whose firm survives today; then John Frederick Fixsen, a wholesale grocer; and then Hammon Paine, a member of the London Stock Exchange.

No 6, when finally completed for occupation in 1804, was leased by William Deschampes (d. 1830), a drug merchant, of St Swithin's Lane. Bankruptcy in 1812 seems not to have deterred him from continuing to trade as a merchant and, by 1816, enjoying an office in Cannon Street. The next owner was Henry Goodwyn (d.1824), a brewer of Smithfield, who lived in various substantial houses in the district over the years (see Registers). After Goodwyn came Thomas Maud, a navy agent of Great George Street; then Edward Sedgwick, merchant, of Great St Helens, and William Christopherson (1802-1853).

No 7 was occupied by only two families from 1807 to 1866: firstly, Isaac Warner (1744-1822), a member of a substantial south London family whose wealth was based on coal. In company with quite a few other residents of the Paragon, he was a trustee of the New Cross Turnpike Road in 1817. Warner and other members of his family, owned extensive lands in Greenwich and nearby, and the Warners seem to have been very keen on Michael Searles' work. A Simeon Warner lived in Surrey Place, Bermondsey, built by Searles, in 1784.

Subsequently, Simeon bought the lease of Colonnade House, also designed by Searles, from the executors of Robert Parry. In 1803, Isaac Warner asked Michael Searles to design him a house near a river (unidentified); although the design was imposing it was never built and Isaac Warner moved into the Paragon in due course. His widow remained at No 7 until she died in 1842, after which the house was taken by Robert Wilcoxon (1801-1866), a looking-glass and plate-glass manufacturer who later added wallpaper to his catalogue. His descendants lived in Blackheath until the 1920s. Wilcoxon's death led to the house being sold to George Martin Hughes (1827-91), solicitor and authority on Romano-British topography.

No 8 – the last Paragon house of the 14 to be completed – was first occupied by Sir Thomas Maryon Wilson, 7th Bt (1773-1821), the principal landowner in Charlton. It passed in 1812 to Sir John Eamer, wholesale grocer and sugar refiner, who had been Lord Mayor of London in 1801-2, when he lived in West Grove. Thereafter the owners were William Castle Damant, a stockbroker, of Damant & Risdon, Throgmorton Street, and then James Cousens, a tea dealer. A later resident was McGregor Laird (1808-1861), merchant and explorer of West Africa who enjoys a fulsome – and fully justified – entry in the *Dictionary of National Biography*.

House No 9, along with its companion in the scheme, No 8, may have been completed later than the rest of the crescent, and was first in the occupation of a Miss Roberts, from 1806 to 1808. Other tenants followed – albeit briefly – until 1817 when the house was home to iron merchant Samuel Bishop until at least 1841. From 1842 to 1865, it was leased by Quarles Harris, Oporto merchant and controller of a family business with its origins stretching back to the 1680s Harris, with offices at No 41 Crutched Friars, specialised in the wines of Portugal and Cadiz: port bearing his name can still be obtained in London up to the present day (2011).

The longest tenancy of any family in the crescent was held in No 10. The house was first occupied, from 1806, by William Ashmead (c.1770-1843), who moved to No 43 Blackheath Park in 1824. He was succeeded by Louis Michael (sometimes written Michel) Simon, a ship and insurance broker with offices in Throgmorton Street. Simon was a leading member of the Stock Exchange and served on its committee of management for many years. He remained at No 10 The Paragon until his death in 1879 at the great age of 93, and his widow, Matilda, until she died in 1882; their unmarried daughter, Emma, lived here for a further year, after which she moved to No 7 Eliot Place, to reside with her nephew and his family. Among the distinguished children of Louis and Matilda was John (later Sir John) Simon (1816-1904), the pioneer of public health.

House No 11 was occupied by a Captain Thomas Mortimer (perhaps the famous gun maker of St James's Square) from 1805; its subsequent owners were merchant banker George Bramwell (d1837), and from about 1825 to 1832 Joseph Dart (1773/4-1866) who was Secretary of the Honourable East India Company. From the 1840s to 1890 the owners were legal men: Sergeant-at-Law Arnold Wallinger, and then solicitor William Walton. The pattern at No 12 was equally varied, starting with Captain Alexander Stupart, an attorney of Greenwich and member of the Blackheath Golf Club. His successor was another golfer, William Geddes, a shipping and insurance broker. Later tenants were solicitors, schoolmasters, Congregational clergymen or their widows, and from 1891 Captain Charles Browne, a retired lecturer on military topics at Woolwich Royal Military Academy.

No 13 was home, from 1801 to 1825, to Godfrey Feise, a City merchant of Upper Thames Street when he moved to the Paragon but who moved his office from time to time, eventually finishing at Laurence Pountney Hill, near Cannon Street. Feise was followed eventually by banker Samuel Lawford

(1778-1864) and later his widow, who occupied No 13 until 1866. For the next 30 years the owner was the Congregational minister Revd Joseph Beazley (1813-99). No 14 had been taken, by 1800, by solicitor/civil servant Charles Rivington Broughton, who worked in the Foreign Secretary's office but seems to have been involved in local deals and was a trustee of the New Cross Turnpike, like many of his fellow Paragon residents (see page 47). From the late 1820s to 1861, No 14 was the home of the Drew family: initially Captain J. Drew, but from 1839 James Drew, a wholesale druggist. For an interval the house was let to solicitor John Meadows White, the principal mover in the scheme to set up a public day school for boys in Blackheath (see below).

The pattern was much the same in Paragon House, except that the first known tenant was a retired army officer, General Sir Robert Stuart (c.1745-1819), another Blackheath golfer and a man with a West Indies connection. His title may have been self-styled (see below). He was followed by Nathaniel Kindersley, a proctor. By 1811 the owner was William Curling, a shipbuilder and whaling fleet underwriter, whose relatives lived at No 1 The Paragon. From the early 1820s to 1858 the occupant was Samuel Turner Prior, a merchant, of Cheapside. The law returned in 1860 with the purchase of the lease by [Sir] John Baptist Hollams (1820–1910), later President of the Law Society. The house remained in the ownership of merchants and stockbrokers until 1926 when it was converted into a hotel by Mr and Mrs William Williams, in which use it remained until damaged by blast in 1941.

The size of No 2 South Row (Bryan House) almost certainly dictated institutional use from the very beginning, despite Cator's general prohibition of schoolteachers. The house indeed took and kept the name of one of the early occupants: the widow Margaret Bryan, who conducted a fashionable school here. As a result, perhaps, the building stayed in school use, through various proprietors, until at least the 1840s. Subsequent lessees were solicitors, ship brokers and merchants, until the First World War when the house was adapted by Dulcie Mildred Ommaney (1875-1925) for a military rest and social centre (the Khaki Club) and, subsequently, was used as a private hotel.

This was the fate of much of South Row after 1920. Nos 3 to 6 South Row were much smaller houses than those of the Paragon, and No 4 as well as Nos 5 and 6 (which were linked for many years) were used as genteel boarding houses after the 1914-18 war. No 3 was, perhaps, the exception, occupied by a succession of merchants, accountants and company executives. No 4 had passed into school use by the 1830s, in the hands of an outstanding cricketer but hopeless businessman, Nicholas ('Felix') Wanostrocht (1804-1876). It later became the home of an East India Company Army man, and then a bank manager, before being taken by Herbert Ford (1834-1903), an architect specialising in the design of warehouses.

Nos 5 and 6 (linked as Albany House Hotel from 1918) were not completed and occupied until about 1805. Little is known about the early occupants of No 5 but by 1837 the house was leased by local solicitor Thomas Watson Parker (1806-1879), later at Montpelier Row. From the 1860s to the mid-1880s the building was a private school run as a tutorial establishment. It passed through a number of brief tenancies until 1918 when it became a hotel with No 6.

The first occupant of No 6 was Lieut.-Col. William Mudge (1762-1820), Lieut.-Governor of the Royal Military Academy, Woolwich, but famous as one of the pioneers of the Ordnance Survey. Merchants and a wholesale cheesemonger (Joseph Henry Warter) were in residence until the late 1840s when the house was taken for the next 40 or so years by Dr John Robertson (1804-1886), later Chancellor of the Diocese of Rochester, and his family. The Robertsons were followed by Charles Willis Troughton, a stockbroker. In 1918 the building was linked with No 5 as an hotel.

Colonnade House (No 7 South Row) was exceptional: it was a large, distinctive building, enjoying substantial stables and four acres of land. It was designed by Searles and fashioned for men of wealth: in this case the Parry family, merchants of Aldermanbury. Later owners were the shipbuilder William Randall, then Simeon Warner, hugely rich on coal, and Richard Wheen, the soap maker of Deptford. The Paterson family (stockbrokers) owned the house from the 1870s until 1908 but, thereafter, its size dictated multi-occupation. By 1917 it was run as a boarding house by Mrs Jeannie Japp, wife of architect Edward William Japp. The Japp family remained the owners until the house suffered bomb damage in 1941.

One firm indication of the size and wealth of the Paragon and South Row households can be obtained from the enumerated census returns of 1841 to 1911. These not only list all members of the family present in the house on a particular night but also the servants and visitors. Except for those buildings which may have been empty on census night, the record shows that all the Paragon and South Row occupants employed resident servants.

Even the empty houses were being looked after, usually by gardeners or housekeepers but these may have been specially employed as 'nightwatchmen' and not treasured retainers. It is worth analysing the numbers and types of live-in servants in the properties (although many servants in those days did not live in) and possible to deduce some patterns from the results. The largest household was that occupied by soap maker Richard Wheen, of Colonnade House: in 1861 there were a dozen servants to look after 13 Wheens (11 children) but because of the large number of children, the ratio of nurses to infants is high. There was also a governess, a butler and a footman. The gardener and coachman lived elsewhere on the site.

Practically every house boasted a cook, and she usually headed the list of employees after governesses and tutors (the latter being regarded as close to professionals but one degree down from the family); there were also countless parlour-maids, ladies' maids and kitchen maids. One or two were long serving: Henry Leeson was employed (as a gardener) by Mrs Rebecca Hensman at No 1 The Paragon in 1841 and 1851, and so was Ann Stump, although she was described simply as a house servant in what was an untypically small household. Elizabeth Jury was cook to the Lawford family in 1841, at No 2 The Paragon, and had returned as a housemaid by 1861.

At the same address, although with different employers, Louisa Burrows, a 21-year-old maid in 1881, had been promoted to cook by 1891 and was still in employment at No 2 in 1901. Otherwise there is scant evidence of faithful family retainers, even for the Simon family who lived at No 10 for 60 years. Although Lambeth born, Mary Ann Chapman is listed on the 1861 and 1871 census returns for No 10. Hers was the only name to survive, although the Simon family is known to have employed a footman and, in 1881, a girl described as 'a useful maid'.

In 1861 the average number of servants across the 21 houses of the Paragon and South Row was three or four, even discounting the 11 employed by Richard Wheen at Colonnade House. The 1841 census does not differentiate between roles: they are all male (or female) servants. But from 1851 there is some description. Small children and the very elderly are usually cared for by nurses and nursemaids. The richer households employed footmen: at Nos 5, 10, 11 and 12, and Paragon House in 1851; at Nos 5, 10 and Paragon House in 1861; at No 10 and Paragon House in 1871. There were no male servants with this description thereafter. Pageboys were occasionally employed, perhaps training to be footmen: at No 5 in 1851; at No 7 in 1871 and 1891. Colonnade House employed a butler in 1851 and 1861 as well as a footman – but this house was so large that it always boasted the greatest number of staff in any year. By 1901 the average number of residential staff in Paragon houses was just three, usually all female and comprising a cook and two housemaids.

It has to be noted that not all these houses were blessed with coach houses and stables which could provide accommodation for staff. Only four of the Paragon houses enjoyed a stable block large enough to house coachmen and grooms if the census returns are to be relied upon. The huge stable complexes initially provided for Bryan House and Colonnade House were rapidly detached from the parent properties and let commercially.

Ten years later, in 1911, the analysis is skewed because eight of the 21 houses in the complex are empty or the householder is away, and hence the pattern of decline in servant employment has been upset. Nevertheless, No 3 The Paragon (Arthur Watson) employed a 21-year-old butler; No 6 (Walter Blandford) four female servants including a nursemaid; and No 7 (the Bath family) seven female servants including four from Compton in Berkshire. The Dolphins, at No 8, needed four female servants to attend their needs. In South Row the balance is upset because a number of the buildings were already in boarding-house use, so that Nos 3 and 4 needed a cook, a waiter and two maids.

There were inhabited garden cottages behind No 3 The Paragon and Paragon House, and perhaps one or two stables. As these were not in use, one must deduce that most of the residents would have hired horses and conveyances from the various commercial operators nearby, as the need arose. Lastly, there was the Lodge, next to No 14 and on the edge of the public highway.

This was occupied by a servant for the whole Paragon block, but who paid his wages is not recorded. It was his job to take in post and parcels, direct visitors to the appropriate houses and keep out beggars, itinerant vendors and other undesirables. Another lodge keeper occupied a house close to the round pond, in Pond Road, in order to guard the wider acres of the Cator Estate to the south; being contiguous to the rear gardens of the Paragon, the residents there no doubt supplied him with some extra money-making tasks.

By modern standards, some of the Paragon and South Row houses were overcrowded. In order to create more living space, extensions were built, notwithstanding the restrictive covenants in the leases. These were added at the rear, adjoining the semi-circular bays, and further rooms were constructed on top of the colonnades. As a result, the beautiful line of the terrace was marred and the Paragon lost some its architectural harmony, becoming, in Bonwitt's word, 'ungainly'. As the 19th century progressed, the crescent must have become positively unseemly, notwithstanding its fashionable position in Blackheath. Interestingly enough, the same fate befell Michael Searles' Kent Road Paragon which, by the time it was demolished, allegedly had lost every vestige of charm or elegance. The story was much the same for the Circus in Greenwich but, in that case, there was the excuse that there was no controlling landlord for the scheme.

That the owners of the houses were able to disfigure the buildings by these additions was partly due to the lack of strict enforcement of the covenants in the leases, and partly because of the lack of enforceable building laws such as we know them today. There were hardly any national or local bye-laws to control development during the major part of the 19th century, let alone the aesthetics thereof. Certainly, anybody who bought or leased a plot of land from John Cator was free to build where and how he liked, without the necessity to obtain building permission. The buyer of a plot could only be bound by private covenants entered into with the vendor – or lessor – of the land. No doubt, a family strapped for space could come to an agreement with Cator's agent and, for an increase in the rent, enlarge its premises.

It is not surprising that the Paragon and South Row attracted men of enterprise and social concern, as well as of commercial substance. The buildings were of a high standard, the setting was congenial and convenient. A number of the residents were well-known in their fields and had achieved professional distinction; others were to reach the biographical reference books for subsequent achievements – some outstandingly so. A schedule of known residents of both the Paragon and South Row houses is given in Part II of this work, together with biographical notes about many of them.
.

Social and cultural concerns

It is worth summarising here the volume of involvement of the Paragon and South Row residents in Blackheath's local administrative, social, educational and cultural interests, almost from the beginning. Many of the early Paragon residents became members of the New Cross Turnpike Trust, joined the

Society of Goffers (later the Royal Blackheath Golf Club), engaged in political activity, were at the forefront of the scheme to establish a Blackheath public day school for boys and, later, one for girls, and were to serve on management committees of the Blackheath preservation groups, the art and music schools and the Blackheath Concert Hall.

The first indication of this can be found in the subscription lists for books for which their authors canvassed support before publication. Mrs Margaret Bryan, the schoolmistress at No 2 South Row (q.v.), published a number of works on astronomy and mathematics which were supported by her neighbours at the beginning of the 19th century. Thomas Noble's extremely dull collection of poetry, *Blackheath: A Poem in Five Cantos*, published in 1808, attracted a good half-dozen Paragon residents. Mr and Mrs Ashmead (of No 10) took two copies, so did Mrs Bryan, but she is the subject of two of the shorter verses. John Kimbell's *Charities of Greenwich* (1816) was also well received but, again, many of the subscribers were mentioned in its pages as trustees of one charitable or parochial enterprise or another.

Turnpike trusts were the administrative arrangement for maintaining the principal highways. The first act authorising Turnpike Trusts was passed as early as 1663 and over the next 100 years there were countless private acts of Parliament, each covering a particular stretch of road and providing local trusts or companies with the legal authority to charge a toll to cover the cost of road building and maintenance. The New Cross Turnpike Trust, which first met in March 1718, looked after the principal thoroughfare from New Cross, via Deptford, to Lewisham. It was a major highway and it earned considerable sums.

Most of the important local gentlemen were foundation trustees, including Sir Gregory Page. Whether the Blackheath gentry became trustees out of a desire to be of public service or for ulterior motives, it is difficult to say. Although there were many trustees, few attended the meetings and the duties seemed minimal, all the work being undertaken by the clerk (a local solicitor), the turnpike keeper, a treasurer and the gangs of labourers employed as the need arose. The New Cross Turnpike stayed in business until 1865, although most turnpikes in London and its environs had disappeared well before the 1860s.

In the period 1810 to 1820 there were more than a dozen members of the trust among the Paragon and South Row residents at any one time (noted against their names in the lists in Part II of this volume). And it was the connection with the Turnpike Trust which led to one of them facing humiliation and scandal. This was Lancelot Loat, resident of No 4 The Paragon from 1811 to 1829 [1826? in Register, p. 37], a man substantially involved in local administration and politics and Treasurer of the New Cross Turnpike Trust. Loat (1770–1841) borrowed close to £3,000 of the cash reserves belonging to the Turnpike for his own purposes and was unable to account for it, when pressed, in September 1836.

To be fair, the Treasurer was expected to look after the money at home, there being no general use of banks and their vaults in those days. It was not thought improper to borrow the money from a charitable trust from time to time, so long as it was there when required. In 1836 it was not, and Loat was forced to assign his property to secure his debt to the Turnpike. He left his house at No 16 St Germans Place, firstly for No 37 Blackheath Park, and eventually moved to his sister-in-law's house at No 49 Lee Terrace, where he was to die two years later.

It was not just the Turnpike Trust which attracted Paragon men: they became Commissioners of the Sewers, Commissioners of the Land Tax (Sir Thomas Maryon Wilson, John Wells, Henry Goodwyn, George Young, Nathaniel Kindersley, Henry Abbott and Charles Rivington Broughton), and Commissioners of the Land and Assessed Taxes for the Hundred of Blackheath and Little & Lessness, Kent (including Henry Goodwyn, John Godby, and Nathaniel Kindersley).

While the gentlemen were concerned with turnpikes and golf, many of the ladies were engaged in 'good works', through the Church or other endeavours. A typical example was the Lewisham and Blackheath Benevolent Society for encouraging and aiding the industrious sick and the aged poor. Most respectable and comfortably placed local families also subscribed and donated to a cause which was largely to help poor married women during their confinements. The visitors who distributed the benefits were urged to discourage idleness and vice. Another scheme which was well supported was the fund to help distressed Irish clergy during the time of reform and curtailment of the Irish Church, the fund being essentially political as it was used in the Conservative campaign to oppose the policy of the 1830s Reform government.

Perhaps the most useful effort for the common good which came out of the Paragon was the establishment of a distinguished day school for boys: the Blackheath Proprietary School. It stood on the corner of Blackheath Village and Lee Terrace from 1831 until 1907 when it was forced to close, unable to compete with the major public boarding and day schools nearby and with no space for expansion. The full story of the BPS (or 'Prop' as it became known colloquially) is told in John Kirby's *History* (published in 1933). The interested reader is also referred to a detailed summary given in Volume I of this series (revised 1993).

It seems sensible to summarise here the events behind the Proprietary School's foundation. When the Paragon and South Row were built, the local population was small and the number of children (boys) requiring education not so large that special schools were needed. Several privately owned establishments had been opened towards Greenwich, the best known being Dr Burney's school in Crooms Hill, a successor to Weston's Academy, near the Park Wall. Later there was Dr John Potticary's school, at Nos 2 and 3 Eliot Place (Benjamin Disraeli being an early pupil), and Revd John Phillips' Chocolate House Academy in West Grove. But these were small, and depended to an extent on the drive (or otherwise) of the proprietor. Not without substance did Dickens parody the Chocolate House Academy as

Creakle's Academy in *David Copperfield*. In 1823, the young Dr William Greenlaw (1791–1850) opened a private day school for boys at No 4 St Germans Place; this survived in the same buildings for many years, styled as Christ's College in recent times. It now flourishes as the Blackheath Preparatory School for boys *and* girls.

The growth of population with the rapidly developing suburb in the period 1810 to 1830, and the planned building for St Germans Place, Lee Terrace and elsewhere, created a need for schools. The Paragon residents were relatively enlightened: they wanted a good school for their boys and they wanted it to be a day school.

Led by solicitor John Meadows White, then renting No 14 The Paragon, and stockbroker Louis Michael Simon at No 10, a small group of concerned gentlemen met at White's house on 26 January 1830. There were nine of them, including White (1799–1863) and Simon, Joshua Andrews (later of No 6 South Row) and Joseph Lawrence. At this meeting a steering committee was formed with the aim of establishing a proprietary school for boys. This meant that the school would be owned by proprietors (those who purchased a £50 share) who would be entitled to nominate boys for the school.

The Chairman was Revd Joseph Fenn, the incumbent of John Cator's chapel in Blackheath Park (now St Michael and All Angels). He remained Chairman virtually until he died in 1878, declining gradually from a youthful, enthusiastic pioneer to a spent force, which effectively prevented the school from moving forward at a critical time in its history.

At the beginning, however, the promoters must have been surprised and delighted by their success. Supporters stepped forward eagerly and the committee was able to commission plans for a building (from architect George Smith [1782–1869]) who had designed Cator's chapel among other buildings in the area, and advertise for a headmaster. They chose Revd Sanderson Tennant, later a resident of No 5 South Row. Many of the 25 boys who enrolled for the first classes in January 1831 were the sons of committee members and there were at least half a dozen boys from the Paragon and South Row. These included the sons of Joseph Lawrence and Joshua Andrews, and John Mason Neale, son of the widow Susannah Neale of No 4 The Paragon. Most of them achieved distinction in various professional fields and details of their success are noted in a later section of this book.

For the next 60 years, countless Paragon and South Row boys attended the 'Prop', despite competition from larger and grander day and boarding schools. And the last headmaster – Edward Provis – was to find a haven in No 9 The Paragon, by then a boarding house, during the final years of his life.

Unfortunately, the new school arrangement was rocked by argument within a few years of its foundation. John White, although Secretary to the School Committee, fell out with the others over policy and formed a breakaway institution: the Blackheath New Proprietary School, with premises in Lee

Terrace. The New Prop flourished for a period but eventually collapsed, despite attempts to merge the rival establishments. White moved to No 48 Lee Terrace shortly after the dispute.

When the Paragon was completed and occupied, the district was still largely rural. There was a continuous string of development stretching from the Paragon to Montpelier Row, along Eliot Place to Dartmouth Row, but little more. All that was to change over the next 45 to 50 years. The rapid expansion of London's suburbs and the increasing population in the industrial and commercial centres of the City led to unforeseen pressures on the amenities of the Heath. What had once been a relatively local playground for schoolboys and golfers (for most of the time, at least) was suffering continuous and, indeed, over-use.

The process of expansion development around Blackheath, on Shooters Hill Road, in Vanbrugh Park, Granville Park and Lee Terrace, may have provided members for the various sporting and social clubs which grew up in the 1840s and 1850s. It also attracted residents tenacious for the quality of their environment.

The Blackheath Improvement Association and the Blackheath Preservation Society (precursors to the present Blackheath Society) were founded in the 1850s and 1860 respectively. The organisers' aim was to keep the Heath in good order, prevent gravel digging and rubbish dumping, and to press for control, firstly by the Lord of the Manor on a voluntary basis and, later, for statutory regulation. Paragon people were in the vanguard of these enterprises: Peter Barlow (No 8 The Paragon), John Bowen (No 3 South Row), Robert Obbard (No 3 The Paragon), and Hammon Paine (No 5), a leading member of the Blackheath Preservation Society committee. Louis Simon (No 10), Griffith Thomas (No 6), William Walton (No 11), Richard Wheen (Colonnade House), Edward Willoughby (Bryan House) and others also played a part. The Association concentrated on getting things done, with the Heath divided into geographical segments and the members turning out to clear litter, discourage rubbish and fly tipping, and keep the ponds clean and clear of dead dogs. The Society's task was primarily one of lobbying government to take the Heath into statutory care – a campaign which resulted in the Metropolitan Commons (Supplemental) Act of 1871. Hammon Paine, the stockbroker, played a leading role in this.

It was, of course, not too difficult for the class of family which lived in houses like those in the Paragon to find the time to support good social causes. Although most found it necessary to earn a living, or – even if well endowed – preferred to do so, they were in professions and callings which provided adequate rewards. There were some exceptions: the Hutchinson family, at No 4, went bankrupt in business; Nicholas Wanostrocht, the cricketing schoolmaster at No 4 South Row, did likewise when his school collapsed. Mark Shattock, a private tutor at No 3 South Row, probably failed to achieve his ambitions because he took too large a house and received too few pupils. But for the majority of Paragon residents, from the outset and until 1914, they felt that they were living in the most fashionable address in south-east London – a circumstance which has probably survived, even in the egalitarian 21st century, despite the houses being converted into flats and the population being more cosmopolitan.

Sports and games

One of the attractions of Blackheath for the mercantile classes in the late 18th century was not simply the quality of the bricks and mortar or the sylvan landscape, but the presence, since about the 1740s, of a golfing society. The game had been well-established in Scotland but had now found a place in Blackheath – the only formally organised golfing society in England at the time, so far as records survive. The Blackheath Society of Goffers continues today as the Royal Blackheath Golf Club (based at Court Road, Eltham) but its most fascinating period is that from the 1750s to 1923 when organised golf finally left the Heath – the club's course for at least 270 years.

Although the origins of the club are lost in mystery (and, in any event, are not part of this book) it is necessary to note that by the 1780s it was supported by a Masonic lodge (the Knuckle Club, or Winter Golf Club) and that the majority of members were ex-patriate Scotsmen, mostly merchants and in the shipping business, tied to the City for professional reasons. Leading members dominated the shipbuilding, insurance and victualling businesses and many lived in Blackheath: in Dartmouth Row, West Grove and Grotes Buildings.

The Captain of the club in 1783 was Duncan Campbell, West Indies merchant and Commissioner of Convicts for the government of the day. The erection of the Paragon and the houses in South Row would have been noticed by the local members and they would have spread the word to those who journeyed to Blackheath on Saturdays for the game and the dinners and the ritual of the lodge in the winter months.

A surprising number of the new residents of the Paragon were admitted as members of the Blackheath Golf Club and the tradition has continued to this day, although the Masonic element disappeared in 1825. Of more than thirty Paragon and South Row names in the club's membership lists from 1800 to 1914, at least five were elected Captain: Alexander Dobie (1796-1876), the solicitor of No 3 South Row and known to the club as 'Attorney-General'; lighterman Samuel Granger, also of No 3 South Row, in 1838; William Hamilton, an early resident but later of No 17 West Grove (a house designed by Michael Searles) in 1788; Charles Boucher Lindsay, of No 9 Paragon, in 1904; and stockbroker Charles Willis Troughton, who lived at No 6 South Row for many years, in 1910. The tradition has been maintained to the present day, with many recent past captains living at some time in the Paragon. The present Field Marshal, Frank Robert Furber [b 1921] was one of the first residents in a flat in the newly converted No 14, in 1948.

Cricket was, of course, the prominent game for public schools and one of the regular fixtures for the Blackheath Proprietary School's First Eleven was against the Paragon Cricket Club which had been formed in about 1830. The club played 'on that portion of the Heath which lies below St Germans Place', i.e., west of St Germans Place and north of the Paragon. The club was strong but no traceable connection with the Paragon has been unearthed, other than that it took its name. It later merged with the Morden and Dartmouth cricket clubs and the conglomeration was resurrected as the Blackheath Cricket Club in 1885.

This club, which plays today at the Rectory Field, Charlton Road, was led by stockbroker Frederick William Prior (1847-1912), grandson of Samuel Turner Prior (1788–1859), resident of Paragon House from 1821 to 1858. Frederick Prior had been one of the founders of the Morden Cricket Club in the late 1860s, and remained a leading player until he retired from active participation in the game in the mid-1880s. He was in the forefront of the move by the Blackheath sportsmen to establish a joint private ground when the Heath became too overcrowded and public for serious competitive play.

Another important cricket connection rested with the establishment of Nicholas Wanostrocht's school, Alfred House, at No 4 South Row, in 1836. Wanostrocht (1804–1876), using the playing name 'Felix', was an outstanding cricketer and was to play for Kent, Surrey and England as well as turning out for the local clubs, including the Blackheath Dartmouth Cricket Club. Unfortunately, his attention to the game led him to neglect the school (and his other business activities) and the Blackheath establishment collapsed. Nevertheless, during his time in South Row Wanostrocht was, no doubt, the street's most famous inhabitant.

The Rugby Union footballers with the Blackheath Lawn Tennis Club acquired the Rectory Field in Charlton Road in 1885. The tennis club withdrew at the last moment but the cricket and football clubs benefited enormously from the arrangement: each remained among the most distinguished amateur teams in the country, playing their sport until 1914.

Although the present Blackheath (Rugby) Football Club (founded in 1862) grew out of the Blackheath Proprietary School, it was not Paragon boys who set it going. It was the Stokes family (brothers Frederic, Lennard and Graham) who raised it to extraordinary heights during the 1870s and 1880s. Graham Stokes (1855-1921) was to live at No 4 The Paragon from 1901.

Croquet was a firm favourite in the district until the advent of war in 1939, at which time most of the croquet lawns were lost to the dig-for-victory campaign. Edward Provis (1850–1941), one-time headmaster of the Blackheath Proprietary School, was foremost in the management of the Blackheath Croquet Club. The club's lawns were originally established at the Rectory Field [in Charlton Road] but were later to be found at the south-east end of Blackheath Park and eventually lost to a development called Streetfield Mews.

Provis was resident at Nos 9/10 The Paragon (then a hotel) from the mid-

1930s until his death in the bombing of that block in 1941. He was Honorary Secretary of the Croquet Club until 1937, when the task passed to another Paragon resident, William Dunn, of No 4. Provis became President instead. The lawns (there were five of them) had been laid out in 1913 by nurseryman Alfred Levett, of St John's Park. The Croquet Club, after recovering from an immediate upset caused by the Great War, took the game seriously, reaching the finals of the Longmans Cup in 1932, and boasted a roll of over fifty playing members. The Second World War also took its toll: three of the lawns suffered bomb damage and one was dug up for allotments. In the end, interest dwindled and the Blackheath Croquet Club was wound up in 1959. By this time, ironically, the game was being played again in Blackheath, but in back gardens and not with the same level of popularity as before.

Cricket on what was the home ground of the Paragon Cricket Club.
Drawing by John Gilbert, May 1832. Royal Borough of Greenwich Heritage Centre.

8   THE BLACKHEATH LOCAL GUIDE AND DISTRICT ADVERTISER.   Aug.

Photo G. E. Boxall]   *By courtesy of " The Kentish Mercury."*

A group of workers of the depot photographed at 11 The Paragon, Blackheath, where comforts for the wounded are large quantities, as described in an article in our last issue.

Blackheath War Hospital Supply Depot

11 THE PARAGON, BLACKHEATH.

FOR VOLUNTARY WORKERS TO HELP THE WOUNDED AND SICK.

Central Depôt of the Greenwich Borough Association for the Administration of all Voluntary Work approved by the War Office.

President : The Right Hon. VISCOUNT HILL, L.C.C.

Chairman of Committee :
The Mayor of Greenwich (ALDERMAN CHARLES STONE, J.P.).

Since July 26th the following requisitions from the Director-General of Voluntary Organisations have been complied with :—

To the Serbian Relief Committee.
250 M.T. Bandages.

To the Assistant Military Forwarding Officer, Le Havre.
100 Handkerchiefs, 56 Shirts, 56 pairs of Socks.

To the Clearing Hospital, Eastleigh.
16 pairs of Surgical Slippers.

To the 3rd Stationary Hospital, Rouen.
100 Slings, 25 Pneumonia Jackets, 25 pairs of Surgical Slippers, 250 Swabs.

To the Military Forwarding Officer, Alexandria.
500 Sun Shields.

To the Military Hospital, Chiseldon.
6 Bed Tables, 6 Bed Rests.

To the Royal Free Hospital.
400 M.T., 100 Roller and 24 Capeline Bandages, 36 Pneumonia Jackets, 50 Davis Slings, 50 Washing Squares, and old Linen.

To the Military Hospital, Pembroke Dock.
4 Bed Tables.

To the Military Hospital, Frensham Hill.
50 Tray Cloths.

To No. 11 Stationary Hospital, B.E.F.
50 Slings.

To the A.D.M.S. Ambulance Trains, Boulogne.
64 Pyjama Trousers.

To the French Wounded Emergency Fund.
48 Pillows.

To the County of London War Hospital.
5 pairs of Crutches.

To the 20th Casualty Clearing Station.
100 M.T. Bandages, 12 H.C. Bed Jackets, 20 pairs of Operation Stockings.

To the 5th General Hospital, Rouen.
200 Slings, 500 Swabs.

To the Military Hospital, Cork.
12 Trays, 7 Leg Rests.

To No. 10 General Hospital, Rouen.
50 Limb Pillows, also 12 Elbow Pads, 12 Splint Cushions.

The above consignments were despatched by Depôt, assisted by :—

THE BOROUGH HALL WORKING AND CLOTHING FUND.—2 dozen Handkerchiefs.

KIDBROOK WAR RELIEF ASSOCIATION.—4 pairs of Pyjamas, 7 pairs of Socks, 13 Bed Jackets.

SIDCUP AND DISTRICT WAR HOSPITAL SUPPLY DEPÔT.—86 Roller and 39 Eye Bandages, 26 Foot and 6 Handkerchiefs, 23 Pneumonia Jackets, 5 Limb Rests (various), 580 Swabs, 22 sets of Ointment Rags, Slings (30 Davis), 37 pairs of Socks, 6 pairs of 42 pairs of Operation Stockings, 83 Washing Squares, 50 Tray Cloths, 36 pairs of Slippers (9 Surgical).

ST. JOHN'S WAR WORKING PARTY.—25 pairs of Socks

The Depôt has also despatched :—

To the Brook Hospital.
6 pairs of Operation Stockings.

To Lady Smith Dorrien.
82 Bags.

To the Hornsea Hospital, Skirlaugh.
6 Bed Tables.

To L'Ambulance de l'Ocean, La Panne, Belgium.
4 dozen M.T. Bandages, 2 dozen Handkerchiefs, Slippers, 12 pairs of Bed Socks, 12 pairs of Pillows.

DOROTHY STONE, *Hon. Secretary.* A. T. WHATLEY, Hon.

Blackheath War Hospital Supply depot – 1st Annual Report, August 1916. BLG

CHAPTER FIVE

FROM THE GREAT WAR TO 1939

Blackheath was a comfortable, thriving suburb at the outbreak of war in September 1914. Its development was virtually complete; its social, cultural and sporting achievements were considerable. Its structure was largely professional and managerial and its support for charitable enterprises always generous. When war broke out, large numbers of its young men enlisted, mostly to be commissioned, and the older generation wrote frequently to the Prime Minister and the press, suggesting how the Germans could be defeated. Everyone would be home by Christmas.

It was not to be. As in so much of Britain, the war caused dramatic social changes. Economy and shortage had prevented the proper maintenance of property. The loss of manpower to the war effort, and the movement of women, once in service, into unskilled and semi-skilled war work, meant that many of the larger houses could not find staff. Coupled with the movement away from Edwardian opulence, it also meant that large houses were both difficult to maintain and hard to let or sell. There was an increasing demand for smaller units and the process of dividing Blackheath's mansions into multi-occupied dwellings, which had begun in about 1910, gathered pace. The conversions were not to the high standard of separation required today and even in the more gracious areas there was surprisingly little permanent division between house sharers.

Of course, a good percentage of the multi-occupied properties were not split up but let out as two-roomed apartments, often with shared bathrooms. Many of these apartments were rented by those engaged in military service and temporarily stationed at Woolwich, the Royal Naval College, the Royal Air Force (from 1918) at Kidbrooke and other establishments nearby. The Army Pay Corps fell upon Blackheath Village with enthusiasm and starting in 1915, commandeered a large number of the public buildings, including the Blackheath Concert Hall, Winchester House (now a branch of the Blackheath Hospital), the Blackheath School of Art and the Blackheath Art Club in Bennett Park. The building which became Lloyds Bank in 1927 had been a meeting hall and swimming bath. In 1915 it was used as a canteen for girl clerks engaged in maintaining army pay records.

A few very large houses were lent by generous-spirited landlords as temporary hostels for Belgian refugees: Woodlands in Mycenae Road, Mill House in Talbot Place, and others from time to time became refugee centres for just a few of the thousands of Belgians fleeing from the German invaders.

It would be easy to assume, from the dry records of the rate books and court directories, that the Paragon and South Row were untouched. But this was not the case. The process of multi-occupation and sub-letting that had started in about 1915 was not to stop when the war was over. The most dramatic changes for the group were the use of No 11 The Paragon as a hospital supply depot and the establishment of the Khaki Club, at Bryan House.

Bryan House was empty at the outbreak of war, No 11 The Paragon by early 1915. The then freeholder – Albemarle Cator – responded to appeals by concerned local people wishing to make some contribution to the war effort, by providing the buildings for free use for the duration. It is interesting to note that despite considerable activity in both houses for five full years, the rate books for the period show them as unoccupied!

The grandly titled Blackheath War Hospital Supply Depot was one of many similar organisations – of a somewhat middle-class character, it has to be said – established to pack medical supplies for the field hospitals. These were largely staffed by volunteers (although each paid 6d [2.5p] a day for the privilege) and organised by a committee of management. The Blackheath depot at No 11 was fitted out and ready for work when it was opened in August 1915 by Lady Mary Scrutton (1857–1940), wife of Rt Hon Thomas Edward Scrutton (1856–1934), shortly afterwards Lord Justice of Appeal and resident at No 99 Mycenae Road. The volunteers, many of them older schoolchildren, worked from 10.30 to 1.00 and from 2.30 to 6.00. The ground floor of No 11 was the department for packing bandages and swabs, and the top floor dealt with items needing sterilisation.

The Khaki Club, at Bryan House, No 2 South Row, was a remarkable enterprise, largely the work of one woman: Dulcie Mildred Ommaney, who was concerned for the welfare of the numerous troops under training and billeted in the area, often in tents at The Cedars, Belmont Hill, or in bivouac on the Heath during transit. Although the local public houses benefited greatly from this influx, many officers and other ranks simply wanted a cup of tea, peace and quiet and a game of cards or ping-pong in their limited leisure moments before being shipped off to the Front.

Dulcie Ommaney (1875–1925), daughter of Lieut.-Col. Edward Lacon Ommaney (1834–1914), of No 42 Kidbrooke Park Road, decided to meet this need. Bryan House had lain empty since 1908. It was a large house, with 25 rooms, and seemed ideal, so Miss Ommaney prevailed upon the Cators to 'lend' the property for the duration as a social and rest club for soldiers under training in the district or in transit.

The initial helpers were members of the Greenwich and Woolwich Division

(London 18) of the VAD, which had grown out of the British Red Cross Society. Marguerita Mermagen – reminiscing in 1961 – wrote of the activities of the VAD in the district and how she and a group of fellow recruits had been directed to help at the Honourable Artillery Company, quartered at The Cedars. Miss Ommaney, who was the local VAD Commandant, decided that they could be put to better use at Bryan House. Having collected funds and furniture and announced an opening date, London 18 was pressed into action to clean the house. No water was yet laid on. Mrs Mermagen continued:

Never mind, there was plenty of water in the Prince of Wales pond out-side. So with buckets of pond-water the house was scrubbed down and the Khaki Club was opened to all Service men. But such a fantastic scheme had never been heard of before. The men were much too shy and we waited in vain until the winter weather, the men getting bolder, and officers began dismissing squads from drill on the Heath for a tea break. Soon the place was packed. A piano, a billiard table and games were secured and concerts arranged.

Fourteen rooms were fitted out quickly and the Khaki Club opened on 21 November 1914, operating every day from 11.00am to 9.30pm. In its first two years it provided beds for more than 4,000 soldiers, and served 9,000 meals. The expenses were met from modest charges and voluntary donations from well-wishers, but the cost of heat and light in the winter was considerable and appeals frequently had to be made. Many local volunteers helped out – 24 women lined up for an inspection in August 1916 – but the driving force was Miss Ommaney, much assisted by Mrs Norah Clough, Mrs Norman McDougall of Kidbrooke Gardens, and countless married women (some already members of the VAD) living nearby, including a number from the Paragon.

The Blackheath Local Guide and District Advertiser reported (24 March 1917):

The Khaki Club, Blackheath, is hospitable alike to the man on leave from the front and to the Tommy who is in training. Artillerymen who come to the district to draw their pay, before proceeding to their homes, sometimes avail themselves of the Club's arrangements for accommodating guests for a night or two. Lately there was a party of five from the trenches. About 250 resident guests have been entertained, including many Australians, who have taken the Club for their headquarters while in London. The charges are proportionately as reasonable for these men as they are for those who visit the place during the day or evening. The recent frosts caused much trouble, and the plumber had as many as ten burst pipes to repair, while some of the rooms were actually flooded out. Miss Ommaney, who is at the head of the ladies who run the club, would welcome any contributions towards the expenses.

Special attention was paid to the wounded: many were fetched from the somewhat dismal military hospitals nearby for the Friday-afternoon enter-tainments, tea on the lawn and so on. The helpers were not averse to organising games for troops camping on the Heath and pushing wounded Tommies around in their bath chairs. Word of its facilities spread so that a number of foreign and colonial soldiers, on leave in London, found their way to Blackheath to spend a few hours or days at the Khaki Club. One French Canadian is alleged to have made it his home for two months.

The club continued for a few months after the Armistice: 110 men enjoyed a hearty Christmas dinner in 1918. In April 1919 Dulcie Ommaney received a 'Special Mention' in the Armistice Honours List. Its work well done but no longer needed, the Khaki Club closed on 25 October 1919. The balance of the fund (of £33.10.0) was donated to the Dreadnought Seamen's Hospital, Greenwich, and a plaque marking the gift remained on the walls of one its empty wards until recent times. That building has since been restructured as the library of the University of Greenwich.

It was Miss Ommaney's intention to reopen Bryan House as a residential club for ex-servicemen but nothing came of the venture, although she remained there until her death, in an accident at the house, in January 1925. But the institutional use of the property did not change, in the sense that it became a private hotel, under a succession of proprietors, until it was bombed in March 1941, the ruins being demolished before the end of that year.

Although there was no physical damage to the buildings during the Great War (the Village was to suffer from a bomb dropped by a Zeppelin in 1916), the process of multi-occupation had been encouraged because of the war. A little discreet sub-letting of spare bedrooms, especially to officers on courses at the Royal Naval College in Greenwich or the Royal Military Academy in Woolwich, grew into a profitable enterprise for some.

After the Armistice, the character of the Paragon and South Row altered drastically. While some of the houses remained in middle-class, single occupation, a large number did not: many became private hotels almost within weeks of the end of the fighting. By the 1930s, all but three of the 17 properties were divided into flats, or in hotel or boarding-house use. Details of some of the proprietors will be found in the Registers at the end of this book. The first to go public, in that it was advertised as a board residence, was Colonnade House (No 7 South Row) but it was so large that perhaps the process was inevitable. In the Paragon itself, No 9 was opened as the Paragon Private Hotel by William Harrison, who effectively controlled all the Paragon hotels until war damage in 1941 destroyed much of his business. In 1923 he had acquired No 10 and in 1928 had bought William Robert Williams' hotel at Paragon House. As though anticipating events (or the end of a lease) Harrison also used No 105 Blackheath Park as a hotel from 1938 and some of his older customers moved to those houses after the bombing of Paragon House.

By 1936 Harrison had renamed the business at Nos 9 and 10 as Leven's Private Hotel. This was not because a Mr Leven had joined the company, but because Harrison had been the butler at Leven's House in Westmorland. Of course, some of these enterprises changed hands from time to time. Another dominating figure in the board-residence business in South Row was Mrs Melitta Hall, wife of George Hall, who put up her plate on No 5 South Row as early as 1918; in naming the enterprise Albany House Hotel, she was reviving an old name for the house. In 1921 she added No 6 South Row and the houses remained in hotel use until the war damage in 1941. These were not the only Hall residences: in 1920 she took over No 11 The Paragon from a Mrs Glasspool, but kept it only until 1925. From 1922 to 1925 Mrs Hall held the lease on No 12 The Paragon but, once again, seems not to have retained the house thereafter.

No 14 was to enjoy fame as a boarding house for schoolgirls from 1918 onwards. Initially, it was the official boarding house for the Blackheath High School, in Wemyss Road, but from 1921 to 1925 it was a private boarding and day school for junior boys and girls, known as Southlands, in the ownership of Miss F. M. Barnes. The tiny garden was inadequate as a playground so Miss Barnes rented a field at the rear of Paragon House and a tennis court was set up. This facility was retained when the High School returned in 1926 to use the house as a Junior Department. The pupils not only filled the house but utilised the small stables and even the rooms over the stable block which became (after conversion and extension) Cator Manor and Cator Lodge. War damage led to evacuation in 1941 and the High School did not fully re-establish itself in Blackheath until 1946 and then not in the Paragon. However, despite these changes some of the Paragon houses kept their style. Some remained, well into the 1930s, as single-family dwellings. No 13 The Paragon was home for Lady Ellen McDougall, widow of Sir John McDougall (1844-1917), a long-time resident in the district. McDougall, a member of the flour [company] family, was Chairman of the London County Council in 1902, for which services he was knighted in 1902. He was also famous (or notorious) for his role on the London County Council's Theatres' Committee which had attempted to censor the music-hall songs of Marie Lloyd.

The Dunn family retained No 4 The Paragon as a single-family dwelling from 1909 until 1946, the last of the houses to be thus occupied. The Baker family occupied No 3 South Row from 1921 to 1940 but after Edward Baker died, in 1932, his widow, Winifred, did take in paying guests.

There were one or two other somewhat unusual enterprises which would not have been tolerated by the old Cators but perhaps the landlords of the 1930s were less concerned by such matters. Mrs Lily Holmes Tennant Cochrane, widow of Lieut.-Col. Robert Cochrane (1871–1925), moved to No 11 The Paragon in 1928. In 1932 she was involved in the launch of a new daily paper, The Call, a venture in which the share capital of £1 million was to be held solely by women. It had been founded by Mrs A. C. Colles but nothing seems to have come of the enterprise. Then, in 1933 and 1934, advertisements appeared in the local press for a miracle household cleanser and soap called Hea-Te-Co (a thinly disguised adaptation of the initials for Holmes Tennant Cochrane). No 11 The Paragon was the registered office of the company but it is unlikely that Hea-Te-Co made a fortune.

Life at the Paragon must have been made more interesting by the presence of William Silas Spanton, at No 1. Spanton (1845–1930) was an artist and art historian and moved to the Paragon on retirement. In 1925 he led a vigorous campaign against a scheme to run a road from the A2, over the Heath in front of the Paragon, across the lawns of Morden College, eventually to lead to the south end of Kidbrooke Park Road. He was supported in this campaign but may not have been in 1928 when he protested at the erection of what he called '… a hideous mud-coloured villa' on the south-west corner of Kidbrooke Gardens. This was a new house put up by William Summerskill, father of the distinguished politician Dr [later Baroness] Edith Summerskill (1901–1980). It was burned down in 1976 and the site redeveloped as Regency Court. Spanton's memoirs, *An Art Student and his Teachers in the Sixties* (published in 1927) were not as bohemian in content as some of his neighbours had hoped.

Another artist, but one of greater distinction, Bernard Hailstone, moved into No 2, in 1937 – probably the youngest Paragon leaseholder to that date – but his stay was relatively short and much interrupted because of the outbreak of war in September 1939. Hailstone (1910–1987) joined the National Fire Service while still practising as an artist, but his home was lost in 1944 when a V-2 destroyed No 1 and reduced No 2 to a burnt-out shell. At some time he shared the house with a fellow painter, Robert Norman Hepple, RA (1908-94). Hailstone brought to the Paragon a connection with the Art Department of Goldsmiths' College, at New Cross, that was to last until the late 1940s, particularly at No 6 The Paragon (see below).

The size of the house and garden dictated the necessity to let off spare rooms and many of the young painters and sculptors at Goldsmiths' were regular visitors and sometime residents at No 2. By then the unusual architectural qualities of the Paragon were being appreciated by artists and some of Hailstone's best landscapes were produced at Blackheath. He was later to live at Hadlow, Kent, the original family base, and after the war divided his time between Hadlow Castle (which he helped secure and restore) and his studio in Chelsea where he gained a reputation as a portrait painter.

By 1939 the Paragon no longer retained the clean, harmonious quality that Searles had created because of extensions and alterations. In part it had become run down, although it never looked really neglected and the overall charm remained. It was this, and a general lack of interest in a terrace which was, after all, only about 120 years old, which could have led to redevelopment proposals. But, somehow, the Paragon was different, perhaps because of its unusual crescent shape.

When the Blackheath Society was formed, in January 1937, it was as a result of a plea by the artist and teacher Douglas Percy Bliss (1900-1984), anxious that many of Blackheath's finest buildings were under threat. His voice was heard and a number of distinguished architectural historians expressed their concern that the Paragon might be at risk of being demolished for a 'packing-case' block of flats. This wasn't true but it was good publicity for the greater cause. Despite its somewhat shabby and altered appearance, the Paragon came to be the symbol of the very best of Blackheath's architectural history and there was a new-found enthusiasm for its quality.

Bliss, writing to the local newspaper *(Blackheath Local Guide & District Advertiser)* in November 1936, spoke eloquently of the threats to the district, reiterating the awful possibility that even the Paragon might be replaced. This did not lead to any dramatic refurbishment of the crescent but it was thought unlikely that there was any intention by the freeholders, the Cator trustees, to redevelop the site. In fact, they had been granting leases since the start of the 1930s on some of the estate's early-19th-century property in Blackheath Park to the architect Arthur Robert Welby (and, later, his assistant Charles Bernard Brown) which led to restoration not demolition. To confirm the point, reference has been found to the sale of a lease for No 8 The Paragon in August 1938. It was for 10 years, at an annual rent of £110 but subject to a premium of £50 for the lease. Also, Lt Col Henry Cator accepted the offer to become one of the Honorary Vice-Presidents of the newly-formed Society.

The Blackheath Society had been established as a spontaneous reaction to what many saw as dreadful damage to the Village and its surrounds: the erection of Selwyn Court at the south end of the Village on the corner with Lee Terrace, the impending unpreventable loss of Clifton House and The Yews, at the top of Crooms Hill, and the factory extensions at the west end of Eliot Place (demolished in September 1994). A signal point made in many of the letters of support for the new Society was that Blackheath people should unite to prevent the loss of buildings of quality – which included, of course, the Paragon. The Society's immediate work was to try to save buildings threatened with total demolition and the Blackheath Preservation Trust was formed for that purpose the following year. Almost as a symbol of Blackheath's architectural quality, the Society used one of artist Gerard Baker's drawings of the Paragon for its 1938 promotional leaflet and Christmas card.

The Society enlisted the advocacy of the young poet [Sir] John Betjeman, who spoke at its public meeting in February 1938. Betjeman (1906-1984) said: '… The new Society must concern themselves not simply with Georgian buildings but those of later periods.' He derided the Historical Monuments Commission which had set 1714 as the latest date for its consideration. Betjeman went on: 'Let it not be supposed that you people believe nothing is worth preserving after that date. How, if you do, are you going to save the Paragon? How do you save Nelson Street [in Greenwich] and Montpelier Row? How do you save those hundreds of unrecorded decent little houses and streets, those shops, pubs and Gothic Revival churches like St Michael's [in Blackheath Park]?'

But the Paragon and South Row were not then at risk. Any plans the free-holders may have nurtured for the restoration or redevelopment of either the Paragon or the houses in South Row remained hidden, if they existed at all. There were development opportunities on the Cators' Blackheath estate and these had been taken in the 1930s, with the building of Parkgate, Manor

Way and Brooklands Park on green-field sites. One of the entrepreneurs – the young architect Charles Bernard Brown – was to develop his talents at this time and bring them to maturity in the 1940s in a remarkable way.

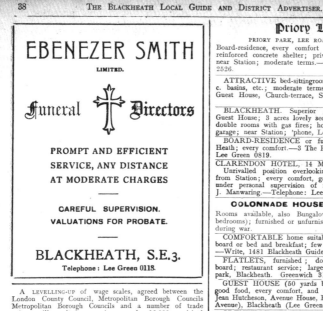

38   THE BLACKHEATH LOCAL GUIDE AND DISTRICT ADVERTISER.   December 16th, 1939.

EBENEZER SMITH
LIMITED.

Funeral ✝ Directors

PROMPT AND EFFICIENT
SERVICE, ANY DISTANCE
AT MODERATE CHARGES

CAREFUL SUPERVISION.
VALUATIONS FOR PROBATE.

BLACKHEATH, S.E.3.
Telephone: Lee Green 0118.

A LEVELLING-UP of wage scales, agreed between the London County Council, Metropolitan Borough Councils Metropolitan Borough Councils and a number of trade unions, will result in wage increases for 16,000 municipal employees at an estimated annual cost of £120,000. The workers affected are engaged in non-trading and miscellaneous manual services and include road sweepers, dustmen, motor drivers, park keepers and main drainage men.

MISCELLANEOUS ADVERTISEMENTS.

Board Residence.

GORDON HOUSE,
109 BLACKHEATH PARK (Lee Green 0263).

This new guest house, associated with Paragon Hotel (proprietress: Mrs. A. Harrison), stands in its own lovely gardens of 1 acre in the most exclusive part of Blackheath. Centrally heated, the rooms are all tastefully decorated and fitted with hot and cold water, gas-fires, etc. Tennis, croquet and garages are available. It is managed by Mrs. E. Wright (née Miss Dorothy Harrison).

GORDON HOUSE, as above, furnished cottage, 1 sitting-room, 3 bedrooms, bathroom, all fitted H. & C. running water; full service and board; nice garden; terms reasonable.   ufn

Priory Lodge,
PRIORY PARK, LEE ROAD, BLACKHEATH.
Board-residence, every comfort and convenience; garage; reinforced concrete shelter; private road; lovely garden; near Station; moderate terms.—Mrs. Gunbie. Lee Green 2526.   ufn

ATTRACTIVE bed-sittingrooms vacant; concealed h. & c. basins, etc.; moderate terms for partial board.—The Guest House, Church-terrace, S.E.13.—Lee Green 0162.   ufn

BLACKHEATH. Superior board-residence in quiet Guest House; 3 acres lovely secluded gardens; single and double rooms with gas fires; home comforts; good table; garage; near Station; 'phone, Lee Green 1907.   D5'40

BOARD-RESIDENCE or furnished apartments, facing Heath; every comfort.—3 The Paragon, Blackheath. Phone Lee Green 0819.   ufn

CLARENDON HOTEL, 14 Montpelier-row, Blackheath. Unrivalled position overlooking the Heath; 3 minutes from Station; every comfort, gas fires in all bedrooms; under personal supervision of resident proprietress, Mrs. J. Manwaring.—Telephone: Lee Green 1591.   ufn

COLONNADE HOUSE, BLACKHEATH
Rooms available, also Bungalow (sitting room and two bedrooms); furnished or unfurnished; special reduced terms during war.   ufn

COMFORTABLE home suitable for business lady; full board or bed and breakfast; few minutes from Lee Station. —Write, 1481 Blackheath Guide Office, S.E.3.   ufn

FLATLETS, furnished; double or single; partial board; restaurant service; large garden.—18 St. John's-park, Blackheath. Greenwich 3118.   ufn

GUEST HOUSE (50 yards buses and Station); quiet, good food, every comfort, and cleanliness assured.—Miss Jean Hutcheson, Avenue House, Blackheath Grove (late The Avenue), Blackheath (Lee Green 5669).   ufn

GRENVILLE HOTEL, 3 Morden-road, Blackheath. Board-residence, terms moderate, every convenience. Lee Green 3987.   ufn

THE LEVENS HOTEL,
Situated in private road; no traffic; beautifully situated and quiet. Single and double bedrooms and sittingroom vacant. Also a furnished Service Flat, will consider unfurnishing, comprising large double bedroom, three single, sittingroom and bathroom; moderate inclusive charge.— W. Harrison, 9 and 10 The Paragon. Lee Green 1939.   ufn

MAYS COURT SERVICE FLATS
54 to 60 CROOMS HILL, S.E.10. (Facing Greenwich Park.) One, two or three bedroom flats. Also double bedrooms and private bath. Terms: all furnished, inclusive of food, service, etc. Central Restaurant. Garages. —A. & S. Slight. Greenwich 1751.   ufn

QUIET sunny rooms, one with bathroom; good cooking; air-raid shelters; also small furnished flat, c.h.w.; close to station and bus.—48 Lee-terrace, Blackheath.   A'40

St. Wolfran's Guest House
Best position, facing Blackheath. No traffic. Single and double rooms; excellent table; gas-fires in bedrooms; terms moderate; under personal supervision of the proprietors, Mr. and Mrs. Jordan, Lloyds-place, Blackheath. Lee Green 4856.   ufn

Furnished Houses, Flats and Apartments.

ATTRACTIVE furnished bed-sittingroom to let, every convenience; moderate rent; board if desired.—Call, 76 Shooters Hill-road, Blackheath.   z

Last advertisements for hotels and boarding houses, December 1939, before the onset of War. *BLG*.

CHAPTER SIX

WORLD WAR II

When war broke out in September 1939, the appearance of the Paragon and South Row had changed considerably from Searles' original creation. The principal pre-war alterations were the extensions which had been built over the colonnades, some as high as the adjoining three-storey blocks. Extra accommodation had been added at the rear of the colonnades, some-times adjoining the bays and completely upsetting the architectural harmony of the crescent. At some time an extra storey had been added to the top of the bay of No 4. As the bay of house No 3 remained only two storeys high, the juxtaposition of the bays was, in Bonwitt's words, 'quite gro-tesque'. There was no doubt that the architectural integrity of the Paragon and South Row had declined by being altered considerably from the original design. But this was not the result of a deliberate act of architectural vandalism – it was simply a symptom of the times and was a natural process of decay and change.

The First World War had left behind a legacy which militated against the large Georgian and Victorian villas, not just in Blackheath but throughout London. As already explained [p. 43], the demand in the 1920s was for small units, flats, trouble-free and easy to maintain modern property: houses which did not require an army of servants to keep clean, warm and tidy. Many of the substantial properties in Blackheath that had been divided into apartments during the Great War and stayed as such. The financial circumstances of the residents had changed, and so did the demographic composition of the district, in that there was a larger number than hitherto of single women whose brothers or husbands had not returned from the war and whose financial circumstances were reduced. Coupled with this was a general decline in the appreciation of Georgian architecture: houses with large rooms that were difficult to heat and costly to carpet, with long windows that were expensive to dress.

During the Great War, No 11 The Paragon had been used for war service and Bryan House, in South Row, had housed the Khaki Club. And after the war, a number of the Paragon houses, and most of those in South Row, had been adapted for hotel and boarding-house use. These were largely occupied as single bed-sitting rooms or two-room apartments on a long-term basis. There was service, for those who wished, but there was also a great turnover of residents. The Paragon House Hotel offered something more, in that it was the base for some social life and the grand drawing room could be hired for wedding receptions and parties. The grounds to the rear provided some modest tennis courts. This was the situation in 1939.

All plans for the substantial development of Blackheath – e.g. a scheme to widen the main road through the Village, plans for a new road running behind Eliot Place, a proposal to upgrade Langton Way as a by-pass for the A2 and a major trunk road crossing the Heath and following the route of Morden Road to the south – were cancelled with the outbreak of war in 1939. However, the subsequent war damage was probably even more dramatic than the realisation of any of these plans. As well as the considerable bomb damage elsewhere in the neighbourhood, Nos 1, 2, 9 and 10 The Paragon were totally ruined. And Bryan House and Nos 3 to 6 South Row were destroyed beyond redemption. It was a catastrophe but, it has to be said, a small disaster in relation to the levels of destruction over the country as a whole and in Europe.

The residents and local population did make some advance preparations in the event of war. Cellars were strengthened, Anderson shelters erected in back gardens, parts of the Heath were entrenched and the wide, flat areas rendered unsuitable for the landing of aircraft. The local Home Defence units and Auxiliary Fire Service practised their techniques well before September 1939. Hose drill was a regular entertainment at the Prince of Wales pond.

The damage to the Paragon and South Row was a result not of direct targeting by Hitler's bombers but almost certainly caused by stray bombs intended for the docks of London. In 1940, the German raids were directed mainly against the industrial areas of the city. During the later raids the targets were wider-spread, which meant that the non-industrial suburbs, like Blackheath, suffered the fallout.

In the Paragon houses, almost all the windows were shattered, slates dislodged and ceilings brought down. During the night of 19 and 20 March 1941 – one of the worst of the Blitz – No 10 The Paragon suffered a direct hit which destroyed it completely, and the adjoining house, No 9, was burnt out. Two people were killed in house No 10, one of whom was the 91-year-old Edward Provis, the last headmaster of the Blackheath Proprietary School. It was on the same night [see above] that a bomb destroyed Bryan House and the neighbouring houses in South Row. The damage was so bad that, for safety reasons, the ruins of these houses were cleared to ground level during 1941. The side effects of this bomb severely damaged both Paragon House to the east and Colonnade House to the west. For-tunately, the basic structures of the two houses were sound and both were considered by the owners as suitable for eventual reconstruction, so the carcases were not demolished.

Incendiary bombs, small anti-personnel bombs and shell splinters from the anti-aircraft shells fired by the 'Z-rocket' batteries stationed on the Heath later in the war, added their toll of damage to the Paragon. The crescent more and more must have resembled a ruin, although those houses not too severely damaged remained in occupation. In April 1941, No 14 The Paragon was slightly damaged by enemy action and the occupiers, the Junior Department of Blackheath High School for Girls, moved to Tunbridge Wells to join the Senior Department, which had been evacuated at the out-break of war. Notwithstanding the reality, the Home Guard and the wardens of the ARP kept in practice. In September 1942 they contrived a 'Battle of Blackheath', with All Saints' Church 'bombed', resulting in the entire congregation having to be 'buried' on the Heath, and Paragon Place was 'in flames'.

There is a remarkable testimony to those early days of the war by a Paragon resident, Edward Provis. On his retirement in 1927, the headmaster and his wife, Margaret Blanche, moved to Harrison's hotel, at Nos 9 and 10 The Paragon, where they occupied a suite of rooms. After Mrs Provis's death in 1936, Edward spent much of his spare time in organising the Blackheath Croquet Club and the Blackheath Bridge Club. He was an enthusiastic correspondent and many of his letters to his daughter (the late Mrs Evelyn Blanche Warrick) survive. Those covering the war period are of particular interest and the quotations below are included by kind permission of his grandson, Anthony B Warrick.

June 3 1940

On your next visit you will see great alterations in the Heath, which will make it more difficult for the German planes to land here. So we are feeling a little safer, and can do without the dugouts which we have not got. Suppose you get buried in your dugout, I do not see how you are going to extricate yourself ... my belief is that you had better throw yourself face-down on the open ground – put cotton wool in your ears and cover your eyes. Unless you get a direct hit you will be safe.

August 9 1940

We are to have a stirrup pump in a few days. Hope Hitler will wait till then before he launches his great attack.

August 25 1940

You will be glad to hear that I have lived thro' the four raids in London that took place yesterday without injury. I got so fed up with them at last that I went to bed without waiting for the All Clear. There were some bangs that sounded rather near ... we have a stirrup pump now but I do not know who is going to use it.

August 29 1940

Two long raids last night beginning at 9 p.m. In the second, bombs dropt [sic] rather near and as they were getting louder and apparently nearer I thought it well to take cover. After that 'O' happened and I returned to my couch ... very sleepy today.

September 1 1940

Our [church] Service this morning lasted from 11 to 11.15 a.m. when the siren sounded, and we all hastened home. I took refuge in Harrison's sitting room. At night when that room cannot be lighted we go into the kitchen of No 10 which seems to be used as a servants' sitting room tho' furnished as a kitchen. I distract my mind by reading the *Old Wives' Tale* by Arnold Bennett. Not very interesting at the beginning but seems to improve judging by the heading of the chapters. You see by the papers we get lots of raids now and occasionally we hear flights in the air and see planes falling to earth. I find a difficulty in distinguishing between guns and bombs. I might stay in bed instead of hurrying to my funk-hole!

November 9 1940

You may like to know how I am after these heavy raids. The first was such a long raid that I scarcely slept at all. Some Nazi seemed bent on keeping us all awake, so he cruised up and down and sent a bomb crashing down now and then. Miss Mavius spent most of the night on my Chesterfield and I lay down on my bed fully dressed, expecting a bomb to strike the house, but that never came. Last night I was bolder and got into bed earlier. The clouds yesterday were full of smoke and so they are today. We can see fresh clouds of smoke rising from the River. I am sorry for the children here. They spent last night sleeping on the kitchen floor ... no harm has been done to The Paragon, not even a window broken. I am surprised not to see any sign of these falling bombs on the roads or the Heath. We hear sounds of fighting now and then, but no outward or visible results thereof. I hope this form of the Battle of London will not last very long ...

September 9 1940

Many thanks for asking me to come and live somewhere near you in the country. No part seems really free from the danger of being bombed. The Paragon is living a charmed life. No harm has been done to any of our houses. There is an AA [anti-aircraft] gun on the Heath and it lets fly if a plane gets too near, and the balloons keep the planes at a good height and so we get on very well. Of course we cannot sleep much at night but I can make up for that by day. I stay in bed as the room is part of the main building ... I think I shall stay on here, as we are not really safe anywhere ... Mrs Webber told me yesterday she saw a basket fall on the other side of a tree in her garden, and as it fell [it] exploded and hurled incendiary bombs in all directions. It was quite a remarkable sight.

September 18 1940

Of course I most heartily wish I could see more of you, but I dislike the journey down to you and do not like the idea of running away. I think the worst is over here. I take refuge in the basement as the others do and they do not seem afraid of anything serious happening. There is a lot of firing from the AA guns. I lie on the sofa in Mr Harrison's room and am well wrapt up. I get a little company in that way and am more cheerful. St Germans [chapel in St Germans Place] has been damaged and we are unable to use it. We go to No 22 St John's Park. Walter Warrick [No 3 St Germans Place] has all his lower windows boarded up. There are several bomb holes near those houses. The AA guns are getting more effective and numerous. There is constant gunfire from them.

September 23 1940

You would not gather from the papers that we have had two very bad attacks on the Paragon, with the result that there is hardly a sound pane of glass left on the north side. Strangely enough we have fared better than most. In the sitting room the right hand window is intact, but the left one has lost its lower portion and Sawers [Norman Clive Sawers] has got his all right, he says, by leaving the door and back windows open. Dunn [No 4 The Paragon] has lost every window on the north side and so have most people. Slater and Fawcett [local contractors based in Tranquil Passage] cannot put in glass just yet, but he has boarded up the window in the sitting room. The raids begin about 9.15 p.m. and last seven or eight hours. Most of us take refuge in the kitchen and scullery. After about two hours of this I lay down on my bed and tried to sleep. This part of the house is safe unless a bomb hits the top of the house and passes thro' it. There is not much danger of this as the balloons keep the planes at a good height. We get a lot of gunfire from the AA gun on the Heath (top of Maze Hill). I am learning to distinguish between the gun shots and bombs. The former is much sharper. We have had two short raids today and I suppose we shall have a night one to destroy what little is left. These raids cause us to get our papers very late.

October 2 1940

Did I tell you about the Molotov bread basket? Quite a remarkable sight. There was one close to us the other day and small incendiary bombs scattered about the Heath – 150 in two lots. A big bomb fell in Liskeard Gardens on Thursday night. One house destroyed and others near badly damaged ... more of my ceiling has come down and I am expecting Slater & Fawcett to come and prop it up after he has taken some more down which looks ready to fall. These long nightly raids ruin our night's rest and make one sleepy during the day. I hear that Lee Park has been badly knocked about. I meant to go and see, but there are so many raids it is difficult to go for a good walk. I spend the evening till 11 p.m. in the servants' hall and am alone for the last hour. There are two very dark places near this hall where Miss Mavius and two others spend the night. I am now in the back room and have had the double bed put in it. My Courier stove in the sitting room is a comfort to me. I burn Coalite and get a good fire with it. There is a man staying here who has invented something for detecting the position of planes. It is called a Predictor and seems to work very well and very quickly. He is trying to invent something else to safeguard us at night. Planes pass over us every night.

October 20 1940

Is there room for one more at your hotel if I get sick of bombs falling about the place and destroying our beautiful houses and take refuge in the country? No 3 [The Paragon] was hit this week and badly damaged. No 4, Mr Dunn's house, was also damaged by the blast which broke all the windows in his conservatory. When we sat down to dinner this morning [?] we heard a bomb coming towards us, so we all disappeared under our tables but nothing happened and dinner proceeded as usual. I am going back now to the front room and use the back as a dressing room. I think this is safer as the attack comes from the back by planes on their way to London. We are truly all in the War and it will not be surprising if one or more of us fall victims. St James' church [Kidbrooke Park Road] and All Saints' [on the Heath] have both been damaged and the congregation invited to go elsewhere.

November

Many thanks for your letter and offer to look for rooms in Cheltenham. I think however it would bother me more to go away than to remain here as it is really much quieter here than it used to be. The night raids are shorter and the machines are attacked and driven back by our own fighters instead of heavy gun fire. My rooms are light enough during the day. The bedroom is pitch dark but that does not matter. I sleep in the small bed but I cannot find sheets suitable for it. Nellie proposes to take a big sheet and fold part of it over and thinks that will do very well. I shall see next week. I find difficulty in keeping the clothes on the bed. The night raid begins about 7 p.m., so after dinner I descend to the basement and stay there until about 10.30. Our noisy kitchen maid has left, so it is pleasanter down there now.

December 17 1940

We have been rather quiet here – very little gun firing and very short raids on London. The raiders go off to other places such as Taunton Road, Lee, where I am told five HE [high explosive] bombs were dropt the other night.

January 18 1941

We are getting along pretty well here. The German planes appear to be driven back by our fighters so that the last two nights have been quiet. I think we have some new planes from the USA – Whirlwind, two engines and very great speed. My trouble has been to exclude the draught from the windows with no glass. Nellie and I are getting over that difficulty.

February 7 1941

The Nazi raiders make it difficult to get to the Village and back unharmed. The banks close at 2 p.m., a very awkward time. Nellie is out till 6 o'clock raid or no raid. She is quite plucky and does not seem to mind if there is no firing. She gets my bedroom ready for me – puts a screen round the bed head to keep the draught out of the broken window. I take in another screen for the end so I am well protected.

March 19 1941
[Edward Provis to his brother-in-law, Canon Frank Manley:]

'Hearty congratulations to you on reaching your xxth year and still keeping fit and able to do such a lot of work in church and garden. We had a long raid here last night. It did not end until 5.30 this morning, after loud firing at 5 a.m. I heard this of course, but not the `All Clear' at 5.30. I must have dropt off to sleep before that came. These late raids rather ruin my night's rest. Our church has been examined and found unsafe.'

This was, almost certainly, the last letter Edward Provis ever wrote. That night No 9 The Paragon was hit by high explosive and two people, including Provis, were killed.

March 20 1941
[Telegram]

Warrick. Great Somerford. Wiltshire
Come at once. Paragon bombed. Telephone Holness Greenwich 0091
Signed: Harrison

It seems that Provis worried about the safety of Nellie, the maidservant who looked after him. She was prone to wandering about the Heath and Provis was waiting for her in his sitting room, although all the other residents were sheltering in the basement. That is where he was killed when the building was hit by high explosive. Mr Anthony Warrick, Provis's grandson, told the author that Norman Clive Sawers, one of Edward Provis's very old friends, was later found sitting in his wheelchair under the stairs in the basement, with nothing but a black eye to show for his experiences.

Despite these catastrophes, life went on for many of the residents: William Harrison moved his Leven's Hotel from the ruins of Nos 9 and 10 to No 5 The Paragon. (Curiously, advertisements for Nos 9 and 10 continued to appear in the local newspaper.)

A R Martin's account

The late A. R. Martin, then a Treasury solicitor whose department had been evacuated to Stratford-upon-Avon, returned to Blackheath as often as his duties allowed. He was acting Honorary Secretary to the Blackheath Society and to the Preservation Trust and was determined that Hitler should not interfere with its work.

In June 1944 he was to stay, as he had done before, a night or two at No 5 The Paragon, part of Harrison's Leven's Hotel after the destruction of Nos 9 and 10. Martin left an account of his time there. After being collected at Charing

Cross Station by architect and town planner William R. Davidge (a fellow director of the Blackheath Preservation Trust).

'He dropped me at No 5 The Paragon, where I had booked a room, at about 6.40 p.m. Found many of the same people still there and some new ones. The company consisted of Mr Pritchard, Capt and Mrs Munford, Mrs King (whose husband and daughter [a WREN] came for the weekend), Mr Harland (Irish), Mrs Madden, Mrs Lovibond, Mr Coverdale and Mr Salmond and a Mr Harper. There were also some others including a young woman and her small son who were there before and who had their meals in the front room. Prof and Mrs Robinson, who formerly lived in Dartmouth Row and whom I had met before the war, came in for meals. They now lived next door [No 6 The Paragon]. Miss Matthews, whom I had met before, was away on holiday. Dr & Mrs Matthews have apparently left.

'After dinner I went for a walk down Morden Road along Blackheath Park to Priory Lane up Lee Road along Lee Terrace and back via Love Lane, Eliot Vale, Eliot Place, Grotes Buildings and Montpelier Row. It was a rather close evening with heavy low clouds. Met Mrs Ord shortly after my arrival.

'Soon after 11.30 p.m. just as I reached my room in the attic of 5 The Paragon the air raid warning sounded, Before long I heard the sound of a single plane and some heavy firing which was taken up by the guns on Blackheath. I had not begun to undress so went downstairs where I found most of the others assembled in the hall. Mr Harper, who is a warden, went out about this time. Hardly had the noise of the first plane died away than we heard another approaching in the distance and again the guns began. The noise sounded rather different from an ordinary plane and they were flying very low apparently under the balloon barrage and in a straight course.

'Then someone who had gone on to the front steps to watch reported that the plane at which they were firing apparently had a light on the tail. When more came at fairly regular intervals we began to wonder what was up. It was obvious that it was something unusual and we began to suspect that they were pilotless planes similar to the one which was alleged to have been bought down at Bow last Tuesday.

'The noise as the battery of rocket guns on Blackheath went off was terrific and slightly reminiscent of several express trains in a tunnel with a loud explosion at the end all compressed into a second of time. It was impossible to attempt to sleep and as some of the planes seemed to pass very close overhead we sat about for some hours on the ground floor, going to the front door from time to time to see what there was to be seen. Still they came on at what seemed to be fairly regular intervals of about 20 minutes.

'The sound began as a faint buzzing growing gradually louder with the guns increasing in ferocity as batteries nearer and nearer took up the challenge. When the guns on Blackheath were in action we knew the plane was close at hand but gradually the sound would recede again into the distance to end generally with a dull quivering explosion the tremor from which shook our building in a different way from the gunfire and told us that a bomb had found its mark.

'At about 3 o'clock (a.m.) it became apparent that it was going on all night so I decided to go upstairs and try and get some sleep. It was of little use, however, as the noise continued with very short lulls and the periodical discharge of the rocket guns made sleep impossible. At about 6.30 a.m. I got up and dressed. It seemed a little quieter but there was another burst of firing while I was shaving. When I got down, things seemed quiet though there had been no all clear. I went out and saw no sign of damage on Blackheath.'

[*Martin then went to London for a meeting of the Blackheath Preservation Trust at Davidge's office, returning on the 6.01 p.m. train.*]

'... a very good dinner again at the guest house. After dinner Mr Ord called to ask me in. They have ground floor rooms at No 7 The Paragon. Went in about 8.45 p.m. and stayed till nearly 10. The very large room on the left, with the huge contemporary fireplace, is used by Mrs Ord as her schoolroom [see below]. We sat in the back room on the right. A fresh warning went while I was there and shortly afterwards I went back. Tonight was not quite so noisy as last night. No rocket guns were fired. Stayed in my room part of the night but came down when things got bad. Mrs Lovibond slept in the hall and most of the others sat around or tried to sleep in chairs. Mrs Lovibond's dachshund very nervous. Her other dog did not seem to mind much. Lay part of the night partly dressed on my bed. At the top of the building the vibration was considerable. Came down after little sleep to breakfast. The others went off to work as usual.'

No 4 The Paragon was still occupied by the Dunn family, despite the broken windows and damaged conservatory, although many of the other houses were virtually empty and, it has to be reported, subject to looting and vandalism. House No 7 was the least damaged. From the summer of 1942 it was part-occupied by the Wricklemarsh School for boys and girls aged between six and ten, run by the brave and enterprising Mrs Caroline Ord. She had married Hubert Ord, who had been both pupil and master at the Blackheath Proprietary School (where he was nicknamed 'Polly' by the schoolboys). Ord had continued his teaching after the Prop closed, largely acting as a crammer, with rooms for many years in the old school building before it was demolished in 1936 to make way for Selwyn Court, Blackheath Village.

The Wricklemarsh School was a rarity. Almost all the other private schools had closed with the outbreak of war and the few that reopened after the Phoney War rapidly put up the shutters at the onset of the Blitz. Most of the pupils had been evacuated [– the Blackheath High School for Girls went to Tunbridge Wells – rcp. p. 51] but the few children who remained needed not only the rudiments of an education but also looking after during the day when many of the mothers were engaged on war work.

Mrs Ord's venture flourished and during the autumn term of 1942 she felt confident enough to throw a party for parents, friends and students at which the children performed dances and songs. She too contributed songs and her husband, always ready to perform with the slightest encouragement, declaimed the stirring and then popular 'Drake's Drum' by England's favourite patriotic poet, Sir Henry Newbolt (1862–1938). Despite the continuing threat of bombs and, later, the V-1 and V-2 menace, the Wrickle-marsh School kept going until early 1946, surviving the war and providing a service for which many parents must have felt some gratitude.

The school was not the only venture at No 7 The Paragon which may not have been tolerated in more genteel days. Ralph and Nancy Price managed to continue with their pre-war enterprise, the riding stables, which enjoyed the grandiloquent name of the Paragon School of Equitation. They also managed the Paragon School of Ballroom Dancing but little detail of this business has survived. One can only guess that one of the grand salons, with which this house was blessed, was the studio.

Miss Price had organised horse shows and gymkhana on the Blackheath High School playing field, at Kidbrooke, in July 1943 and, by 1944, was advertising the Paragon riding school, based at stables in Pond Road. Mrs Maureen Bryant, then Miss Black, remembers that when she took a room at No 7 it was necessary to push past sacks of horse feed stacked in the basement. In 1946 the riding school found more suitable premises in the stables at Heathfield House, Eliot Place, where its meadows were used as a paddock from time to time; the school continued to function until 1950, shortly afterwards she was declared bankrupt.

The bombing raids eased from about mid-1942 but in 1944 a new danger arose with the appearance of the so-called 'V' weapons, particularly the first of these, the V-1 flying bombs. Their range allowed them to reach the centre of London. Aircraft, anti-aircraft batteries and barrage balloons were employed to intercept their flights. Some of these defences were stationed on the Heath. These measures did not always destroy the V-1s in the air but sometimes brought them down, the bombs exploding on impact with the ground, causing widespread damage. Greenwich and Blackheath were particularly vulnerable to these attacks and on 3 July 1944 No 1 The Paragon suffered a direct hit, which destroyed it and the adjoining outhouses completely. In the ensuing conflagration, house No 2 was completely burnt out (see illustrations). This house was owned by the artist Bernard Hailstone (1910–1987), ironically then serving with the Auxiliary Fire Service as both a fireman and an official war artist.

When the war ended, any independent observer must have considered the reconstruc-tion of Paragon House and Colonnade House as an impossibility. Further, although the Paragon had lost only four of its fourteen houses, another half-dozen were in extremely poor condition and the integrity of the crescent had been seriously impaired. South Row was mostly an empty bombsite.

By this time, plans had been laid for the reconstruction of London and the other bombed cities. A dramatic shift by the public in their party-political support from right to left meant that any attempts to turn back the calendar to a pre-war society under a Conservative government would not succeed. The people had won the war and the people were now in charge. Hitler had destroyed much of London's industrial heartland but not all of its slums and substandard housing. Each metropolitan borough and the London County Council had its own agenda for the future and post-war construction, even before D-Day (6 June 1944).

28   THE BLACKHEATH LOCAL GUIDE

ROYAL ACADEMY.
PICTURES BY LOCAL ARTISTS.

The Academy this year is particularly interesting in view of the large number of Local-Artists.

"Suburban Wits," one of the six works shown by Mr. Francis Dodd, R.A., 51 Blackheath-park, suggests a casual meeting and chat on a pleasant summer pre-war day in one or other of the residential thoroughfares off the Heath.

The "wits" in question are a tall woman, in straw hat, pink coat and pleated skirt, and an elderly man, in sports coat, flannel trousers and boater with his old school ribbon, and white spats. His gesture suggests that he has something very good to relate. Errand boys, a nurse and dogs, with the background houses and trees, complete a very attractive composition.

"Prudence in her Bath," a happy painting of a child, and "Gardens Under Snow" by Miss Phyllis Dodd, of 38 Lee-park, Blackheath, suggest again that in the pursuit of subjects, winter and war artists have looked near home. "Head of a Dwarf" and "Rosy" are oil portraits by Norman Hepple and Bernard Hailstone, of 2 The Paragon, Blackheath. The former is well modelled.

"A Lady in Black" is a distinguished work in the art of portraiture by Mr. Dodd. The technique and drawing of the hands, one gloved, is remarkable. "The Garden in Winter" is another interesting oil, while "Suburban Elms" is suggestive of a point near the Roan School, Maze Hill.

"The Rev. Canon F. H. Gillingham," a portrait in charcoal by Mr. Dodd, well modelled and characteristic, will appeal to many friends of the Rector of Lee, particularly now that he is leaving for St. Stephen's, Walbrook. Another charcoal "A. S. Owen, Esq.," a fellow of Keble College is the artist's sixth contribution.

"My Garden under Snow" and "Pre-Raphaelite Spring" are not only excellent examples of the art of Mr. Douglas P. Bliss, of 38 Lee-park, Blackheath, but faithfully present his garden, and embrace in the background, houses and trees in Lee-road, Blackheath. As a third oil, he shows "Ayrshire Bridge."

Exhibitors at the Royal Academy Summer Exhibition. May 1940. *BLG.*

The Village in 1935. B Soc

The Village in March 1945. B Soc

CHAPTER SEVEN
RESURRECTION

T**he first of the** London redevelopment and assessment plans had been concocted by the London County Council in 1943. It was an imaginative document and recognised the value of relatively small and self-contained residential communities like Blackheath: '... that preserve their mellow beauty and which, indeed, might even be damaged by the injudicious zeal of the planner.'

Greenwich and Lewisham borough councils had different ideas. Blackheath was clearly suitable for the developments each had in mind. It was full of open spaces, and large gardens behind old houses that had come to the end of their useful lives. The 1944 plan (compiled under the direction of Sir Leslie Patrick Abercrombie [1879-1957]) proposed a series of ring roads and outer suburban new towns. The 1952 plan was more specific. Large chunks of the Blackheath Cator estate would be compulsorily purchased by the local authorities and the land intensely redeveloped.

One disaster was averted. In 1945 Greenwich Borough Council had considered a scheme in which the gaps in the Paragon would be replaced with groups of prefabricated houses. These would be the temporary first part of a huge new estate stretching south to Blackheath Park. Lewisham Borough Council would develop its side of Pond Road in the same way. Its scheme would encompass the whole of South Row and a new road, from west to east, would run along the north side of the railway line, thus linking Pond Road directly to Blackheath Village.

Word of all this had leaked out well before the conflict ended. Blackheath Society activists A R Martin and town planner W R Davidge had kept in touch during the war years. In February 1944 Davidge (1879-1961) wrote to Martin (1901-1974) that he was already lobbying the Cator trustees on the fate of the Paragon and other Blackheath Park buildings, and that he had contacted Professor A E Richardson for his support. He finishes his note to Martin: *"When we meet [Mr J C] Habgood [Cator's agent] I will sound him as to figures. It would be a great thing if we could save the Paragon."*

Matters were not helped a few months later when it was announced that the principal of the Cator family: John Cator (1863-1944), died in April that year and that his son, Major Henry J Cator was away serving with the airborne forces. A keen supporter and committee member of the dormant Blackheath Society was Philip Arthur Wayne, resident in Morden Road but Headmaster of St Marylebone Grammar School [your author's alma mater]. Wayne (1889-1963) wrote to Martin in May 1944:

"Dear Martin – I hope you are well and that the day may not be too far distant when we shall meet again upon our errands of mercy towards the things of old decency and dignity in Blackheath ... I believe that the old Cator was an admirer of Colonnade House and one of his last ventures forth was to visit it. I will, subject to you views, try to spy out the land regarding this fine old house: I have a fear that [a] syndicate already aims at profiteering flats there. And it seems that our leading local agent [he meant Committee member estate agent and surveyor Capt W F Dyer] *is engaged with interest."*

In November that year Martin received a letter that sent a chill to his marrow: "A Mr Ellis wrote: *"Dear Mr Martin I have been told by a sister of a resident that she has been informed by the Cator estate that 'fate of the Paragon is in the balance', and I understand that there is to be a meeting about it.* The Cassandras were at work and there was no meeting – at least, not one to which the public were invited.

Martin must have been hugely relieved when a counter rumour became fact to be learned of in a letter of September 1947 from Charles Brown telling him (Martin) that his intention with both Colonnade House and The Paragon was to replace them externally exactly as originally built and convert them into high class self-contained flats internally. Also, he would be removing the ugly Victorian excrescences and modern additions even though it would mean the loss of accommodation and rental.

With the arrival in about 1946 or 1947 of this scheme for Brown's restoration of the Paragon, the Greenwich plan was immediately curtailed and the Paragon was removed from its boundary. Although it is much quoted that the Paragon was saved by a public inquiry into a compulsory purchase order (CPO), this does not accord with the discovered facts. No inquiry seems to have taken place, if indeed there was an order for the Paragon. The author is therefore driven to the view that Greenwich realised the opposition it would face if it attempted to remove what was left of the crescent when there was a valid and economic repair programme on the table.

Lewisham's intention for South Row was severely restricted as a result of protests at the subsequent inquiry into the plans in March 1947. This was largely because private plans (by Charles Bernard Brown for the Cator trustees) had been published showing the restoration of Colonnade House and the replacement of the remains of South Row with buildings in harmony with the predominant character of the surrounding buildings. In the end, Lewisham was allowed to develop only the garden ground behind Colonnade House and Bryan House with frontages on Paragon Place and Pond Road.

The saving of the Paragon came about because of the determination of two men: the landlord, Lieut-Col. Henry John Cator, and the 34-year-old architect, Charles Bernard Brown, who had undertaken a large number of restoration and conversion schemes on Cator's estate before the war. Bonwitt felt that Brown's name should always be coupled with that of Michael Searles: for without his vision and energy, and the support of Henry Cator, a descendant of John Cator, the Paragon and Colonnade House might not be there today.

Curiously, there are some interesting parallels in the life and work of Michael Searles and that of Brown. Searles obtained his train-ing from his father and became an architect in all but name without the benefits of university training, architectural school or the necessity to pass examinations. He learned the art of surveying while on the job as a young man and his artistic talents as a designer would have developed from his apprentice days.

Charles Bernard Brown, who was born in 1910, started his career in his mid-teens and his training was similarly informal. Brown's father had died when the boy was 14 years old and after he left school (at the age of 15) he had to help his mother to main-tain a household and bring up two younger children. He became an office boy in the practice of Arthur Robert Welby, an architect, at £1 per week. The office manager died six weeks after Brown had started work and thereafter he was expected to cope with the administration of the business while Welby worked at the drawing board.

Gradually, Brown mastered his side of the work but was drawn more and more towards the architectural design elements in the practice, eventually working alongside Welby until August 1934, when Arthur Welby died. Brown was, by his own recollection, working 'excessive hours' and although he started attending evening classes, firstly at the Regent Street Polytechnic and, later, at the Central School of Arts and Crafts, he was unable to complete either course. He claimed that this was through overwork.

Certainly, Welby's practice was busy. An architect who had retired from the Army with the rank of Lieutenant-Colonel, Welby had anticipated the demand for small units and flats in the Blackheath area and had picked up many of the larger houses at bargain prices. Accompanied by his somewhat juvenile assistant, Welby must have earned a good living through the 1920s and early 1930s, converting at least two houses a year and selling on the results. Houses in West Grove, Heath Lane, Dartmouth Row and Grotes Place benefited from his attention. But perhaps most important was his work on the Cator Estate.

Welby was not in the full sense a designing architect and most of the work he undertook was in the repair and conversion of period property. As a result, Brown's apprenticeship provided him with the opportunity to examine and repair old buildings and he came to appreciate in particular the Georgian classical styles, of which Blackheath and Greenwich were rich in examples.

Welby had no children and, according to Brown, had promised to make a will in his assistant's favour. But the architect is alleged to have changed his mind frequent-ly and threatened to cut out the youth every time they had a disagreement – which, according to Brown, happened quite often. Thus, on Welby's untimely death, Brown found himself to be an executor with an obscure reversionary in-terest but no cash. Mrs Welby felt that the practice should continue and decided that Brown, by now in his mid-twenties, was competent enough to carry on the process.

Henry Cator's support for Welby was transferred to Brown and he continued his late mentor's pioneering work of acquiring Cator property and converting the larger houses into flats and the coach houses into attractive 'period' dwellings. When he took over the practice, Brown claimed that he possessed just £8 in his Post Office Savings Book. By the time the Second World War broke out he had increased his savings to £3,500 through successfully buying and converting properties and other deals.

Brown was more enthusiastic about new design than Welby had been. He is best remembered for a number of distinctive houses on the Blackheath Cator estate: the Parkgate estate, in particular Nos 1 to 9, and Nos 2 to 20, and in Foxes Dale with No 12 (Park House) and Nos 14 & 18. Conversions of this period included Park Lodge in Meadowbank, Nos 53, 101 and 103 Blackheath Park, No 9 Pond Road and No 4 Morden Road, for example.

On the outbreak of war, Brown enlisted in the Royal Air Force and served in Bomber Command. When he was demobilised he claimed that he felt 'too old' (at 35) to resume his studies, but his financial circumstances required him to pick up the threads of his business. Thus, although he was able to style himself as a Licentiate of the Royal Institute of British Architects (because he had worked with and been 'trained' by Welby, a member of the RIBA), he was not a registered architect as such and had passed no examinations. He was just innately skilled at what he did.

Brown had remained in contact with the Cators' and their surveyors during the period 1939 to 1945, and must have discussed with them what should happen to the Paragon and the remains of South Row. In the months imme-diately following the end of the war, it was agreed by the Cators that Brown could attempt to rescue the Paragon and repair both Paragon House and Colonnade House. The gap in South Row would, if the local authorities could be persuaded, be refilled with a pastiche of what had been there until 1940. Brown possessed an intense feeling for Georgian architecture and his dream must have seemed to be little more than that in 1945, when there was considerable difficulty in obtaining materials, all major building work was subject to permits, and money was short. He claimed that he was inspired at this time by his old master's philosophy that 'Honour, beauty and art must always come before commercial gain' – a noble sentiment which could easily lead to bankruptcy, as it had done for Michael Searles 150 years earlier.

The Paragon reconstruc-tion costs were estimated at between £80,000 and £100,000 in 1945. This may not seem untoward compared with 2011 values but, at a time when the average take-home pay for a skilled man might be not much more than £3 a week, it was a considerable sum. In 1946 Henry Cator, encouraged by Brown's enthusiasm and also holding a great affection for the Paragon, granted to the architect's holding company, Paragon Preservation Ltd, a building lease for 90 years, at £350 per annum, subject to a successful negotiation for a claim for war damages.

Brown's initial agreement with the Cator trustees was on a piecemeal basis, house by house, but in January 1950 he was granted a 99-year lease on all the Paragon property from the newly-created Lodge at the east end to the three small houses created within the footprint of the old garage and store next to Paragon House. Along with the houses numbered 1 to 14 The Paragon Brown now possessed the entire crescent. He paid the Cator's £20,000 but needed, of course, to provide from his own resources or by borrowing, the costs of repair and rebuilding the damaged property. Even those houses not bomb damaged were in need of renovation and upgrading to a then sufficiently high standard to tempt buyer's of the social level Brown was hoping to attract.

An early obstacle to the financial possibility of economic restoration was the fact that the civil servants at the War Damage Commission interpreted the regulations covering war damage claims rather narrowly. Compensation was supposed to be provided only for partly destroyed buildings and not for those which had been totally destroyed. Structures such as Colonnade House and Paragon House were judged to be beyond repair and therefore not eligible for compensatory payments.

The rules dictated that compensation could not be obtained for houses 1, 2, 9 and 10 The Paragon or for the surviving houses in South Row. However, Brown argued a special case for the Blackheath houses. He later boasted that, in the absence of Sir Trustram Eve, head of the War Damage Commission, he had convinced the deputy head that the Blackheath houses were special. The Paragon must be treated as a whole. The fact that four houses in the crescent had been damaged beyond repair meant that 10 houses remained and, therefore, only part of a structure had gone. In which case, compensation should be paid, as it should for Paragon House and Colonnade House, because these buildings could be repaired and restored much more economically than by redevelopment. Having managed to persuade the bureaucrats to amend the official view, Brown obtained full com-pensation for all the war damage including that for the totally destroyed houses. In the following year, the Finance Act removed the ambiguity upon which the Commission had relied.

Brown maintained that maximum commercial gain was sacrificed to 'honour, beauty and art' in his repair and reconstruction of the Paragon and the two surviving houses in South Row. He wanted to recreate the appearance of the crescent as it must have looked when it was finally finished in about 1805. He claimed to have 'sacrificed' available space which could have provided as many as 12 (one claim was 26) additional flats. These areas were largely to be found in the Victorian additions and accretions to the original buildings. Aesthetic considerations and a desire to restore the harmony of the crescent prevented Brown from considering any other course. The accretions were demolished, where not already devastated by war damage. It must be said that both Cator and Brown probably guessed that a smaller number of units in a restoration of extremely high quality would, in the end, pay higher dividends than a quick conversion into a large number of bedsits

It would have been relatively easy to recreate the basic appearance of the Paragon houses without troubling over infinite details because there were no legal controls at that time governing the replacement of architectural ornament and decoration. Indeed, Brown had deliberately knocked off all the fancy Victorian details on No 19 Morden Road and No 102 Manor Way when he converted those houses into flats. But, fortunately for the Paragon and Blackheath, Brown was determined to be as accurate as possible in restoring the original facade of the crescent, down to the smallest period detail. A good deal of the ornament was still intact in the houses that had not been destroyed, so measurements could be taken of what remained to provide templates for remodelling the missing fragments on the damaged buildings. Thus, he was prepared to go to endless lengths to recreate various seemingly small and relatively unimportant ornamental features. Some scale drawings of No 1 The Paragon and Colonnade House had also been published in *Small Georgian Houses and their Details 1750-1820*, a photo-graphic survey compiled by Stanley C. Ramsey and J. D. M. Harvey, in 1919.

However, Brown claimed that he had seen none of these, which is surprising for a well-read man and a student of Georgian architecture.

The obstacles presented by his attention to detail were formidable. Wartime building restrictions being still in force, the difficulties in obtaining materials of any kind were enormous. Knowing exactly what he wanted, Brown scoured builders' yards and antique and junk shops 'all over the country' and often had architectural features recreated to his own design. The 'stone' rustication on Paragon Cottage and No 15 The Paragon (the erstwhile gatehouse) is typical, in that he had to instruct his contractor to fabricate the individual blocks from fine cement – no mean feat in those days.

It is also remarkable that Brown achieved such a faithful reconstruction of the Paragon, and the two period houses in South Row, without having seen the original Michael Searles' drawings, now safe in the British Architectural Library. Until their acquisition in 1961, the existence of these drawings was hardly known. All Brown's work had been aided by old photographs, b intuition and his innate sense of style, helped, of course, by those parts of the Paragon which survived reasonably unscathed.

Brown's knowledge of the private housing market indicated that to reinstate the Paragon, Paragon House and Colonnade House as single-family dwellings would not have been economic in the 1950s when the demand was for small, affordable units, easy to maintain and support. The cost of staff required to run such large houses was prohibitive, even if there had still been a ready supply of domestic servants. Therefore, it was decided from the outset that the houses would be restored into flats. In the end, over 80 flats were constructed behind the facades of the 14 Paragon houses; the west-end lodge was altered and upgraded and a new house created on the ashes of the stable block allied to Paragon House and Colonnade House were also converted into six and seven flats respectively.

This was not at that time an act of commercial vandalism, as some may now think. The internal qualities of the two free-standing houses and at least two-thirds of the Paragon houses had been indifferently treated during the early decades of the 20th century, with massive alterations and subdivisions. Four of the Paragon houses had been destroyed and many others shaken and blasted. Subsequent neglect had led to vandalism, looting, and dry and wet rot. Most of the interiors had been damaged so badly that total replacement of the plaster, woodwork, staircases and fireplaces was required in any event.

All the services (gas, electricity, water, drainage) were in poor repair, dangerous or non-existent. The evisceration of the houses to replace these utilities to meet modern regulations must, alas, have helped in no small measure to remove further surviving fragments of the original fittings and decorative work. Therefore, Brown did what was most sensible: he created elegant, mostly small, modern flats with the spaciousness of the Georgian period but with all the then-latest modern conveniences. The old coal-burning fireplaces and kitchen ranges were replaced with central heating and modern gas and electric cookers. Some of the flats did, and still do, enjoy a fragment of the original decorations: the odd fire surround, a few feet or so of ornamental plasterwork or cornice.

Paragon House and Colonnade House

It was fortunate for Brown that the Planning Department of the London County Council was sympathetic, and granted development permits fairly quickly and regularly. This enabled him to begin the repair and conversion of Paragon House into six flats by May 1946. Few alterations were re-quired to the front to restore it in keeping with Searles' original plans (although Brown had no knowledge of these). A shallow but considerable extension which had been built on the west side was taken down and the entrance, always from Pond Road, was enhanced by a 'new' door and architrave – in fact, it was one salvaged from No 2 Adam Street, in the London Adelphi. This was installed in the correct position but the flight of steps leading to the door was reversed to lead from the south (see illustration).

The disfiguring kitchen and bathroom block, on the east side, was removed. The windows were restored to their original position and to a correct line and scale, the damaged Victorian substitutes removed and replaced with glazing bars conforming to the Georgian proportions. Considering that the house had been much ill-used as a hotel from 1926 and then savagely dam-aged by bomb blast in 1941, it was a remarkable feat of reconstruction. What was left of the semi-circular bay at the rear of Paragon House was taken down and completely rebuilt to a pattern subsequently used on Nos 1–3 and

5–12 The Paragon, with the object of enlarging the bay windows and thus allowing more light into the sitting rooms.

The finished work stimulated an article in *House & Garden* (Autumn 1948) by journalist Ann Johnson, who wrote of the far-sighted and magnanimous co-operation by Cator and Brown which had averted the tragedy of demolition and replacement by prefabricated houses, and that '… 18th century traditions of architectural elegance have triumphed over that iconoclasm which so often masquerades as necessity'. She guessed that the architect might have been one Michael Soame (sic).

The restoration of Colonnade House continued the story. This was, in some ways, more difficult in that Lewisham's intention had been to acquire the whole South Row frontage. Only one house – Colonnade House – out of seven had survived the Blitz and it seemed to municipal surveyors that it was beyond repair. Brown and Cator thought otherwise. Brown obtained consent from the London County Council for a conversion into flats andthey started work immediately. Shortly afterwards, Lewisham served a compulsory purchase order for the land, presumably, wrote Christopher Hussey (1899–1970) in *Country Life* (December 1950): '… under the general policy of restricting works by private enterprise'. Lewisham was defeated (although it kept much of the garden ground at the rear) after an appeal inquiry.

Colonnade House had suffered internally well before the war. Its use as a boarding house/hotel completed the thoughtless alteration which had been going on since mid-Victorian days, with extensive additions and alterations at the rear. The huge families which had occupied it since the early 19th century had taken their toll. Marble chimney-pieces had been replaced by Victorian equivalents, plasterwork had been supplemented or replaced by 19th-century versions, commented Hussey. He also explained that the house had not only sustained considerable bomb damage but had deteriorated for lack of immediate protection after 1941, and had been looted.

It was openly reported that the 1949 restoration work and replacement proved to be considerable: the whole of the back wall had to be taken down and rebuilt, giving the opportunity to remove many of the late-Victorian accretions which had survived the war. Two extensions which heightened the wings were retained (the space was valuable) and, in any case, these did not detract from the architectural harmony of the building. The date of these rooftop extensions is not known but in 1861 Richard Wheen commissioned 'additions, alterations and other works' from local architect Francis Freeman Thorne. They cost over £1,500, which was a considerable sum in those days. Now that the original scheme has been deciphered, it can be seen that Thorne (if he was the architect responsible for these 'improvements') did, according to some opinion, improve on Searles' creation.

The second (or servants') staircase was removed in order to create more space for the flats, but otherwise the main hall and corridors were retained. Modern services – wiring, plumbing and so on – were quite advanced for their period (late 1940s) and included back boilers for central and water heating. Hussey wrote, when discussing the interior decoration: 'A Regency note was indicated by the chimney pieces, of composition and wood, which have been made by the firm (founded in 1780) which originally supplied them for the house and was able to produce the original moulds.' How did they know – when all knowledge of the date and designer of the house had been lost at that time? Hussey even guesses at the architect of Colonnade House: *'The architect is not known for certain: one Leroux has been named, or Michael Searle [sic] ... whoever it was, one suspects that he was a pupil of James Wyatt.'*

The triple windows in the rear bays were enlarged; the garden ground lowered so that the basement flats would be brighter and more open, and face a sunken rose garden rather than a bank of earth. More important, perhaps, the iron railings above the front canopy were replaced in the style still evident in the rusting remains found by Brown in the rubbish-strewn garden when he first took over the building. What were not replaced were the front garden railings – to judge from the lead-filled holes on the coping which survives on the street boundary, of a tightly-packed complicated design. The gates had also gone but the huge Portland stone gate piers remain, statutorily listed in their own right. Modern ironwork in plain spears finally replaced the front railings in the early 21st century

Not only was the restoration of Colonnade House an extraordinary act of unselfish enthusiasm for a private house at the time, but the method of recouping the cost by selling the seven flats on 99-year leases for a premium (starting at £1,800) at a modest ground rent (from £15 to £25 per annum) was novel. Brown calculated that the annual outgoings would be £138, which would include three per cent of the £1,800 and an annual share of wear and tear on the common hall carpet. So, for a deposit of £600 and a mortgage of £1,200 over 20 years, the flat owner could enjoy Georgian elegance for £84 a year over this period. He could not, of course, anticipate either inflation or the massive rise in property values during the 1970s and 1980s and onwards: the £1,800 flats changed hands at sums more than 525 times that figure in the first decade of the 21st century.

THE POND ROAD HOUSING SITE

The Ministry of Health, in conjunction with the Minister of Town and Country Planning, and after consultation with the Royal Institute of British Architects, has nominated Professor A. E. Richardson, R.A., M.A., F.R.I.B.A., to act as architect for the development of the Pond-road housing site at Blackheath. At a meeting between Professor Richardson and the Town Clerk and Borough Engineer of Greenwich, it has been established that the architect will confine himself to the design and layouts of the proposed development, which it is intended shall harmonize with the surrounding Georgian properties.

*   *   *

Pond Road housing. Prof Richardson appointed July 1950. *BLG.*

THE DEVELOPMENT OF BLACKHEATH

The County of London Development Plan as it affects Blackheath over the next twenty years is a matter of much interest to local inhabitants, and these notes are set out with a view to explaining its main features.

Density

The first matter of importance is that of density of population. So far as the London Suburbs are concerned, the average for the residential areas is planned to be 70 persons per acre. In terms of houses, this would amount to about 19 houses per acre on the basis of each household having an average of 3.6 persons. This density is, of course, considerably greater in Central London. Open spaces are not part of the residential areas and consequently are not included in the over-all acreage.

In places on high ground or adjacent to open spaces, this average density may be exceeded but, on the other hand, it may be less than average if the architectural unity of the locality would be upset by buildings allowing of greater density.

Open Spaces

The second feature of importance are the open spaces. These are classed as either public or private and, of course, in Blackheath the Heath itself and Greenwich Park are designated as public open spaces. The areas scheduled as private open spaces to be kept free of buildings are:
1. The allotments and sports grounds at the end of Blackheath Park extending across to Kidbrooke Park Road;
2. The grounds of Morden College;
3. The sports grounds alongside the Manor Way;
4. The sports ground at the end of Brooklands Park; and
5. The green in front of the Paragon.

Development Plans

Having specified the open spaces the next stage in the plan is to specify the remaining area as "residential," "industrial," "shopping," etc., and to set out the proposed developments. These fall into two categories, namely, development during (a) the first five years and (b) the next fifteen years. It must be emphasized at the outset, however, that these proposals are tentative only and are regarded as subject to amendments as circumstances may require.

First Five Years

Working round in a clockwise direction from the Village, the plan shows that residential development is to take place:
1. Immediately behind Colonade House, between Paragon Place and Pond Road. Work on this project of 104 flats has, in fact, already started under the Lewisham Borough Council.
2. Immediately behind the Paragon, extending from Pond Road (east side) along the railway cutting to Morden Road.
3. "Drakecourt" Estate of about 14 acres, extending from Brooklands Park behind the south side of Blackheath Park down to the Ordinance factory along to just short of the allotments.
4. "Casterbridge" Estate of about 8 acres, also in Brooklands Park and adjacent to "Drakecourt." The plan allows for a Primary School to be built on part of this site, if considered necessary.
5. "The Hall" Estate in Foxes Dale of just over 4 acres, extending up to the Bowling Club in Brooklands Park.
6. Two areas along both sides of the railway line, extending up to Eliot Place on the north and Lee Terrace on the south.

Next Fifteen Years

During this period the plan in its present form shows three areas on which residential development will be considered.
1. Pond Road (west, or Village, side), between the railway cutting and the present development area referred to in paragraph (1) of the five-year plan above.
2. A large area that runs behind the north side of Blackheath Park. It incorporates the houses and gardens on both sides of Pond Road down to the railway cutting, it also includes both sides of Morden Road and borders the grounds of Morden College up to Kidbrooke Grove. The grounds of St. Michael's Church and the gardens of the houses on the north side of Blackheath Park are excluded
3. The area between Priory Lane and The Manor Way, including "The Priory" grounds in Park Gate and the houses in Lee Road on the east side. In this area there is provision for a "Further Education" establishment.

In connection with this second part of the plan, it is to be explained that the areas marked are those considered likely to be eligible or ripe for residential development during the period, and regard will be taken of the age, condition and general conformity of buildings already in existence on the areas scheduled.

The detailed plans setting out the above details are on view at the County Hall. They are also on view at present at the Town Hall, Greenwich, so far as they relate to the Greenwich area.

J. H. M. CLARK.

Details of the London Development Plan. *BLG.*

CHAPTER EIGHT
THE RECONSTRUCTION OF THE PARAGON

The resurrection of the Paragon began with the appendages to house No 14, the lodge, the stables – which had been converted into garages during the inter-war years – and the outhouses. The lodge became No 15 The Paragon, a radically re-built single-family dwelling in the Georgian style with rustication exploiting the late 18th century style. Small as it is, No 15 has many unique features, not least a circular staircase with bowed treads winding round a fluted column. A similar house was built on the eastern end, in the shell of a broken garage, to be known as Paragon Cottage. No 15, together with those of the Paragon houses completed by that time, earned the project a Plaque of Distinc-tion for good urban design in connection with the Festival of Britain in 1951. The plaque can be seen today above the entrance to No 15.

In 1953–54 the other outbuildings at the western end (see illustrations) were taken down and remodelled into three new houses called Paragon Close, Manor and Lodge. The new building blends well with the Paragon and Paragon House but is unashamedly new and the brick was not weathered down to make it look otherwise. It is a tribute to Brown's skill at creating a neo-Georgian architectural style that it did not prove embarrassing subsequently (as did other examples in the district built later (Parkside, on Vanbrugh Park). At the same time, south of Paragon House in Pond Road, Brown built a block of garages on part of the Paragon House gardens. They were consciously designed to resemble 18th-century stables. These garages are such a skilful imitation that many passers-by believe them to be adapted from genuine Georgian stables, particularly as the forecourt is cobbled.

Brown claimed to have laid most of the cobble-stones himself, being unable to obtain skilled tradesmen to do this work, but it is more likely that he designed the scheme, started it off, and then spent his time more profitably on those professional matters for which he could engage no better man than himself.

During the conversion of the Paragon into flats, the fronts of the houses were rebuilt faithfully to replicate the original and now look exactly as they did when completed by 1805, but not as clean. Where new brick-work was required, second-hand London stock bricks were obtained. These were often paler by comparison and failed to blend with the original bricks, so all new work was liberally soot-washed when pointing took place. Thus the entire facade presented a har-monious aspect by the time the task was completed in 1957 (see illustration). The fact that the clean air legislation did not come into force until the mid-1950s certainly helped – Greenwich was notorious for suffering worse air pollution from London's coal fires and industry, it was alleged at the time, than any other borough in the capital.

The first houses to be finished were Paragon House and Colonnade House (the recreation of which Brown was to detail in a book, *The Conversion of Old Buildings into New Homes for Occupation and Investment* [1955]) and Nos 13 and 14 The Paragon. The completed works demonstrated that the scheme was not only possible but also might be commercially sound as well. The next to be restored were houses Nos 11 and 12. During the refurbish-ment of Nos 3 and 4, Brown commenced the major recon-struction work on those blocks that were once Nos 9 and 10 and Nos 1 and 2, in that order. By 1952, when 10 houses had been completed, monetary con-siderations slowed the pace despite the fact that only four of the Paragon houses remained unrepaired or still to be converted.

However, the Housing Acts of 1949 and 1954 enabled Brown to obtain building grants which, in the case of houses Nos 5 and 6, amounted to £7,427 out of a total cost for their conversion of £25,434. Grants also became available for the reconstruction of the last pair, Nos 7 and 8; although one of the condi-tions of the grant was that the number of flats had to be increased: there was still a housing shortage at the time and 'under-development' was more of a sin than over-development. As a result, this pair were planned to contain 14 flats, instead of 12 as in all other blocks. Curiously, one of the early lessees combined two flats at the time of purchase so the actual number of flats in the block of Nos 7 and 8 today is 13. In the following decades some other units were merged to create larger dwellings but that is not part of the story at this point.

Where Brown did not attempt to recreate Searles' scheme will be found in the rear (south) elevation of the Paragon, which differs considerably from the original. As with Colonnade House, Brown took liberties in the interests of light and air for the basement units. Before the war damage, the basements had been servants' quarters and kitchens; after the war, such space was too valuable to be left as utility rooms but since the front rooms (which faced north) looked straight on to the brick walls retaining the front footpath, these spaces were planned for utilitarian purposes. The rear rooms could be arranged as sitting rooms and, by substantial excavation and lowering of the ground levels (see illustrations), enjoy the benefit of the south light through much of the day.

The amalgamation of the gardens into a single pleasure ground helped in this respect and the basement dwellers had one great advantage: immediate access to the gardens at ground level. The gardens were made more 'interesting' by the piling up of the excavated material and redundant rubble into hillocks. Inevitably, not all the new Paragon residents were pleased by the garden re-arrangements. Wilfred ("Bunny") Teagle (1920-2008), a distinguished ornithologist, and his then wife Rosemary [nee Gault] kept a careful notebook of his time in the Paragon from March 1953 to 1961. Shortly before he died I received his permission to quote from his notes:

"I moved to Blackheath in March 1953, having escaped from a dreary part of north west London where I had lived from the age of seven. It was a new world, with an immense expanse of grass and sky, and there trees around the Heath that had been allowed to grow to their full height, in marked contrast to the brutally pollarded trees in the road I had left behind. My flat at the top of No 2 The Paragon was reached by a climb of sixty-four stairs. I therefore had an excellent view of my new territory. My bedroom window overlooked the Heath, and my living room opened on to a small balcony that looked across the partially developed Paragon garden towards the area still Blackheath Park. A caravan site was visible from the balcony and further out, beyond the railway cutting, there were piggeries.

The Heath was in a transitional state when I appeared on the scene. The Nissen huts had gone, but the prefabs were still there and were to remain for some time. There were large areas where the vegetation had been left more or less unchecked and these provided suitable conditions for the skylark, a species that had taken advantage of the of the unmown vegetation on Hampstead Heath and Wormwood Scrubs.

The year 1953 was to see the end of such favourable sites on Blackheath. Fences were erected and notices appeared that announced that the ground was being "reinstated". Some of enclosures acted as sanctuaries, however, for larks were heard singing there until late June. During that month most of the rough area was ploughed up but two birds were still frequenting the enclosed expanse east of Talbot Place on 22 August.

More devastating were the changes which took place to the ground south of the Paragon:

'All too few visits were paid to the wilderness behind The Paragon before the axes and bulldozers got to work. Half of the Paragon garden was in an unformed state when I moved in on 26th March [1953]. It was, in fact, a bare expanse of mud, peppered with Blackheath's characteristic pebble-pellets, and it was not until the well into the spring that it began to turn a timid and insipid green. The garden door of No 2 was locked ... for the outside steps had yet to be provided. The steps appeared in due course, but the door remained locked for a good time afterwards.

It was this difficulty of access which made my visits to the "wilderness" very few indeed. My first penetration in fact was made on 11 May and force of circumstances made it a very brief one. I found the Hamiltons (Sir George & Lady H) of Paragon House fussing around a mother mallard and her brood of three in their front garden [in South Row] – just at the time I ought to have been running for a train. We caught the ducklings with the idea of putting them on to the Prince of Wales pond. But the duck flew to the lawns of Paragon house – in the opposite direction – and so Sir George and I took the ducklings through the garden and set out for a quite different pond [the round pond – filled in by the municipality in the alter 1950s] which lay beyond the wilderness.

We passed from the garden of Paragon house into a tangle of vegetation – a mixture of cultivated and wild plants covering the remains of out-buildings – tall willows, walls of bramble and a sort of cartouche-shaped concrete pond choked with aquatic weeds. The, beyond the willows, the pond – a sheet of duckweed littered with fallen branches -, and a waving forest of reed mace. It was not the sort of pond one expected to find so near the centre of London. It did not survive for long.

On 29 June [1953] I found that the waters upon which we had launched three cheeping ducklings little more than a month before had disappeared. There was only mud – very wet and still covered with the green confetti of duckweed. The habitat was soon to be swept away. Lorries made Pond Road their highway, walls fell and fences went up. As I crossed the top of the road each morning I looked down to see if the green of the reed mace still showed. It was there for quite a while, then brick and rubble buried the dried mud of the pond, and the remaining willows were left standing in a pinkish desert where moorhens had paddled and newts had lurked. Yes. The pond and all that remained was its name, preserved in Pond Road. During the autumn the brambles followed suit, and in the wake of the bulldozers came the cement-mixers and brick-layers. *[Author's note: This would have been building work for the Fulthorp Road houses].*

Although I rarely went down to the "wilderness" (behind the Paragon) its voices came to me from across the garden throughout the spring and summer. Some of the voices were undoubtedly those of m migrants. Chiffchaffs did not sing between 15 May and 2 August and no willow warbler was heard between 21st April and 26th July. But blackcaps often sang and whitethroats were persistent. The first one (whitethroat) I saw and heard on that hurried dash to the pond, three ducklings in hand. That particular bird may have been a (passing) migrant, but other most certainly stayed, and almost every morning in June and often in July I would hear the scratchy song. One was seen in song-flight in The Paragon garden itself on 28 June. Then on 2nd August a female was seen feeding three well-fledged young.

Throughout most of 1953 the ground behind the two blocks that formed Nos 5-8 in the crescent lay untended; the houses themselves were untenanted and uninhabitable, having been damaged by bombing during the war. Before the finch population could exploit the seeding weeds, however, work began on the houses and by the end of the year this part of the garden had been changed into something resembling that behind No 2-4 at the time of my arrival.

Building work continued throughout 1954, not only behind the Paragon, where flats had been erected, but on the ruined part of the Paragon itself. Whereas in 1953 it was possible, by leaving the living-room window open, to hear the voices of the warblers as they arrived, in 1954 one could rarely hear anything for the noise of cement mixers,, lorries and all the mechanical dinosaurs that are put into service by the building industry.

Much of the area behind the Paragon remained un-built on event at the end of the year, but it had little attraction for birds. But thrushes, blackbirds, starlings and sparrows continued to frequent the Paragon lawn, and jays, woodpigeons and goldfinches still haunted the trees. The green and great spotted woodpeckers seemed less frequent and no breeding spotted flycatchers were noticed...

The Heath itself remained much the same. The areas which had been "closed for reinstatement" remained all through the year, developing their grassy covering and providing secluded restring places for common, black-headed and lesser black-backed gulls, and feeding places for crows, jackdaws and starlings. The arks sang bravely but any nesting attempts they made must have been frustrated by the mowing and rolling which took place periodically.'"

Whatever was done to the garden ground all the semi-circular bays were rebuilt, except those of houses Nos 4 and 14. No 13 The Paragon always lacked a bay and none was added during the conversion. The other bays were all carried right to the top of the buildings, whereas originally these had stopped short by one floor. The bay of No 4 The Paragon, which extended to the top floor in any event, was not rebuilt (see illustration).

The restorative treatment of the rear of the colonnade sections varied from house to house, as did the staircases leading from the ground floor to the garden. There were few surviving drawings or photographs to show the aspect from the garden, which could have acted as a guide. Brown had to use his ingenuity and the compromise he achieved is by no means as successful as the facade and certainly not always in a true Georgian style. Georgian houses often appeared as elegant from the rear (known, curiously, as the back front) as they did from the front elevation. Colonnade House, originally, may have been one such building. But it was necessary to provide as much space and light as possible and huge, almost picture, windows were inserted.

During the conversion, the opportunity was taken to remove all the dividing garden walls from the Paragon houses as well as from Paragon House, to create a communal garden. Only Cator Lodge and Cator Manor (as Brown named the west-end outhouses on the turn of the crescent to South Row proper) enjoyed their own little private spaces. This has always been regarded as a masterstroke and, indeed, it was. But it should be remembered that many of the garden walls had fallen down, or were in danger of so doing, and the cost of repair would have been huge. There would also have been the necessity of imposing the garden arrangements and responsibilities on the occupants of the six flats or so in each house. Brown had benefited from long experience of property management and the difficulties that could ensue when lessees disputed the rights and wrongs of horticultural management. One big garden laid to lawn would be simple to maintain and easy to use. Those desperate for a little gardening could potter at their planters and tubs, while the basement dwellers would quickly take responsibility for those tiny scraps of defensible space outside their windows.

Paragon House was converted into six units; Colonnade House lent itself to seven apartments. And each of the 14 Paragon houses was converted to offer a basement flat and five other flats, one on each of the upper floors and two on the ground floor – all self-contained. Nos 7 and 8 have thirteen between them. The basement flats, except in Nos 7 and 8, have five rooms, kitchen and bathroom; all the other flats have two rooms, kitchen and bathroom.

Houses Nos 7 and 8, the last to be completed, were combined. In the centre of that block is a spiral staircase with a fine wrought-iron banister rail and this is probably the most graceful interior feature of the entire rebuilt terrace. The flats are all of the two- or three-room variety, with one exception on the ground floor, and even the basement flats are no larger. But as this block is deeper than the other six, the floor area of each flat is greater than those of the corresponding flats in all the other houses.

The flats were completed and offered for sale or let from about 1948 onwards, some with short leases but most with leases of 84 years at an annual ground rent of £25. In view of the then prevailing housing crisis, the flats were occupied as soon as they were ready, even if the other flats in the house were still unfinished. Some early occupiers remember being unable to use the front entrance to their house for several months because it was obstructed by scaffolding and stacks of building materials – a situation which must also have faced the occupiers in the period 1794 to 1805.

The quick sale of the flats greatly benefited Brown's financial arrangements and the investment started to climb out of deficit. In 1955, flats in Nos 5 and 6 The Paragon were offered for sale at prices ranging from £3,950 (the basement flats) to £1,795 (the attic flats). The rateable values varied between £32 and £48 per annum at rates then of 20/3d (101.5p) in the £, and the London County Council offered 80 per cent mortgages at four per cent per annum interest. In the prospectus for these two houses, the total annual outgoings per flat for ground rent, rates, water rates, insurance and a fair share of the cleaning of the common parts and staircases and gardening, were estimated at about £103.9.4 (£103.47) for the basement flat and at £76.4.1 (£76.20) for the top flat.

The rebuilding of the Paragon was completed in August 1958 when the flats in Nos 7 and 8 were offered for sale. Prices were higher than in the other houses, but the flats were larger: they ranged from £3,000 to £3,850 for most flats, but one flat, with four large rooms, was offered at £6,500. Ground rent and rates were identical to those of Nos 5 and 6, except for the one large unit for which the ground rent was £35 a year.

Whether the venture was a financial success is difficult to judge but there was no doubt about its aesthetic success. The reconstruction was highly praised in many newspapers and periodicals, and by many architectural writers. The LCC Historic Buildings Council had listed the Paragon and Paragon House as buildings of exceptional architectural and historic merit, scheduling the Paragon immediately as Grade I in 1951, and Paragon House as Grade II*.

There is some mystery about the cost of the exercise although Brown was quite frank in revealing his outgoings on some of the repair works. The financial story of Colonnade House, for example, is well-detailed in his book. A lot of money was obtained from grant aid in the form of War Damage Commission payments and, later, from a form of historic buildings' grants. At the public inquiry in 1952, into the compulsory purchase order for the backlands to the south of the Paragon, Brown is quoted as claiming that he had spent £250,000 on the Paragon and South Row houses. This was why he said that he was particularly angry that his lessees (who had paid for their flats) would be looking into the kitchen windows of municipal dwellings if the town hall scheme went ahead. It did – but his lessees managed to survive the embarrassment. Also, when the last Paragon flat (at No 7) had been sold in the autumn of 1958, *The Times* reported (4 November) that the cost of the project, once estimated at around £80,000 to £100,000 had, in the end, come out at £360,000. Brown had to fund the difference between grants and costs but he could, of course, retain the proceeds of sales.

It would be fair and reasonable to suggest, from information gleaned by the author in discussions with Charles Bernard Brown, and subsequently with those who knew him well, that he may not have become very rich from his redevelopment of the Paragon and South Row, but he certainly did not become poor. His other property dealings in Blackheath and elsewhere (particularly the conversion of Trumpeter's Lodge in Richmond) ensured that he was comfortably placed and could enjoy the rewards his work had earned.

Brown was pardonably proud of his achievement in Blackheath. He was also concerned about the future upkeep of the buildings which he had so faithfully and painstakingly resurrected. He was the sole proprietor and freeholder (the freehold obtained from the Cator trustees in 1955) and was concerned that, as he was a bachelor, there would be no family to inherit the title to the property and ensure that his efforts would not be eroded by neglect and mismanagement.

In 1969 he successfully negotiated the sale of the freeholds of the Paragon, Paragon House and Colonnade House to the trustees of Morden College, along with the benefit of some of the short-lease flats as well. Thus, some of the ground on which these buildings stand com-pleted a full circle. From being in the possession of Sir John Morden and, thereafter, of the trustees of the College which he founded and to which he gave his name, the ground was sold to Sir Gregory Page in 1723. In turn, his heirs sold it to John Cator in 1783, with whose family the freehold remained until 1955. Thereafter the ground passed to Paragon Preservation Ltd (Charles Brown's holding company for the property) and, finally, in 1969, it reverted once more to the trustees of Morden College.

Gardens – front and back

When Searles laid down the shape of the Paragon, he built it behind a crescent of grass, separate from the Heath. It was planned as a single open space, the houses enjoying only back gardens. In South Row, the buildings enjoyed both private front drives and back gardens.

To keep out the public and grazing animals (sheep, in particular, grazed Blackheath during the 18th and 19th centuries), the Paragon green was protected by a ditch with a high mound on one edge. There is much controversy about this: in modern times it has been elevated to the status of a ha-ha, and the 1847 plan of Blackheath (by the Driver brothers, of Southwark) marks the ditch quite clearly as such (see illustration). But formal archaeological excavations in 1974 revealed the original profile of the ditch and the archaeologists claimed that the ha-ha theory could be firmly discounted. For more details on this see Chapter 9.

Nevertheless, as late as the 1850s the Paragon remained open to public gaze until, eventually, on the Paragon side of the ditch there grew a screen of elms which acted as a windbreak and tended to hide the crescent. The spread of Dutch elm disease in 1975 led to the felling of these trees although, by then, the ground had been invaded by epicormic growth and various self-seeded shrubs. The loss of the trees had one unexpected benefit, in that it became possible to enjoy a magnificent view of the terrace, in all its restored beauty, from the Heath: a view that had not been available, in the summer at least, for almost a hundred years. The front green has boasted a number of other trees over the years, and a few remain (chestnut, for example), providing a somewhat park-like setting for the Paragon.

When Blackheath was taken into public care by the Metropolitan Board of Works in 1871, an argument developed as to whether the Paragon green was part of the Heath or not. If so, then the Board would expect to reclaim it and restore it to the Heath – this would allow public access. In the end, it was agreed that the green was not part of the Heath but, in 1931, as an extra security precaution, it was deemed protected by the London Squares Preservation Act. In this way, it could remain in the possession of the Paragon owner or owners and it was safe from development and building.

Wartime neglect led to the ground being covered in long grass as well as the invasion of weeds, shrubs and saplings. In the early years of the restoration, a good part of it was used for the parking of contractors' huts and building equipment. Brown's treatment of the front green led to a mildly acrimonious correspondence with A. R. Martin, then acting as Honorary Secretary to the Blackheath Society had learned that Brown intended to plant up the land with what the Society suspected might be artificially introduced flowering shrubs, better suited to, and more reminiscent of, a municipal recreation ground or a suburban garden. The Society considered that species native to open heathland would be a more appropriate choice. Brown's retort was that he had had enough difficulty as it was, restoring the houses and dealing with looters and vandals, and that he would do exactly as he wished. Martin replied, politely, that Brown's hands were tied because of the London Squares Preservation Act – a piece of information which was new to both Brown and his then landlord.

The Society, it has to be said with hindsight, misjudged the architect: Brown simply cleaned up the ground and sought the advice of one of his lessees – Miss Kate Gaussen (later Mrs Phillips), then living at No 14 – a horticultur-alist. The end result was plain but dignified and the scene was immortalised in Geoffrey Fletcher's sketch of the part-restored Paragon, published in the *Manchester Guardian* in November 1951 (see illustration). Kate Gaussen is the lady sweeping up the autumn leaves.

John Gower's Panorama of the Paragon and South Row,
Society of Architectural Historians of Great Britain, 1987

8 THE REPORTER

E. WOOKEY & CO. EST. 1882

B. WILLSON-PEMBERTON
F.A.I., A.R.V.A.

CHARTERED AUCTIONEERS · SURVEYORS · VALUERS · ESTATE AGENTS

| 2 CHARLTON RD. S.E.3 | 119 BURNT ASH RD. LEE, S.E.2 | 8 HIGH STREET CHISLEHURST, KENT | 245 HIGH STREET BECKENHAM, KENT | MAURITSWEG 31A ROTTERDAM, HOLLAND |

SURVEY DEPARTMENT . . . 5, TRANQUIL PASSAGE, S.E.3. E. J. WATTS, A.R.I.C.S.

25 MONTPELIER VALE, BLACKHEATH, S.E.3

Manager : MICHAEL BARDEN   *Telephone* : LEE 4353 (10 lines)

OUR ENLARGED AND MODERNISED OFFICE IN MONTPELIER VALE IS NOW ABLE TO SHOW PROJECTED COLOUR SLIDES OF THE FOLLOWING PROPERTIES (AMONG OTHERS).

BLACKHEATH. NEW DEVELOPMENTS:

200 yds. from Heath. Freehold Town Houses, 6 Rooms. Cloakroom, Kitchen, Bathroom. Full Central Heating. Garage. Garden.   **£7,850 Freehold**

In Rural Lane. Very near Heath. Detached Freehold Houses of superb construction. 8 Rooms. Cloakroom, Kitchen-Diner, Double Glazing, Vanitory Units in Bedrooms. Double Garage. Full Central Heating. Garden.   **£14,000 Freehold**

THE PARAGON, BLACKHEATH
Ground Floor Colonnade Flat. One Bedroom, One Reception Room, Kitchen, Bathroom.
£5,250 Leasehold

TARNWOOD PARK, ELTHAM
Two Storey Maisonette. Two Large Bedrooms, One Reception Room, Luxury Bathroom and Kitchen. Garage.   **£4,950 Leasehold**

SURVEY DEPARTMENT, 5a Tranquil Passage, Blackheath, S.E.3. LEE 4353/1-9.

THE FOLLOWING PROFESSIONAL STAFF HAVE NOW JOINED THE FIRM:

EDWARD T. WISHLADE, B.Sc. (Estate Management), A.R.I.C.S., A.A.I.   MAURICE YOUNG, A.R.I.C.S.
Consultant Architect: BRIAN DAVID MEEKING, A.R.I.B.A.

The above are selected at random from our well-stocked register. We would be happy to send a property list **ON APPLICATION.**

Advertisement for Messrs Wookey, estate agent, 1962. *BLG*.

CHAPTER NINE
MORE MODERN TIMES

T**he completion of** the works to the Paragon, Paragon House and Colonnade House in the late 1940s and early 1950s marked the end of a major task for Charles Bernard Brown, promoting the cause of post-war historic building restoration. The national and local authorities in England and Wales, alas, decided that there was also encouragement to clear sites and rebuild in a contemporary form, albeit quite often with little concern for the historic style of surviving neighbourhoods. At the same time they took the chance to clear communities that had not suffered from bombing. There was a strong party-political influence on housing policy, with, by and large, the Conservatives eagerly supported by the building industry and the Labour councils anxious to become the largest landlords in their municipalities.

Blackheath was one such area, having to fight both sides from the middle. Fortunately, there were forces for good in the district which had kept going through the years of conflict despite lack of resources. The Blackheath Society had been held in suspended animation although the Secretary, A R Martin, did his best (even when posted as a Treasury solicitor to Stratford-on-Avon) to keep a watchful eye and a firm grip on SE3, engaging, often successfully, in battles with minor bureaucracy. His attempt to retain the Georgian and early-Victorian ironworks to many of the houses fronting the Heath was frustrated less by Mr Jobsworth of the Town Hall than by thieves arriving at 6.00 a.m. with false papers and oxyacetylene torches.

Brown replaced all the street railings in the Paragon and South Row in keeping with the original ironwork where these had survived; some could be hammered straight and refurbished. The Colonnade House ironwork is a good example of this, although the street railings were not replaced until the present century.

Thus, the Paragon houses, filled with eager new flat dwellers, settled down to a period of mannered calm. It was a stupendous example of what could be done and Brown's achievement was much praised in the national press. The younger members of his profession were not always as enthusiastic, however, as he would discover in the early 1960s.

Festival of Britain plaque, 1951

Brown received no civic honour for his efforts in Blackheath and Richmond. But perhaps one accolade might have pleased him more. This was the Festival of Britain Award for outstanding achievements in matters of building design. The symbol – the work of graphic designer Abram Games (1914-1996) – was reproduced as a metal plaque and mounted above the Paragon Lodge (No 15) in the summer of 1951. Other 'winners' from a restricted list were developments designed by distinguished architects of their day, still respected in 2011.

There was a school in Catford designed by Yorke, Rosenberg & Mardell; two housing schemes by [Sir] Frederick Gibberd. Maxwell Fry & Drew submitted flats at Catford. Brown's contribution was described as the Paragon, Paragon House, Nos 2-6 South Row and Colonnade House, even though the site of Nos 2-6 South Row was still holes in the ground. Maybe the schemes were judged partly from plans but, if so, no Brown drawings for replacement Nos 2-6 South Row have been discovered.

It was this level of recognition that most of the new Paragon dwellers appreciated. But this was not always the case, as the local press, including the *Kentish Mercury*, was eager to report. Interviews with the new council tenants in Ryculf Square (on the Lewisham side of Pond Road) revealed much appreciation of the improved conditions and facilities compared with their previous homes, but arrangements were not, in the tenants' view, wholly well thought out: for example, 'electric plugs in the bedrooms get hidden behind furniture because the windows are in the wrong position'. There was another – much bigger – grumble: the coal bunker. In many cases 'it is right down the length of the hall, opposite the living-room door'. 'Every time the coalman calls it is operation spring-clean,' said one housewife.

Nevertheless, because the designer (Sir Albert Richardson [1880-1964]) had striven to harmonise his scheme with the Paragon, the press referred to Ryculf Square as 'the Beau Brummell Estate', because of its Georgian feel.

Just as the municipal tenants in Ryculf Square had mixed views, so had the residents in Brown's restored Paragon, especially when it came to increases in rent. The landlord could not just put up the rent – he (or she) had to convince the local court. Landlord and tenant could state their case but were obliged to accept the court's findings. Brown made a powerful case for increasing the rents as these had been fixed at pre-war values but, equally, he was all too well aware of post-war costs. In December 1954 the rent for No 1 Paragon House was £166.8.1; Flat 4, £180.4.1; and Flat 3 in No 11 The Paragon was £95 per annum. Brown wanted to register 'a fair increase'. He made the point that many of those who resented this had lived for years in the Paragon and had benefited hugely as the value and sale price of their flats climbed and climbed.

The following week the residents turned out in force, represented by surveyors who would plead their case. Because of the council estate at the

rear of the Paragon, Mr Norman Singleton said that 'the area is rapidly deteriorating'. Another advocate for the residents was Mr W. Wilson Pemberton (later proprietor of estate agents Wookey & Wookey). He said that the view from the Paragon flats was hardly pleasing, and added that there was a caravan site and pig farm at the back as well. (These had been there during the war and the pig farm was some distance away.)

Mr Singleton claimed that there were serious disadvantages to living in the Paragon flats, 'but this was not surprising with buildings erected more than a century and a half ago … They do not and never did contain many of the basic requirements for good-class flats.' He pointed out that the flats were not sound-proof and the walls not entirely –proofed against penetrating damp so it was difficult to keep the rooms warm as there was no central heating. He added that the tenants had to walk downstairs to the coal store and dustbin sheds which were under the roadway. The larders were inadequate and frequently unventilated.

The Paragon tenants felt that they should not be expected to pay for the outside beauty of a building; that the comforts of a home were the things that mattered. At least eighteen of the residents were represented at the rent tribunal, including the Countess of Enniskillen, businessman Brian Farmer, the son of Mr Wilson Pemberton, and the distinguished long-term Paragon resident Mr Victor Serebriakoff, founder of Mensa (who died at Flat 1, No 6 The Paragon in January 1987, aged 87, 33 years later).

Most of the new Paragonians – as they quickly became known (or Paragoons, following the example of the popular radio show: the Goon Show). But although families did settle there, the turnover of flats was brisk once building societies became used to funding mortgages for leasehold dwellings. This was a scheme Brown claimed to have pioneered, encouraged by local chartered surveyors and estate agents Stocker & Roberts (since dissolved).

One initial drawback was that many of the flats were too small once a child or two had arrived .The Furber family (still living in Blackheath at the time of writing) were one of the first to take a Paragon flat (at No 14). Geoffrey Fletcher's drawing of the Paragon west end in 1948 depicts a pram on the lawn – almost certainly holding the infant John Furber QC, still a Blackheath resident. Mr and Mrs Furber produced more children, making a move essential, although they retained affection for the Paragon and its occupants, attending the 200th anniversary dinner in 1994.

Although the Paragon houses boasted small gardens – relative to the number of residents – the Paragonians made good use of what there was. The basement and ground-floor dwellers in particular were known to place a few pots and planters in front of their windows and to enjoy picnics in suitable weather. Surveyor Jonathan Stocks remembers his time as a small boy in the 1970s, finding much to keep him and his friends occupied, and reminisced about the 'secret footpath' also known as the Grove memorial wall and garden, on the site of the old tennis court, which then led from the west end of the garden through to the block of garages on Pond Road. He was a co-author with H L Masterson of the Paragonian song:

> *The yellow bricks of the Paragon*
> *The artists' praise have always won.*
> *Right opposite the Greenwich Park*
> *It spreads around its noble arc,*
> *It claims attention as you pass.*
>
> *It is a refuge where we store*
> *A wealth of friends whose kindly ways*
> *Support us through our nights and days.*
> *Through all life's cares it is the hub;*
> *More than a building, it's a club*
> *Where neighbours lend a hand to each,*
> *Heart warming all within their reach:*
> *Doctors, poets and specialists,*
> *Civil servants and journalists*
> *The barbecue with joy resounds*
> *And with our friends we stroll the grounds.*
>
> *Happy he or she who can*
> *Say: 'I'm a Paragonian.'*

One distinguished author, who even set one of his novels in and around the Paragon, found that life there was not always easy, however. He regretted the lack of private gardens, no amenities for children, and the fact that he had to avoid the Air Vice-Marshal's dog. Also, not all of his literary friends knew where Blackheath actually was.

The new South Row

It was the replacing of South Row in the early 1960s which sparked the final major controversy between developers, planners and the conservationist lobby. Brown's intention was to rebuild the bombed-out remains of South Row in replica. Photographs of the original buildings can be found in this book, so the reader will be able to gain a good idea of what was in the architect's mind.

Public inquiries and lobbying had decided the fate of the Paragon's backlands, within the Borough of Greenwich. There were to be municipal flats. When the landlord (Colonel H. J. Cator) learned from his agent that the ground would be taken by compulsory purchase, he decided not to appeal. One slightly curious element in the Paragon history was Searles' (or Cator's) parsimonious attitude towards the private gardens. None was very long and the south boundary was more or less as it is now, marked by the line of Fulthorp Road. Nevertheless, there was a considerable acreage of meadowland between the back garden walls and the Kid Brook which flowed through the round pond (quite close to the present railway line,

which arrived in 1848–49). Paragon residents took these small plots in good measure but on short leases, initially expiring in 1828. Many households kept a cow or two here, one or two boasted small fish ponds, or were able to make use of the land for their horses. Only four of the houses boasted serious stabling.

But the garden grounds behind Bryan House (No 2 South Row) and Colonnade House (No 7) were so extensive that post-war development would have taken place in any event, whether private or municipal. The only difference with a private scheme was that this would probably have permitted larger back gardens.

Instead, the land was utilised by the municipality (the LCC working hand-in-glove with Lewisham Borough Council) for a series of three-storey blocks called Ryculf Square. There was fierce objection to this; with local people angry at what they thought was violation of the historic environment of Blackheath by philistine planners.

One objector in 1953 (architect Frederick Thwaites Bush) spoke of the dreadful prospect for the residents in the newly-restored Colonnade House. They would be unable to avoid the view of the dustbins, washing and rubbish of the people in the new flats, he claimed. As it proved, the slope of the ground precluded most of that and trees subsequently shielded the eyes of even those in the attic rooms. Charles Brown had been equally horrified that, having spent a fortune on restoring the Paragon, his new lessees would have a full-on view of the Greenwich flats in Fulthorp Road and what some old Blackheathans considered socially ill-behaved Council tenants.

These were the views of the early 1950s. Nevertheless, all parties survived, little knowing that most of the municipal flats would eventually become privately owned and populated by the middle classes (i.e., people with money).

Meanwhile, the South Row site lay fallow. It was cleared in June/July 1941 as a hazard, following the bombing. Initially, it was used as ground for a small group of prefabricated houses, euphemistically known as 'The Bungalows'. Many enjoyed a few years in the wide and overgrown garden of Colonnade House.

It had been Charles Bernard Brown's intention to replace Nos 2-6 South Row with replicas of what had stood there from about 1800 to 1940: Bryan House in particular was very fine. But although the shells of these houses were repairable, the local authority would have none of it and they were demolished on grounds of safety. The author remembers taking a short cut over the bombed area from the Prince of Wales pond to Pond Road, when in his teens, to visit a relative in Blackheath Park. At the time he didn't consider what may once have stood on the bombsite and what would happen next.

Its future was decided by the following circumstances: firstly, Brown could not raise the capital to proceed with his plans, although there was much encouragement for them; secondly, his friend and erstwhile informal partner in building matters – Leslie Bilsby – was by then eagerly engaged in promoting the cause of the modernists in building design.

Bilsby's company – Span Developments Ltd – applied for planning consent to clear the site and erect a block of flats on the Heath frontage, with a row of houses on the south edge of the plot. They would be designed by the architect Eric Lyons (1912–1980) and be unashamedly in a modern idiom. At least, some felt, Lyons would respect the building line of Colonnade House and the roof height (more or less). Brown promoted his own scheme of things.

After much lobbying by the Blackheath Society, the Royal Fine Art Commission and, *inter alia*, the Georgian Group, the Span scheme was rejected by the London County Council. Such had been the level of concern that the amenity societies briefed learned counsel to plead their case at the public inquiry. Span appealed, as it had the right to do. The outcome was a triumph for Span but a disaster for the amenity groups.

The government's Planning Inspector wrote: '*... the facsimile building proposed by Paragon Preservation Ltd [Brown] would cast doubt on the authenticity of the adjacent buildings and assume an importance which it could not justify or maintain*'.

The Blackheath Society was enraged. It made a firm public statement that the Inspector's opinion may have been valid if it had been proposed to fill the gap with a vaguely 'period' buildings but this was not what had been suggested. The proposition was that the external elevations should reproduce exactly what had been destroyed, following the pattern established with the restoration of houses within the Paragon..

The LCC planning committee, local residents and many architects were in favour of this and appealed to the higher authority in the shape of the Minister of Housing. Unfortunately for the conservationists, the Minister's department saw fit to recommend that the Inspector's view be upheld in favour of Span. It was the scheme designed by Lyons, later President of the Royal Institute of British Architects (1975–77). The Blackheath Society responded: 'It is a matter of great regret that the Minister of Housing [Rt Hon. Henry Brooke] should have seen fit not only to reject the opinion of the LCC Planning Committee, but also to have ignored local opinion, which some of his predecessors were more ready to take into account.' They should not have been surprised. Brooke was a fan of Span and in 1959 had planted a tree at Corner Green Span estate, off Pond Road, to mark the notional one-millionth private house built since the end of the war.

Work started on the new South Row in 1961, after which members of the public were able to make up their own minds whether the modern replacement enjoyed the same aesthetic quality as Searles' original. The owners of the new flats thought them splendid and, being untrammelled by protective legislation (other than conservation area status), seemingly without problems.

The Blackheath Society could not leave it at that, but made a few, not altogether negative, points about the development in its Annual Report for 1962: 'Members will have noticed that the Span flats between Colonnade House and Pond Road, which were allowed on appeal after being turned down by the LCC, are now at last taking shape. Criticism will undoubtedly be levelled at some of the qualities of design, the heaviness of which is emphasised by the gracious refinement of detail in the neighbouring buildings, but at least the colouring of the new brickwork blends well with the old, and the skyline of the flats is relatively unobtrusive among the fine trees that have been preserved on the site."

The design team, consisting mostly of young architects, found the South Row scheme most exciting. What they did not like was the view of Sir Albert Richardson's municipal blocks of flats, designed in a Georgian style, which they could see every day from their drawing boards. So they erected screens in order to avoid being offended.

All property, of whatever age and style, needs attention from time to time, with periodic redecoration and repair. Controversy arose in 1968 when some of the householders on the Span estate decided that they would replace their windows with non-conforming styles which would, they thought, being plastic (uPvc), be cheaper to install and easier to maintain.

The owners were split – daggers were drawn. However, the conservation lobby, backed by the Blackheath Society, won the day, not only by repelling the installation of modern non-conforming windows throughout the development; it also saw the whole block being listed Grade II in June 1996, which gave an extra dimension of protection. It was the first Span estate in Blackheath to be statutorily listed, despite being less than 33 years old at the time: a badge which all the residents would wear with pardonable pride. English Heritage wrote of it: 'The group makes a careful, well-landscaped but nevertheless powerful contribution to a sensitive historic setting.' Alas, neither Leslie Bilsby nor Eric Lyons was alive to enjoy this remarkable accolade for a modern housing estate.

Bonwitt book & the Blackheath Centenary 1871-1971

There was a heartening revival of interest in local history in the late 1960s and early 1970s. The author of this work, then Press Officer for the Blackheath Society, was commissioned by the Greater London Council in 1971 to write a pamphlet to mark the 100th anniversary of the local authority assuming responsibility for the care of the Heath: the result was *Blackheath Centenary 1871-1971*.

It proved to be a success and soon called for a reprint. Variant editions, entitled The Heath, have been published over the years and the book, in a much expanded form, has remained in print ever since. One reader of the Blackheath pamphlet was German-born William Bonwitt, resident of No 6 The Paragon. He had long had an interest in his house and the attractive crescent of which it was a part. Bonwitt (1910–1992), who was born in Stettin, then in Prussia, fled the anti-Semitism of his home town a few years before the outbreak of war. He remained in Britain long enough to be granted British citizenship and eligible to join the Intelligence Corps, for which he acted as an interpreter of captured Nazi officers under interrogation.

 After demobilisation, Bonwitt set up as a manufacturing stationer, with a substantial factory in north-west Kent. He also developed a collector's penchant for what we, in our ignorance, would call 'valentine cards' but he knew as 'paper cuts'. In 1975 he decided to write a history of the Paragon and Paragon House and record a schedule of some of its inhabitants. His interest encouraged, he worked with characteristic thoroughness and his 54-page book, published in 1976, soon sold out. Copies became increasingly rare and currently (2011) change hands for substantial sums.

Bill Bonwitt was not interested in revisions and reprints. The book had been published and he was satisfied. What attracted him next was an investigation into the life and career of the architect Michael Searles, designer of the Paragon and the other South Row houses. The result of all his painstaking research was his monograph, *Michael Searles: a Georgian Architect and Surveyor*, which was published in 1987 by the Society of Architectural Historians of Great Britain. While he was disappointed that the Searles book was much thinner than he had expected due his publisher's rigorous editing process, he did appreciate the fact that the Society had recognised his outstanding scholarship, even though he was not an architectural historian.

Ha-ha investigation, 1979

Another element of the rise in interest in local history embraced a new approach to urban archaeology. A number of enthusiasts set up local groups, working as professionally as it was possible with limited resources but with a tenacious discipline in recording all findings.

One topic was of particular interest: was the Paragon protected on its north boundary by a ha-ha, or just by a plain ditch? The Driver brothers' survey of 1847 clearly marks the ditch as a ha-ha – and the Drivers were some of the best land surveyors of their time – but the general view was that it was not.

In 1979, by invitation of some Paragon residents, a group from the Greenwich archaeological and historical societies, led by D. T. Jones, BA, Dip. Arch investigated the Paragon ditch to establish once and for all whether it was a ha-ha. The findings were quite clear: a single trench was dug which revealed that the original Paragon ditch was a broad U-shaped construction about 6 metres wide by 2 metres deep.

Although many 19th-century fragments were discovered and a few possibly from the 18th century, little of value was found. However, the team positively established that the Drivers were wrong and that the Paragon could not boast a ha-ha. Some were deeply disappointed, having conjectured that

there had been a ha-ha in the Drivers' time (1840s) which had been removed. This is doubtful, partly because the digging team was able to confirm that the trench had been cleared out at some time early in the 20th century and no trace of any ha-ha wall had survived.

The purpose of a ha-ha would have been to keep livestock away from a lawn or private garden. But the only livestock known to have grazed freely on the Heath in the 18th and 19th century were sheep, which had almost certainly gone by the 1860s.

Paragon Bicentenary

There was no dispute in June 1994 when, by general agreement of various parties, it was decided that the Paragon was then 200 years old. There was evidence of construction by 1794, the boundary stone fixed on the Heath by the Greenwich parish being one firm indicator. Another had been placed (or replaced) in 1890 to mark the division between Greenwich and Lewisham parishes. Two events marked the Bicentenary: the erection of a carved slate plaque between Nos 13 and No 14 to mark the work of both Michael Searles and Charles Bernard Brown, and a dinner in a marquee in the gardens. The author, who was a guest at the dinner, was honoured to be asked to propose the toast to Michael Searles' memory, and to the Paragon, which he did with enthusiasm. The response was given by Paragon resident Commandant Vonla McBryde (1921-2003), one-time Chief Officer of the Women's Royal Naval Service (the Wrens).

The Paragon Bicentenary plaque was jointly sponsored by the Paragon residents, the Blackheath Society, and the then landlords, Morden College. It was carved in slate by stonecutter Bernard Klose, who insisted on erecting it on the building himself to ensure a proper job. The Brown trustees were represented on this splendid occasion by Mr Frank Boswell, Charles Brown's executor. Following the event, he donated some of Brown's photographic surveys of the Paragon to the images collection of the Blackheath Society. This valuable resource has enhanced this volume in considerable measure, especially the extraordinary scenes of wartime damage.

The plaque was unveiled by John Cator, of Woodbastwick Hall, Norfolk. He was an indirect descendant of the John Cator (1728-1806), of Beckenham, who had granted the development lease to Michael Searles which had brought the Paragon and South Row into being. Mr Cator (1897-2000) was a very genial guest and admired the scheme which his ancestor had encouraged. But even though his father, Lieut-Col. Henry John Cator (1897-1965) had backed Charles Brown's restoration plan, Mr Cator remained a little puzzled by the invitation. Shortly before receiving it, he had disposed of the last vestige of Cator property in Blackheath; he had even surrendered his patronage of the living of St Michael and All Angels parish church, once the Cator Proprietary Chapel, in Blackheath Park.

With the post-war enthusiasm for costume dramas both on the silver screen and on television it was inevitable that directors would seek suitable locations. The restored Paragon held such attraction so long as the residents cooperated and cars and other modern paraphernalia could be moved away.

One of the first was a film called *Secret Partner* (1961) starring Stewart Granger (1913-1993) as Brent, a shipping agent living in the Paragon, but it was the colourful productions which found the Paragon most useful, especially with its replica gas lamps. In 1972 *Lady Caroline Lamb* (directed by Robert Bolt and starring his wife, Sarah Miles) while notorious in content flopped both critically and at the box office.

Portrait of a Lady (Henry James) in 1995, and *Great Expectations* (Charles Dickens) in 1998 were made for television and were more successful. Not all the Paragon residents were pleased with the tiny amounts which ended up on the screen in relation to the time taken by the production teams, notwithstanding the fees to the management company.

Paragon 1 to 8 about 2003.

CHAPTER TEN
EPILOGUE

Michael Searles' Paragon is one of the glories of what remains of Georgian London. It was described by the late Sir Leslie Patrick Abercrombie (1879-1957) in his report on London in 1944 as '... the most important surviving ex-ample of Georgian domestic architecture in the country'. This may have been going somewhat over the top, considering the riches to be found in Bath and Edinburgh alone. Nevertheless, the Paragon provided gracious living for its occupants during its first two centuries, with a short break between 1939 and 1952, and continues to do so for the present residents. As Bill Bonwitt wrote in 1976, '... one must hope that this pleasant state of affairs will last for many more years.'

Although the modern Span block in South Row may seem, to some, a regrettably modern intrusion in what had been a fine piece of late-18th-century townscape when designed by Michael Searles (not that he would have recognised it as such), there is no doubt that Eric Lyons, in his turn, produced another piece of 'gracious living' but one attuned to the fashions and needs of the mid 20th century. Since it was listed Grade II in June 1996, South Row has settled, self-managing and relaxed and has welcomed/suffered as many coach loads of architectural students coming to admire Mr Lyons' smart new block of flats as those wanting to visit the restored Paragon. Eventually, the generation which could remember the pre-war South Row dwindled in number and those who could recall it as a bombsite also shrank. Within thirty years, South Row had become one of the familiar features of Blackheath; only the huge oak tree on the corner with Pond Road remained to bridge the pre-war years and the 21st century.

There was, briefly, a chance that the municipal flats in Pond Road would, in their turn, be scheduled as historic monuments. This would provide as much satisfaction for the Blackheath Society as did the scheduling of the Paragon, Paragon House and Colonnade House in the early 1950s. In some ways the process of appreciation had started in the late 1980s with a growing acceptance that Richardson's talents were to be found not just in pastiche.

In 1995 the local authority (Lewisham) served enforcement notices on those flat owners in Ryculf Square who had had the temerity to change their windows without consent, substituting plastic materials (uPvc) for the carefully proportioned wooden glazing bars which Richardson had specified in 1952 to match the Georgian pattern of the Paragon. Lewisham had come to recognise the design qualities of the municipal flats which it had found exasperating when imposed by an unusually sensitive Minister of Housing.

Ironically, when the window frames of the flats on the Greenwich side of Pond Road were suffering decay, the local authority replaced them with uPvc, requiring those few flats in private ownership to contribute to the cost whether they wanted to or not. Lewisham Council, for its side of the road, capitulated, imposing plastic windows on its own properties as well as on those tenants who had purchased their flats under the right-to-buy schemes.

With the replacement of the front doors by a myriad of poor designs from DIY stores, the chance of the houses in Ryculf Square (Richardson's scheme) becoming listed buildings in their own right was lost, probably for the foreseeable future. But this did not stem the advance of the owner-occupier: by the time this volume is published it is likely that over 75 per cent of the flats will be privately owned and changing hands for large sums. They have become fashionable pied-à-terre, a sort of Blackheath Barbican, ideal for second homes or as investment properties.

This was a state of affairs which has become applied to the Paragon and South Row flats. A considerable number of the units have been acquired by absentee landlords for "investment" purposes – a reliable estimate puts the current (2012) figure at between 30 and 40 per cent. A circumstance highlighted in the national press when Mr Nick Leeson, late of Barings Bank, and his wife Lisa, were revealed by the Daily Telegraph (March 1995), to be the owner of a long lease on a Paragon flat, described by the reporter as a "large house", purchased for investment.

Charles Bernard Brown was pardonably proud of his achievement in Blackheath. He was also concerned about the future upkeep of the buildings which he had so faithfully and painstakingly resurrected. He was the sole proprietor and owner of the freehold (obtained from the Cator trustees in 1955) and, since he was a bachelor, there would be no family to inherit the title to the property and ensure that his efforts would not be eroded by neglect and mismanagement.

In September 1969 Brown's holding company, Paragon Preservation Ltd, wrote to all its lessees and tenants to say that the burden of freehold ownership of the Paragon and some adjacent properties was proving to be a problem. The letter stated that the company might not exist beyond the lifespan of its directors and so the need to find a successor had become increasingly urgent.

To that end the company had approached the trustees of Morden College. The letter continued: 'We felt that the Morden College trustees, with their wonderful record over centuries, would be ideal in ensuring control virtually in perpetuity.' The College had agreed to take over the Paragon, Paragon

House, the Close, Cator Manor and Cator Lodge, between the Paragon and Paragon House. This seemed ideal and there great relief among all concerned.

Some of the ground on which these buildings stand, completed a full circle. From being in the possession of Sir John Morden and, thereafter, of the trustees of the College which he had founded, the ground was sold to Gregory Page in 1723. In turn his heirs sold it to John Cator in 1783, with whose family the freehold remained until 1955. Thereafter it passed to the Paragon Preservation Co Ltd before, finally in 1969, reverting once more to the trustees of Morden College.

The College charity remained the owners of the Paragon and Paragon House until 2007 when the residents and other local people with an affectionate interest in the Paragon were astonished to learn that the College trustees intended to auction the freehold of the whole lot to the highest bidder. Somewhat bizarrely, the Morden College trustees had put on the market the two garage blocks as separate titles. Paragon House and Colonnade House were to be treated for separately.

So much for Brown's confident forecast of 'control virtually in perpetuity'. Rather than placing themselves in the hands of absentee landlords with little more than a pecuniary interest and possibly even becoming part of a foreign holding company, the Paragon residents decided to buy the property. Even with the freehold enfranchisement laws on their side there were, of course, considerable difficulties in raising the funds; and to contriving a deed of agreement that would please all the parties and not give endless work to learned counsel in years to come. The residents, using the existing instrument of the Paragon Preservation Company Ltd, purchased the equity at a cost of £1.8 million and, from 2009, have self-managed their own property.

The Paragon story will, hopefully, never end and the houses will remain an architectural delight to please local residents and visitors alike for another 220 years at the very least. To paraphrase Bill Bonwitt, the Paragon's first historian "A particularly beautiful piece of Georgian urban development on the smaller, domestic scale lies modestly at the extreme south eastern edge of Blackheath. The name of the crescent-shaped development is The Paragon which name well describes its perfection of style, situation, appearance and quality of construction."

In this he was absolutely right thanks to Michael Searles and Charles Bernard Brown.

PARAGON REGISTERS

**Being a schedule of all those residents
discovered living in Nos 1-15 The Paragon
from the beginning to about 1940**

Below and opposite:

The Paragon on the 1866-1867 Ordnance Survey (published 1869)
and the 1893-1894 map (published 1897)

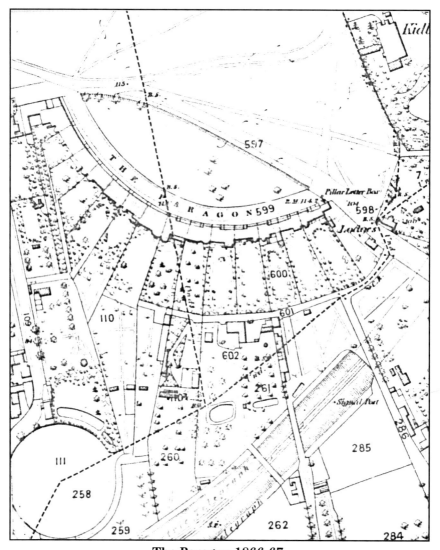

The Paragon 1866-67

108

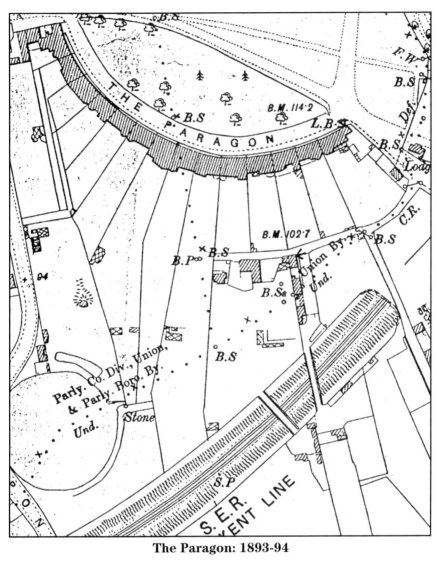

The Paragon: 1893-94

No 1 The Paragon

1800-1801
William Thompson (d. April 1815): insurance broker of No 8 Over Royal Exchange, until at least 1804

Thompson also held a stable, to the east and what was described as a farmyard. His house lease, when offered for sale, had 78 years to run, but the land at the rear was held only until 1827. Thompson died at his house on Laurence Pountney Hill after '... repeated attacks of apoplexy' (*The Times*).

24 October 1801: *The Times* advertisement:
Capital family residence with nine acres of land, Paragon, Blackheath, the residence and property of William Thompson esq, who will give immediate possession. By Peter Coxe, Burrell & Foster, at Garraway's, Friday November 13 1801, unless disposed of by private

contract on or before the 10th. Those very valuable substantially built leasehold premises, constructed and fitted up at a most considerable charge and with the greatest attention, situate at the end of The Paragon, Blackheath, next Morden College, replete with every convenience for use, comfort and elegance, abounding in pleasant views in every direction, with lawn, pleasure ground, cold bath etc. The family apartments consist of two handsome drawing rooms, fitted up with great taste; a spacious eating parlour, a gentleman's room, library and boudoir; and excellent entrance hall and light staircase; eight family bedchambers, dressing rooms, water closets; and admirable nursery and storerooms complete. The servants' apartments are suitable and the domestic offices are of every description with good cellaring and dairy. The out-door offices are laundry, men's room, stabling, coach house, attached farm yard, with every requisite for pleasure and economy. The kitchen garden well-stocked and in most excellent heart and the pasture land is immediately attached and in high condition for produce. The whole abundantly supplied with fine water. The lease of the premises has 78 years to run and the terms on which the land is held is to Michaelmas [September 29] 1827. May be viewed 12 days preceding the sale by tickets only ... The whole of the singularly elegant and excellent household furniture with other effects suitable to the premises may be taken by appraisement.

17 December 1801: *The Times* advertisement:
The furniture and effects of Wm Thompson to be auctioned 17 December and the following days by Messrs Peter Coxe, Burrell & Foster.

1802-1808
Henry Waddington (d.1840): merchant of Bridge Street, off Blackfriars

He tried to sell his Paragon house in March 1804 and again in May 1805, seemingly without success. The advertisements were similar to that of October 1801 but expanded thus: ' ... the views on each side are sufficiently known to be recollected without the aid of accurate description, it is sufficient to say that the site on which the premises stand comprises part of the park belonging to the late Sir Gregory Page bart.' (Page had been dead for 33 years at this time!) The dining room had become 'a commodious eating parlour', and an aviary had been added. The residue of the lease had, of course, dwindled a little.

Waddington was successful by the end of 1808, when it was noted that the contents of the house had been sold by Mr Burrell, on the premises, on Friday 30 December. The contents included copious quantities of Madeira wine and port, as well as pigs and chickens. Waddington, who had been in business with a partner (S. & H. Waddington, merchants) continued his company after he left the Paragon (probably residing over the counting house). By 1824 he had moved to Great Winchester Street but disappears from the London pages of the commercial directories by about 1827.

The date may be made significant by the announcement in The Times (15 March 1828) of the marriage of Joshua Thompson of Denmark Street, to Hannah, widow of the late Samuel Waddington, of Leman Street, London. The Times noted the death , at Sienna, ItaLY, of Joshua, his oldest son, Waddington, on 21 December 1840.

1809-1819
Edward Spencer Curling (d.1838): shipbroker, and underwriter for whaling vessels

A trustee of the New Cross Turnpike, Curling, who lived previously (from 1802 to 1808) at Layard's House, Crooms Hill, was a member of a substantial family involved in the shipping business. Curling, who traded as Curling & Domet, ship and insurance brokers, of Castle Street, Birch Lane, and Limehouse, was related to William Curling, the shipbuilder, who lived at Paragon House (q.v.) from 1809 to 1818. A William Curling died (aged 81) at Chatham Place, Walworth, in November 1823. The company not only conducted an insurance business but also acted as merchants, with premises at Limehouse Hole and, in the 1820s, at George Yard, Lombard Street. The shipyard at Limehouse Hole was still trading, as Curling & Young, as late as the 1840s. Edward's wife, Mary Ann, died in May 1827, aged but 46, at Deal in Kent – whence the couple had retired by the early 1820s. Edward died in Thanet towards the end of 1838.

1820-1829
Charles Bankes (1789-1830): sugar refiner

His name is sometimes written as Banks. Charles Bankes was of Little Distaff Lane and Upper Thames Street. He was the son of George Bankes, a sugar refiner of the same business address in 1814. After Charles's death, on 31 August 1829, the business was continued by George Bankes, possibly his son, although the boy would have been very young, no more than 20 say, and had left the Paragon. His eldest son, also Charles, died on 30 October 1830. The second boy, F. W. Bankes, died at Clifton, Bristol, in February 1844.

1830-1831
Mrs Elizabeth Bankes (d.1839): widow of the above

Elizabeth Bankes (whose first name is not revealed in the notice of her death placed in The Times) died at her mother's house, in Grove Terrace, Peckham, on 17 July 1839.

There was a double wedding on 8 June 1841 of Mary, youngest daughter of the late Charles Bankes, to William Brookes, son of J. Y. Brookes, of Ilfracombe, and Elizabeth, daughter of the same, to Robert William Soady, barrister, of Lincoln's Inn.

1832-1836
House let to Mrs Hensman (see below); rates paid by Bankes' executors

1832-1851
Mrs Rebecca Hensman (1777-1851)

The widowed mother of Boswell Hensman, solicitor, of No 12 The Paragon (q.v.). George Hensman, probably another son, was in partnership with Peter Bruce Turner in the 1840s, at Basing Lane, Bread Street. After Mrs Hensman's death, the lease and the contents were sold. A local agent, Felix Gilbert, handled both and there is an item in his notebook charging cab hire for ' ... going to Mr P. Cator's for permission to sell'. The contents fetched £145.14.6 and that sum, less Gilbert's commission, was sent to George Hensman.

1852-1856
Major Henry Barkley Henderson (c.1790-1860): army officer in Bengal

Henderson was based in India during the early years of the 19th century, where he enjoyed a reputation as a poet, publishing at least three volumes: The Goorkha, by a Young Officer (1817), Violanthe, a Tale of the Twelfth Century (1818) and his most famous work: The Bengalee, or Sketches of Society and Manners in the East (1829). Bengalee was the language of Bengal but Henderson's prose in is English. He served on the committee of the Great Western Railway of Bengal in 1845, and became officiating auditor-general of the firm Carr, Dawarkanauth & Co. in Tagore, Calcutta. He returned to London in about 1845 but went back to India a number of times. In 1859 he was appointed Secretary of the Indian Mutiny Fund.

Henderson married Elizabeth Hawkins in India, in 1822, and their children included Elizabeth Mary (d.1824), Henry, Elizabeth Jane, James Lumsden (d.1845) and Frances Mary, who married Colonel Keith Young in 1852.

Henderson's eldest son - also Henry Barkley Henderson, which makes research difficult – was born in Calcutta in 1825/6. He joined the government service, rising to the post of 1st Grade Deputy Commissioner in the Bengal Civil Service. He was living with his wife Mary at No 48 Eastbourne Terrace, Paddington, in 1861.

1856-1876
The Misses Hadley· *School for Girls*

The Hadley family seems to have consisted of at least eight girls and one boy (William A. Hadley), all of whom were born in Smethwick, Staffordshire. They first appear locally when Mrs Sarah Hadley, a clergyman's widow, with three of her daughters, Fanny, Ellen and Sarah, ran a girls' school at Wintoun Place, Blackheath Road, in the mid-1840s. The business must have

prospered despite considerable local competition. The family then moved to No 22 Dartmouth Row, which they conducted as a boys' school from 1849 to 1855. They also leased No 22 Dartmouth Hill for the girls and flourished from 1849 to 1860. With the closure of the Dartmouth Row establishment, they took No 1 The Paragon and remained in business there until 1876. The names of the Hadley family, none of whom married, were Amelia, Jane, Sarah, Marianne, Annette, Ellen Ann, Jane, Maria and Fanny.

It has to be said that the two census returns covering the Hadley occupation (1861 and 1871) list few pupils: in 1861 only three; in 1871 only seven, but one was born in India, another in New South Wales, and Jane Guill, aged 14, came from the South Pacific. It could be that there was a missionary service connection harking back to the days of the Revd Hadley.

1877-1881
Thomas Walker (1809-1889): solicitor

Walker was a solicitor at Furnival's Inn for his entire career. The family moved from Oakley Villas, Hampstead, to No 16 Northbrook Road, Lee, in 1871, but by April 1881 had left Blackheath for St John's Wood, where Thomas died, at No 5 Loudon Road, on 15 January 1889. All the children, at least seven of them, were given Mewburn as their middle name. Walker's sons, Arthur and Edward, were educated at the Blackheath Proprietary School. The Revd Edward Mewburn Walker (1857-1941) was a distinguished and much honoured classicist, one-time Provost of Queen's College, Oxford, and Chaplain to HM George V.

1881-1907
Franklin Richardson Kendall, FRSA, FRGS (1839-1907)

Franklin Kendall was the second son of Lieut. Edward Nicholas Kendall, Royal Navy hydrographer with Sir John Franklin (1786-1847), who served with merit on several Arctic expeditions. Lieutenant Kendall ended his maritime career as Superintendent of the Peninsular & Oriental Steam Navigation Company [(P&O)] base at Southampton. Edward married, on 8 May 1832, Mary Anne, eldest daughter of Joseph Kay (1775-1847), architect and surveyor to the Greenwich Hospital estates and best known for his designs for the centre of Greenwich and the Trafalgar Tavern.

His son, named after the two famous explorers, was educated at Christ's Hospital school and joined P&O in 1856. He served the company for his entire working life, being stationed at Bombay, Singapore, Hong Kong and Melbourne. Kendall retired in 1906, having achieved the post of Chief General Manager of the P&O shipping company.

His marriage to Frances Margaret (1840-1930) was blessed with six sons and a daughter, Mary, who died young in 1902 All the boys were educated at the Blackheath Proprietary School, of which institution F. R. Kendall was a shareholder. Most did well, especially Sir Charles Henry Bailey Kendall (1878-1935), who became a High Court judge in India. Nicholas Fletcher (a surgeon) and Franklin Kaye (an architect) married (25 April 1906) Kathleen and Annie Frances (d1944) respectively, who were daughters of Walter George Izard, of No 10 The Paragon (q.v.). The Kendall occupation of this house somehow typified the late-Victorian ideal of the happy family in comfortable circumstances, with children bright enough to succeed in their professions and adventurous enough to fill their lives, from their schooldays onwards, with much of interest. Fortunately, the record survives and details of this have added measurably to the content of this book. (See also Chapter 5 and Appendix I).

Sadly, this picture of family joy was dreadfully upset on 23 December 1907 when Franklin Kendall committed suicide by cutting his throat. It was said at the inquest that he had become seriously depressed since his retirement. His widow, Frances, survived him by 23 years and died on 29 November 1930, aged 90.

30 January 1908: Contents of house for sale

1910-1912
Arthur Mason Worthington, CB, MA, FRS, FRAS (1852-1916)

Worthington, born at Cheetham House, was educated at Trinity College, Oxford, where he obtained his MA. He worked at Owen's College, Manchester, and, subse-quently for a short while, at Helmholtz's laboratory in Berlin. On his return to Eng-land in 1877 he became head-master of Salt's School, at Shipley, Yorkshire, until, in 1879, he obtained the position of head-master and Professor of Physics in the Dockyard School, Portsmouth, and the Royal Naval Engineering School, Devonport. From there, he went on to become Professor of Physics at the Royal Naval College, Greenwich. The ap-pointment lasted from 1909 to 1910 and during most of that time he lived in the Paragon. He died in retirement at Exmouth, having first moved to Southernhay East, Exeter, in 1911.

1913 Empty

1914-1930
William Silas Spanton (1845-1930), artist and art historian.

Memoirs: An Art Student and his Teachers in the Sixties (Robert Scott, London, 1927). In May 1925 Spanton protested loudly about a plan to run a road in front of Morden College. The scheme was abandoned by the London County Council after public protest. In March 1930 he was in print again, protesting at the loss of a wild garden, to be replaced by 'the stumps of trees and the erection of a hideous mud-coloured villa', on the south-west corner of Kidbrooke Gardens. It had been built by William Summerskill and ended its days in ruins after vandalism in 1976. The site has since been redeveloped with the equally hideous Regency Court. Spanton died in December 1930 in a motoring accident. His wife, Sarah (née Pechey), died here in 1917. Their son, Arthur, serving with the Honourable Artillery Company, was killed in action in January 1917. Spanton's eldest daughter, Helen Margaret Spanton, who was a prominent suffragette (see below), also died at the Paragon in 1934.

1931-1934
Helen Margaret Spanton (1877-1934)

Helen Spanton was closely involved in the militant suffragette movement with the composer Dame Ethyl Smyth and joined Smyth and others in smashing the windows of government offices in Whitehall, in June 1912. She was sentenced to two months' hard labour in Holloway and shared a cell with her more famous colleague.

Spanton took this in her stride and was much involved in helping to rally the spirits of the inmates, organising games of hopscotch in the exercise yard. She played down her role as a suffragette after the Great War of 1914-18, becoming a dedicated pacifist, and was one-time Honorary Secretary of the Blackheath branch of the League of Nations Union. She abandoned this eventually because she thought many of its committee members were too timid. In 1917 she was probably the first Paragon resident to join the Labour Party.

Her first attempt at a career was as an artist, training at the Slade School and joining the New English Art Club. In her last years Helen Spanton abandoned art to study Aristotelian philosophy and aesthetics, which occupied her time to the point of obsession for the rest of her active life. She died on 17 September 1934.

Flats:

1935-1936 Arthur James Stevenson

1935-1940 William Parr Foster-Smith

1937-1941 Mrs Charlotte Sheraton Lamont

April 1937 Cecile Foster-Smith opens 'Food Clinic' here

12 April 1937 letter to the *Blackheath Local Guide and District Advertiser:*

Sir – In response to the newly awakened national interest in Nutrition and Physical Fitness I have decided to open a Food Clinic at the above address and your readers may like to hear of the work I propose to do.

It is at last become widely known that there is far more to be learnt about correct feeding than can be picked up from newspaper articles or even books on the subject. Food is such a personal matter that generalisations often fail to satisfy, and the main work of a Food Clinic is found in this adjustment of the individual.

I have made a very close study of Dietetics for many years both here and abroad, and have been running a Food Clinic in town for some time. Being a native of Blackheath and descended from one of its oldest families, I feel that in view of this National Campaign, it would be returning some of my debt to the neighbourhood to open a local branch of my work for the benefit of those who realise their responsibility to feed themselves and their families in the best manner possible.

I propose to give lectures and individual advice by appointment. Where special diets have been prescribed by the doctor for illness, I am also prepared to elaborate on them for the benefit of the puzzled cook or caterer.

Those wishing further particulars should apply by postcard or telephone to the appended address.

C. Foster-Smith
The Food Clinic, No 1 The Paragon, Blackheath SE3. Lee Green 1574.

1937-1941 Mrs Charlotte Sheraton Lamont

1938 Edith Geary

1946: The voters' list shows Cecile Foster-Smith despite the fact that there was no house on the site.

January 1948: Charles Bernard Brown appeals for old pictures of the Paragon which would show No 1 and small lodge 'formerly on the site of present static water tank'.

House badly damaged by V-2 rocket, 3 July 1944. Rebuilt and occupied by autumn 1951.

No 2 The Paragon

This was the house assigned to Mrs Elizabeth Coade, a major creditor, because Searles had not paid for the Coade Stone pillars and embellishments he had specified for the Paragon. Some of the columns of the Paragon have the Coade trademark cut into the base, still readable today. See sale notice below.

1800-1808
Thomas Barnard

Either a merchant, of Jeffries Square, St Mary Axe, or possibly the owner of a shipyard at Deptford.

1809-1821
Revd Dr Richard Jenkins Runwra Jenkins, DD (*fl.* 1775-1821)

Son of William Jenkins of Tenby. Educated at Corpus Christi College, Cambridge, where he matriculated in November 1793; gained his doctorate in 1808. He was formerly the Master of a school in Bridgwater, Somerset but had settled at the Paragon by January 1809 where he also conducted a boys' school. At the same time he served as curate at St Margaret's, Lee, staying until 1819. For a short period he was a trustee of the New Cross Turnpike.

1821-1842
John Lawford (1766-1842)

Described as of 'independent means' in the 1841 census but probably the John Lawford, an ironmonger and nail merchant, of Leadenhall Street, in the 1820s. His wife, Rebecca, died in October 1823, aged but 52 years. In April 1826 one of his daughters married a Mr Knaggs, of Laurence Pountney Lane. He lost his son, John, on 27 December 1835 at the boy's house at Mitcham Green. John senior died in the Paragon on 24 August 1842, aged 76.

6 November 1822: Head lease for sale on the orders of the executors of Mrs Elizabeth Coade, deceased. Eight closets. Let at £80 p.a. Held for 58 years from Christmas 1821, at £7.10.0 p.a.

1842-1863
Miss Ann Lawford (1798-1863), sister of the above

During this time the house was also home to Lawford's nephews: Arthur, a bank clerk, and Sidney who worked for a wine merchant and was still living in Blackheath in 1901, from 1887 at No 81 Foyle Road. Ann died at No 2 The Paragon in the summer of 1863.

1864-1865
Mrs Sarah Mary Gillespie (1820-1869)

Mrs Gillespie was the widow of merchant George Gillespie, and resident for some years in Wellington Place, Mount Ephraim, Tunbridge Wells, and later in Kensington. On his death in the autumn of 1861 she moved to Blackheath, but did not stay here very long. George was sufficiently hard of hearing to be declared 'deaf' on the 1861 census return. Sarah Gillespie died at Ashby-de-la Zouch, Leicestershire, in the winter of 1869, aged only 49.

1865
William Henry Peel, JP (1803-1883): farmer and magistrate

Peel was the owner of a substantial farm at Taliaris Park, Llandilofawr, Carmarthenshire, inherited from his father, Robert Peel (1770-1838). Born at Church Bank, Lancashire, Peel was to flourish sufficiently to need 10 live-in servants at his house and employed an additional 16 workers on his 430-acre farm. As a JP and magistrate, he clearly enjoyed great influence in the county. His son Herbert Peel, BA, DL, JP, joined him on the Bench in an unusual father-and-son team.

In 1864 William Peel journeyed to Blackheath to place his son – Alan – in the Blackheath Proprietary School, renting No 2 The Paragon while he made the arrangements. Neither the boy nor the man stayed long, with Alan at the Prop only for a year from midsummer 1865 and William already back home in Wales before the year ended. .

1865-1874
John James Andrew (1816-1874): solicitor

John Andrew was born in Cornwall. Before moving to the Paragon, he had lived at No 15 Shooters Hill Road, from 1856. He was in practice as Atkins & Andrew, Lombard Street, but also, by at least 1847, at 1 Church Street, Deptford. The family lived at Deptford before moving to Shooters Hill Road. The business expanded and by the 1860s was trading, somewhat clumsily named, as Atkins, Andrew, Atkins & Irvine, both in the City and Deptford. John Andrew was a member of the Blackheath Improvement Association in 1858. Mrs Harriett Andrew, his widow, moved to Northbrook Road, Lee, in 1874, the year in which their only son, Burney Weld Andrew (b.1852), died. He had been educated at the Blackheath Proprietary School and Caius College, Cambridge.

10 July 1874: Sale of lease (expires 1896) direct from freeholder. Nine bedrooms, hot water in bathroom. Raised croquet lawn.

1876-1917
Edward Robert Robson, FSA, FRIBA (1835-1917): architect

Previously at No 6 St Germans Place. Edward Robson was one of the most distinguished architects of the late 19th century and his work for the London School Board set standards for educational buildings that have been retained today. Many of the schools he designed in London function more than adequately in the 21st century.

The elder son of Alderman Robert Robson, JP, of Durham, he left school at 16 and worked for a builder for three years to gain experience of the industry. He then worked with Sir George Gilbert Scott (1811-1878) and was appointed, at the early age of 22, architect to Durham Cathedral, a post he held for six years. From 1864 he worked as architect to the Liverpool Corporation. In 1870 Robson was appointed Chief Architect to the London School Board and remained its head man, latterly as a consultant, until 1904.

The Board was established, after the passing of the Elementary Education Act of 1870, to serve as the the the forerunner of the Inner London Educa-tion Authority. In its first few years, six different architects were invited to compete for the design of each school and 30 schools were designed in this way. This method was expensive and disastrously slow, so it was decided to make Robson, who 'had given abundant showing of his qualities', responsible for the design and construction of all the London Board's schools. His salary was fixed at the then amazingly high figure of $1,000 per annum and from 1872 until his retirement in 1889, he was personally responsible for the design and construction of every Board school in London. With a staff of eight assistants, he completed one set of drawings per week. On Robson's insistence, the staff was increased to 15 and by 1876 he and his small team had completed 134 schools, with 40 more under construction or contracted. The design and drawing-office costs for each school worked out at about one per cent of the building costs whereas private architects charged five per cent.

However, the reduction in costs invariably led to a similarity in style of building not always suitable for its neighbourhood. The Board decided that it needed some variety and the competitive system was re-established. Robson's preferred style was what is now called 'Queen Anne revival'. He liked to build high and ensure that his schools stood out from their sur-roundings. In his book, *School Architecture*, published in 1877 – a standard text both in the UK and on the Continent for many years – he says that the schools were 'henceforth to rank as pub-lic buildings, planned and built in a manner befitting their new dignity. In its aim and object it [a school] should strive to express civil rather than ecclesiastical character.' Robson travelled widely and studied school-building methods in other countries, especially in Germany.

Robson operated an independent practice and his buildings include the Royal Institute of Painters in Water Colours, Piccadilly (1880), and the People's Palace (1886-88), on the Mile End Road. His local buildings which survive include the Blackheath Road School (designed with John James Stevenson [1832-1908]), Blackheath High School for Girls in Wemyss Road (1879-80) – his wife was on the original committee and Robson donated his design – and No 99 Mycenae Road which is one of the few of his domestic buildings to survive and be accurately attributed.

Robson refused the formal civic honours he was offered and so richly deserved. He died on 19 January 1917, aged 81, earning generous entries in the *Dictionary of National Biography*, *Who Was Who* and the major architectural reference books.

His wife, Marion, died in 1900. She served on a number of local social welfare groups, including acting as Secretary to the Association for Befriending Young Servants.

Their children were educated locally, the two sons at the Proprietary School and daughter Ethel at Blackheath High School. Leonard Gray Robson became a solicitor. The second son, Philip Appleby Robson (1871-1951), was also an architect, specialising in church work; he lived at No 21/23 Dartmouth Row for many years until his death. His passion was for hockey and he became an authority on the history of the game (see his entry in *Who Was Who*).

1917-1925
Miss Ethel Mary Robson (1863-1936)

Daughter of the above. Educated at Miss Octavia Hill's school, at Nottingham Place, before attending Blackheath High School. Ethel Robson shared her brother's enthusiasm for hockey, becoming Secretary of the All England Women's Hockey Association. She was responsible for the arrangements of the 2nd Women's International Match, at Rectory Field, in 1899. She was for many years Manager for Schools for the London County Council. Ethel Robson died at No 21 Dartmouth Row (her brother's house) on 16 May 1936.

1925-1934
Mrs Annie Belton Clark (1877-1965)

Widow of Lawrence Clark, of No 1 South Row (Paragon House). Mrs Clark eventually moved to No 116 Westcombe Park Road

1929
Mrs Jane Greene, aged 84, widow of Alfred Greene, died here on 7 October 1929. (Estate valued at £6,121 - personality at £5,947)

1935-1936 Empty

1937-1941
Bernard Hailstone, RA (1910-1987): artist

Robert Norman Hepple, RA, PPRP (1908-1994): artist
Both were to serve with the National Fire Service as official war artists. For full details, see Chapter 5. Hailstone and his family moved to Hadlow, Kent.

House badly damaged and burnt out as a result of a direct hit on No 1 in March 1944.
Reconstructed and fully occupied by autumn 1951.
Flat dwellers included Commandant Vonla McBride, CB (1921-2003), Director of the WRNS.

No 3 The Paragon
Cottage in garden

1800-1801
Misses Charlotte Sharpe and **Eliza Frances Robertson**

Charlotte Sharpe conducted a boarding school at No 21 Gloucester Circus from 1792 to 1794 and then moved to No 66 Crooms Hill, at which time she met Miss Eliza Robertson. The Crooms Hill school was sold, in 1799, to Mrs Jane Smallwood and her daughter. In 1800, the ladies took a lease on No 3 The Paragon and spent a considerable fortune on fitting it out in a most luxurious manner. The bills were never paid. The extraordinary story of these events is told in Appendix III of this work.

4 April 1801: *The Times* advertisement:
Blackheath, Paragon, by Mr Winstanley, on 17 April.
An elegant, substantial and well-finished leasehold house, being No 3 in The Paragon, Blackheath, with newly-built double coach house, four stall stable, cow house, dairy, laundry and other convenient out buildings, lately erected at very considerable expense; pleasure and kitchen garden recently laid out with much taste and planted with young wall and standard fruit trees etc, and a newly-built circular greenhouse and rich meadow. The premises are beautifully situate on part of Sir Gregory Page's park commanding rich and extensive views; the neighbourhood is of the first respectability and the distance from town easy. The house is furnished in a style of very superior elegance, complete with every requisite accommodation for a genteel family and held for a long term at an easy rent. Immediate possession may be had and the fixtures taken at fair appraisement. View by tickets only which, with descriptive particulars may be likewise had from Mr Searle, solicitor, Inner Temple Lane, and of Mr Winstanley, Paternoster Row.

8 April 1801: *The Times* advertisement:
Sale to be at Garraway's, Cornhill, on Friday April 17, at 12 o'clock, by order of the trustees.

16 April 1801: *The Times* advertisement (as before)

1801-June 1802 Empty

1802-1805
Henry Smithers: of Smithers & Hill, coal merchants, 12 St Mary Overy Stairs, Southwark

3 August 1803: *The Times* advertisement:
The Paragon, Blackheath.– by Peter Coxe, Burrel & Foster on Friday 19th August, at 12 o'clock, at Garraways. Elegant residence with lawn, plantation, offices and garden. An eligible elegantly fitted family residence, the third house from the east in that admired range of buildings, the Paragon Blackheath, with lawns, pleasure ground, plantations and pastureland occupying a site of ground part of the extensive park belonging to the late Sir Gregory Page, bart., abounding in beautiful views on all sides and richly wooded with capital offices, coach house, stabling, servants' rooms and various conveniences.

The dwelling contains every accommodation a respectable family can require in spacious apartments on the ground floor, appropriately decorated and judiciously enriched in basso relievo and other paintings, a singularly handsome, cheerful entrance hall, various family bed chambers, water closets, nursery rooms and servants' apartments, gentleman's room etc. The domestic offices are uncommonly convenient and numerous, fitted up with the utmost attention, with excellent cellaring and the whole premises in complete repair. These most eligible premises comprise altogether a site of 4 acres held for the long term of 27 years to run at the moderate rent of £140 per annum. May be viewed by tickets only six days preceding the sale upon application to Messrs Peter Coxe, Burrel & Foster, Throgmorton Street, of whom particulars may then be had and at Lloyd's and Garraways.

1806-1808
George Elliott: Madras merchant, of No 16 South Street, Finsbury Square
(*many variants on the spelling of his name*)

The Times, 3 October 1807: 'On the 21st ult, of an apoplexy at Revd Mr Greenalls, at Cranbrook, where she had resided for some months, Miss Mary Elliott, of The Paragon.' Another daughter, Hester Maria, married William Ashburner, of Bombay, in July 1815. Their son, Maj-Gen George Elliott Ashburner (1820-1907) came to reside in Blackheath in 1882 at No 18 St John's Park where he stayed until his death.

15 December 1808: *The Times* advertisement:
On March 2nd, by order of the assignees of Mr George Eliot [sic] an excellent family residence replete with every convenience, fitted up with peculiar taste and uncommon care, with out-door offices of every description and every other accommodation; walks, shrubberies and plantations, ornamental forest trees, kitchen garden and four acres of land and commanding beautiful views in every direction. The premises are in perfect order and the sitting room and family apartments equally elegant and commodious as well as numerous, with suitable domestic offices.

2 February 1809: *The Times* advertisement. As above but with the additional information:
Term of 21 years unexpired. The purchaser may have the option of taking the elegant furniture and effects on the premises at a valuation; if not so taken they will be shortly sold by auction on the premises. May be viewed eight days preceding the sale with tickets only, which, with particulars, may be had of Mr Peter Coxe, Throgmorton Street, particulars likewise at the Green Man, Blackheath and of Lloyd's and Garraway's coffee houses.

1809-1811
William Barr (1776-1840): wharf owner
(sometimes written Barre)

Wharfinger, of Symond's Wharf, Tooley Street, Southwark, from at least 1798 to 1814. He was to live at No 17 West Grove from 1816 to 1834, and died at Peckham, on 8 September 1840, in his 65th year.

1812-1818
John Hayes
(sometimes written Hays)

Probably the John Hayes, bookseller, of 153 Cheapside and, later, of 252 High Holborn. His infant son, also John, died here in February 1817.

1819-1822
John Stockwell

Stockwell was living in Blackheath (at an address not discovered) when, in September 1813, his daughter, Mary, married Henry William Smith, of Peckham.

1820 and 1821
George (sic) **Stockwell**

This may have been a mistake in record-keeping or else there were two Stockwells living here at the time.

1823-1826
John Allen (d. 5 April 1826): merchant of Size Lane, Bucklersbury

Son of William Allen, of Clifford's Inn and Lewisham High Street. In July 1810 John married Mary, daughter of Isaac Warner, of No 7 The Paragon (q.v.).

1826-1827
Mrs Mary Allen (1785-1827): d.13 June 1827

1827-1828
Miss Mary Ann Allen, possibly a daughter of the above but, if the daughter of John and Mary Allen, then she was very young to have been the recorded householder.

20 March 1838, *The Times:* Marriage of Persis, 2nd daughter of the late John Allen, of Blackheath, to William Woxen Rooke esq., of Lymington.

28 July 1842, *The Times:* At Sutton-at-Hone, [marriage of] George Gipps Jnr, of Lincoln's Inn, elder son of George Gipps, of Howlett's, Kent, to Elizabeth, 3rd daughter of the late John Allen, of Blackheath

1832-1836: Executors of Mrs Allen. Probably sublet.

1837-1849
Lawford Richardson (1802-1870): stockbroker

Son of James Malcott Richardson (1770-1854), bookseller, of No 97 Blackheath Park. Lawford Richardson lived previously at No 11 St Germans Place, then (by 1850) at Court Yard, Eltham. His wife, Anne Emily (1816-1866) (daughter of Joshua Andrews [d. 1834], of No 6 South Row), and daughter Emily Jane (1836-1866) both died of diphtheria on the same day: 21 January1866. A son was born on 3 March 1833 at St Germans Place. Their children living at No 3 The Paragon were Lawford Andrew, Emily, Sophia, Herbert and Walter. Another son, Gerald Murray Richardson, died in September 1849, aged only two days.

1850-1873
Robert Obbard (1789-1873): window-glass and lead merchant

Offices at No 14 Bride Lane, Fleet Street, and warehouse at 12 Bridgehouse Place, Newington Causeway. Lieutenant of the City of London and a member of the Court of Common Council for

41 years. His retirement from this was marked by the presentation of a silver salver and tea service of exceptionally high quality. Obbard, who was born in Westminster, lived in Tooting and then Brixton before moving to Blackheath. The Obbards employed three or four servants and a resident gardener – James Carter – who lived in the garden cottage. Obbard was a member of the Blackheath Improvement Association 1857-62

The family were major glass and lead merchants in London, the business having been established by the early 1820s. The company traded as Robert & Joseph Obbard (or sometimes as Obbard & Co.), Joseph probably being Robert's brother. It moved its premises from time to time and by the 1830s was established in Newington Causeway. By the 1840s there were two branches: Robert Henry Obbard, at Old Street, and Obbard & Co., at the Crescent, Blackfriars, until the late 1860s. Because Robert, of the Paragon, seems to have had no child with that name, it must only be guessed that Robert Henry was related directly to Joseph.

Robert's wife, Sarah Ann (b.1797), who was the elder daughter of Henry Hammond, of Camberwell, survived him; their children living at the Paragon were Elizabeth, Harry, Emily M., Fanny, Adelaide, Catherine, Arthur, a merchant, and Thomas. Most of the girls remained unwed and were resident at No 3 when Robert Obbard died. His will was sworn at under £30,000 (even so, a respectable sum) with Sarah Ann and John Obbard and Alfred Sayers Edmunds as executors.

There were 17 children in all: eight boys, and nine girls. The seventh son, Harry Smith Obbard (1824-1891), achieved distinction in the Indian Army. Commissioned in 1842, he ultimately became a Lieutenant-General in the Bengal Staff Corps, having helped to raise the 21st Punjab Infantry Regiment at the time of the Mutiny (1857). He also commanded the 41st (Gwalior) Regiment of the Bengal Infantry for 19 years! Like all good old soldiers from the Indian wars he retired to Cheltenham, where he died in 1891.

John Obbard (b.1823) also served in India but as a master pilot and river surveyor for the government dockyard at Kidderpore. Thomas (b.1835) was commissioned in 1853 and served in India and Abyssinia. He became, ultimately, Major-General in the Madras Staff Corps retired in 1886 and lived in Cornwall until his death in July 1921.

Robert Obbard died at the Paragon on 9 March 1873. A memorial stone was erected in his honour in the crypt of St Bride's Church, Fleet Street, detailing his achievement in City governance.

1874-1877
Mrs Sarah Ann Obbard (1797-1877)

1879-1882
William George Larke (1825-1882): builder and contractor

Larke was born in St Luke's, Middlesex; he lived previously in Islington and locally at No 11 Walerand Road from 1866, and at No 77 Granville Park from 1877. His stay in the Paragon was short and from there he moved to No 8 Lee Terrace where he died shortly afterwards. Nothing has been discovered about his career. Whether the Paragon house was too large or too expensive to maintain is not known. Whatever, Mrs Martha Larke stayed at Lee Terrace only until 1887, then she returned to No 77 Granville Park where she remained until 1902. Children living with William and Martha at the Paragon were: Alfred, a Merchant Marine officer, and Ernest Octavius, a building clerk probably working with his father. In June 1881 Alfred Larke was fined 5/- for carving his name on a Greenwich Park bench. While admitting the offence, he did complain bitterly that the local newspaper described him as a 'seaman' when, in fact, he was a 2nd officer, in the Merchant Marines.

1882-1900
William Richard Minter Glasier (1836-1914): auctioneer and surveyor

The eldest son of William Richard Glasier, W. R. M. Glasier was born in Lambeth in1836. The family lived at No 5 Grotes Buildings (from 1871-81) before moving to No 3 The Paragon on William's retirement. In 1900 they moved to Tunbridge Wells. His wife, Leonora Charlotte, daughter of Sir Ebenezer Howard [the distinguished town planner], died in January 1930 at the age of 88. Glasier, who was a Justice of the Peace, supported local endeavours, owning shares in the Blackheath Concert Hall Company and the Proprietary School where both his sons received some of their secondary education. William and the boys were members of the Blackheath Golf Club and all appear in a group photograph of the then membership taken in 1891. One son, William, was a chartered accountant, and the other, Howard, a distinguished Cambridge physician; the daughters were Ethel and Leonora. W. R. M. Glasier died on 29 October 1914, aged 78.

1898-1900
Howard Glasier, MA, MB (Cantab) (1872-1932): son of the above

1901-1907
John Walters (or Walter) Wilson, JP (1836-1912) Spanish wine merchant

Wilson removed to No 3 The Paragon from No 7 and, by 1910, was living at No 14 Kidbrooke Grove. Two of his daughters married from No 3: in July 1902 Ellen Blanche married Herbert R. Killick; and in November 1903 Gertrude May married Major R. J. McCormack, MD, RAMC. There were two sons living at the Paragon: Herbert J. and Charles E.; the youngest daughter was Constance. It took four residential servants to attend their needs.

1905
Edmund Wrigley Severne (1835-1914)

Severne stayed at No 3 The Paragon just for 1905 (according to Kelly's Directory for that year). Why he came to Blackheath is not known because the family, of considerable substance and property, lived from the 1870s at Thenford, Brackley, Northamptonshire. Edmund died there in the winter of 1914, aged 79. He indicates no professional calling and was away on the nights of the enumerated census returns for 1881 and 1891.

1905-1915
Arthur Watson (1873-1927): antique dealer

Arthur was born in Snaresbrook, Wanstead, Essex. He married Katherine (1872-1933), daughter of shipbroker Edward Pembroke (1831-1911) of No 5 Vanbrugh Park. In 1901 they were living at Foots Cray, Kent, but had moved to No 3 The Paragon by early 1905, when he attended a meeting of the trustees of St Germans' Chapel. This was the Pembrokes' church. In 1911 the three Watsons required four servants, including a valet and a butler, to look after them. They had moved to Hay Hill, Mayfair, by 1918. The only son, Gerard Arthur Watson, married Jean MacFarlane and their child is the distinguished actor Moray Watson.

1916-1919
Arthur [Aubrey?] Patrick Hughes Gibb

1920-1921
Robert Daniel Bradford

1922
W. Mackenzie

1922-1926
Frank Howard H. Hamilton

1926-1941
Sidney William Clayton
Offered board residence throughout the 1930s, placing advertisements in the *Blackheath Local Guide* from 1935 onwards. The telephone number in 1935 was Lee Green 0819.

House restored and reoccupied as six flats by 1949

No 4 The Paragon

1800-1810
Samuel Weyman Wadesdon (1754-1821): attorney, of Austin Friars

Wadesdon seems to have been engaged in a number of partnerships: in 1798 it was Wadesdon & Hardy, from 1804 Wadesdon, Barlow & Grosvenor, and from 1819 Wadesdon, Barlow & Wadesdon. The second Wadesdon was probably Edward Weyman Wadesdon, his son, with chambers in Great Knightrider Street, although the 1830 directory notes Wadesdon & Dingwall, solicitors, at 11 Austin Friars. Samuel's wife died in 1816 at their house in King's Road, Bedford Row, and Samuel himself in November 1821.

1811-1826?
Lancelot Loat (1770-1841): sand and gravel merchant, brick maker, land developer and speculator. Commissioner of Land Tax for the Liberty of Kidbrooke; Trustee of the New Cross Road Turnpike Trust in 1817; Guardian of the Poor for the Hundred of Blackheath in 1817.

Later at No 16 St Germans Place 1832-6; at No 37 Blackheath Park 1836-7; died at No 49 Lee Terrace.

Loat was one of those Paragon residents whose efforts to raise himself from humble origins to the same social class as most of his neighbours may have led to his eventual downfall. His original calling was a dirty trade, that of a sand and gravel extractor and merchant. Most of these materials he dug from 'Loat's Pits', a piece of ground bordered by Lewisham Road, Black-heath Hill, Morden Lane and Morden Hill. Its name persisted until the be-ginning of the 20th century. Loat's initial wealth had been made during the great rush of building in Greenwich and elsewhere in south-east London in the early years of the 19th century. Inevitably, he saw an opportunity in building speculation rather than just supplying the raw materials to others. He prospered and aspired to join the ranks of the gentlemen.

In company with many other Paragon residents Loat was appointed a trustee of the New Cross Turnpike Trust in 1817. In the same year his name appears as one of the Guardians of the Poor for the Hundred of Blackheath and he was also Commissioner of Land Tax for the Liberty of Kidbrooke. In about 1812, Loat bought one of the oldest and most important houses on Crooms Hill, sometimes known as Cottle's House, or Olivier's House. He demolished it despite its antiquity (it is mentioned in Pepys's *Diary*) and replaced it with the present Nos 42 to 48 Crooms Hill and King George Street, Greenwich. Other developments he undertook were in Charlton, Lee Green and Burnt Ash Lane. Loat also owned a large brickworks – late Ffinch's – where St Donat's Road is now, in New Cross.

In the mid-1820s Loat moved from No 4 The Paragon and may have rented another of the houses because his wife, Mary, died at the Paragon in January 1829, aged 53. He next appears in local records (1832) as the lessee of No 16 St Germans Place. It was when resident there that he fell into financial difficulty and was revealed to have misappropriated considerable sums of money belonging to the Turnpike Trust, of which Loat was the Treasurer (see also pages 40 & 47). It was not considered too dreadful to have borrowed the money entrusted to him, only that he couldn't pay it back when called.

He escaped the humiliation of bankruptcy because his guarantors (who included Thomas Leverton, the architect and Loat's in-law) were required to cover the debts and his property was assigned to his creditors. Most of it was sold, including his interest in No 4 Shooters Hill Road and the Barley Mow public house in Greenwich. The scandal did not deter his fellow liverymen at the Tylers' and Bricklayers' Company from electing him as their Master for two terms: 1834-5 and 1836-7. A later Master was John Moreland (see below).

After moving to No 37 Blackheath Park in 1836-7, Lancelot Loat died at his sister's house, No 49 Lee Terrace, in 1841, aged 71, clearly a broken man.

1826-1827
Charles Browne: probably the mast and block maker of Vine Yard, Pickle Herring Wharf, Southwark, from before 1814 until at least 1826.

1830-1832
Jonathon (sic) Blunt: probably the attorney, of Pay Office Chambers, Broad Street

There was a considerable family of legal men of this name in the period 1810 to the late 1830s, including both barristers and solicitors. (Blunt is included in the 1832 *Pigot's Directory* as resident in the Paragon.)

1832-1837
Mrs Susannah Neale, daughter of John Mason Good, and widow of Revd Cornelius Neale (d.1823)

Mrs Neale was the mother of Revd Dr John Mason Neale (1818-1866), the hymn writer. He was one of the first pupils at the Blackheath Proprietary School, proceeded to Trinity College, Cambridge, where he took his BA, and achieved his doctorate at Hartford College, Connecticut. His career was not to be as a parish priest but as a theologian and writer of hymns. Neale wrote many tales and stories for the young, but is chiefly remembered now for the astonishingly rich contribution he made to the hymnals. No fewer than one-eighth of the entries in long-standing editions of *Hymns Ancient and Modern* were from his pen: originals, adaptations or translations. Perhaps his most famous works, still sung with enthusiasm today, are his versions of 'Good King Wenceslas', and 'O Come, O Come, Emmanuel' .

Mrs Neale had previously lived at No 52 Blackheath Park (much damaged during the 1939-45 war) and moved to the Paragon by Christmas 1832.

For some reason undiscovered, Mrs Neale's house was the subject of an inventory, which was conducted by local surveyor George Felix Gilbert in October 1833. The list of contents of the house is not only fascinating, in that it is a record of the time, but it is quite extraordinary. The quantity of glass and china is considerable and must have been way beyond the needs of a widow and her son. The inventory is printed as Appendix III of this volume.

1838-1843
Matthew Hutchinson, Snr (1780-1843), dealer in hemp and flax

1843-1861
Matthew Hutchinson, Jnr (1806-1874), dealer in hemp and flax

The Hutchinson family occupied No 4 The Paragon for nearly 35 years but it is difficult – due to a paucity of records – to differentiate between them because both father and son were called Matthew. The 1841 census lists Matthew Hutchinson, aged 60, and trading as a merchant. Living with him is his daughter, Martha Hutchinson, then recorded as aged 30 (but who was certainly older (see below). They had two servants to attend their needs. The enumerated census conducted on 7 June1841 reduced adult ages to the next-lowest multiple of five. Martha could have been 34 pushing 35, but was regarded officially as 30. Matthew senior died at home in the winter of 1843.

The entry for the 1851 census records another Matthew, a 45-year-old bachelor, also listed as a dealer in flax and hemp. Martha, his sister, had remained in the house but by then has had to report her age accurately, as 45.

The Hutchinsons first appear in the London commercial directories in 1835 with one of the Matthews trading as a Russia merchant, with offices at No 48 Mark Lane. By 1837 the company is in business as hemp and flax dealers and a son has joined the family firm. It was to remain in this trade, and at that address, until April 1861 when Matthew junior was declared bankrupt, with a deficiency of £18,826.

This was also the year the family left the Paragon. The April 1861 census notes that the new occupant of No 4 is the widow Harriet Panton, aged 48, born in Norwich. She is shown as a housekeeper while the house is under repair.

Matthew junior moved to No 13 Delacourt Road, a somewhat humbler address, where he lived from 1861 until at least 1866, in business as a flour merchant. Later he is a lodger at the even

more humble Leonard's Place, off the Old Dover Road, listed as a retired Russia merchant in 1871. Matthew senior died there in the winter of 1874, aged 68.

The name of Hutchinson, as hemp and flax dealers, returns to the commercial directories in 1866, by which time John and Henry Hutchinson occupy the offices at No 48 Mark Lane. The company was still trading as late as the 1880 – an interesting circumstance but outside the scope of this volume to investigate.

1862-1863
Revd Thomas Wilson, MA

1864
Revd Joseph Betton (1813-1876), BA of Christ's College, Cambridge

Cambridge-born Betton was ordained in 1833, held various curacies, and was eventually appointed Rector of Stamford, then Rector of Frocester, Gloucester, 1869-70. He had retired by 1871, when just 58. His widow, Emily, went to live with her artist sister, Sarah, in Bristol on his death in 1876, but then moved, with daughter Ada, to Mount Ephraim Road, Tunbridge Wells.

1865-1868
George William Petter (1823-1888): printer and publisher

Petter, who was born in Barnstaple, Devon, set up as a printer in 1848 at Crane Court, off Fleet Street. In 1852 he moved to No 4 Playhouse Yard and took into partnership Thomas Dixon Galpin. In 1858 he bought out John Cassell's list and also took Cassell into partnership. After Cassell's death in 1865, Petter became sole proprietor but kept his partner's name, which survives today as Cassell plc. Petter published *The Echo*, the first 1d London newspaper, *Cassell's Illustrated Family Bible* and *Popular Natural History*. These, and subsequent popular publications, achieved considerable success. Petter retired in 1883 when the firm became a limited company, and moved to Bournemouth. He left a fortune of over £520,000.

Petter was related through marriage to the Rock family, publishers of engraved letterheads of views and prospects which became hugely popular in Victorian times as the precursors of picture postcards. Another Barnstaple family, the Rocks also settled in Blackheath, in Hyde Cliff House at the top of Crooms Hill (the site of St Ursula's Convent school). Petter's sister Fanny married Richard Rock (1808-1871), partner of the publishing business with brother William and brother-in-law John Payne. Petter's mother Mary was living at Hyde Cliff in the 1870s. It may have been Petter's residence at No 4 that led the Rock Brothers to publish a card depicting the Paragon (reprinted in this book).

1869-1877
Edward Basil Jupp (1812-1877): solicitor

Jupp's father, Richard Webb Jupp (1767-1852), also a solicitor, took his son into the family practice. Jupp senior was Clerk to the Carpenters' Company and, later, father and son were joint clerks, with Edward becoming sole Clerk to the Company after Richard's death. The Jupp family served the Carpenters' Company over four generations: Richard Jupp, Master in 1768; his son William (1734-1788); his son William (1770-1839); then Richard Webb Jupp, and finally Edward Basil Jupp. He was an avid collector of Thomas Bewick's woodcuts, and wrote a history of the Carpenters' Company in 1848.

Edward previously lived at No 3 Grotes Buildings, from 1855 to 1868. He was a member of the Blackheath Improvement Association from 1857 to 1862. As a Blackheath Proprietary School shareholder from 1874, he educated his sons at the school. Children living with Jupp and his wife, Elizabeth, at No 4 were: Edith; Richard Franklin; Herbert Basil; and William Theodore Jupp who was ordained. Another son, Edward Kaye Jupp, was killed in an accident in 1870, aged 20. Edward Basil Jupp died on 30 May 1877, at the age of 65.

1877
Mrs Elizabeth Mary Jupp (1819-1897): widow of the above

Mrs Jupp was the daughter of architect Joseph Kay (1775-1847), designer, among other projects, of the Trafalgar Tavern and Greenwich town centre (Nelson Road and the market) in the period 1828-39. She eventually lived at No 12 Eliot Place.

Mrs Elizabeth Jupp died at Tunbridge Wells, on 2 December 1897, in her 79th year. The Times refers to her as Elizabeth Margaret (sic) Jupp. See also No 1 The Paragon – sister Mary Anne Kay married Edward Kendall, in 1832.

1878-1892
John Brogden Moreland (1836-1910): builder

Moreland, who may have been related to Mrs Frances Moreland, of No 108 Shooters Hill Road, was born in Hoxton. Before moving to No 4 The Paragon the family – wife Caroline and four children – had lived in Margate and Leytonstone. His business must have been successful because in the 1881 census he is described as living on rents and dividends, despite being only 45 at the time. Children living here were: Homer J. B.; Ethel Grace; Mary F.; Jessie. Grace Moreland died at Wickham Road, Beckenham, on 11 November 1921, aged 81. John Moreland was elected Master of his livery company, the Tylers and Bricklayers, in 1887-8. Various other Morelands held that office during the period 1866 to 1920 and the dynasty ended with Homer Moreland (John's son), who was Master for the session 1919-20. John Brogden Moreland died at Beckenham, in the autumn of 1910, aged 74.

1893 Empty

1894-1896
Rt Revd John Harold Greig, DD (1865-1938): Bishop of Guildford 1927-34

Greig was ordained in 1888 and held various posts – including that of incumbent of St Germans' Chapel, St Germans Place, from December 1893 to 1896. It was his term there that led to the taking of No 4 The Paragon as a parsonage. After various posts he was appointed Archdeacon of Worcester and Rector of Hartlebury from 1911, and in 1921 was translated to the See of Gibraltar. He was appointed the first bishop of the then newly-created diocese of Guildford in 1927 and held the post until his retirement in 1934. He married Lilian Sophia, daughter of William Owen Robinson, in 1890.

1898-1899
Charles W. Clement Smith

1900 Empty

1901-1909
Graham Stokes (1855-1921): solicitor

Stokes was a member of a distinguished and talented sporting family that dominated Blackheath football, cricket and golf for many years at the end of the 19th century. The son of Henry Graham Stokes (1816-1875), solicitor, of No 2 St John's Park, Graham entered the family practice along with brothers Frederic and Henry B. Stokes. Graham excelled on the cricket field and was capped for Blackheath and Kent, as well as playing on the rugby football field for the mighty Blackheath Football Club.

Frederic (1850-1929) was not only Captain of Blackheath FC but also Captain of the England side in the first-ever formal international game in 1871. Another brother, Lennard (1856-1933), was a GP, and followed the family sporting interests, becoming President of the Rugby Football Union in 1886. Graham Stokes lived at No 17 Church Terrace from 1889 and moved to No 4 The Paragon on his marriage to Esther Frances, daughter of Edward Henry Bath (see No 7 The Paragon). They resided at Heathfield, Priory Lane (now Priory Park), from 1914 until his death in December 1921.

125

1909-1946
William Dunn, MA, LLB (1866-1948): solicitor

Dunn was a member of a large family that occupied Nos 20 and 22 St John's Park for many years. The son of William (1815-1895 [*see comment on p.67*], he was educated at the Proprietary School. On his marriage in 1897 to Margaret Elizabeth, daughter of Henry Smith (1840-1908), of No 72 Beaconsfield Road, he moved to the newly built No 11 Eliot Vale. While resident there he joined, in 1908, the committee of the Blackheath Conservatoire of Music and remained on it until 1947, having served as Chairman from 1918 to 1938. He was also a member of the Board of the Blackheath Concert Hall Company from March 1914 until 1938, resisting all offers of the Chair.

The Dunn family remained in the Paragon during the war, despite periodic damage – their house being the last in single-family occupation. Daughter Christine Margaret married Captain Richard Turbutt, on 2 May 1923. William moved house on the death of his wife, Margaret, in November 1946.

House fully restored, converted and occupied as six flats by 1952.

No 5 The Paragon

1800-1801
The parish records indicate that this house was not fully finished until 1801. It must have been one of those which fell victim to Searles' financial difficulty and Cator was presumably anxious that it be occupied. The reason for this view is that it was taken, by midsummer 1801, by a Cator relative. The head lease had passed to William Bennet, a master carpenter and one of Searles' principal creditors. When the Sparkes family (see below) moved away, the house was advertised for sale, along with No 6, with the benefit of a 90-year lease, at £7.10.0 (£7.50) per annum. The sale also included Nos 3, 19 and 20 The Circus (now Gloucester Circus} in Greenwich, once part of Searles' personal investment in that development.

1801-1803
Joseph Sparkes, Jnr, of the Bank of England
(sometimes written Sparks)

The third son of Joseph Sparkes (d.1790), who had married John Cator's sister Mary (1742-1794). The family had previously lived at No 97 Blackheath Hill and then, briefly, at Point House, No 18 West Grove. It was to George (d.1824) and Henry Sparkes (d.1818) – brothers of Joseph junior – that the bulk of Cator's estate was left in trust, but neither lived long enough to enjoy it.

13 March 1804: *The Times* advertisement:
At Messrs Skinner, Dyke & Co, at Garraway's, on March 23rd, 12 noon, by order of the assignee, Mr William Bennet. Eligible leasehold estate pleasantly situate at The Paragon on Blackheath and at the Circus, Greenwich and in Creed Lane, Ludgate Hill, London, let at rents amount-ing to £331. Lots 1 & 2, two genteel modern built brick dwelling houses with proper offices and gardens delightfully situate at The Paragon, Blackheath in the possession of –Deschamps, Esq,[No 6] and ... Sparkes, Esq [No 5], held for 90 years at £7.10.0 per annum .

1804
Lady Burnaby: No information discovered

There is no certainty to link our Lady Burnaby with what follows: *The Times* recorded that on 2 February 1823 occurred the death, aged 85, of Lady Burnaby, of Stoke Cottage, Guildford, the relict of Admiral Sir William Chaloner Burnaby (d.1794) of Broughton Hall, Oxford. She was 85.

1804-1805
Thomas Gowland: merchant, of 16 Muscovy Court, Tower Hill

Gowland, whose name is sometimes written Gouland and even Goulding, was previously of Savage Gardens, near Fenchurch Street. He had moved his office, at the very least, to No 28 Great Winchester Street by 1809 where his presence is recorded until 1814. His stay in the

Paragon was brief and nothing more has been discovered about him or his activities.

1806-1808
Henry Alexius Abbott (1765-1820): navy agent and Calcutta merchant

Abbott's office was at No 10 Essex Street, Strand, later (by 1812) at No 12 Clement's Inn, and eventually in Great Russell Street. Abbott, who was a subscriber to Thomas Noble's poem, Blackheath: A Poem in Five Cantos (1808), lived previously at Littlecote, Hertfordshire, and later on Blackheath Hill, before moving to the Paragon. A number of children were born at No 5. The Abbott family later lived at Lindsey House, Grotes Buildings. Abbott died in February 1820 and was buried at St Mary's, Lewisham.

Three of Abbott's sons achieved high rank in the Indian Army. Maj.-Gen. Augustus Abbott (1804-1867), an authority on ordnance, was once described as '... one of the finest artillery officers of his time'. He was Inspector-General of ordnance and magazines at Bengal from 1853 to 1858 and was Commander at Meerut in 1858 at the time of the Mutiny. The journals of his experiences in the Afghan War were published, posthumously, in 1879. Curiously, he died at No 4 Paragon Buildings in Cheltenham. Maj.-Gen. Sir Frederick Abbott (1805-1892), distinguished himself as an engineer with the Bengal Army in Kabul and in the Burmese campaigns. An authority on bridge building, he retired from active service in 1847 and was knighted in 1854.

The youngest of the brothers, General Sir James Abbott (1807-1896), who was born at No 5 The Paragon, may have been the most illustrious member of the family. Commissioned in the Bengal artillery in 1823 he was, in 1839, sent to negotiate a treaty between Khiva and Russia, signing the terms in St Petersburg in 1840. He was Commander of the garrison at Hazara in the Sikh War of 1849-50, and held it so tenaciously that he enjoyed the thanks of both Houses of Parliament. Abbottabad, now in Pakistan, was named after him. His memoirs of the Khiva campaign were published in 1843. Abbottabad – '... a remote city in a valley ...' – suffered dreadfully in an earthquake in October 2005. The town became internationally known when, on 1 May 2011, the notorious terrorist Osama bin Laden was killed there by American Special Forces.

8 August 1807: *The Times* advertisement:
Blackheath. Elegant residence, offices, garden and land. By Messrs Winstanley & Sons, at Garraway's, on Friday, 21st instant, at 12 o'clock. A very desirable leasehold house replete with every requisite convenience for a family of the first respectability containing suitable bedrooms, two handsome drawing rooms, fitted up in a state of superior neatness and communicating by large folding doors, good proportioned eating parlour, breakfast room, boudoir, enclosed verandah (sic) [should be sq br , as below, unless in original] or summer room, excellent offices, well supplied with water, detached newly-built coach house, four stall stable, poultry house and yard, walled pleasure ground and lawn cloathed [sic] with full bearing fruit trees, a large productive kitchen garden, fish pond, cow house, tool house and two pieces of meadow land, containing about four acres and a half. The premises are in the most perfect state of repair, and beautifully situate, [at] No 5 The Paragon, Blackheath, and early possession may be had. To be viewed by tickets only, with particulars which may be had of Messrs Winstanley & Sons, Paternoster Row; particulars likewise at the Green Man, Blackheath, and Garraway's.

1808-1826
Charles Lewis Muller: exchange broker
(sometimes written as Charles-Louis Miller)

Charles Muller, whose father was also called Charles Lewis, was in business by 1804 at No 10 Great Winchester Street as an exchange and discount broker. In the same offices was Samuel Muller, a notary public, perhaps a brother. Charles Muller may have moved to Blackheath on his marriage to Mary, daughter of Dr Edward Long Fox, MD, of Bristol, in February 1808. Whatever, Muller stayed both at his home and his office address for many years (this was unusual at the time). His last appearance in the commercial records was in 1828, still at Great Winchester Street, but in 1830 the occupant is S. A. Muller. The latter was also an exchange broker, but what his relationship was to Charles has not been discovered. Charles Muller's mother, Anne, died at No 5 The Paragon, in November 1809, aged 73. Charles died in the winter of 1839, in the Palace of St James, Westminster .

9 June 1827: *The Times* advertisement:
For sale on 18th instant [June] 1827 No 5 The Paragon. Two drawing rooms; seven bedrooms; 2ac 1r 10p [sic?] garden and paddock. Unexpired lease of 16 years from Michaelmas next. Also the sale of its furniture.

1827-1841
Joseph Laurence (1791-1878): stockbroker

Of all the Paragon residents, perhaps Joseph Laurence (often written as Lawrence) was one of the most successful and influential in business. Born Joseph Levi he was, very early in his professional life, a successful stockbroker, trading as Laurence, Whitmore & Co. and a member of the London Stock Exchange by 1824. In 1826, Levi formally changed his name to Laurence. A contemporary at the Exchange was Philip Cazenove (1798-1880) and in January 1836, along with Charles Thomas Pearce (a colleague at Laurence, Whitmore), they formed the partnership of Laurence, Cazenove & Pearce. Their descendant partners are in business today as Cazenoves, and Rathbone Bros Ltd, which absorbed Laurence Keen in 1995.

Laurence took an active part in Blackheath life, being one of the founders of the Blackheath Proprietary School. So keen was Joseph's advocacy for the new school that his son, Sydney (1819-1895), was one of its first pupils before going up to Caius College, Cambridge. Another son, [Revd] Perceval Laurence (1829-1913), received his schooling there and partner Philip Cazenove enrolled his son Henry, despite living in Clapham. Charles Pearce (who died in 1847 in Camberwell) was succeeded in the company by his son, also Charles, in 1851; he became a partner in 1853. Sydney Laurence joined his father as a clerk in 1843 and was a partner by 1846. In December 1854 the partnerships were dissolved (amicably), with one branch continuing as Laurence, Son & Pearce, and the other as Cazenove & Co.

Joseph Laurence and his wife, Penelope, had moved to Beddington, Surrey, by 1843. While at the Paragon they had the sad misfortune to lose two of their children: a son, Edward, in 1829 at the age of 11, and Penelope Louisa, aged only 14, in August 1830.

1841 enumerated census return: Thomas Hards, aged 40, gardener, lived in the cottage at the rear of No 5.

1842-1860
John Frederick Fixen (1782-1860): wholesale grocer and merchant.

His name bewildered the record keepers and it was sometimes written as Fissen, Fisson, Fixson or Fixsan. John was in business as early as 1823 at No 3 Garlick Hill. The trading name continued into the 1860s but to judge by Fixen's age, it may be that by then the company was under the control of others. For a period in the 1830s it was trading as Fixen, Harris & Inceson and, in 1839, as Fixen & Meeson. But by the 1840s the offices were at No 35 Queen Street and the company had become John Frederick Fixen & Co., the name it retained after Fixen's death. The family moved to No 5 The Paragon at about the time of the company's move to Queen Street, having previously lived in Clapton (in the 1830s) and then Clapham. John's widow, Elizabeth, remained in the Blackheath house for a further year or so.

Fixen's son, also John Frederick, did not enter the family business. After attending the Blackheath Proprietary School, he was admitted to Trinity College, Cambridge, and took holy orders. He was eventually the Vicar of Ugborough, Devon (1869-85) and of Bucknell, near Clun, in Shropshire from 1885 until his death in 1909. In 1854, Fixen's eldest surviving daughter, Elizabeth, married Revd Arthur Rawson Ashwell (1824-1879) who enjoyed a distinguished career in theological education, eventually becoming Canon Residentiary and Principal of Chichester Theological College. He also had a high reputation as a writer and preacher, earning him a place in the Dictionary of National Biography and Boase's *Modern English Biography.*

The Fixen children known to have lived at the Paragon included: [Revd] John Frederick (d. 1909); Elizabeth; Emma (who died in 1856, aged only 27); Sophia; Louisa; and Fanny Edelman. Footmen were among the family's living-in servants in 1851 and 1861. The gardener's cottage was occupied by William Robinson in 1851 and, in 1861, by Samuel Peak, his wife Lydia, and no fewer than seven children aged from 13 years down to 1.

1861-1862
Mrs Elizabeth Fixen (1797-1881): widow of the above

The widow Fixen and her unmarried daughters lived at Bishop's Croft, Guildford, after they left the Paragon in 1862. Eventually, Louisa entered the Church, joining the order of the Sisters of Mercy at the Penitentiary Church in Oxford. The last surviving daughter, Fanny Edelman Fixen, died at Bishop's Croft on 5 May 1915, aged 78. Elizabeth (miswritten in the record as Mrs Fixsen) died in the spring of 1881 at the family house in Guildford.

1863-1894
Hammon Paine (1824-1894): stockbroker, landowner

His first name is sometimes (erroneously) written as Hammond. Paine was the son of Cornelius Paine, a stockbroker in partnership as Kensington, Paine & Young in the 1840s. By 1861 the company was Paine, Morris & Co. and by 1866 Hammon Paine & Co., stock jobbers, of No 31 Throgmorton Street. Hammon Paine was a member of the London Stock Exchange. His four sons (George, Hammon D. Jnr, Harold and Gerald (1864-1885) were all educated at the Proprietary School and all entered the business.

The firm survives today (2011) as Paine, Webber, of the London Commodity Exchange. Hammon Paine, who was born in Hythe and lived in Peckham for many years before moving to No 5, was much involved in local concerns, serving on the committee of the Blackheath Preservation Society. This group, a precursor to the present Blackheath Society, was largely instrumental in ensuring that the Heath was taken into public care in 1871 (see page 50). After retirement, Paine spent part of his time at Folkestone; when he died, he left an estate valued at £135,015.

Paine and his wife, Helen (who died at No 5 The Paragon in January 1890, aged but 51), were blessed with a large family, although they suffered the loss of a son in 1874 at the age of 17 and another, Gerald, died at 21 in 1885. Besides those mentioned above, the children at No 5 were: Alice, Helen, Gertrude, Florence, Norah, Louis, Conrad and Albert. The last named not only did not attend the Proprietary School but was not to join the family firm, choosing instead to enter the Army. This was Lieut.-Col. Albert Ingraham Paine, CMG, DSO (1874-1949), who served with distinction in the South African War as well as in the 1914-18 conflict.

1895 Henry Hampton

1896 George Leeds Paine: stockbroker, son of Hammon and Helen Paine (above)

5 October 1896 Contents for sale

1897-1899 Empty

1900-1906
Charles Clifton Shurey (1862-1906): journalist and publisher.

Charles Shurey entered the newspaper business quite young. By the time he was 29 he was a wholesale newsagent, by 1891 a newspaper proprietor, and he was to publish a long list of popular magazines. None lasted long but none was intended to. A new title would attract both old and new readers, always hungry for novelty. Magazines like Boys, Monster Monthly, Pals, Spare Moments and Police News earned him a small fortune. His offices were at Caxton House, Gough Square – the heart of old Fleet Street.

Shurey died young but his estate was valued at a comfortable £29,948. The Shurey family were previously of No 95 Lee Road. They were away from the Paragon on the night of the enumerated census return in April 1901, on holiday at a seafront boarding house in Brighton.

On his death, his widow, Laura Florence Shurey, and the boys Harry, Reginald and five-year- old Gordon Lindsey, moved to No 42 Lee Road. Later the family moved to Eastbourne, eventually to reside at the Mostyn Hotel. It was while living here that Laura married the Revd Tudor Thomas, MA, of Gravesend, in August 1928

1907-1914 Empty, possibly let on short-term agreements

1915-1940
Percy John Rendall, MD (Brux), LSA, MRCS, FZS (1861-1948): physician and surgeon

Rendall initially gained much medical experience in Central and Southern Africa. Later he was an authority on venereal diseases: he was the Medical Officer in charge of the VD wards at the Royal Surrey County Hospital and at the Royal Herbert Hospital, Woolwich, from 1917 to 1919. He was awarded the OBE in 1920 for his work in this speciality. In April 1922, his daughter, Joan Dorothy, married war hero Harold George Rickwood, DSO, MC. The Rendalls lodged briefly at No 22 Lawn Terrace, Blackheath Village, before moving to No 5 The Paragon.

1930-1940
Mrs Edith Rendall (1876-1942)

Listed as the ratepayer for the property, with her son Anthony Rendall, a chartered accountant. Mrs Rendall let rooms in the house during the 1930s; she died aged 66, in 1942, on the Isle of Wight.

21 October 1931: Death of **James Edward Wilson** aged 70. Keen cyclist.

1932
Harold Lancelot Newman, CIE (1878-1949)

Chief Conservator of Forests, Bombay, India. Retired in 1933 and moved to Redcliffe Gardens, London SW10.

18 July 1932: *The Times* reports the wedding at St Paul's, Knightsbridge, of Hilda Suzanne Newman, daughter of Harold Newman, No 5 The Paragon, to James Derek Deuchar, of Dissington Hall, Northumberland.

1941-1946
Leven's Private Hotel, Proprietor: **William Harrison**

This building was taken by Harrison after his hotels at Nos 9 and 10 The Paragon were bombed during the night of 19/20 March 1941.

House restored by Charles Bernard Brown and in occupation as flats by 1955.

No 6 The Paragon

House in the parish of Greenwich; most of the grounds in Lewisham; part of the rear garden in the parish of Charlton. This was the only house in the Paragon to remain occupied throughout the 1939-45 war.

1800-1803 House unfinished

March 1804: A 90-year lease was offered for sale (coupled with No 5) on 31 March 1804, along with houses in the Circus, Greenwich, and elsewhere. For full details, see No 5 The Paragon.

1804-1811
William Deschampes (1774-1830): drug merchant, of No 52 St Swithin's Lane
(sometimes written De Champ)

Bankrupt 1812; died at Datchet on 27 December 1830, aged 56. Deschampes was a widower, his wife having died at Ringwood, Hampshire, in November 1799. Another company of merchants, trading as W. W. Deschamps (sic), was operating from a bewildering variety of City addresses from before 1810 until at least 1816 when their location was No 58 Cannon Street. In July 1830 William Deschampes suffered the death of his (unnamed) daughter, the wife of army officer Lewis Walsh, RA. His son, George Edward Deschampes, died at the residence of Charles Dyer, a surgeon, at No 5 Devonport Street, Hyde Park, on 23 August 1841.

15 January 1812: *The Times* advertisement:
Sale on February 12 1812 of a 12_ years unexpired lease on ' ... a genteel family residence and land ... in The Paragon, by the assignees of William Deschampes, bankrupt. Rent £92.18.6 per annum. Harvey & Warne, solicitors.'

The house boasted marble chimney-pieces and the estate included a handsome lawn and walled pleasure ground, statuary, a two-acre paddock of rich grassland, and a walled garden.

1813-1824
Henry Goodwyn (d.1824): brewer

Goodwyn was a very rich brewer, in various partnerships (with Messrs Skinner, Thornton and Hoare at different times) but always based in a brewery at Lower East Smithfield. He was on good terms with many of the rather grand Blackheath and Greenwich families through his connection with the Enderbys and the Larkins. The Enderby family were owners of substantial whale oil and shipping businesses, trading in the South Seas and Antarctic waters, and Larkins' fortune was based on trade and shipping through membership of the East India Company. Two of Goodwyn's daughters married into these families, in a joint ceremony at St Botolph, Aldersgate, in April 1787: Elizabeth (1769-1846) married Charles Enderby (1753-1819) and her sister, married Samuel Enderby (1755-1829). Goodwyn's son married Laura Larkins in 1804. His third daughter, Mrs Catherine Ryder, died on 5 October 1832; the fourth, Amelia, on 27 February 1841.

Henry Goodwyn, who was a trustee of the New Cross Turnpike, among other public offices no doubt, lived in some of the best property in the district: from 1787 to 1792 at Cambridge House, West Grove; at Vanbrugh Castle from 1793 to 1804; at Clifton House, on the north-west edge of the Heath close to what is now Hyde Vale, in 1804 and 1805; and at Point House, West Grove, from 1807 until he moved to No 6 The Paragon – where he died in 1824. Vanbrugh Castle, Point House, and No 6 The Paragon all survive.

1825-1826
Thomas Maud

Probably the Thomas Maud who was a navy agent and merchant of Great George Street, from before 1798 until at least 1820. No other references have been discovered. According to the Land Tax return of 1826, this property is shown as 'late Maud'.

1826-1837
Edward Sedgwick (d.1835)

Edward may have been the son of Thomas Sedgwick, merchant, of Clement's Lane, then Great St Helens and, finally, 137 Fenchurch Street from 1812 to 1832. He died on 17 October 1835, at Brighton, where, according to The Times, he went '... for the good of his health'.

The ratepayer on this house, from 1837, is given as Mrs Jane Sedgwick although Edward is recorded as the ratepayer for the strip of land which fell within Charlton parish as late as 1843. Even so, the 1841 census accepts that Jane was then a widow. Their daughter, Helen, born at No 6 in 1824, married Edgar Harry Howell, a coal and wine merchant, in 1849.

1837-1847
Mrs Jane Sedgwick, widow of the above

Jane was only 45 at the time of the 1841 census, with three children living at home: William, 15; Elizabeth, 15 [perhaps twins?]; and Helen, 13. Jane Sedgwick had moved from the Paragon to Catford House, Catford Hill, by 1848.

1848-1849
William Christopherson (1802-1853): wholesale and shipping ironmonger

Christopherson was in business at No 55 King William Street by 1845, residing at No 2 Gloucester Circus, Greenwich, from 1841. He moved to No 6 The Paragon in the summer of 1848. His

descendants were to remain in Blackheath until the 1950s, with his grandchildren having a profound and lasting effect on the social and sporting welfare of the district. This was largely because his son, Derman (1835-1907), a stockbroker, raised at least eleven children. William's first wife, Harriet (née Green, of Eltham), died in May 1849 and this may have led to his removal to No 15 Church Terrace. He married his second wife, Jane (1805-1858), another daughter of John Green of Eltham, in October 1850.

William's son, Clifford (1838-1914), a merchant and chemical agent, who lived in Blackheath Park, became Chairman of Consolidated Goldfields; the third son, William Bayley Christopherson (1846-1939), also resident for many years in Blackheath Park, was Managing Director of Hubbard's, a leading paint manufacturer. More details of the Christopherson dynasty can be found in Volume II of this series.

In 1849, part of the far south end of the garden of No 6 was sold to the South East Railway Company for the development of the railway-line tunnel from Blackheath to Charlton.

1851-1860
Griffith Thomas (c.1814-1884): solicitor

In 1824 Griffith Thomas was articled to solicitor Anthony Brown (d.1853) and, after a brief spell of working independently, he became his partner in 1833. The practice specialised in banking but also undertook much work for railway companies and the Kent Water Works Company. On Brown's retirement, Thomas became second senior partner, and senior partner in about 1860. The business prospered and entered an outstandingly successful period when, in 1844, a Blackheath resident, John Hollams (later Sir John, and President of the Law Society in 1878), became a junior partner. The legal firm of these two Blackheath men grew into the internationally respected company of Coward Chance, which merged with solicitors Clifford Turner in 1987 to become Clifford Chance, one of the largest legal practices in the world. The story of Thomas & Hollams' practice is well told in a (1993) monograph on the origins and development of [the legal firm of] Clifford Chance by Judy Slinn. More details about Hollams will be found in the entry for Paragon House, South Row.

Thomas had previously lived at Camberwell but moved to Blackheath in 1851, where he remained for the next 11 years. He took an active part in local affairs and was a committee member of the Blackheath Proprietary School and of the Blackheath Improvement Association. His son, Harry Brockholes Thomas who attended the Prop, went on to Trinity College, Cambridge, and then read for the Bar as a member of the Inner Temple. In 1862, Thomas (with his wife, Martha) moved to Queen's Gate Terrace, Kensington, and to Englefield Green in Surrey when he retired from the practice in 1873; he subsequently became a director of the Central Bank of London (later part of Midland Bank). When Griffiths Thomas died, he left an estate valued at £52,000.

The children, along with Harry Thomas, who lived at Blackheath, were Fanny, Charlotte, and Catherine. The latter was to marry Thomas's successor in the practice, Cecil (later Sir Cecil) Coward (1845-1938), and Griffith Thomas provided a generous dowry of £2,300.

1860-1880
Henry Clarke Hills (1819-1897): manufacturing chemist
(sometimes written as Henry Charles Hills)

Henry Hills, the son of Thomas Hills and Sara (née Clarke), was born in Bromley-by-Bow, and spent many years in Amlwch, Anglesey, before a brief spell in Birmingham. He may have moved to London (he was resident in Camberwell in 1857) to take over a company run by his father (or uncle Frank) because he first appears in the London commercial directories as a manufacturing chemist at Brook Terrace, Deptford .

Thomas Hills had been active at the Bromley-by-Bow Steam Mills as early as 1811; Frank Hills was a manufacturing chemist, trading under his own name by 1837, and Henry is named as the proprietor from 1851. The family companies (they were numerous) were involved in copper mining or processing in Wales, Spain and Wallsend in Northumberland. Thomas had patented a process for the manufacture of sulphuric acid in the early years of the 19th century and is

supposed to have cornered the market in a method of gas purification.

The Hills family lived at No 6 The Paragon for 20 years. With Henry and his wife, Charlotte, were: George A., Charles H., Emily J., Augusta, Ellen St Clair, Fanny F., Fredericka F. (all born on Anglesey), Alice M. and Caroline (who was born in the Paragon). In 1880 they moved to No 6 Northbrook Road, Lee, where Henry died in the spring of 1897 aged 78. Charles H. Hills was listed in commercial directories as a copper smelter, at Wallsend-on-Tyne, in 1882.

1880-1891
Revd Ebenezer Evans Jenkins, MA (1820-1905)

Jenkins, a Wesleyan Methodist, was a widower aged nearly 60 when he came to No 6 The Paragon, accompanied by two young children: Elizabeth Fearnley Jenkins, born in Southport, Lancashire, and James Heald Jenkins, born in Highbury. In 1881 Emily Anne Dorey, his niece, was living with them and she may have acted as a housekeeper/companion for the children. Jenkins' career had been spent largely in India, where he lived from 1845 to 1867, excluding the Mutiny years. On returning home, he was appointed to the Hackney circuit but spent much time travelling widely, including to Japan and the United States. From 1877 to 1888 he was General Secretary for Foreign Missions and President of the Wesleyan Conference in 1880. He married twice and both his wives died young: firstly, Elizabeth (née Drewett) – the mother of his children – who died in Madras in 1869; secondly, Margaret Heald (née Wood), of Southport, who died in childbirth in 1875. Jenkins, who retired to live in Southport, enjoys a modest entry in the *Dictionary of National Biography*.

1891 census: Empty

1892-1894 No entry in directories

1895-1909
Wilhelm Friedrich [?] August Arnold (1839-1910): marine underwriter

Arnold was born in Germany but generally known as William Arnold. He was a partner of Danzig-born Dr Ernst Emile Wendt, DCL (1818-1892), who lived at No 8 Vanbrugh Park and then at No 50 Shooters Hill Road. Arnold was one of the first shareholders in the Blackheath Concert Hall Company. He had lived earlier (1876 to 1882) at No 7 Lee Park and afterwards at No 3 Mercator Road (then known as Marlborough Road), Lee, until he moved, with his wife, Mathilde Christiane Floriane (1848-1925), to the Paragon in 1895.

In April 1898 the Arnolds hosted a reception here after the marriage of William King Webster, son of Revd E.Webster, of Lincolnshire, to Agnes Heinken. William Arnold died at No 20 St John's Park on 15 May 1910, aged 71. His estate was valued at over £47,000.
1910-1922

Walter Fielding Holloway Blandford, MA (1864-1932): solicitor

Blandford was the son of the eminent physician George Fielding Blandford, FRSM (1829-1911), of Wimpole Street. On George's death, at Tunbridge Wells, in August 1911, he was described as 'one of the leading consultants on insanity in the country'. He enjoyed an entry in *Who's Who*.

Walter lived at home in London until his thirties. He was a lecturer at the India College [where?] in 1891, and described only as a solicitor's clerk in 1901. It may be that the huge wealth enjoyed by his father (he left over £107,000) helped towards the purchase of the lease on No 6 The Paragon.

Walter's son, Henry Fielding Blandford, was born at the Paragon on 2 February 1912. The family moved from time to time, and Walter died at No 12 Lee Road. Unfortunately the death registrations for 1932 record a Walter Fielding Blandford, aged 58, from Fulham. He cannot have been the solicitor who lived in the Paragon, born in 1864-5. Molly (née Smith), the widow of our Walter Fielding (if indeed they had been married), eventually moved to No 6 Lee Road.

December 1922: advertisements for board residence (allied to No 5 The Paragon)

Paragon Registers

1923-1924
Romeo Censi

1925-1938 Mrs E. F. Censi

1929-1930 *Sutherland Private Hotel*
Advertisement of 18 May 1929: '... under entirely new management'.

1931-1932 Mrs McDonald-Wilson: Private Hotel

1933-1936 James McConville: Private Hotel

1937-1940 Mrs Evelyn Marjorie Wickham: Private Hotel

1941-1950 William Harrison (proprietor): Leven's Private Hotel

Post-war residents included:

1946-1950 Mildred Gascoigne

1946-1951
Arnold Fation Bideleux (1870-1953): German-born merchant banker who retired to the UK
in 1933. Arnold and Anna Maria Bideleux celebrated their golden wedding in November 1948.

1948-1949: Mrs Vera L. James, LRA

House restored and converted into flats by 1955.

No 7 The Paragon

1800-1806
The pair of houses Nos 7 and 8 The Paragon were ready, to judge by auction particulars, well
before the end of 1804, but purchasers were not found until at least 1806. Pending that sale, a
strip of land (1 acre, 1 rood and 30 perches) at the rear of the houses, was let to the then
occupant of No 8 (q.v.), Sir Spencer Maryon Wilson. The equity in Nos 7 and 8 the Paragon had
been assigned to William Pitcher, of Salisbury Square, a carpenter, and Thomas Cartwright of
Miles Lane, Thames Street, a bricklayer. Pitcher & Cartwright were creditors of Searles and, no
doubt, received the leases on these houses in lieu of payments.

20 September 1804: *The Times* advertisement:
*Messrs Peter Cox, Burrell & Foster respectfully inform the public that they shall submit for
sale in the month of October next two very capital family houses built in an elegant and
substantial manner, being the two centre houses in The Paragon, Blackheath. Any gentleman wishing to purchase either of them by private contract in the meantime may be
informed of the particulars on application to their offices in Throgmorton Street.*

19 March 1805: *The Times* advertisement:
*Capital house, Blackheath, with immediate possession. To be peremptorily sold. By Peter
Coxe, Burrell & Foster, at Garraway's, on Thursday, April 14, at 12 o'clock, by order of the
proprietor in two lots. Two substantial, elegant family residences, held for a long term at
trifling ground rents, situate in the centre of that regular ornamental pile of buildings, The
Paragon, Blackheath, a spot very dry and healthy and commanding beautiful views over a
great extent of country; the premises are finished in the present style; the principal storey a
spacious hall, two lofty drawing rooms, enriched ceilings, 52 ft by 18ft, opening with
folding doors, windows to the floor and solid, statuary chimney pieces, dining parlour,
gentlemen's dressing room, store room, nine excellent bed chambers with good closets; in the
basement lofty kitchen 25 feet by 18, housekeeper's room, butler's pantry, wash-house,
scullery, larder, front area and arched vault, walled garden etc., with two acres of pasture
land to each house. May be viewed by ticket 12 days preceding the sale when particulars may
be had at the Bull, Shooters Hill; Green Man, Blackheath; at Lloyd's and Garraway's; and of
Messrs Peter Coxe, Burrell & Foster, Throgmorton Street, and No 88 Pall Mall.*

9 June 1806: *The Times* advertisement:
Capital residences with land, Blackheath, by Mr Burrell, at Garraway's, on Thursday June 12th, at 12 o'clock, in two lots by order of the proprietors. Two substantial and elegant family houses held for the long unexpired term of 74 years at £18.8.0 per annum, situate in the centre of that regular ornamental pile of building, The Paragon, Blackheath ...(rest as before)

12 August 1806: Agreement

1807-1822
Isaac Warner (1744-1822): coal merchant

Warner was a member of a large family involved in the coal trade, both as merchants and coal factors. Isaac's son, Simeon (1786-1866), resided at Colonnade House, South Row (q.v.), from 1823 to 1852. Warner was a founder member of the London Coal Exchange, established by Act of Parliament in 1807, probably the year he retired. He was a trustee of the New Cross Turnpike Road in 1817. Isaac was buried in the churchyard of St Margaret's, Lee, in January 1822.

His daughter Mary married John Allen, son of William Allen, of Clifford's Inn, in October 1810. The young couple later resided at No 3 The Paragon (q.v.). A son, also Isaac, died at Blackheath, aged 36, in 1817. Warner and other members of his family owned extensive lands in Greenwich and nearby, and they seem to have been impressed by Michael Searles' designs. A Simeon Warner lived in Surrey Place, Camberwell, in a house designed by Searles in 1784.

Subsequently, Simeon bought the lease of Colonnade House, also designed by Searles, from the executors of Robert Parry (see below). In 1803, Isaac Warner asked Michael Searles to design him a house near a river (unidentified) but although the design was imposing it was never built, so far as one can tell.

1822-1842
Mrs Mary Warner (1756-1842): widow of the above

Mrs Warner gave £5 to the Distressed Irish Clergy Fund in January 1836.

2 July 1842, notice in *The Times:* No 7 The Paragon for sale – late Mrs Warner, deceased. Lease to be sold 2 July [sic] and the effects on 4 July 1842.

1843-1867
Robert Wilcoxon (1801-1866): plate-glass manufacturer

Wilcoxon was the son of a wholesale looking-glass and cabinet maker, of Lombard Street, whose company was in business by the 1820s. For many years it traded as Wilcoxon & Harding and by 1835 had moved to Monument Yard. Robert must have taken over the business at about this time (he lived on the premises and many of his children were born there) and was in partnership with his brother, Arthur, who lived at No 5 St Germans Place from 1845 to 1857. They added paper staining and wallpapers to their trade in due course and, clearly, prospered considerably from the growing demand for plate glass for shop windows. The family settled in Blackheath in 1843 and was to remain there – with the exception of Robert's son Arthur (1839-1920) – until the late 1940s. He and his brother, Charles, both entered the business.

Robert married Lucretia (1807-1883), daughter of Thomas Brocklebank (1776-1843) of Westcombe Park and, as a result, inherited some useful property at the west end of Westcombe Park Road, now the site of Nos 3-9. After her husband's death in 1866, Lucretia moved to No 9 Vanbrugh Park Road West, then to No 15 in the same road and, finally, to No 30 South Vale Road, where she died in December 1883, aged 76. Arthur Wilcoxon took over the company and had moved to No 14 Annesley Road by 1883. His family remained in that house until the death of his youngest daughter, Alice Elizabeth, in 1948.

The children living with the Wilcoxons at No 7 The Paragon were: Lucretia, Mary, Charles, Arthur, Annie and Emily.

27 November 1866, notice in *The Times*: 12-year lease for sale on No 7 Paragon. £100 p.a.

1867 Empty

1868-1874
George Martin Hughes (1827-1891): attorney and solicitor

Hughes, who may have moved to the Paragon because he knew the Wilcoxon family (one of the Wilcoxon daughters was a visitor here in 1871), was a solicitor by profession but devoted much of his time to the study of Romano-British topography. He published a number of books on the topic. Such was his authority on the subject that he enjoys an entry in Boase's *Modern English Biography*. The family had lived in Hampstead for many years, where Hughes' wife, Catherine, had been born. Children living at No 7 were: Catherine F., George C., Mary W., Lucy E., Emily M., Alice B. and William A. Hughes (the last two children and another girl were born at here).

1875-1888
Revd Charles Bullock, DD (1829-1911): clergyman, author and publisher

Bullock was a clergyman who enjoyed a considerable reputation – and no small wealth – as an author and editor of popular religious magazines, which would account for the ability of a relatively young clergyman to live in such a grand house. He was born in King's Lynn, Norfolk, and was ordained at Rotherham in 1855. After various curacies, he served as Rector of St Nicholas, Worcester, from 1860 to 1874. During this time he developed an enthusiasm for the Sunday observance movement and wrote copiously on this and other topics. Among the magazines which he founded and edited were *The News*, *Home Words* and *Fireside Magazine*. In 1884 he was appointed Principal Chaplain to the Army, at Woolwich, a sinecure that allowed him to concentrate on his publishing. Bullock, who justified an entry in *Who's Who*, retired to Eastbourne, where he died in 1911. He was married twice, secondly to Hestor (née Savory) (1845-1925) in 1866. Children at No 7 were: Edith E., Charles A. H. (from his first marriage), [Revd] William Charleston (1867-1929), Hubert Somerset (1871-1963), Hettie Lena, [Revd] Reginald W. (1876-1953) and Ernest H. Bullock. William, Reginald and Hubert were enrolled at the Blackheath Proprietary School.

In March 1881 there was the need for a new parlour-maid, but in April 1887 the requirement included a daily governess for the three children: two girls aged 13, and a boy of 6. The governess was expected to teach them music, drawing and elementary Latin as well as German and French.

1889-1900
John Walters (or Walter) Wilson, JP (1836-1912): Iberia (wine) merchant

Wilson, the son of Daniel Wilson, an importer of Spanish wine, was to move to No 3 The Paragon (q.v.) where he lived from 1901 until 1907. He returned to Blackheath to live at No 14 Kidbrooke Grove for the last two years of his life. Wilson, who had lived previously in Liverpool, then at No 85 Eltham Road and, in the 1880s, at Oatlands Park, Surrey, came from Wirksworth, Derbyshire. His wife, Ellen, was born at Stoke-on-Trent. Children living at No 7 were: Gertrude M., Ellen B., Amy F., Georgina F. and Constance M. Wilson. The third daughter, Amy Ford Wilson, married Arthur Kirby on 13 August 1896.
1901 enumerated census return: Empty

1901-1921
Henry Bath (1875-1921): ore and metal broker

Bath, the oldest son of Edward Henry Bath (1851-1908) was the owner of estates at Allt-y-Ferin, Nantgaredig, Carmarthenshire. His family firm was the ship breaker, Henry Bath Ltd of Old Broad Street, which purchased the SS Great Eastern in December 1887 for £16,700, solely for scrap. The vessel was broken up in August 1888 and the remains sold for £58,000. The ship, sometimes called The Leviathan, was designed by Isambard Kingdom Brunel (1806-1859) and built at Millwall by Messrs Scott, Russell & Co. She was launched, after much difficulty, in January 1858.

Paragon Registers

Bath was the brother-in-law of Graham Stokes, of No 4 The Paragon, and it may have been this connection that led him to Blackheath. Henry Bath died at Lynton, Devon, on 19 April 1920, leaving an estate of about £24,000.

1921-1940
Mrs Kathleen Mary O'Calahan Bath (1875-1940): widow of the above and daughter of Wyndham Pryce Lloyd

The Bath family regarded No 7 The Paragon as their town house; their principal interest was in the estates in Wales, where Henry Bath spent much of his time. Nevertheless, Kathleen and Henry Bath Jnr (1904-1970) are named on the voters' lists for this house for the period until 1938. There were a number of family occasions in Wales: engagements, marriages, deaths, and young Henry's 21st birthday party (which took place at Allt-y-Ferin in January 1925), the details of which the Bath family felt were of sufficient importance to be noticed in the Blackheath press. One Bath daughter, Kathleen Margaret Eileen Gwyn (1900-1955), married Major John William Gaisford, RAOC, at All Saints' Church on 1 March 1919 (divorced 1944). Her sister, Sioned Cordelia Gladys (1901-1962), who was married there on the same day to George Arthur Oscar Champion de Crespigny (d.1962), was also divorced (1932). Kathleen Bath died in Carmarthenshire, in 1940, aged 65.

The younger generation's reminiscences about life at No 7 in the 1920s and 1930s indicate generally ramshackle domestic arrangements and make mention of a long garden left to run wild – which the children adored. Beyond the official garden was a substantial plot leading down to the round pond, on Pond Road, probably the extra acre leased by Sir Thomas Maryon Wilson in 1806.

1940-1953

From 1940 until Charles Bernard Brown commenced the task of restoring and converting Nos 7 and 8 The Paragon into self-contained flats, these buildings were in guest-house use. They remained habitable throughout the Second World War, albeit suffering damage and broken windows on a number of occasions. Some idea of the cosmopolitan life that was led here is given in Chapter 6 of this book. Among the more noteworthy residents of No 7 during and after the war were:

1940-1952
Hubert William Ord (1869-1953)

Mrs Annie Caroline Ord (1899-1975)
Hubert William Ord, MA, was one of the last surviving masters of the Blackheath Proprietary School. He came to Blackheath in 1880, with his widowed mother, Mary, and was a pupil at the Prop from 1880 to 1886. After taking his degree at Oxford he joined the staff of the school (where he earned the nickname Polly, which stuck throughout his life) and remained there until it closed in 1907. Thereafter, he worked as a tutor and crammer, for many years in the old BPS building in Blackheath Village. He was a keen member of the Greenwich and Lewisham Antiquarian Society and served as its President in 1914 and 1925. In 1936 he published his autobiography, Adventures of a Schoolmaster.

1940-1946
Wricklemarsh School
Headmistress: **Mrs Annie Caroline Ord**

A school for small boys and girls and one of the handful that kept going through the most difficult days of the war. The Wricklemarsh School was a rarity. Almost all the other private schools had closed with the outbreak of war and the few that reopened after the 'Phoney War' ended in May 1940 rapidly put up the shutters at the onset of the Blitz. Most of the school-children had been evacuated – the Blackheath High School for Girls went to Tunbridge Wells – but a few remained and they needed not only the rudiments of education but also looking after during the day when many of the mothers were engaged on war work.

Mrs Ord's venture flourished and during the autumn term of 1942 she felt confident enough to throw a party for parents, friends and students, at which the children performed dances and songs. She too contributed songs and her husband, always ready to perform with the slightest encouragement, declaimed the stirring and then popular 'Drake's Drum' by England's favourite patriotic poet, Sir Henry Newbolt (1862-1938). Despite the continuing threat of bombs and, later the V-1 and V-2 menace, Wricklemarsh School kept going until early 1946, surviving the war and providing a service for which many parents must have felt some gratitude.

1943-1946
Paragon School of Equitation
Proprietors: Ralph E. and Nancy Price

Nancy Price had organised horse shows and gymkhana on the Blackheath High School playing field, at Kidbrooke, in July 1943 and, by 1944, was advertising the Paragon riding school (to be run from stables in Pond Road, near the railway bridge).

1944-1945
Paragon School of Ballroom Dancing

Ralph E. and Nancy Price also managed the Paragon School of Ballroom Dancing but few details of this business have survived. One can only guess that one of the grand salons, with which this house was blessed, was the studio.

1945-1950
Lieut. Cecil Leslie Stranack, RAOC (1883-1950)

Stranack was born in Poona and commissioned in the 3rd Derbyshire Regiment.

1945-1951
Cecil Ernest and Annie Louise Jamieson

House restored and converted by Charles Bernard Brown through the years 1952-8. The completion of this pair (Nos 7 and 8) represented the end of Brown's monumental task, although progress was considerably delayed, partly because of shortage of funds.

No 8 The Paragon

House not finished until 1806.

A lease on this house for a term of 75 years from 25 December 1804, at £11.10.0 a year, was granted by John Cator to William Pitcher, a carpenter of Salisbury Square, Fleet Street, and Thomas Cartwright, bricklayer, of Miles Lane, Thames Street, on 12 March 1805. In August 1806 the benefit was assigned to Thomas Maryon Wilson, to the approval of Cator's executors (his brother Joseph and one Richard Johnston) for the sum of £1,300. Shortly after the agreement was finalised, Maryon Wilson rented some land at the end of his plot: a long, irregularly shaped strip of more than one acre, for £6.0.9 a year for a term of 21 years.

1806-1811
Sir Thomas Maryon Wilson, 7th Bt (1773-1821): Lord of the Manor of Charlton and Sheriff of Kent

Maryon Wilson was resident here when his daughter, Margaretta Maria, was born to his wife, Elizabeth, in May 1808. They had married in 1799 (she was the daughter of Captain James Smith [1723-1786]) but did not always reside in the family home, Charlton House. This was probably because it was still the home of his mother, Lady Jane (1747-1818), widow of the 6th Bt, Sir Thomas Spencer Wilson (1723-1798). Maryon Wilson took much interest in the estates of the family, both in Kent and Essex, and was frequently away from Blackheath. His wife died in November 1818, aged only 47.

1812-1817
Sir John Eamer, Bt (1750-1823): sugar refiner and wholesale grocer
Director of the West India Dock Company. Lord Mayor of London, 1801-02

Eamer, who had previously lived in a house on the site of No 13 West Grove, took an under-lease from Maryon Wilson for No 8 The Paragon. He was an alderman of the Langbourn ward in the City from 1795 until his death, being knighted in 1795, and Lord Mayor in the session 1801-2. Eamer, whose detractors claimed that he 'formerly kept a small grocer's shop in Leadenhall Street', grudgingly acknowledged that, from his offices at No 3 Wood Street in the early 1790s, '... he carried on a great trade in the wholesale grocery business'. Eamer was later based in Rutland Place and Upper Thames Street. He was one of those local men of sufficiently high social standing to be a regular visitor to HRH Caroline of Brunswick, Princess of Wales (1768-1821), when she lived at Montague House on the south-west corner of Greenwich Park.

As well as enjoying the usual privileges and duties of a City man, Eamer was also Lieutenant-Colonel in the London Militia from 1803 to 1820, a police magistrate at Southwark from 1814 to 1823, and Director of the West India Dock Company [date/s?] As a member of the Salters' Company, he was elected Master in 1805. His political aspirations failed, in that he stood unsuccessfully as a Tory candidate for the seat of Ilchester in 1796. Sir John was, for a short while, a member of the Blackheath Golf Club. Many of his business colleagues with West Indies connections were also members so this was possibly more for the club's social interest (the dinners) than for a love of the game. His heir, Charles Samler Eamer, died at Ghazeepore, India, in August 1805. His second daughter, Harriet, died at No 8 The Paragon in June 1816. Sir John himself died on 29 March 1823, at his house in Bedford Square, Brighton, in his 74th year.

1818-1826
William Castell [sometimes written Castle] **Damant** (1774-1841): stockbroker
Damant had lived at Hatton Garden before moving to the Paragon as a tenant of Maryon Wilson. The family enjoyed a private pew at St Mary's parish church, Lewisham, during their time in Blackheath. When Maryon Wilson died, Damant purchased the unexpired lease of No 8, in October 1822, for £1,240. He was a stockbroker in partnership with John Risdon, and their relationship was extremely stable, lasting from before 1819 until Damant's death, at No 38 Kensington Square, in June 1841 at the age of 67. They worked from No 8 Shorters Court, Throgmorton Street, and both were members of the London Stock Exchange. Risdon, who lived at Brunswick Square, took an active part in the management of the organisation. While at No 8 The Paragon, Damant's younger brother, Edward, emigrated to South Africa, taking passage on a ship called The Ocean, which sailed from Deptford. William Damant married a widow, Mrs Wightwick, of Tettenhall, Staffordshire, in August 1815. In later years they lived at Yelverton House, Tavistock, in Devon. In August 1829 his daughter Caroline (d.1867) married the distinguished architect George Wightwick (1802-1872), of Plymouth, who, somewhat curiously, was William Damant's stepson. The second daughter, Maria, married William Payne, of Lavender Hill, on 13 January 1842.

1827-1831
William Scott Preston (1797-1852): barrister, of New Square, Lincoln's Inn

He married, in May 1822, Margaret Grace Gordon, daughter of Peter Lawrie (d1828), of No 93 Blackheath Hill. By 1832 No 8 was in occupation by James Cousens. Preston had moved to his late father-in-law's house and by 1851 he was no longer in professional practice.

1832-1842
James Cousens (1782-1861): tea merchant
(sometimes written Cousins or Couzens)

Previously at No 12 The Paragon (q.v.). In 1809 his company was trading as James Cousens & Kemp, from No 25 Coleman Street, but by 1843 it was James Cousens & Son, tea dealers; the office was at14 Sherbourne Lane, where it was still in business in 1855. Cousens' erstwhile partner, James Kemp (1788-1844), lived at No 45 Blackheath Park. The family may have moved to No 8 because of its size: there were10 children in the house on census night in April 1841 – no wonder the parents (James and Caroline) were away on that date. Also, No 12 The Paragon enjoyed only a small garden. Cousens must have been a head lessor for the property because he was entitled to the vote in 1832. He also gave a generous £5 to the Distressed Irish Clergy Fund, in January 1836.

The family tea business continued under the direction of Stamford Cousens, the older son. Another son, James (1823-1867), remained in the area, living at No 71 Shooters Hill from 1848 and finally moving to Sidcup House, Foots Cray, where he died on 9 April 1867. James senior and Caroline eventually moved to Waverley House, West Hill, Sydenham. Caroline died in the summer of 1861and James senior in the winter of that year, aged 79.

Children living at No 8 during the Cousens' occupation were: Stamford; James; Edward; Sydney; Caroline; Kate; Frances; Isabella; Mary; and Louisa. Not surprisingly, there were seven servants in residence in 1841 to attend the needs of the household. Caroline junior married, in April 1842, John Shorter, a merchant of Oporto.

1842-1845
Frederick Luck (d1845): timber merchant

There is much confusion about the Luck family in the surviving records. Firstly, in the late 1820s/early 1830s Frederick Luck lived at the Paragon in New Kent Road, Searles' first exercise in crescent design. A brother, Edward, lived at No 11 The Paragon, Blackheath, in 1844-5, although Frederick is recorded for that address in 1837 and 1839. Unfortunately, 'Mr Luck, The Paragon' was all that was considered necessary for most purposes at that time and it is difficult to know which Luck was which. Frederick's widow, Jane Lee Luck, did move to No 53 Blackheath Park for a few years, and then to Onslow Square, Kensington, where she died in June 1859, aged 47. She was also of the Luck family and had married Frederick on 3 December 1829 when he was a resident at the Kent Road Paragon. The wedding notice refers to her as Jane, oldest child of Michael Lock (sic), of Brompton, Kent. Certainly, the sons of these men – C. L. Luck, E. J. Luck, Michael G., George and Henry Luck – were pupils at the Blackheath Proprietary School at various dates between 1842 and 1856.

Frederick and Edward were members of the Luck family of The Hermitage, West Malling. The line was well established by Thomas Luck (1765-1857) of Went House, West Malling, who was blessed with seven sons; their descendants were still at Malling as late as the 1960s. In the 1820s there was a timber company, Luck & Steel, with offices at Rotherhithe and wharves at Cuckold's Point. This company became George Luck & Co. and was still in business there in 1839. By 1843 Frederick Luck was in partnership with one Engstrom (a Swede), as merchants, based at No 9 Great St Helen's.

1847 Mrs Mary Coburn (sic)
This name and its distinctive spelling is recorded for No 8 The Paragon in Bagshawe's 1847 *Directory*, the only reference to Mrs Coburn found in any local record.

1848-1851
James P. Davidson (1801-1874): civil servant

Davidson was only in his late forties when he retired from the Bengal Civil Service but his stay in Blackheath was short – about two years, previous to which he had lived at Eltham. With him and his wife, Mary, at the Paragon were their children: Ann Mary, born in India; Eleanor; Susanna F. and Charlotte E. (both born in Blackheath); and Fanny. There is no trace of the family in 1861 (records may have been lost) but Davidson was a widower by 1871, living with his daughters at No 20 Lansdowne Terrace, Cheltenham. James Davidson died there in the summer of 1874, aged 73.

1853-1858
McGregor Laird, FRGS (1808-1861): merchant, shipping-line owner and Africa explorer

Bill Bonwitt wrote in his Paragon book (1976) that Laird personified the spirit of enterprise, initiative and sheer guts of the Victorian age, probably more than any other Paragon resident of the time. This was no exaggeration and the pages of the *Dictionary of National Biography*, Boase's *Modern English Biography* and other works provide evidence to support such a claim.

McGregor was the younger son of William Laird, founder of the Birkenhead shipbuilding company, and the boy joined the firm after leaving school. His brother, John (1805-1874), took over the company in 1833, by which time McGregor had given up active employment with the family firm - not to serve with a rival business but, with characteristic enthusiasm, to establish his own in Liverpool. This was in 1831 when he was only 23.

His plan was to exploit for commercial purposes the then recent discoveries on the Rivers Niger and Tchadda, in West Africa. In early 1832, Laird fitted out and despatched two small vessels; one of which, the *Alburka*, a paddle steamer, was the first iron vessel ever to make an ocean voyage. McGregor Laird accompanied this expedition, which sailed from Milford Haven and reached the mouth of the Niger at the beginning of October 1832. The hardships were such that of the 48 Europeans on board the two vessels at the beginning of the journey, 39 were dead before the end. Notwithstanding, the survivors explored the rivers and the interior of the Niger basin, not returning until 1834.

Laird's health was much impaired due to the privations he endured, from which he never fully recovered. In 1837 he published a narrative of his expedition and was subse-quently elected a Fellow of the Royal Geographical Society. He married Eleanor Hestor, second daughter of Lieutenant-Colonel Nicolls, of the Royal Marines at Woolwich, in August 1827 [should this be 1837? He would only be 19 in 1927]. In the same year he was one of the promoters of the British and North American Steam Navigation Company that built and owned the steamship British Queen, designed to outrun the Great Western that was created for them by Isambard Kingdom Brunel (1806-1859). Laird's ship – which was broken up in 1841 – was built by Curling & Young of Limehouse: members of the Curling family lived at No 1 The Paragon and at Paragon House (q.v.). Henry Bath & Co. dismantled Brunel's *SS Great Eastern* in 1887 (see No 7 The Paragon).

Laird was of an inventive mind. He filed numerous patents connected with improvements in shipbuilding. Much of his later life was devoted to establishing trade with, and developing the resources of, West Africa. His principal moral concern was to combat the Arab slave trade that still flourished in the interior. Many expeditions were sponsored and supported by him with little or no prospect of material advantage. In the early 1840s he established a base as an Africa merchant, at No 3 Mincing Lane, and moved his home to south-east London. While here, he floated the Africa Steamship Company and built at least three vessels for African exploration, entirely at his own expense.

Laird lived at many addresses in Blackheath but why he moved so regularly is not satisfactorily explained. His wife, Eleanor, must have been a very tolerant woman. They lived at Phoenix House, Blackheath Village, from 1841 to 1845; were at No 12 Crooms Hill in 1851; then at No 8 Lee Terrace from 1852 to 1853, after which they settled for a long five years at No 8 The Paragon. Shortly after arriving here, the Lairds suffered the loss of a son, aged 14. Two of their boys, Edward and McGregor junior, were educated at the Blackheath Proprietary School. While at No 8, the Lairds were forced to bring a court case restraining one George Tryon who had become infatuated with their daughter.

In 1858 the family moved to Brighton, probably because of Laird's poor health. He died on 9 January 1861, at the early age of 53. Mrs Laird still suffered from itchy feet: following her husband's death, she moved the family no less than five times between 1861 and 1890. Eleanor died in at Tonbridge, Kent, in the winter of 1898, aged 85.

1859-1867
Peter William Barlow, CE, FRS (1809-1885)

Peter Barlow stood in the shadow of his father, also called Peter, and has been confused with him. Peter the elder (1776-1862) was a distinguished mathematician, physicist and optical scientist, becoming Professor of Mathematics at the Royal Military Academy, Woolwich. It was inevitable that his son would follow a scientific career but, instead of physics, the boy turned to engineering. He was one of the leading railway and bridge engineers of his day: he worked on the construction of the Liverpool and Birmingham Canal and the New London Docks, and served as resident engineer for the London to Dover Railway (later the South Eastern), planning and designing many branch lines for the company, as well as railways in Ireland. Barlow designed and constructed Lambeth Bridge (opened 11 November 1862) for the astonishingly

low cost of just £30,000. Unfortunately, his design was not to last and the bridge was replaced in 1929. He was elected a Fellow of the Royal Society at the comparatively young age of 45. Before moving to the Paragon, Barlow and his wife Bethia (a daughter of William Caffin, of the Royal Laboratory, Woolwich – they married on 5 July 1836) lived at No 8 Eliot Place. Children living with them in the Paragon were: Bethia E., Selina H., Katherine G. and Robert William (all born at Tonbridge); Ellen F., the youngest daughter, was born at Eliot Place. While at Blackheath, Barlow was a member of the Blackheath Improvement Association. He died at Notting Hill, in May 1885.

1868-1869
John Jacob Lidgett (1829-1869): merchant and shipowner

Lidgett was the son of John Lidgett (1800-1859), shipowner, of Brandon House, Morden Hill. John Jacob and his brother George (1832-1907) entered the family business. They were devout Methodists and were instrumental in the campaign and cause that led to the building of the Wesleyan Methodist church, in Blackheath Grove, in 1863. (It was a victim of a V-2 in March 1945 and was never repaired; its remains were demolished in the early 1950s.) For 10 years John Jacob and his family lived at No 6 St Germans Place, moving to No 8 The Paragon early in 1868. Unfortunately, he died in May of the following year but despite this, the family seems not to have been plunged into financial hardship and it remained at No 8 until 1880.

1869-1880
Mrs Maria Elizabeth Lidgett (1826-1911)

Mrs Lidgett (née Scott) was an enthusiastic worker for the Methodist cause, particularly for the Methodist Missionary Society. Her father, John Scott, was a leading layman in the movement and twice President of the Methodist Conference. In 1880 Mrs Lidgett went to live at No 69 Shooters Hill Road where she resided until her death in May 1911.

The children living at No 8 The Paragon were John Scott, Lucie Maria (1856-1953) and Alfred Edward (1859-1945), shipowner, member of the Baltic Exchange and art connoisseur. Of the wider Lidgett family, John Scott Lidgett (1854-1953) was to achieve the greatest distinction, being appointed a Companion of Honour in 1933. Educated at Blackheath Proprietary School, John spent two years in a shipping and insurance office before entering University College, London, where he took a BA in 1874 and an MA in philosophy and logic the following year. In 1876 he entered the Methodist Church and was appointed to a number of duties on the circuits. His driving ambition was to work in some of the poorer areas of London and, in 1891 he helped establish the Bermondsey Settlement where he served as Warden until 1949. The Settlement and its various enterprises transformed Bermondsey by inspiring and integrating its social, educational and administrative services.

Lidgett combined this with many other tasks, such as the editorship of journals (including the Methodist Review) and a considerable volume of authorship. He also served on the Committee of the London School Board, representing the nonconformist view, and was an alderman of the London County Council. In addition, he was Chairman of the Methodist Conference in 1908, and first President of the United Methodist churches in 1932. He remained physically and politically active into his nineties, not retiring finally until his 96th year when he moved to Epsom. He was an outstanding man and richly deserved the honours that were bestowed on him over the years, including the award of the Companion of Honour in 1933. Shortly before his death, Lidgett was made a Freeman of the Borough of Bermondsey. In spite of these weighty preoccupations, he retained his sense of humour. When, on his 95th birthday, a young photographer took Lidgett's portrait, the journalist asked whether he might be allowed to do so on his 100th birthday. The great man looked him over gravely and said: 'Yes, my lad, I think you'll make it.'

1880-1881 Empty

1881 census:
William Johnston, 62, Greenwich pensioner, acting as caretaker, with his wife Charlotte.

1882-1891
George Francis Legg (1819-1904): architect and surveyor

Legg was a working architect with a central London practice, and is quite often confused with his more famous namesake, George Legg (1799-1882). For some reason, Legg lived at many addresses in Blackheath: No 11 Belmont Grove from 1852 to 1856; No 9 Church Terrace 1860-67; No 105 Blackheath Park, 1867-80. He moved to No 65 Shooters Hill Road in 1891, and to No 14 Montpelier Row in 1896 where he remained until 1899, when he was in his late seventies.

Little has been discovered about Legg's work but he may have designed No 11 Belmont Grove (since demolished). Photographs show it to have been a heavy, not hugely attractive building, much of its period. He was elected a Fellow of his professional institute (FRIBA) in December 1877 and served as District Surveyor for West Hackney for some years. His wife Anne (1818-1898) died at No 14 Montpelier Row. There were at least three children: George (who was educated at the Blackheath Proprietary School), Eleanor J. and Lancelot H., the last two still living at home in their thirties in the 1890s. Instead of entering his father's profession, Lancelot worked as a contractor's agent.

1891-1931
James Dolphin (1842-1931): stock and share broker

Resident at No 23 Shooters Hill Road from 1872 to 1876 and at No 5 Vanbrugh Terrace from 1876 until the family moved to No 8 The Paragon. His wife, Jane Georgiana (1846-1931), who was born in India, was the daughter of Maj.-Gen. Edward Lacon Ommaney and sister of Colonel Edward Lacon Ommaney (1834-1914), of No 84 Shooters Hill Road. Jane Dolphin, who died in December 1931, survived her husband by only a few weeks.

Children of the family included Edward James (1876-1944), Jane Isabel (see below), William Heathcote (1881-1921), Agnes Muriel, Vernon O. and Helen Gladys. Vernon was killed in action in June 1917, aged 31. Jane Isabel married Walter Field Soames (1876-1933), son of Walter Kolle Soames (1849-1934), of Maze Hill House, in July 1905. Agnes married, in 1912, Captain Francis Loder Symons, who was killed in March 1915. She married again in June 1921: Lt Col Colin Trevelyan Robertson, OBE (1877-1957), of Paragon House and, later, headmaster and proprietor of Shirley House School, Cherry Orchard, Charlton.

29 July 1905, *Blackheath Local Guide and District Advertiser:*

A wedding of considerable local interest was solemnised at All Saints' Church, Blackheath, on Tuesday, the 18th inst. The contracting parties were Councillor Walter Field, eldest son of Alderman and Mrs W. K. Soames, of Maze-hill House, Greenwich, and Janie Isabel, eldest daughter of Mr & Mrs J. Dolphin, of The Paragon, Blackheath. The Revd W. H. K. Soames (uncle of the bridegroom) officiated, assisted by the Revd H. Welsford Snell; and Mr H. Gisby, the organist, played a number of appropriate selections. During the service, which was choral, the hymns: *Lead Us, Heavenly Father, Lead Us*, and *O, Perfect Love*, were sung. The bride, who was given away by her father, wore a gown of ivory duchesse satin, the bodice being swathed with satin and draped with lace and folds of chiffon, embroidered with silver, and caught up with real myrtle blossom, while the transparent Court train, which hung from the shoulders, was of ivory chiffon, draped with antique Limerick lace, with a wreath of orange and myrtle blossoms. She wore a tulle veil and a diamond and pearl pendant, the gift of Mrs W. K. Soames, and carried a bouquet of lilies of the valley and orchids.

The bridesmaids were the Misses Muriel and Gladys Dolphin (sisters of the bride) and Miss Florrie Soames (cousin of the bridegroom), while little Miss Esther Stokes and Master Bennett Abrahall bore the bride's train. Mr E. J. Dolphin (brother of the bride) was best man. The brides-maids' dresses were of ivory chiffon taffetas, trimmed with lace and silver, and embroidered with forget-me-nots, and they wore picture hats of ivory crinoline with pale blue feathers. Their bouquets were of yellow carnations, and they wore pearl and diamond pendants, the gifts of the bridegroom. Miss Stokes was dressed in crepe de chine and lace cap, and wore a pearl heart, the gift of the bridegroom, while Master Abrahall wore a white cloth suit and three-cornered hat. A reception was afterwards held at The Paragon, and during the afternoon Mr and Mrs Field Soames left for the continent. The bride's travelling costume was of pale blue radium silk faintly shot pink, with a cream crinoline hat trimmed with pale blue ribbon and velvet and pink roses. The presents, which numbered 240, included a sold silver fruit stand from the staff of the works of Messrs Wilkie & Soames Ltd,* together with a pair of brass candlesticks and letter rack from the workmen. In honour of the event a quarter-peal of Stedman triples was rung upon the bells of St Alphege Church, Greenwich. The dresses were made by Mrs Standing, of Brewer Street, Woolwich.

To commemorate this marriage the employees of Messrs Wilkie & Soames Ltd, were entertained to dinner by Mr Walter K. Soames, at the Trafalgar Hotel, East Greenwich, on Wednesday the 19th inst. Mr J. Stenson Turner, the manager, presided, supported by Mr W. H. Stacey (secretary) and others. Numerous toasts were proposed and responded to, including 'Prosperity to Wilkie & Soames Ltd', and 'the health of Mr and Mrs Field Soames', the latter being accorded musical honours. A capital programme of music was performed between the toasts, which was contributed to by a number of capable performers.

(Sadly, the happy couple were divorced a few years later. Mrs Soames remarried as Sandeman.)

* Soap and candle manufacturer which, in 1920, was taken over by Lever Bros.

10 March 1932: Contents for sale: Dolphin deceased

1932-1934 Empty

1935-1937
Albert John Wadman (1877-1937): son of Deptford architect and surveyor's assistant, William J. Wadman

August 1938: 10-year lease for sale: £110 per annum, plus £50 for residue of the lease. Purchased by Ralph Price.

1938-1940: Ralph Price

194 Empty

1945-1948:
Mrs Phyllis M. Horsborough and **Alan M. Horsborough**

10 March 1945: Advertisement for riding stables at No 7 The Paragon. These were conducted by Mrs Nancy Price, of the same address.

Until the mid-1950s Nos 7 and 8 The Paragon were run as somewhat ramshackle boarding houses with a great turnover in tenancies. Many students of the Goldsmiths' College Art Department stayed here from time to time: see Chapter 7.

House restored and converted into flats; fully occupied by autumn 1957.

1957-1967
Flat 5
Sir George Rostrevor-Hamilton, MA, FRSL (1888-1967), previously at No 2 Paragon House.

No 9 The Paragon

Nos 9 and 10 The Paragon may not have been fully fitted out for immediate occupation until about 1805. This block was totally destroyed in the blitz of 19 March 1941, and rebuilt in replica by Charles Bernard Brown in 1951.

1806-1808
Miss Roberts

Nothing has been discovered about Miss Roberts but she must have been a woman of substance to have taken on the house. It may have been fitted and furnished for others who then underlet the property. *The Times* advertisement of 31 July 1807 does not indicate the length of the lease for sale:

Genteel residence, Paragon, Blackheath, with immediate possession, by Messrs Skinner, Dyke & Co., at Garraway's on Thursday August 13 at 12 o'clock. A genteel residence, No 9, with offices and gardens, delightfully situate in The Paragon, Blackheath. The premises are handsomely fitted up in good repair and contain two elegant lofty drawing rooms of good dimension, a capital dining parlour with recess, 19 feet by 16; breakfast parlour, four principal bedchambers, servants' apartments etc. To be viewed 14 days preceding the sale when printed particulars may be had on the premises; also at the Green Man, Blackheath; place of sale and of Messrs Skinner, Dyke & Co., Aldersgate Street.

The property was advertised again, on 8 March1808, with almost identical particulars as the July 1807 advertisement, but with the addition of a coach house, stabling and walled garden. The auctioneers by this time had grown into: Messrs Skinner, Dyke, Tuckin & Forrest.

1809
Mr Irwin: probably J. Irwin: merchant of Muscovy Court, Tower Hill, in 1812

The company was still trading in 1819 but at 1 Lime Street Square.

1813
Mrs Rebecca Edwards (proprietor): *School for Girls* [or No 12]

Mrs Edwards advertised her school with a leaflet. The surviving account book of a local solicitor, Thomas Watson Parker, refers to bills rendered to Mrs Edwards, of the Paragon, Blackheath, for advice received in 1813. If the 1813 date is correct, then Mrs Edwards may have occupied this house or No 12. No advertisements for her school have been found in *The Times*, where it might be expected that she would have publicised it, since there were no local newspapers at the time. The lack of Vestry rate records for Lewisham parish for the period removes a primary opportunity for reliable confirmation of the occupant of this house at the time. The fees for Mrs Edwards' school were quite high for such an establishment and it may be that she achieved too few enrolments to justify continuing.

The handbill informed that 'Mrs Edwards, Paragon, Black Heath, instructed ladies in "Useful Attainments and Elegant Accomplishments". General tuition and French grammatically. 45gns per Annum; entrance 3 gns. The elements of Astronomy and Geography scientifically £3.3.0; music £6.6.0; drawing £4.4.0; writing £3.3.0. Latin, Greek and Italian by respectable Masters.'

1817-1841
Samuel H. T. Bishop (fl.1781-1841): iron goods merchant

Bishop, whose business was flourishing at Bankside, Southwark, by 1812, owned an iron foundry with a John Bishop (possibly a brother). Although the foundry address changes from time to time, in the London commercial directories it remained in the Upper Ground area of Blackfriars, and can be documented until at least 1839 when Bishop was nearly sixty. This may mean that he then retired. Items manufactured by the company included iron hoops and chains; in 1837 there is mention of copper as well as iron goods available on wholesale supply. Nothing has been discovered about the Bishop family life in Blackheath although Samuel junior was one of the first pupils to enrol at the Proprietary School, in January 1831. He attended the school for five years and may have left to join the family firm. With Samuel and his wife, Mary, at No 9 The Paragon in 1841 were the following children: Elizabeth, William, Henry, Samuel and Richard.

1842-1865
Quarles Harris (1791-1876): Oporto merchant

Harris, the son and grandson of men also called Quarles (and, perhaps, even earlier generations), was a merchant trading in wines from the Iberian peninsula, particularly Oporto. The company boasted that it had been founded as long ago as 1680 and the commercial London

directories certainly confirm it back to the middle of the 18th century. When Quarles, of the Paragon, took over the business is not known but before 1798 it was trading as Quarles Harris & Son, and operating from No 41 Crutched Friars. It remained at this address until at least 1835 when it moved to No 9 Billiter Square; in later years the counting house was as No 3 Savage Gardens. Quarles and his wife, Anne (née Harris; 1800-1877), had previously lived at East Wickham Hall, in Kent, for many years. A few years were spent in Lewisham, where two children were born, but by 1842 they had taken No 9 The Paragon.

Harris was a generous supporter of charitable endeavours (giving 10 guineas to the Distressed Irish Clergy Fund in 1836), and actively supported the foundation, in 1838-40, of the Hospital for the Cure of Club Foot and other Contractions (later [1907] amalgamated with other hospitals to form the Royal National Orthopaedic Hospital, initially at Great Portland Street and now at Stanmore, Middlesex. The family company collapsed in 1865 but the trademark continues and it was possible to buy Quarles Harris vintage ports as recently as 2011, the label still boasting of its 17th-century origins. Quarles junior continued trading as a wholesale wine merchant, from 30 Jewry Street.

The Harris's second surviving son, Walter George, died in December 1857, aged 21, when on a voyage to the Cape of Good Hope, undertaken, ironically, for health reasons. Three daughters married into the Army, including Isabella Anne, the second daughter, who married, in April 1858, William Addis Delacombe of the Royal Marines Light Infantry. He was to become Military Governor of the St Juan Islands, British Columbia and, later, Chief Constable for Derby. Their son, Lieut.-Col. Addis Delacombe, DSO (1865-1941), achieved a distinguished record during the Great War.

The Harris children living at No 9 were: Eliza Dorothea (died here on 24 January 1842); Georgia G.; Charles E. (who entered his father's office); Isabella Anne; Walter G.; Letitia B.; Maud Mary (d. 1871); Quarles J. junior (1843-1891); and Clarissa [?] C. Harris.

1866 Empty

1868-1882
Jesse John Tustin (c.1815-1899): colour manufacturer

Charles Driscoll Tustin (1868, 1870, 1872 and 1874 commercial directories)

The names Charles and Jesse John are listed in alternate street directories for this address during the Tustin years, but Jesse John alone is listed as head of the household in the 1871 and 1881 enumerated census returns. There is no mention of Jesse John Tustin, colour manufacturer, in the London commercial lists until 1876. In fact, Jesse, who had been born in Bishopsgate in about 1815, was living at Woodlands Terrace, Trafalgar Road, in Greenwich in 1851. He was described as a mercantile clerk. Jesse was married to Stepney-born Jane Anne (née Ericson), who was the same age. Children living at the Paragon in 1871 were: William Bucknell, colour manufacturer, born in Limehouse c.1844; and Susan, 23, Jessie Susannah, 21, and Miriam, 19, who were all born in Greenwich. Staying with them in that year was Susannah Ericson, Jane's sister. In 1881, only Miriam was still living at home with her parents. By 1891, Jesse, now in his mid-seventies, was living on his own at Eastbourne. He died at Reigate in the summer of 1899, aged 84.

From the 1870s Tustin, colour merchants, were firmly established in Tustin Street, New Cross. The Tustins – Edward Erskine and William], as well as Jesse Tustin – were based in Camberwell and active Methodists. There was a Methodist chapel next to the colour works, well supported by the family. The close proximity of their works and church may have led to the street being named after them. The firm was still trading in 1907 – in the name of Charles Driscoll Tustin (who lived on Denmark Hill, Camberwell) – after which it was merged with the neighbouring company of Horace Corey & Co., chemical colour manufacturers. Corey was to remain in business until the 1930s. The site was redeveloped in due course but the municipal estate on the site retains the Tustin name to this day.

1883-1887
Charles Boucher Lindsay (fl.1848-1916): merchant with interests in the United States

When Lindsay took No 9 The Paragon he was only 25 and recently married to Maria (née Justin). Their first child, Eleanor, was born here in 1883. The family moved to No 5 Pond Road in 1887 and remained at that address until 1910. An enthusiastic golfer, he was a member of the Royal Blackheath Golf Club from 1886 until at least 1916 and served as Captain of the club in 1904.

After Lindsay's departure from the Paragon (which may have coincided with the ending of the original lease) the house was subject to considerable repairs and alterations. These were undertaken in February 1888 'on the instructions of Mr Cator, the ground landlord'. The architect was Robert W. Collier (1854-1923).

1890-1894
William George White (1837-1895)

In 1891 the census taker recorded William White, 53, born in Southwark and listed him as a retired builder. In fact he was rather better than that and had been a marble mason, with a staff of 10 hands. He may have settled at the Paragon when he retired from business. His wife was Ann, born about 1841 in Luton. The family had lived in Kensington for many years.

The White children were William G., 26; Alice K., 18; and Arthur V – only 4 when he was registered as a voter in 1891. In October 1893, young William married Kate, daughter of Frederick Parkinson, of Fryerning, Essex.

By 1901 White's son, also William and trading as a Russia fruit merchant, was living at The Crescent, in Barnes, with his sisters and mother, Ann.

1895-1903
Frederick Wissler (1855-1924): sugar merchant

Wissler, who was Swiss-born, had retired from the sugar business by 1901, in his early forties. In his wider subsequent activities, he was to become Chairman of the Marmite Food Extract Company in 1902, the year the trademark for that distinctive vegetable paste was registered. Wissler and George Hunter acquired a 20-year licence for £11,000 from the Vereinigte Nahrextract works of Dresden, which had patented the process of manufacturing a yeast extract. They floated the Marmite Food Extract Company Ltd on a capital of £50,000 in February 1902. It was a huge success – as we all know to this day. In 1912 they also sold vitamin pills and in 1920 acquired the Bovril trademark. Eventually, the products were sold to Unilever.

Despite having lived in England for 53 years Wissler was obliged, in September 1914, to insert an announcement in the *Blackheath Local Guide* denying that he was a spy for Germany and threatening libel actions against those who continued to spread the rumour. Many local people with German-sounding names did the same and some even changed their names, especially after the sinking of the *SS Lusitania* in 1915. Wissler moved to No 1 Shooters Hill Road in 1904 where he remained until his death in 1924. His wife, Alice Maud Mary, died in July 1952, aged 87, at Bromley, Kent.

1904-1917
Revd John Francis Kendall, MA (1862-1931): incumbent of St Germans' Chapel from 1904 to 1917

Kendall was the son of John Kendall, bailiff of the Angerstein estates, at Woodlands, Westcombe Park (now No 90 Mycenae Road and the Steiner School in Greenwich). In 1888, Kendall married Julia Augusta, the eldest daughter of his father's employer, William Angerstein, MP (1812-1897), of Woodlands and Weeting Hall, Norfolk. He was ordained the year of his marriage, after obtaining First Class honours in English at London University, followed by a First in history at King's College, Cambridge.

After a couple of incumbencies, Kendall was appointed, in 1895, Rector of Hempstead with Lessingham, Norfolk, but instead took over St Germans', Blackheath, in 1904, in which year the family moved to the Paragon. He was Vicar of Richmond and Rural Dean from 1917 to 1928. On his retirement he was appointed a residentiary canon of Norwich Cathedral, and died in the Cathedral Close in August 1931 following a motoring accident. Mrs Kendall died in November 1936. One of the Kendall daughters, Ruth Medea Angerstein, died young, in May 1913.

For a short period the family lived at No 2 St Germans Place but moved back to No 9 The Paragon for reasons unknown. While incumbent at St Germans', Kendall was able to arrange for the Church authorities to purchase the freehold of his chapel and he saw it consecrated as a full Anglican church within the Diocese of Southwark. A previous minister of St Germans' – Revd John Harold Greig – had also used a Paragon house (No 4, qv) as a vicarage.

NB: *No names are recorded for this house in the street directories for 1906-8 despite the Kendalls' tenancy.*

1919-1941
Paragon Private Hotel: sometimes Leven's Private Hotel (combined from 1923 with No 10)
Proprietors: **Mr William and Mrs Annie Harrison**

This was the first of many of the Paragon and South Row houses to be used as a hotel or commercial boarding house. They were easily adapted into a series of bedsitting rooms or two-roomed apartments with a modicum of service and a common dining room. Harrison, who had worked at Leven's Hotel, Westmorland, before coming to Blackheath, enjoyed a monopoly of the Paragon hotels from 1919 until 1941, when the bomb on Nos 9 and 10 forced him to shift his base to Nos 107 and 109 Blackheath Park.

The first advertisement, in September 1919, offered high-class board residence. Numerous people came and went but a number became long-term residents. Perhaps the most distinguished was Edward Provis, last headmaster of the Blackheath Proprietary School, who lost his life in the hotel during the air raid of March 1941. Provis's wartime experiences are recorded in a series of letters he wrote to his family, quoted in Chapter Six.

Other residents at this address, combined with No10, included:
1923 John Gwynne Howell, MC (1891-1923): late Major in the Royal Air Force. Died 21 December 1923, aged 32; husband of Jessie.

1926
William Gick
Ernest Honey
Mrs Lily Holmes Tennant Cochrane (see also No 11 The Paragon)

1926-1936
George Edward Wright (1875-1936): electrical engineer, much interested in croquet, the Church, and psychic phenomena. The Wright family previously lived at No 32 Shooters Hill Road. His mother, Mrs Elizabeth Annette Wright, died here in 1932. She was the widow of Frederick Charles Buckley Wright, of the India Office.

1927-1936
Edward Provis and **Margaret Blanche Provis**. They were married for 50 years. Mrs Provis (daughter of the late Major Manley, 32nd Madras Native Infantry) died here in June 1936.

1930
Miss Frances Baker, ARIBA, an architect who won a prize, in a competition in February 1930, for a design that encouraged the use of electricity in a room

1938-1941
Norman Clive Sawers (1877-1951), Hon. Secretary of the XL [?] Lawn Tennis Club, who lived previously at No 69 Hervey Road

Severely blitzed 19 March 1941. House demolished along with No 10.

Rebuilt in replica, but as flats, and occupied by autumn 1951.

No 10 The Paragon

No names discovered before 1806.

1806-1823
William Ashmead (1770/71-1843)

Despite his long residence in Blackheath, little has been discovered about Ashmead other than that he and his wife, Rhoda Armstrong, of Highgate, were married in June 1803, and subscribed towards the publication of Noble's poem, *Blackheath: A Canto in Five Verses*, in 1808. Before they moved to the Paragon they lived in Kentish Town. The Ashmeads were living at No 43 Blackheath Park in 1824. Rhoda died in October 1842, aged 78, and is buried in the churchyard at St Margaret's in the parish of Lee. William died in March 1843, aged 74, and was buried next to his wife.

1823-1879
Louis Michael (otherwise Michel) Simon (1782-1879): ship and insurance broker

The Simon family occupied No 10 The Paragon for a longer span than any other residents in either the Paragon or South Row. They lived there from 1823 until 1883 – a total of 60 years. Before moving to the Paragon, Louis Simon lived, from 1821, at No 37 Lee Road (since demolished).

Simon, of French origin and the son of a refugee from the Revolution, occupied offices as a broker at his home in Gould Square, and then at No 13 George Street, in the Minories, from 1817 to 1824, separating his home from the counting house when he moved to Lee Road in 1821. In 1826, as a stockbroker, he was at 10 Warnford Court and, from 1834, at No 7 Warnford Street, Throgmorton Street. Despite his relative youth he was an early member of the London Stock Exchange and a leading member of its committee for many years. Nowadays, perhaps, he is most famous for being the father of Sir John Simon (1816-1904), the public health reformer, who lived with his parents in the Paragon from 1823 to 1834.

Louis Simon retired from the Stock Exchange at the age of 76, in 1858. He was married twice: his first wife died in 1810, aged only 26. His early married life was also blighted by the loss of four of his first five children in infancy. Simon was then to marry his first wife's sister, Mathilde (née Nonnet), who bore him another nine offspring. The Simon children known to have lived at No 10 were: John; Louisa; Maximilian Frank (who entered the family firm and later lived at No 32 Lee Terrace); Emma; Annette; and Mary. Over the years, various grandchildren lived here, including Louis Faulkner; Herbert and Annette Carey; Maximilian F. Simon Jnr (later Dr Simon, CMG, MD, MRCS, the distinguished colonial surgeon) and his children, and Cornelia. Two boys, Frank and Max, were educated at the Proprietary School.

1879-1882
Mrs Matilde (sometimes Mathilde) Simon (1787-1882), née Nonnet, second wife of the above

1882-1883
Miss Emma Simon (1827-1900): daughter of the above

She moved to No 7 Eliot Place to live with Herbert Simon Carey (1856-1947), a civil servant, and his sister Annette (Emma's nephew and niece).

Sir John Simon (1816-1904)
Some details of the Simon family can be gleaned from the memoirs (*Personal Recollections*) of John Simon (later Sir John) which were privately published in 1898. He was born in 1816 in the City and he considered that living there had disastrous effects on his family. Three out of four brothers and sisters died as well as his father's first wife, after less than five years of marriage. John was educated firstly at a preparatory school in Pentonville and then, from the age of 10, at Dr Charles Parr Burney's school at the north-west end of Crooms Hill, Greenwich, where he remained for nearly eight years. Burney (1785-1864) was the grandson of the famous musicologist Charles Burney (1746-1814) and the nephew of Fanny Burney (Mme D'Arblay; 1752-1840).

The school, which had been started by Charles Parr Burney's father (also Dr Charles; d.1817), was distinguished in its time but when Sir John wrote his memoirs, at the age of 81, he had some revealing comments to make:

Of the education, especially of the moral education at Dr Burney's I hesitate to speak a dispraise which perhaps represents chiefly the fact of my individual unfitness to make the best of it ... but the great faults in myself ... might have been cured ... by better guidance than my boyhood received. Probably the shortcomings which existed in the school where I received most of my educa-tion were common to all public and other large schools at the time.

After matriculation, John spent ten months in Germany and, on 1 October1833, was appren-ticed to Joseph Henry Green (1791-1863), surgeon at St Thomas's Hos-pital and Professor of Surgery at King's College. This apprenticeship bond cost his father the then considerable sum of £500. John undertook practical work at St Thomas's and attended lectures and dissections at King's, in the Strand. 'On three mornings of the week when I had to be at the college at 9 a.m. for chemical lectures and when as yet there was no coach early enough to help me, l had to start from Blackheath at 7 o'clock for my walk of eight miles. On three nights in the week, when Mr Green used to lecture from 8 p.m. to 9 p.m., I used not to reach home until nearly 11 o'clock.'

Louis Simon considered these exer-tions as being too strenuous for his son and arranged for lodgings near the college for the nights of the lectures. From October 1834 onwards, John became a permanent lodger in town and did not again, except on social visits, live for any length of time in the Paragon.

John Simon became a Member of the Royal College of Surgeons in 1838 and was elected a Fellow of the Royal Society in 1844, at a remarkably young age. He was appointed Senior Assistant Surgeon at St Thomas's in 1847 with a salary of £200 a year. He was married in 1848 (to Jane O'Meara) and in July that year became the first Officer of Health for the City of London. Simon's career and fame rested thereafter in the field of sanitary and public health reforms although his distinction as a surgeon was well recognised. After seven years in this post, he was appointed Medical Officer to the Central Board of Health, a place he continued to occupy when, in 1858, the Privy Council took over the duties of that Board.

The first Public Health Act, for which Sir Edwin Chadwick (1800-1890) had laid the founda-tions, was a considerable advance but the Act did not satisfy Simon's ambitions, especially in view of his memories of the unhealthy conditions suffered by his family when living in the City. The Medical Act of 1858, which introduced regulations covering the qualifications of practitioners in medicine and surgery and which, in turn, led to the formation of the General Medical Council, was largely due to his endeavours. He wrote and lobbied widely for reforms to prevent cholera and promote vaccination, and on all matters pertaining to public health and the spread of disease through inadequate sanitary and sewage systems. When the Local Government Board was formed in 1871, he became its first Medical Officer and worked to secure the passage of the Public Health Act of 1875.

In his private life Simon was a close friend of Charles Kingsley, H. T. Buckle, John Ruskin, Edward Burne-Jones and many other eminent intellectual Victorians. During his holidays he travelled ex-tensively abroad, often in the company of Edward Chadwick. The academic world honoured him with Degrees, he became a Governor of St Thomas's Hospital, a Crown Member of the General Medical Council, President of the Royal College of Surgeons and Vice-President of the Royal Society. In 1897 he was created KCB.

But Simon never fulfilled his principal ambition that, as the government's Chief MedicalOfficer he would enjoy the freedom of action that he had been led to believe would be his right. He was thwarted by Treasury officials and, after many battles, his office was abolished. John Simon retired in 1874 on a generous pension despite being only 58, with much energy and drive still to expend. Other than taking an active part in the development of his professional associations he was never able to complete the huge tasks he had set for himself. Nevertheless, Simon's success in his work led him to become known as the 'Father of Public Health'. He died on 23 July 1904 in his house in Kensington Square, where he had lived since 1867. An oration at a memorial meeting in 1905, delivered by Sir Richard Douglas Powell, read: *'He was a man gifted with true genius and inspired by the love of his kind. He will ever remain a noble figure in*

the medicine of the 19th century, and will live in history as the apostle of sanitation.'
Historic hindsight indicates that John Simon was, perhaps, one of the most influential residents
that the Paragon has enjoyed.

1884-1888 Probably empty

January 1888: Alterations and repairs at No 10, on behalf of Albemarle Cator (the freeholder),
were organised by Robert W. Collier, architect. After 60 years in one-family occupation, the
house probably needed some attention.

1890-1917
Walter George Izard (1840-1918): civil and railway engineer

Izard, who was born in Brighton, spent most of his career in foreign parts, building railways in
India (from 1858 to 1871) including the line from Bombay to Asrigahr [Asirgarh?], in Brazil, and
in South Africa (in the 1880s) where he built the railway from Durban to Pietermaritzburg. After
further work on the ground, in Argentina, he eventually returned to London permanently, to a
desk job with Argentine government railway interests.

In the last twenty years of his life he devoted himself to many charitable causes including that
of the Blackheath Cottage Hospital, Shooters Hill Road, and he was Vicar's Warden, Treasurer
and correspondent at All Saints' Church, Blackheath.

With his wife Letitia (1856-1940), born on Alderney, Channel Islands, the family consisted of
G. Walter, Letitia Addison, Kathleen and Annie Frances Izard. Two of the girls, Kathleen Addison
(d. 1926) and Annie, married Nicholas (in 1901) and Franklin (in 1906) Kendall respectively, of
No 1 The Paragon (q.v.). After Walter Izard's death (on 2 January 1918) his widow moved to No
23 Shooters Hill Road where she remained until shortly before her death at St Leonard's-on-Sea,
at the age of 85. The unmarried daughter, also Letitia (b.1885), was still resident at Shooters Hill
Road in 1947.

1918-1922
Rt Revd William Woodcock Hough, DD, MA (1859-1934)
Suffragan Bishop of Woolwich 1918-32

Hough, the son of James Hough, FRCS, was educated at the Perse School and Corpus Christi
College, Cambridge. After a spell as a schoolmaster at Wimborne, Dorset (where he met and
married, in 1886, Georgina Elizabeth Druitt [d.1933]), he was appointed curate at the Corpus
Christi Mission in Bermondsey, and became Clerical Secretary of the South London Church
Fund for the period 1901 to 1905. During part of this time Hough lived at No 23 Blessington
Road, Lee. From 1905 to 1916 he was Vicar of St Mary's parish church, Lewisham, where he
was succeeded by Revd Arthur Llewellyn Preston, MA (1884-1936). In 1918, when his family
moved to No. 9 The Paragon, Hough was appointed Suffragan Bishop of Woolwich, which he
coupled with the Archdeaconry of Lewisham; he was also Canon of Southwark Cathedral. After
retirement in 1932 he moved to Carshalton, Surrey, where he died in March 1934.

1923-1936 *Paragon Private Hotel*
Proprietors: **Mr and Mrs William Harrison**

7 July 1932, *The Times:* Death of Elizabeth Annette Wright, wife of F. C. B. Wright of the India
Office; last surviving daughter of George Cattermole

1936-1941 *Leven's Private Hotel* (same proprietors)

In 1923 No 10 was combined with No 9 as Harrison's Boarding House and Hotel. Details of this
enterprise and some of the residents will be found in the section relating to No 9 The Paragon.
27 December 1923: Death of Helen le Suer Honey, aged 73, wife of Ernest Honey, at No 10 The
Paragon.

8 April 1939: Death of Ernest Honey, aged 84, at No 10 The Paragon. The family previously
lived at No 21 Shooters Hill Road.

House demolished as a result of enemy action in March 1941. Rebuilt in replica externally and occupied as self-contained flats by autumn 1951.

No 11 The Paragon

1805-1807
Captain Thomas Mortimer: probably the Thomas Mortimer (1755-1824), gun maker

Mortimer was of No 44 Ludgate Hill and, later, No 21 St James's Square when the company was trading as Thomas Mortimer & Son. Captain Mortimer, who was a contractor to the East India Company, was in partnership with his brother, Henry Wartlake Mortimer. Thomas noted the birth of his daughter in *The Gentleman's Magazine* for October 1805. This was the first reference to him living at the Paragon and the first published information about any resident of this house.

1808-1813
The Hon. Mrs Anne Charlotte Murray (d1824)

Lady-in-waiting to the Princesses Augusta and Elizabeth, daughters of HM George III. The local connection was probably through the fact that Chesterfield House (now Rangers House) was home for Augusta (1737-1813), Duchess of Brunswick and sister of George III, from 1807 to 1813. She was the mother of Caroline Amelia Elisabeth, unhappily married to the Prince of Wales and resident at Montagu House, Park Wall, Blackheath, to the south of Rangers House, from 1799 to 1812. Considering Mrs Murray's duties, it is difficult to be sure how often she resided at the Paragon; nevertheless, she paid for a pew at St Mary's parish church, Lewisham, until 1813. She was the daughter of Lieut.-Col. Francis Ludovic Grant, MP, and the widow of Lord George Murray (1761-1803), Bishop of St David's from 1801.

Their fourth daughter, Amelia Matilda (1785-1884), an excellent artist and an enthusiastic botanist, devoted much of her time to the plight of destitute children. She was a maid of honour to HM Queen Victoria in 1837, but eventually resigned from royal duties in order to be free to write and publish her anti-slavery views. Her recollections of the period 1803-37 were published in 1868.

1817-1822
George Bramwell (d1837): solicitor/banker

George Bramwell insured this house (wrongly written as No 12 The Paragon) and his office with the Sun Fire Company [also written as Sun Insurance Company and Sun Life Insurance Company]: the renewal cover for the house, in July 1822, was £800, with the household goods, apparel, books and plate being valued at £400, jewels at £20 and china and glass at £50. The coach house and stabling (brick and slate) were put in at £200. With other small items, the overall cover was £2,700 but that included £1,200 for his office and its contents at No 3 Paper Buildings.

Bramwell was married to Elizabeth, daughter of Joseph Firth, at St Luke's, Old Street, in November 1800, and the couple first lived in Enfield, where their two sons were educated. He enjoyed a pew in St Mary's parish church, Lewisham, from September 1817 when the family moved to the Paragon. George died on 5 November 1837 at his house in Balham and his widow, Elizabeth, died at Bury St Edmunds, in the winter of 1841.

Two of the Blackheath Bramwell sons were knighted: Sir George William Wilshere Bramwell, PC, LLD, FRS (1808-1892), later 1st Baron Bramwell of Hever, retired as Lord Justice of the Court of Appeal and had served on the Royal Commission on the Courts of Law and Equity from 1867 to 1874; and Sir Frederick Joseph Bramwell, DCL, LLD, FRS (1818-1903), a civil engineer whose early interests lay with railways and who was a pioneer of the short-lived 'atmospheric railways'. He was President of the Institution of Mechanical Engineers in 1874-5, President of the Institution of Civil Engineers in 1884-5, and President of the British Association in 1888 - probably a unique treble. He was a remarkably all-round man, as much at home in the law and the arts as in the world of the engineer and scientist. Both men enjoy generous entries in the *Dictionary of National Biography*.

It was long thought that the George Bramwell here was a partner in the firm of Dorrien & Co., bankers, of Finch Lane, Cornhill [he is described as a solicitor initially]. The company later merged with Glynn, Mills & Currie Bank

1825-1831
Joseph Henry Dart (1773-1866): Secretary to the Hon. East India Company, 1818-29.

Dart lived 'over the shop', so to speak, in his early career, but eventually moved to the Paragon. On final retirement he moved to Budleigh Salterton, Devon, where he died in November 1866. His son, Joseph Henry (1817-1887), who was born at India House, Leadenhall Street, and lived at No 11 The Paragon during his schooldays, was a barrister and was to become senior conveyancing counsel to the High Court of Justice from 1875 to 1886. Joseph junior married Adeline Pennal, daughter of Richard Humber, one-time resident of No 4 South Row. Joseph Henry Dart enjoys a short entry in the *Dictionary of National Biography.*

24 March 1832, *The Times:* No 11 The Paragon and other properties for sale as investments.

By 1835-1847
Edward Luck (1799-1865): timber merchant and land proprietor

Brother of Frederick Luck, of No 8 The Paragon (q.v.). Edward was to marry, in May 1835, Harriett, oldest daughter of Joseph Jackson, Blackheath landowner and businessman but then living at Court Lodge, West Farleigh. It may have been this union which led the Luck family to the Paragon, a few minutes stroll from Jackson's house, Kidbrooke Lodge, at the south end of St Germans Place. Unfortunately, the Lucks were away on the night of the 1841 enumerated census return. It is possible that Frederick may have lived at No 8 before moving to No 11. His children, C. J. Luck and Edward John Luck, were educated at the Blackheath Proprietary School but the registers do not record in which Paragon house the family were living at the time. (See No 8 The Paragon, for further details.) Whatever, Edward Luck died in the summer of 1865, aged 66, at the family seat of West Malling, near Maidstone.

25 September 1844, *The Times:* Head lease for sale. Fuller & Nash, auctioneers, Mansion House.

1847-1851
John Arnold Wallinger (1797-1860): Serjeant-at-Law
Wallinger was called to the Bar as a member of the Middle Temple in 1824, and practised as a special pleader from his chambers at No 5 Pump Court. He was appointed Serjeant in 1848. This was a superior order of barristers which was to be abolished in 1880, to be superseded by Queen's (or King's) Counsel.

He was the son of William Arnold Wallinger (d.1798), a merchant of Millbank Street, Westminster. John Wallinger, who worked mostly on the Norfolk, Suffolk and Aylesbury circuits, inherited family estates at Hare Hall, Essex. He had married, in August 1823, Anne Nasmyth Marsh, daughter of Thomas Marsh, of Norwich. Their son, James Nasmyth Arnold Wallinger (fl.1829-1863), was admitted as a solicitor, and lived at No 71 Lee Road from 1854 to 1859, and then at 25 Eltham Road until his untimely death. The other son living at No 11 was Henry, described as a scholar even at the comparatively late age of 19.

In August 1851, Wallinger assigned his lease to solicitor William Walton who was then 'in occupation'.

1851-1889
William Walton (1805-1889): solicitor

Walton, and his wife Caroline Kean (née Oliver), were both born in St John's parish, Wapping. They must have married somewhat late for the period because Mrs Walton was 38 when their first known child, Ada, was born at No 11. Walton, who was in practice in Wapping from at least 1837 until the end of the 1840s, later moved his offices to Bucklersbury. By the early 1860s he was listed as Secretary of the Imperial Continental Gas Association, based in Lombard Street.

He may have had professional dealings with Wallinger and, as a result, took over Wallinger's lease of No 11 in 1851. Walton was a member of the Blackheath Improvement Association from 1857 to 1861. The Walton children who lived here were Ada, Georgina, Caroline and William.

1890 Empty

1891
George Henry Clarke Lea: solicitor of Old Jewry

Stepney-born George Lea was resident mostly in north London – at Highgate (where three of his children were born) and Enfield. Why he moved to the Paragon for a single year is not known. Perhaps the family were not happy south of the Thames.

1891-1900
Captain Charles Orde Browne, RHA (1838-1900): military lecturer

Lecturer at the Royal Military Academy, Woolwich. His name was frequently miswritten as Ord-Browne or Orde-Brown. Despite the lack of a hyphen he is often listed under his first sur-name. Browne, who served in the Crimea with the Royal Horse Artillery, was an authority on armour but spent much of his career as a teacher and moved from Woolwich to No 11 The Paragon on retirement. His wife, Annie Maria (née Michell), who was born in Leicester, bore him at least seven children. Those living at No 11 were: Mary Ethel Stanley, Maysie K., Florence, Mabel L., Alice Fancourt, Sybil and Granville – their only son – later Sir Granville St John Orde Browne, CMG (1883-1947).

Captain Charles served with distinction in the Royal Artillery in the Zulu Rising of 1906 and the East African campaign during the 1914-18 war, and then in the colonial service in Africa where he became an authority on native labour.

1900-1915
Mrs Annie Maria Orde Browne (1855-1917): widow of the above.

The Orde Browne daughter, Mary Ethel Stanley Browne, married Colonel George Wingate, CIE (1851-1936), of the Indian Army, and the Wingates frequently stayed at No 11 when on leave.

Their son, Orde Charles Wingate, DSO (1903-44), spent many of his early years in this house rather than having to suffer the rigours of the Indian climate when his father returned to active duty. Orde Wingate was not only a great adventurer, but also a man of devout faith and extraordinary administrative abilities. He was to enjoy a most distinguished career in campaigns in Palestine, Abyssinia and Burma, and it was his brilliant organisation of the Chindits (indigenous troops) in action behind the Japanese lines in Burma which earned him decorations, promotion at a very young age to Major-General and the status of a public hero. He was killed in a plane crash in Assam in March 1944, and was buried in Arlington Cemetery, Washington.

The Orde Browne daughter Sybil (d.1962), married Captain (later Lieut.-Gen. Sir) William George Shedden Dobbie, DSO, RE (1879-1964), in 1904. They returned to Blackheath in due course, to reside at No 37 Kidbrooke Park Road from 1914 to 1916, and then lived at No 9 Rochester Way from 1917 to 1920 (house since demolished). Dobbie, who earned a place in the *Dictionary of National Biography*, was General Officer Commanding in both Malaya and Singapore at the outbreak of war in 1939. He further distinguished himself as Governor and Commander-in-Chief of Malta from 1940 to 1942, sharing the hardships and privations of the island's inhabitants during the constant German and Italian onslaught. Like the Orde Browne family, Dobbie was a deeply committed Christian and had become a member of the Plymouth Brethren during his early military days at Woolwich.

1915-1918:
Blackheath War Hospital Supply Depot

With the departure of Mrs Orde Browne, the house fell vacant and reverted to the landlord. The

outbreak of the Great War, in August 1914, led to a dearth in buyers of property of this size. It also coincided with the spontaneous enthusiasm by the civil population to 'do their bit' and No 11 The Paragon was 'kindly lent by Mr Cator' to the organisers of the Blackheath War Hospital Supply Depot (an official war charity). It took some while to organise (after a public meeting in July 1915) and Lady Mary Ellen Scrutton (1857-1940), of Glenwood, Mycenae Road, formally opened it on 3 August 1915. The volunteers (about 130 in all and mostly local women and schoolgirls over the age of 17) wore white overalls and sleeves and muslin caps. They each paid a nominal 6d (2.5p) a week towards the running expenses. They made and packed bandages, splints, surgical dressings and other war hospital requisites. Clothing and comforts were added later.

The ground floor was for bandages and swabs; the first floor occupied by makers of pyjamas, suits, dressing-gowns and bed-jackets, and a swab room where 20 helpers made more than 6,000 swabs and surgical dressings every month. One floor up was the splint room; and the top floor was the department for sterilisation. It functioned continuously until March 1919, also acting as a depot for the production of hospital requisites by smaller groups elsewhere. The volunteers enjoyed a reunion meeting in October 1919.

1919
Mrs Glasspool: board residence. Advertises for staff, September 1919.

1920-1925
Mrs Melita E. Hall (1876-1955): board residence

Mrs Hall and her husband George ran boarding houses at Nos 5 and 6 South Row as well as at Nos 11 and 12 The Paragon until 1926. The Halls had lived in Bennett Park before starting their business in South Row and the Paragon.

Tenants included:

1924 Miss D. M. Wilkins

1924 Lieut.-Cdr. Francis G. Hunter, RN

1925 Herbert Lancaster
In February 1925 Mrs Hunter arranged an 'at home' to support the Liberal Party.

1926-1928 Empty

1929-1941
Mrs Lily Holmes Tennant Cochrane (1878-1951): widow

Lily Cochrane (1871-1925) was the widow of Lieut.-Col. Robert C. Cochrane, CBE, FRCVS, a member of the Royal Army Veterinary Corps. Mrs Cochrane, who was the third daughter of Oliver Tennant, of Bethlehem, Orange River Colony, previously lived at No 45 Westcombe Park Road for a period but returned to Blackheath after her husband's death, initially to a flat at No 9 or 10 The Paragon. She became involved in various business ventures, including the launch, in 1931, of a new daily paper, *The Call*. The founder of the enterprise was a Mrs A. C. Colles, and the share capital (of £1 million) was all to be held by women. Nothing came of the promotion. The next Cochrane scheme was the eponymous Hea-Te-Co furniture cleaner and soap. It was advertised in the local press from 1933 to 1937 as the 'famous' furniture cleaner but it is unlikely that the landlords (the Cator family) really approved of a Paragon house being used for this sort of business. The Cochranes' only child, Margaret Gough Harper Cochrane, died here in 1934. Mrs Cochrane is alleged to have lived at No 11 until March 1941 but she would have had to move out then because the house was severely damaged when Nos 9 and 10 were destroyed. She died at Brighton in the summer of 1951, aged 73.

The house was rebuilt and converted into six flats in 1948-9 and occupied by the end of 1950.

No 12 The Paragon

Bonwitt claimed that this house was built and mortgaged by 1795. If so, it seems odd that its other half, No 11, seems not to have been occupied until 1805. Nevertheless, it was in car-case form by April 1795 and ready for completion, as the following advertisement in The Times for 15 April (and subsequently) confirms. Despite the paucity of records for Lewisham parish, it does seem reasonable to place Captain Stupart in this house by 1797/98.

LEASEHOLDS, PARAGON, BLACKHEATH

*By Messrs Griffith & Co. At Garraway's Coffee-house, Change-alley, Cornhill,
on Monday 27th inst .[April 1795] at 12 o'clock, in two lots,*

A VALUABLE LEASEHOLD BRICK DWELLING-HOUSE, truly eligibly situated in the Paragon, a short distance from Morden College, on Blackheath, numbered 14. The premises contain a Drawing-room, a Dining-room, Breakfast Parlour, 4 good Rooms on the principal floor, and 8 Bed-rooms on the upper stories [sic]*; a good Kitchen and every necessary domestic office on the basement; detached, is a double Coach-house, Stabling for 6 Horses, and a good Garden, in the occupation of Mr Searles; the annual value £100.*

Also, a HOUSE in the said Paragon, No 12, built nearly to the same plan, but with the addition of a circular bow at back front; at present unfinished, but to be completed in the like manner as No 14; are held for a long term of years, and subject to very low ground rents. May be viewed and particulars had on the Premises; at the Green Man, Blackheath; the Tyger's Head, Lee Green; the Bull, Shooters Hill; the Greyhound, Greenwich; at Garraway's; and of Messrs Griffith & Co., Blackman-street, Southwark.– N.B. Grass land may be had near the Premises, if required.

1798-1802
Alexander Stupart

In 1788 a Captain Alexander Stupart was a member of the Blackheath Society of Goffers. He may have been the son of Alexander Stupart, who married Diana Hughes, in 1746, at St George's, Mayfair. In December 1799 the Lewisham parish records note the death of Mrs Ann Stupart. Whether these people were related has not been discovered. From 1804 to 1810, a Charles Stupart, an attorney, was working in Royal Hill, Greenwich.

1802-1811
William Geddes

Geddes was a ship and insurance broker but where his office was situated at the time of his residence in Blackheath is not known. He was, later, at No 7 London Street, Greenwich, and then Fenchurch Street until 1819. Arthur Geddes, possibly his brother, was running the business by the 1820s, from an office in East India Chambers. William Geddes, who was a member of the Blackheath Society of Goffers by 1806, previously lived at the then newly built No 18 Tranquil Vale (now the site of Barclays Bank). He married Elizabeth Grice at St Luke's, the Charlton parish church, in March 1800. Elizabeth was probably the daughter of James Grice who had been responsible for building the Tranquil Vale house. Although they enjoyed a pew at St Mary's church, Lewisham, their first son, James, was baptised at St Luke's, Charlton, in February 1801; a daughter was born in September 1802.

1812 Empty

1813
Mrs Rebecca Edwards: *School for Girls*

Mrs Edwards' school was either here or at No 9 The Paragon (q.v.). The school may have been little more than a prospectus. The Cator leases usually forbade the use of their houses for schools although there are many instances where the condition was waived. Mrs Edwards, of the Paragon, sought the advice of a local solicitor in 1813 for some undiscovered reason, but no evidence in the form of advertisements for her enterprise has been found in the London press.

Section A: *In the beginning*

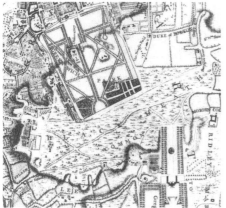

1. Rocque' London 1745

2. Sir John Morden

4. Sir Gregory Page

3. Morden College of 1695

6. Wricklemarsh House 1775

5. Wricklemarsh House of 1723

7. Wricklemarsh House in pieces.
Nos 13 & 14 Paragon on extreme left

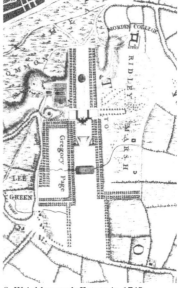

8. Wricklemarsh Estate in 1745

I

9. Green Man, Blackheath Hill. Local landmark from 1629

12. Cator John

10. Lydia & Sherwell. Landmarks since 1776

13. John Cator signature

14. Michael Searles signature

11. Heathfld House

15. Alexander Doull's signature

16. Beckenham Place. The columns and pediment removed from Wricklemarsh

17. Gloucester Circus, Greenwich

18. Paragon New Kent Road

19. Paragon New Kent Road

20. Paragon New Kent Road

21. Paragon New Kent Road

22. Paragon New Kent Road

23. Blackheath Paragon version 1

24. Blackheath Paragon version 2

25. Blackheath Paragon version 3 (adopted)

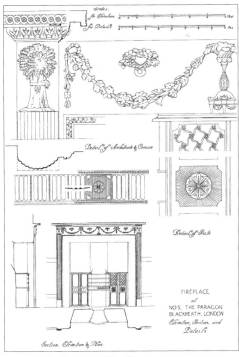

26. No 5 The Paragon (detail)

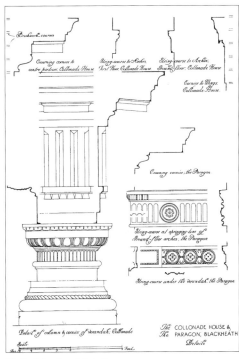

27. Architectural detail

28. Paragon bounds 3 January 1794

29. Boundary stone east

30. Boundary stone west

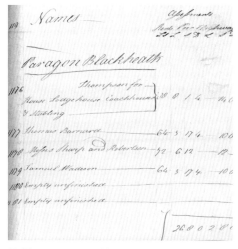

31. First rate record (Greenwich) 1800

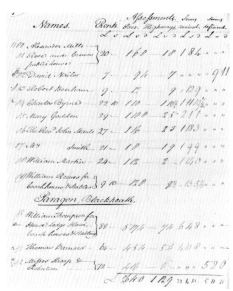

32. Rate record (Greenwich) 1801

33. Coade stone pilaster on No 13 The Paragon

35. Water post and steppping stone etc

34. Creenwich Parish boundary stone replaced 1890

Section B: *19th century*

Paragon, Blackheath.—Elegant Residence, with Coachhouse, Stabling, Pleasure Grounds, Garden, and Offices; Household Furniture, Plate, China, Books, Wines, &c.—By Mr. PULLEN, on the Premises, on Wednesday, May 11, at 11, under a Writ of Extent issued against Charles Rivington Broughton, esq.

A Valuable Leasehold Estate, held for 55 years, at a ground rent of 16l. 7s. 6d. per annum (very desirable for occupation or investment); comprising a capital and substantially built residence, with coachhouse, stabling for 5 horses, extensive garden, lawn, shrubberies, cold bath, and excellent attached and detached offices, delightfully situate—No. 14, Paragon, Blackheath. On the same and following day will be sold all the household furniture, 400 ounces of plate, fine old china, glass, scarce prints, library of books, 160 dozen of port and madeira wines, and miscellaneous articles of value. The house may be viewed 6 days and the effects on Monday and Tuesday preceding the sale. Particulars of the estate had on the premises; also of H. Legatt, esq. Solicitor for the Affairs of Taxes, Adelphi-terrace; and Mr. Pullen, 80, Fore-street, Cripplegate; catalogues of the effects to be had on the premises at 6d. each, and of the auctioneer.

1. No 14 Paragon 1825

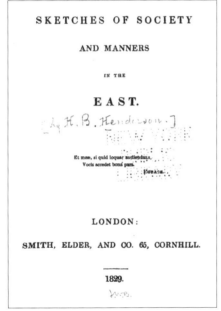

3. Major Henderson (later at No 1 The Paragon) author of Bengalee

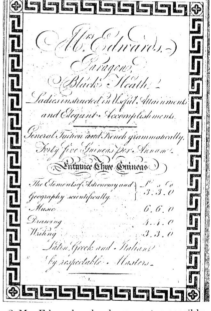

2. Mrs Edwards school prospectus possibly for No 9 The Paragon, 1813

4. Quarles Harris Oporto merchant at No 4 Paragon

5. Blackheath Proprietary School in 1833

6. Blackheath Proprietary School in the 1860s

7. Blackheath New Proprietary School

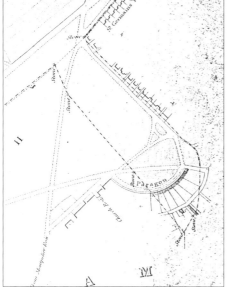

8. Morris map of Greenwich 1834

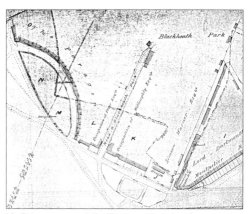

10. Drivers map of the Paragon showing the so-called Ha-Ha

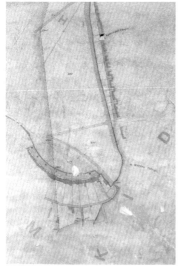

9. F W Simms' map of 1837

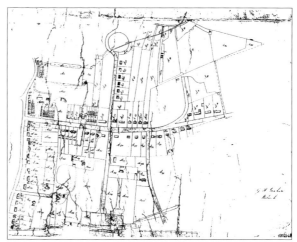

11. Charlton tithe schedule 1839. Land below the red line rented by some Paragon residents

14. Morden College and Paragon lodges in about 1870

12. Pond Road pond and Lodge

13. Nos 3 to 8 The Paragon in the 1870s

15. The Paragon as it may have been in the 1870s

16. Boundary stone – replaced 1890

DYER, SON & HILTON
Auctioneers & Surveyors,

30 BUDGE ROW, CANNON ST., E.C., and BLACKHEATH.

On MONDAY NEXT.

5 The Paragon, Blackheath.

MESSRS. DYER, SON & HILTON will Sell by Auction, on the premises, on Monday, October 5th, at Two punctually, the remaining Furniture, three capital wardrobes, cottage pianoforte by Broadwood & Sons, 9ft. billiard table, four wheel chaise and numerous effects.

May be viewed the Saturday prior and morning of sale, and catalogues had of the Auctioneers, 30 Budge-row, E.C., and Blackheath.

On FRIDAY NEXT.

"Bellefield," Blackheath Park.

MESSRS DYER, SON & HILTON will sell by Auction, on the premises, on Friday, October 9th, at Two punctually, the remaining Furniture, including mahogany dining-room suite in leather, dining table, an 8ft. billiard table by Thurston & Co., two enclosed bookcases, a cottage pianoforte by Broadwood, an expensive bath chair by Carter, a mangle by Baker, stove and greenhouse plants and outdoor effects.

May be viewed the day prior and morning of sale, and catalogues had of the Auctioneers, 30 Budge-row, E.C., and Blackheath.

18. Water post & mounting block

17. Contents of No 5 The Paragon for sale. October 1896

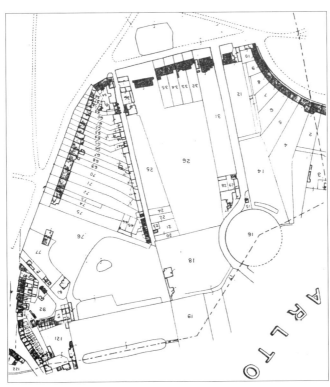

19. Lewisham Parish tihe 1843

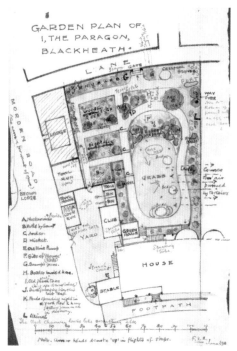

1. No 1 The Paragon garden 1900

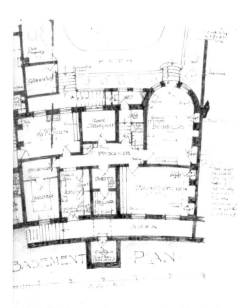

2. No 1 Paragon basement. West side. 1900

3. No 1 The Paragon basement. West side. 1900

4. No 1 The Paragon. Ground floor. East side. 1900

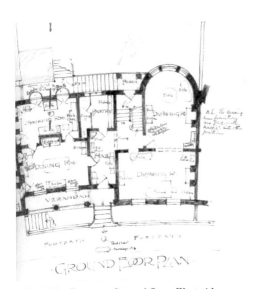

5. No 1 The Paragon. Ground floor. West side

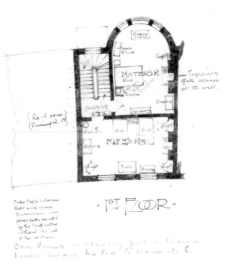

6. No 1 The Paragon. 1st floor. 1900

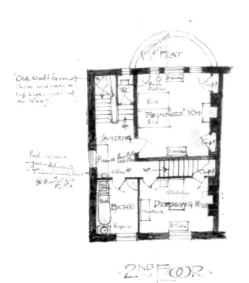

7. No 1 The Paragon. 2nd floor. 1900

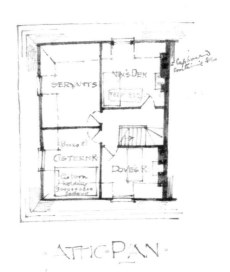

8. No 1 The Paragon. Attic

9. No 1 The Paragon. 1910

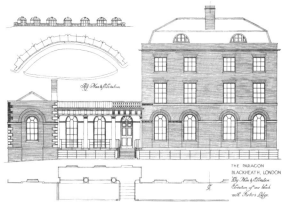

10. No 1 The Paragon. 1923

11. No 1 Paragon & Lodge pre 1939

12. Nos 2-5 The Paragon. 1903

14. The Paragon c1919

13. No 6 The Paragon. Before 1910

MARMITE FOOD EXTRACT.

'Marmite' is the name given to the new food extract, which is made from yeast. The food value of yeast has been long known. No plant contains a larger proportion of the nitrogenous elements, to obtain which mankind usually resorts to flesh food, and in none is such a valuable array of phosphoric salts and other mineral constituents necessary for the nutrition and health of the human frame to be found.

The Marmite Company, by a process the rights of which they control, are able to extract from the yeast cells that portion of their contents valuable for human sustenance, and to reduce it to such a concentrated form that the resultant extract, which closely resembles in appearance extract of meat, has an equal food value and is more easily digested than any of the meat extracts on the market. The company, in short, by the clean and tidy process of fractional distillation and synthetic chemistry, produce a similar or a better result than is obtained by passing vegetable food through the stomach of a living animal, and then killing that animal for the sake of extracting from its flesh the product resulting from the chemical changes the vegetable food it has consumed has undergone in traversing the digestive tract. The chemical process of the Marmite Company, in addition to being cleanlier, is much cheaper than that of first feeding an animal and then killing it to secure the chemical results of such feeding, and therefore the Marmite Company is able to place its extract on the market at a popular price.

The company have erected large works at Burton-on-Trent, so as to be quite in the centre of the brewing industry. These premises are fitted up with special new machinery, for the purpose of washing and cleansing the yeast, as it is received from the breweries, and carrying out the subsequent extractive processes.

The Marmite Company, as the holders of the solution of a problem which many of the best chemists of Europe have striven for the past half century unavailingly to solve, and as the producers of an extract whose unique value for human food is not a matter of experiment, but has been fully proved in Germany, believe that their industry has a great future before it. It has one great advantage even over its fellows in Germany, and that is that the yeast used in Burton is more suitable for the process, and contains more valuable nitrogenous bases and nutritive albuminoids and mineral salts, than are to be found in the lager beer varieties of yeast, to which the German extract manufactories are confined.

We have tried 'Marmite' as a cup and as sandwiches, and can assure our readers that in both instances it is equal in every respect to meat extracts; and—note well—it is but half the price of the latter.

15. Paragon 9 Apr 1903

16. No 9 The Paragon. October 1918.

Blackheath War Hospital Supply Depot
11 THE PARAGON, BLACKHEATH.
FOR VOLUNTARY WORKERS TO HELP THE WOUNDED AND SICK.
Central Depôt of the Greenwich Borough Association for the Administration of all Voluntary Work approved by the War Office.
Registered under the War Charities' Act, 1916.
President: The Right Hon. VISCOUNT HILL, L.C.C.
Chairman of Committee:
The Mayor of Greenwich (ALDERMAN CHARLES STONE, J.P.)

The Committee beg to acknowledge with most grateful thanks the receipt of Donations and Gifts from the following Donors:—

Donations (from August 21st to October 15th).
£5 5s.—Mr. E. F. White.
£5 (each)—Rugby Football Committee (per Mr. Rowland Hill), Mr and Mrs. Burrell (quarterly), Miss Hope.
£3 3s.—Mrs. Sidney Prestage.
£3—Mr. and Mrs. Stanley Day.
£2 10s.—Vanbrugh Castle Hostel Girls' Tennis Tournament.
£2 2s. (each)—B.E.A., Mr. F. G. Previté.
£2—Mrs. Leslie (2 M)
£1 15s.—Burnt Ash Club Bowling Competition (per Dr. Tolmie).
£1 10s. (each)—Mr. and Mrs. R. Whyte, Mrs. Haddon (3 M), Mrs. and Miss Greenside (3 M).
£1 1s. (each)—Mr. W. H. Adams, Mrs. Dunn (2 M), Mrs. J. Spink, Mr. J. McCarthy, Mrs. J. Cooper.
£1 (each)—Mrs. Alison, Misses C. and H. Robinson (M), Mr. Hobson, Mr. and Mrs. Briggs (4 M), Mrs. Miller, Mrs. Pownall, Mrs. Tilley (2 M), Anon.
10s. 6d. (each)—Mrs. Harrison, Mrs. Saw.
10s. (each).—Miss E. Goddard Jones, Miss East, Miss Williamson, Mrs. Harcourt, Mrs. Friday, Misses C. and H. Robinson (M). Mrs. Hough, Miss Swinton and Mrs. Ingham-Thompson (2 M).
9s.—Miss Boeltzer
7s. 6d.—Mr. R. Eicke (3 M).
6s. (each)—Miss Elsie Whyte, Anon. (per E. L.)
5s. (each)—Mrs. Trotman, Mrs. Spencer, Miss Purcell, Mrs. Hardcastle, Mr. Holland (2 M).
4s.—Miss L. Robinson (2 M).
3s.—Anon. (per E. F.)
2s. 6d. (each)—Mrs. Holland (M), Mrs. Percy Smith.
M—Monthly Payments

Gifts.
Anon., Lady Scrutton.
Mmes. Binning, Bradram, Bush, Buttenshaw, Day, Deasen, Dodds, Edwards, Franklin, Gordon, Gover, Haddon, Hamilton, Hobbs, Howitt, Jacquet, Marchant, Morris, Moller, Morant, Muller, Marten, Naresse, Penny, Pownall, Pumphrey, Priday, Rosselli, Salt, Sawyer, Simpson, H. Smith, Snell, Swinton, Trego, P. Walker, Ed. Wilson, Worthington.
The Misses Binning, Carr, Carter, H. N. Clarke, Cook, M. L. Dewick, Fox, Hanson, Hope, Houghton, Hutchinson, Japp, Jenning, Keen, Lawrence, Levett, Martin, Matthews, Morgan, Osmond, Purcell, Roberts, Tideman, Trueman.
M Dickson, Esq.
Maze Hill Working Party.
Gifts received:—162 Knitted Washing Squares, 120 Swabs, 54 Pyjamas Girdles, 43 pr. Socks, 32 pr. Mittens, 31 Mufflers, 30 Hospital Bags, 10 Lavender Bags, 9 Anti-Vermin Shirts, 5 Caps, 4 pr. Operation Stockings, 3 Bed Jackets, 3 Helmets, 3 Pyjamas, 2 Pyjamas Coats, 1 Pneumonia Jacket, 1 Walking Stick, 1 pr. Gloves, Material, Soap, Old Linen, Nail Brush, Cretonne, Linoleum.

Since September 15th consignments have been despatched to:—
B.E.F.
"Comforts' Pool," Le Havre.
°2nd Canadian Casualty Clearing Station.
12th General Hospital (St. Louis, U.S.A.).
56th Casualty Clearing Station.
10th General Hospital.
74th General Hospital.
°Dobson War Relief Hospital.
Miller Hospital, Greenwich.
Heavy Woollen District War Hospital, Dewsbury, Yorks.
Administrators Office War Hospital, Nottingham.
§Rangers' Lodge A.S.C.
‡1st London General Hospital, Myatt» Park.
Military Hospital, Syeamore Road, Nottingham.
•Lewisham Military Hospital.
•Lord Derby War Hospital, Warrington.
°Seamen's Hospital, Greenwich.
French Red Cross, Knightsbridge.
°Queen Mary's Military Hospital, Whalley, Lancs
Military Hospital, Preston Hall, Aylesford.
Spaghum Moss Depôt, Edinburgh.
Lady Smith Dorrien's Bag Fund.
•Military Hospital, E. Dulwich Grove, Southwark.
2/1st Southern General Hospital, Dudley Road, Birmingham.
Military Hospital, Sutton Veney, Wilts.
* Monthly Requisitions.   † Fortnightly Requisitions.
‡ Weekly Requisitions.   § Private Appeals.

Articles Despatched.—11,866 Swabs and Dressings, 6,061 Spaghnum Moss Bags, 1,510 Roller Bandages, 308 Hospital Bags, 302 pr. Socks, 300 Knitted Squares, 250 pr. Mittens, 232 Sewn Bandages, 200 Mufflers, 150 Bed Socks, 150 Caps, 128 pr. Slippers, 103 Pyjamas, 98 Day Shirts, 92 Handkerchiefs, 58 Bed Rests, 52 Helmets, 42 Pneumonia Jackets, 36 Slings, 36 Triangular Bandages, 20 Bed Jackets, 12 Limb Pillows, 12 Milk Covers, 6 Splints, 6 Crutches.

The above consignments were despatched by the Central Depôt, and included the undermentioned contributions from affiliated Societies:—
SIDCUP AND DISTRICT WAR HOSPITAL SUPPLY DEPÔT.—2,000 Dressings, 200 Washing Squares 145 Sewn Bandages, 135 pr. Socks, 130 Roller Bandages, 80 Caps, 40 Operation Stockings, 30 Bed Socks, 30 Milk Covers, 29 Shirts, 20 Mufflers, 20 Slippers, 15 Ointment Sets, 15 Hot Water Bottle Covers, 10 Handkerchiefs, 8 Pneumonia Jackets, 5 pr. Pyjamas, 1 Limb Pillow.
CHURCH OF THE ASCENSION WORKING GUILD—20 Capeline Bandages, 10 Hospital Bags, 5 Shirts, 5 pr. Socks, 5 pr. Mittens, 4 Mufflers.
KIDBROOK WAR RELIEF ASSOCIATION.—16 pr. Socks, 12 Handkerchiefs, 10 Pyjamas, 8 Mufflers, 7 Shirts, 6 Helmets, 5 Bags, 5 Bed Socks, 3 pr. Mittens.
ST. JOHN'S WAR WORKING PARTY.—39 Shirts, 28 pr. Socks, 21 Pyjamas, 5 Caps.
BOROUGH HALL WORKING AND CLOTHING FUND.—23 pr. Socks, 1 pr. Mittens, 1 Muffler.
BLACKHEATH CONGREGATIONAL CHURCH RED CROSS SOCIETY.—10 Hospital Bags, 9 pr. Socks, 7 Mufflers, 2 Knitted Squares, 1 Bed Jacket, 1 pr. Mittens.

MORE WORKERS ARE VERY URGENTLY NEEDED AT THE DEPÔT.

We are making 5,000 Hospital Bags from 200 Surgeon's Coats, and 500 Pneumonia Jackets for the American Red Cross from material provided by them. This is to save shipping the Bandages, etc., from the United States. In order to help in this useful and practical scheme we shall need more

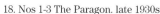

17. No 14 The Paragon (Southlands School)

19. No 11 The Paragon 1930s

18. Nos 1-3 The Paragon. late 1930s

20. The Paragon by Bernard Hailstone. 1938

21. Hailstones relaxing. No 2 The Paragon

22. Paragon 1 rear pre 1939

Section D: *Damage & Decay 1939-1947*

1. No 1 & 2 Paragon

3. Nos 1 & 2 The Paragon. 1944

4. Rear Nos 1 & 2 The Paragon

2. No 1 Paragon.

5. No 1 & 2 The Paragon 1944 b

6. No 2 Paragon – fanlight

7. Nos 1-5 The Paragon

8. Pediment from No 2 The Paragon

12. Nos 3 & 4 The Paragon

9. No 3 The Paragon 1945

13. Nos 3 & 4 The Paragon

10. Nos 3 & 4 The Paragon

14. Nos 3 & 4 The Paragon – part repaired

11. No 4 The Paragon (Levens Hotel)

15. No 4 The Paragon 1950

16. No 5 The Paragon during repair

20. Nos 4-6 The Paragon 1945

17. No 5 The Paragon

21. Nos 5 & 6 The Paragon

18. No 6 The Paragon 1945

22. Nos 5 & 6 The Paragon 1946

19. Nos 3-8 The Paragon 1945

23. Nos 5-8 The Paragon 1946

24. Nos 7 & 8 The Paragon

28. Nos 7-10 The Paragon

25. Paragon 5, 6, 7, 8 – late 1940s

29. Paragon 9 & 10 gap

26. Nos 7 & 8 The Paragon (garden)

30. No 11 The Paragon

27. No 8 The Paragon

31. No 11 The Paragon

32. No 11 The Paragon

36. Nos 11 & 12 The Paragon

33. Nos 11 & 12 The Paragon

37. Nos 11 & 12 The Paragon

34. Nos 11 & 12 Paragon

38. Nos 11 The Paragon

35. Nos 11 & 12 Paragon

39. Nos 11 & 12 The Paragon

40. Nos 11-14 The Paragon

41. Nos 11-15 The Paragon

44. Nos 13 & 14 The Paragon

42. No 13 The Paragon

45. Nos 13 & 14 The Paragon

43. Nos 12 & 13 The Paragon

46. Nos 14 & 15 The Paragon

THE PARAGON—A UNIQUE GROUP OF GEORGIAN BUILDINGS SWEEPING ROUND IN A MAJESTIC CRESCENT—IS ADJACENT TO THE PROPOSED NEW BUILDING SITE.

period in England. Just beyond it are the picturesque old brick almshouses known as Morden College (1695-1702), a hitherto unspoiled work of Wren's prime. The unsightly prefabricated houses, which have so seriously depreciated from the beauty of Blackheath, have now been followed by the proposal to build working-class flats along the south side of the heath, on the site of South Row and Colonnade House, immediately next to the Paragon it: A public enquiry into the proposed compulsory purchase order for this purp was held at Catford Town Hall on March 25 when the matter was adjour for the final decision of the Minister of Health. On these pages our artist, Cap Bryan de Grineau, depicts some of the fine buildings which are now endange

47. Paragon west end in 1951

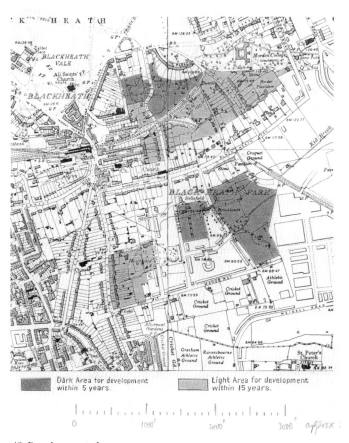

Dark Area for development within 5 years.

Light Area for development within 15 years.

48. Development plans

Section E: *Restored: 1949-958*

1. Aerial 1958

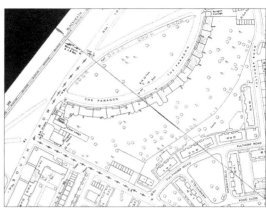

2. Ordnance Survey

4. Wine from No 1 The Paragon

THE BLACKHEATH SOCIETY.

—

VISIT TO THE PARAGON AND
COLONNADE HOUSE.

SATURDAY, 16th JULY, 1955.

MR. C. BERNARD BROWN, L.R.I.B.A., has kindly
consented to conduct members of the Society round
the buildings and gardens and to explain the work of
reconstruction.

The party is to meet at No. 8 The Paragon at 3.0 p.m.

3. Blackheath Society visit July 1955

5. Paragon Lodge

6. Paragon Lodge

7. Paragon Lodge and Nos 1 & 2 restored

8. Nos Paragon 1 & 2 The Paragon 1994

9. Nos 3 & 4 The Paragon

10. The Paragon

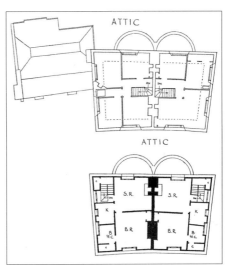

11. Nos 5 & 6 Paragon attic plan

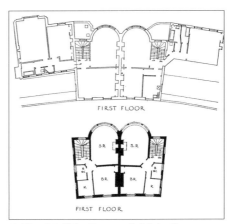

12. Nos 5 & 6 The Paragon 5 & 6 1st floor

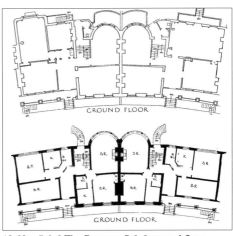

13. Nos 5 & 6 The Paragon 5 & 6 ground floor

14. Nos 5 & 6 The Paragon

18. No 9 The Paragon – under restoration

15. No 6 The Paragon

19. Nos 9 & 10 The Paragon

16. Goldsmiths student picnic

17. Nos 9 & 10 The Paragon (new built in carcase form)

20. Nos 9 & 10 The Paragon

21. Nos 9 & 10 The Paragon

25. Nos 11 & 12 The Paragon

22. Nos 9 & 10 The Paragon

26. Nos 9-11 The Paragon

23. Nos 9 & 10 The Paragon

24. Nos 9 & 10 The Paragon

27. Nos 11 & 12 The Paragon

31. Nos 13-15 The Paragon

28. Nos 11 & 12 The Paragon

32. Nos 13-15 The Paragon

29. Nos 11-15 The Paragon

33. The gardens without dividing walls

30. Nos 13 & 14 The Paragon

A drawing by Geoffrey S. Fletcher of The Paragon, Blackheath

One of the most interesting of the recent restorations is that of the Georgian crescent the Paragon at Blackheath, in the process of which the original elevations have been preserved while the interiors have been remodelled where necessary to form moderately-priced flats. The crescent is not a true semi-circle on plan, but is flattened at the centre of the arc, and it consists of seven blocks of three storeys and an attic storey. It is of yellow stock brick connected by arcades based on the Roman Doric order, of five columns and two pilasters. The two centre blocks and three of the arcades await restoration. At the extreme ends of the crescent are shorter arcades joining the main blocks with a lodge, and on the pavement in front of the crescent the mounting blocks for carriages still remain. The whole represents a dignified, if somewhat academic, elevation in the late Georgian manner, in which Palladian attic windows are combined with traces of Adam influence in the fanlights and string-courses. A slight departure from too rigid a convention is the use of a cable moulding on the bases of the columns in the arcades. The restoration has gained an award of merit from the Festival authorities.

35. The Paragon west end 1951

34. Charles B Brown demonstrates

36. Festival of Britain award 1951

THE PARAGON
BLACKHEATH,
S.E.3.
The ten years rehabilitation of this
FAMOUS GEORGIAN CRESCENT
CIRCA 1794
is nearing its end with the completion of Nos. 7 & 8, The Paragon,
where immediate vacant possession of
TWELVE FLATS
can be given.
Preference will be given to selected applicants appreciating the atmosphere, quality and craftsmanship of bygone days.
THE BOW WINDOWS, FINE CHIMNEY PIECES AND OTHER PERIOD FEATURES, THE SUNNY OPEN HEATH AND GARDEN VISTAS AT BOTH FRONT AND REAR ONLY EMPHASISE THAT THESE MUST BE AMONGST
THE FINEST AND MOST EXCITING FLATS EVER OFFERED.
LEASES WITH 80 YEARS TO RUN AT £25–£35 P.A. ARE
FOR SALE from £3,000.
VIEW ANY TIME
(including evenings and weekends.)
LEE Green 9496.
PARAGON PRESERVATION LTD., 182, BROMPTON ROAD, S.W.3.
KEN 5634.

37. The final flats. A *Times* advertisement June 1958

1. Paragon 1-8 The Paragon and Lodge 2003

4. Nos 5 & 6 The Paragon 1994

5. Nos 6-10 The Paragon 1994

2. No 6 Paragon & Fulthorp Road (above) 1994

6. Nos 7 & 8 The Paragon 1994

3. No 4 Paragon

7. Dinner a deux 1994

8. Evening in The Paragon gardens 1994

12. Social life 1970s

9. Evening in The Paragon gardens 1994

10. Nos 7 & 8 The Paragon 1994

13. The Secret path

11. Paragon play 1970s

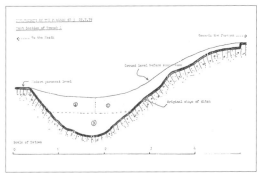

14. Ha Ha investigation 1979

15. Paragon Ha Ha 1994

16. Paragon Ha Ha winter 2000

17. Placing the plaque

18. Plaque unveiling

19. Plaque 1994 cut by Richard Klose

20. Plaque plaque party

21. Plaque plaque party

22. Plaque for No 14 The paragon

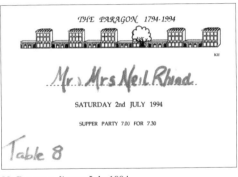

23. Paragon dinner July 1994

27. Paragon dinner July 1994. Commandant Vonla McBryde responds

24. Paragon dinner July 1994

28. Film set 1995

24. Paragon dinner July 1994

29. Film set 1995

26. Paragon dinner July 1994. The author proposes the toat

30. Film set 1995

31. Film set 1995

35. Paragon aerial 1997

32. Film set 1998

33. Film set 1998

34. Film set 1998

36. Nos 13 & 14 The Paragon

37. Paragon for sale

38. Paragon for sale

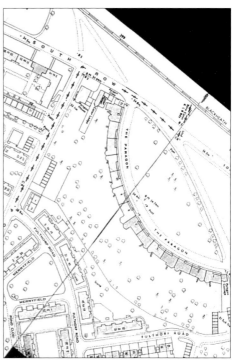

39. OS map 1960s

Section G: *The Cator Lodges – Nos 15-18 the Paragon*

1. Nos 11- 14 The Paragon & Lodge (No 15)

4. No 15 The Paragon before

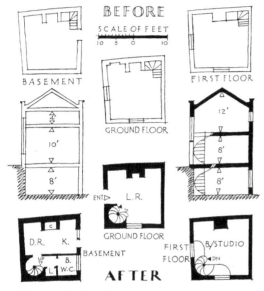

2. Paragon Lodge plan

5. No 15 The Paragon before

6. No 15 The Paragon before

3. No 15 The Paragon conversion

7. No 15 The Paragon

11. Paragon Hse stables 1945

8. No 15 The Paragon

12. Cator Manor befoe

9. No 15 The Paragon

13. Cator Manor before

10. 1951 Festival of Britain plaque

14. Cator Manor rear before

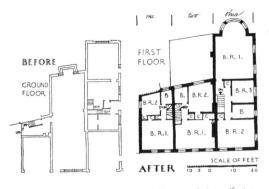

18. Cator Lodge to south.

15. Stables conversion plan

19 Cator Lodge to north.

16. Cator Manor prospectus 1952

20. Cator lodge 1950

17. Cator Manor half done

21. Cator lodge

22. Cator Manor

26. Cator Lodge after

23. Cator Lodge after

27. No 17 The Paragon – Cator Lodge.

24. Cator Lodge after

28. Cator Manor after

25. No 18 The Paragon – Cator Lodge.

29. Cator Manor after

30. Cator Manor after

31. Cator Manor after

32. Cator lodge 1954

33. Cator Manor after

34. No 18 The Paragon
(Cator Manor) 1994

31. Cator Manor after

36. Nos 16-18 The Paragon 1994

37. View from Cator Manor 1950

Section H1: *South Row – historic*

1. South Row 1906

2. South Row 1906 (cropped version)

4. No 1 South Row – original drawing

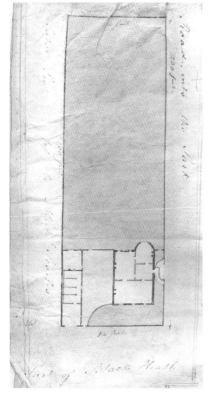

3. No 1 South Row 1790 plan

5. No 1 South Row – Paragon House (personal adverts)

THE ARCADIA CLUB

To those interested in TENNIS (Hard and Grass Courts), BRIDGE, MUSIC, DANCING, etc.

A Select Club

has been opened at

1 SOUTH ROW, BLACKHEATH.

Blackheath Residents will be well advised to write early for membership of this Club, with its Beautiful Grounds, Gaze's Hard Court and a Grass Court, Clock Golf, most comfortable Lounges for Bridge, Music, Reading, Bagatelle, etc. In fact everything is provided for the comfort of Members & Visitors.

Non-Members 3/- per hour for Hard Court and 2/- per hour for Grass Court

REFRESHMENTS, MORNING COFFEE, LIGHT LUNCHEONS AND DAINTY TEAS SERVED.

Write or 'Phone for Particulars.
1 South Row, Blackheath.   Lee Green 2189.

LAWN TENNIS COACHING by MISS E. D. HOLMAN

Miss E. D. Holman, Silver Medalist, Olympic Games; Wimbledon Semi-Finalist; Winner of World's Hard Courts Championships; Winner of World's Covered Courts Championships; Winner, London Covered Courts Championships; is now Coaching Lawn Tennis and open to take pupils at "ARCADIA," 1 SOUTH ROW, BLACKHEATH. Miss Holman recommends the "Arcadia" as possessing the finest Gaze's Hard Court she has ever played on.

AUCTION BRIDGE AND CONTRACT

6. No 1 South Row advertisement

LADY offers comfortable home to one or two Paying Guests; terms moderate.—Write, 35, L.G.O., S.E.3.   κ

MRS. RENDALL, of Five The Paragon, Blackheath, offers large double and single Bedrooms; private sitting-rooms, general dining-room (separate tables).   W-31

ONE or Two Gentlemen received in lady's own house.—2 Liskeard-gardens, Blackheath.   ufn

PARAGON HOTEL, 1 South-row.—Open to non-residents; weddings, luncheon and dinner parties catered for; double and single rooms; non-residents are specially catered for; hard and grass tennis courts will shortly be available.—'Phone, Lee Green 2189.   ufn

PAYING GUESTS received by Mrs. Macdonald Wilson, of 6 The Paragon, Blackheath; efficient service; well-appointed garage.   ufn

W. HARRISON, 9 & 10 The Paragon, Blackheath. Single and double Bedroom now vacant; personal supervision.—Lee Green 1939.   κ

WANTED, one or two Rooms, furnished or unfurnished, with full board and attendance, for elderly couple (wife partial invalid); Blackheath, Westcombe Park or Charlton district; state terms, etc.—Write, 40, L.G.O., S.E.3.   κ

8. No 1 South Row advertisement

The Ideal Rendezvous . .

Situated in a quiet part of Blackheath in beautiful surroundings, the Paragon Hotel represents the pre-eminent local venue for social occasions of all kinds. Double and single rooms are available at moderate charges, and the hotel and tennis courts are open to non-residents. Social gatherings, wedding receptions, children's parties, dinner and luncheon parties are catered for under Mrs. Harrison's personal supervision.

THE   Telephone LEE GREEN 2189

•PARAGON HOTEL

PROPRIETRESS — MRS. HARRISON

SOUTH ROW, BLACKHEATH, S.E.3.

7. No 1 South Row advertisement

9. No 1 South Row in 1938 as a hotel

10. No 1 South Row – advertisement

12. No 1 South Row 1946

13. No 1 South Row 1946

11. No 1 South Row – entertainments

14. No 1 South Row stables 1945

15 No 1 South Row 1945 fragment

18. No 1 South Row repaired 1948

16. No 1 South Row 1946-47

19 .No 1 South Row restored 1948

17. No 1 South Row 1 1946-47

20. No 1 South Row restored 1948

21. No 1 South Row 1994

22. No 1 South Row 2011

23. No 2 South Row – original drawing

24. No 2 South Row (Bryan House)
about 1805

A

COMPENDIOUS SYSTEM

OF

ASTRONOMY,

IN A

COURSE OF FAMILIAR LECTURES;

IN WHICH THE PRINCIPLES OF THAT SCIENCE ARE CLEARLY
ELUCIDATED, SO AS TO BE INTELLIGIBLE TO THOSE
WHO HAVE NOT STUDIED THE MATHEMATICS.

ALSO

TRIGONOMETRICAL and CELESTIAL PROBLEMS,

WITH

A KEY to the EPHEMERIS,

AND

A VOCABULARY OF THE TERMS OF SCIENCE
USED IN THE LECTURES;

WHICH LATTER ARE EXPLAINED AGREEABLY TO THEIR APPLICATION IN THEM.

By MARGARET BRYAN.

These are thy glorious Works, PARENT of GOOD,
ALMIGHTY! thine this universal frame,
Thus wond'rous fair; THYSELF how wond'rous then!
Unspeakable! who sit'st above these Heav'ns,
To us invisible, or dimly seen
In these thy lowest works; yet these declare
Thy Goodness beyond thought, and Pow'r Divine.   MILTON.

LONDON.
PRINTED FOR THE AUTHOR,
And fold by LEIGH and SOTHEBY, York Street, Covent Garden;
And G. KEARSLEY, No. 46, Fleet Street.
1797.
[Entered at Stationers' Hall.]

25. No 2 South Row. Frontispiece Mrs Bryan's textbook

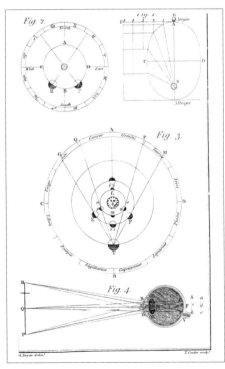

26. No 2 South Row – page from
Mrs Bryan's textbook

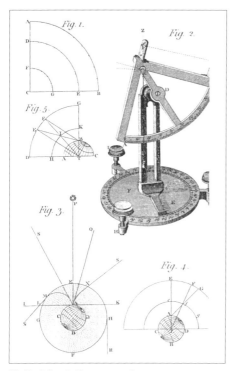

27. No 2 South Row – page from
Mrs Bryan's textbook

28. No 2 South Row (Bryan House) 1938

29. No 2 South Row (Bryan House hotel) 1938

30. Nos 3 & 4 South Row original drawing

31. Nos 3 & 4 South Row 1938

32. Nos 3-6 South Row 1938

33. Nos 3-7 South Row late 1938

34. Nos 5 & 6 South Row original drawing

38 South Row war damage 1947

35. Nos 5 & 6 South Row – 1920s

39. South Row prefabs 1944

36. Rear of Nos 2-5 South Row after air raid

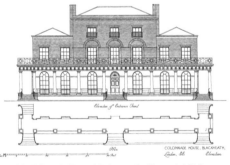

40. No 7 South Row (Colonnade House) 1910

37. Front of Nos 2-5 South Row after air raid

41. No 7 South 1938

42. No 7 South Row 1946

45. No 7 South Row and fragment of original stable

43. No 7 South Row 1946

46. No 7 South Row damaged

44 Rear of Nos 3- 7 South Row after air raid

47. No 7 South Row 1948

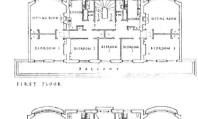

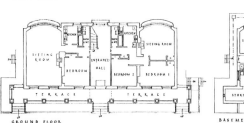

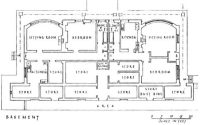

48. No 7 South Row – reconstruction and conversion plans

CONVERSION FOR INVESTMENT

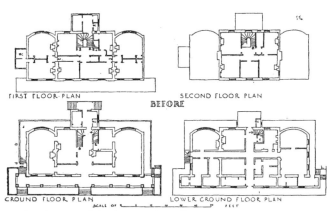

FIRST FLOOR·PLAN   SECOND FLOOR PLAN

BEFORE

GROUND FLOOR PLAN   LOWER GROUND FLOOR PLAN

49. No 7 South published conversion scheme

50. No 7 South Row before repair

53. No 7 South Row before repair

51. No 7 South Row before repair

54. No 7 South Row before repair

52. No 7 South Row before repair

55. No 7 South Row before repair

56. No 7 South Row before repair

60. Rear of No 7 South Row 1948

57. No 7 South Row – Hall before repair. 1950

61. No 7 South Row

58. No 7 South Row – Hall restored

62. No 7 South Row after

63. No 7 South Row after

59. No 7 South Row after

64. South Row late 1940s

Section H2: *South Row – modern*

1. Leslie Bilsby

2. Eric Lyons

5. South Row east end early 1960s

3. South Row 1960s

6. South Row & pond early 1970s

4. South Row 1960s

7. South Row, with Paragon House, late 1960s

8. South Row late 1960s

9. South Row east end 1994

10. South Row rear 1970s

12. No 41 South Row. 2012

11. South Row 2012

Section I: *Paragon Place and its neighbours*

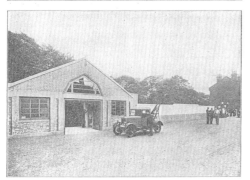

1. Paragon Place 1934

2. Paragon Pce riding 1938.

3. Paragon Place 1938

4. Paragon Place 1938

5. Paragon Place

6. Wemyss Cottage, Paragon Place, 1969

LI

"GEORGIAN" TOUCH FOR BLACKHEATH FLATS.

An impression of the proposed flats to be erected by Lewisham Council at Paragon-place, Blackheath, viewed from the South East corner. The designer is the Borough Architect, Mr. M. H. Forward, F.R.I.B.A., who has aimed at conforming to the Georgian character of the Paragon and other buildings in the vicinity.

7. Paragon Place 1949

8. No 32 Paragon Place 1966

11. Paragon Place last vestige of 19th century

9. No 32 Paragon Place 2012

10. Pond Road Lodge 1938

12. Fulthorp Road back 1994

13. Paragon Garages Morden Road

14. Fulthorp Road, Pond Road prospect 1994

15. Paragon Garages Pond Road

16. Paragon Garages Pond Road

17. Paragon Garages Pond Road

18. Ryculf Square early 2012

POST-WAR BUILDING DESIGN
Festival Awards

The Festival of Britain—on the recommendation of the Council for Architecture, Town Planning and Building Research—selected 19 architectural and landscape designs to receive awards for works of architecture completed since the war and considered to be of an exceptional high standard. There were 173 entries and the list of winners includes the name of Mr. C. Bernard Brown, L.R.I.B.A., chartered architect, of 182 Brompton-road, Knightsbridge, whose award was made for the group of buildings—The Paragon, Paragon House and Colonnade House—which will be linked together by building 2-6 South-row to a similar standard, when licenses can be obtained.

Our halftone illustration shows 9 and 10 The Paragon, which has just been completely newly built, after a direct hit which demolished both houses. There are twelve flats in this pair, and the ambition has been to keep the premises as they were first built in 1794 externally, with flats inside, but absolutely no indication from outside, such as little kitchen and bathroom windows, plumbing, etc., which most flats seem to suffer from. The whole crescent is being treated in this manner; 10 houses providing 60 flats have already been completed since 1947, and the remaining four houses should be completed within the next year or two.

On the morning of the 12th inst., an interesting ceremony was held in the Royal Pavilion of the South Bank Exhibition, when Mr. Bernard Brown, with his contempories, was presented with a Certificate commemorating the honour, together with a Plaque—similar to those affixed on buildings formerly inhabited by distinguished personages—which will be built into the wall of The Paragon. Present at the ceremony were General Lord Ismay, Chairman of the Festival

Mr. C. Bernard Brown, L.R.I.B.A.

Council, Mr. Gerald Barry, Director-General' of Festival of Britain, and the members of the Cc for Architecture, Town Planning and Bui Research.

1.Blackheath Local Guide. Festival of Britain plaque 1951

THE "VANDALISM" OF THE PARAGON

A PRIZE may be offered to the architect who can best solve the headache of the week—the great gulf of disagreement between the Cator Estate, Blackheath, and London's planners.

This solution was offered by despairing representatives of the Estate at County Hall on Wednesday, after two days of furious argument.

For those two days the Estate tried to convince the planners that theirs was a unique part of London, jealously guarded for generations, and splendidly developed—it would be desecration to intrude, they argued.

And for two days the planners tried to convince the Estate that their housing schemes to bring in 1,200 people would be a benefit to the community, and no hurt to the amenities.

The case began on Tuesday when Mr. E. J. Rimmer, Q.C., led for the residents. The Estate Company followed with their objections on Wednesday.

Star Witness

The star witness in the affair was one of Britain's top architects, Mr. Charles Bernard Brown. He is the man who won the Festival of Britain Award for the finest architecture since the war—his restoration of the Paragon, the beautiful semi-circle of Georgian houses that crowns the north end of the Estate on Blackheath. And he is the architect retained by the Cator Estate.

Mr. Brown told how he first stumbled on this area in 1926 and realised that it contained priceless architecture of the Georgian period.

"Since the war I have been determined to perpetuate all this for posterity," he said. "I realised that it was one of the few backwaters left where the sort of work I enjoy could be appreciated."

He described how over the

they had been doing for 20 years. By the time the Development Plan was completed they would be finished, he said.

Money no Object

Finally he paid his tribute to the Cator Estate. After the war he told them they could get £20,000 for the site of the Paragon. But they replied they were only interested in the buildings. They did not mind serious financial loss—"The terms they made with me were quite ludicrous; they had no bearing on businesslike terms at all," he said.

Mr. Harold Marnham, for the L.C.C. told him: "You are protesting about something which, as far as is known, is not even contemplated. Because t h e s e properties are in a blue area* it does not mean any firm decision has been taken."

Mr. Brown replied: "Then I think it is a very sad thing that we have all been put in such a panic."

"Destruction, Freezing, and Congestion"

The principal witness on Tuesday was Mr. R. Bessant, chairman of the Cator Estate Residents' Association.

He voiced their objections on the following counts: It was an estate with private roads maintained by the residents; the L.C.C. proposals envisaged the destruction of much high-rated property and the"freezing" of others; there were historic amenity values which should be preserved; an increase of population would increase congestion on already over-crowded services; any development of the estate should be left to private enterprise.

"We would welcome housing development in the area as long as it will preserve the

character of the estate," he said.

"We feel we are custodians for life of this quite exceptional estate—not only for ourselves but for posterity."

Mr. E. J. Rimmer, Q.C., summed up for the residents. He accused the L.C.C. of putting forward their proposals for the estate on the basis of housing and not of town planning.

"The development which the L.C.C. proposes is entirely inconsistent with the character of the area and really shocking town planning," he said.

He pleaded for any development which may be made to be kept well below the figure of 70 persons to the acre indicated in the plan. He demanded not more than 30 to the acre.

A Careful Plan

Mr. Michael Rowe, for the L.C.C., denied that housing need had overridden the needs of good planning.

"The two have been taken in conjunction," he said. "The solution put to the Minister is a very carefully thought out solution."

It was Mr. E. J. Harris, counsel, making the final speech for the Estate on Wednesday, who suggested that the building schemes on the estate must come, should be put open to competition to find the best architect.

He suggested that the entries should be judged by an expert team appointed by the Minister.

"It is imperative that such an estate should be preserved for posterity," he declared. "Everything nowadays is being swept away—why, why can't we preserve just something?"

*The blue areas on the plan indicate proposals for the 6 - 20 y e a r period. Red colouring shows the 0 - 5 year schemes.

Greenwich High Road Reprieve

ath. Right : A rear view of the Paragon. [Photographs by Adolf Morath.

3. Paragon February 1953 Manchester Guardian

THE MANCHESTER GUARDIAN TUESDAY FEBRUARY 17 195.

4. Paragon February 1953. Manchester Guardian

DECEMBER 18, 1954 THE SPHERE 517

A FAMOUS GEORGIAN CRESCENT WHICH EMBODIES STONE MADE TO A SECRET FORMULA : The Paragon, seen here, has been extensively restored since the war. The building is attributed to Michael Searle in the 1790's. It comprised fourteen houses built in pairs and linked by colonnades. The column bases and caps, w triglyphs, modillions and cornices, are of Coade stone. Some are signed with the dates 1794-1796. Coade is a stone of remarkably enduring quality, made to a

formula which died with Elizabeth Coade. It consists of Roman cement, glass, and other constituents. Kiln-fired to a high temperature, they produce a material which weathers much better than natural stone. The Paragon was altered indiscriminately and mutilated by a succession of owners and severely damaged during the war. The restoration, estimated to cost over £250,000, has taken seven years and is nearly completed. The restorers have replaced the exteriors as they were originally designed and converted each pair of houses into twelve flats.

5. Sphere Magazine December 1954

SOCIAL UNIT

MODERN HOMES IN OLD HOUSES
By Our Special Correspondent

The division of large Georgian and other old houses into flats, which is proving to be an excellent way of preserving some of the best architecture in London squares, suburban crescents, and country towns, has led to the birth of a new social unit: the flat-owners' committee.

This has come into existence because the purchasers of new flats in these old buildings usually have to share the cost of incidental repairs, maintenance of the fabric of the house, the cleaning and lighting of the staircase and hall, and the upkeep of the shared garden. When the unexpected happens, this is the committee which meets to decide what shall be done. Before the new owners move in they have obviously employed architects who see that the building work has been done soundly and that the plumbing and equipment is likely to operate satisfactorily; indeed, the developer knows that there would be no sale if a heavy repair bill could be foreseen.

In the case of the Paragon at Blackheath, the developers, who might well be acclaimed the saviours of this magnificent crescent, also had to restore the houses to their original appearance while building modern, well-equipped flats into the shells.

SHARING COSTS

But even in the best conversions an unpredictable crisis may come after the flats have been bought. The roof may be damaged in a storm, or there may be trouble with the drains. In many of these converted houses such a crisis calls for a meeting of the flat owners to decide what action is to be taken, and when the bill comes in the cost is shared by all the owners in proportion to the rateable value of their part of the house. The same happens with recurring bills. In the event of a dispute there is usually an arrangement whereby the aggrieved flat owner can appeal to the freeholder or leaseholder for judgment. The committee can also go to the freeholder or leaseholder for advice.

Where a property is converted into flats by a leaseholder the plans must have the approval of the ground landlord, and houses of architectural value are often saved from despoliation by a condition that any conversion must leave the outer fabric unchanged or restored. The holder of a dying lease may well strike a bargain with his ground landlord and, in return for improving the property, obtain a 50 or 60 years' extension of his lease.

On the other hand, the ground landlord may ask for a capital sum or an increase in the ground rent in return for the new lease. Usually the ground rent is shared by the new flat owners, but the wise freeholder makes sure that he is secured in case (and this has happened) the leaseholder, having got his flat-owners' committee functioning smoothly, vanishes into the blue. Some "men of straw" have left ground landlords with a much reduced income and a legal headache. Some leaseholders retain a larger interest in the property and undertake to carry out all repairs and maintenance. This is obviously reflected in the price paid.

In London the building societies do not seem to have got used to the idea of buying flats of this kind. At Blackheath only one society could be found to grant a loan, up to two-thirds of the value, but the London County Council has advanced as much as 90 per cent. Recently one of these flats, sold originally for £2,400, changed hands for £3,500.

levied upon them, but they can be very expensive. Some of the big new blocks now being built in the residential sixteenth *arrondissement* are being advertised at three million francs and even more a room.

The fortunate Parisians are those who are still living in a leased flat, at a small rent fixed by law and secure in their tenancy, provided they pay their rent and do not make a public nuisance of themselves. In Paris to-day, possession is ten-tenths of the law, for, provided the simple conditions are fulfilled, scarcely anyone can be turned out by the landlord, even though the original lease, which was for three, six, and nine years (there are no long leaseholds in France) may long ago have run out. Consequently, there is virtually speaking no such thing as a leasehold apartment with possession. The hapless foreigner who, expecting to be here for some time, seeks accommodation, is obliged, if he cannot raise the capital to buy an apartment, to take a furnished flat at more than £200 a year for each principal room.

The rebuilt Paragon Crescent, Blackheath, which has been completed after 12 years' work at a cost of more than £360,000.

LAST FLAT LET IN REBUILT PARAGON

12-YEAR TASK COMPLETE

FROM OUR PROPERTY MARKET CORRESPONDENT

With the letting of the last flat in the newly rebuilt Paragon Crescent, Blackheath, one of the most interesting of London's building rehabilitations is complete.

The work has taken about 12 years and the original cost estimate of between £80,000 and £100,000 had to be revised even in the early stages. The final figure is something over £360,000. Restoration was much helped by the decision of the War Damage Commission to regard the crescent as an architectural whole.

When work began in 1946 10 houses were badly damaged and four missing out of the seven pairs, joined by a colonnade, which formed the residential space of the crescent. To-day there are 85 flats and two small lodge houses, and the appearance of the whole is claimed to be virtually as it was in the year of its building, about 1794. Detailed work was assisted both by old prints and details of the original construction work which became apparent as the work progressed.

Certain later building carried out over the colonnade between the main buildings some time before the Second World War has been done away with at a sacrifice, it is estimated, of about 12 further flats in order to restore the original appearance of the façade.

The restoration and conversion has been carried out by Mr. C. Bernard Brown, architect to Paragon Preservation, Ltd., the freeholders. About one-third of the present residences have been let on 21-year leases and the remainder sold on 90-year leases.

7. The Paragon: The Times November 1958

Property Problems

Clash at Blackheath

"**D**O you want a modern house or flat? Or do you prefer period?" The glint in the eye, the challenge in the voice are sufficient warning that, in Blackheath, this is by no means such a simple question as it seems.

For there is a very strong clash of opinion. To some of the inhabitants the glories of Blackheath are the famous Paragon, and the wonderful Georgian and Regency houses. On the other side is the school that is excited by modern Span estates. The house-hunter who thinks of looking for something in Blackheath—"the poor man's Chelsea," as Mr. Roy Brooks describes it—should, before he starts his search, decide what he really wants and which side he is on.

Along the fringes of the argument is the local council. Its policy can obviously influence the future development of Blackheath, and one can say at once that it is responsible for a very pleasant and peaceful estate at Beaconsfield-close, imaginatively built round a magnificent oak that makes the Basque Tree of Guernica seem a sapling. The council does not appear to have been so successful at Pond-road, an estate of neo-Georgian flats, houses and cottages. Some people feel that it blends into the surroundings only when seen from the top storey of the Paragon.

The sensitive need not be too frightened that anybody will commit a monstrosity. Blackheath has several admirable societies which are ceaselessly on guard. These are the Greenwich and Lewisham Antiquarian Society, the Blackheath Preservation Trust and the Blackheath Society.

Broadly, the private buyer has a choice between Span and the other modern estates; the Paragon and forty-odd Georgian and Regency houses which Mr. Bernard Brown has converted into flats and flatlets; or a period home of his own.

Snapped Up

In order to buy a period house you will certainly have to get up very early in the morning. "If one comes into the market," a local agent says, "it is snapped up before we can even advertise it in the window." Prices greatly vary. A semi-derelict Regency relic can be as low as £1,600 freehold, and it may be four storeys high with nine rooms and will have a garden. You will probably have to spend at least £1,500 to modernise it. On the other hand, in Blackheath Park—and it is one of the most beautiful roads imaginable—the prices will be about £6,000 to £10,000. Even so, you would be paying half what you would be asked for the same thing in Chelsea or Belgravia.

Span is a very interesting communal experiment on a private enterprise basis. The houses, if you have an eye for these things, are gay, modern and full of light and air. The prices are reasonable. Span offer you ninety-nine-year lease on a house with three bedrooms, one reception, kitchen, bathroom, central heating, refrigerator, masses of glass, a tiny garden for £3,450 and all in a private park. What is more, they do not lose interest once you have paid your cheque. There is a full-time manager who helps with problems that you would normally have to handle yourself. Is your drain bunged up? Does the clicking of your neighbour's knitting needles annoy you? The estates manager will be your ally. And there are other attractions. You can choose your own decorations, mortgages are easy, and no one, Span claim, has yet sold a house for less than he gave for it.

Span is for the young and adventurous—for the up-and-coming man with, let us say, a minimum of £1,500 a year; for the person who has his feet firmly planted in the year 1958. The middle-aged and the elderly might not be so excited.

The Paragon was built in 1794 and is attributed to Michael Searle. It consists of fourteen houses built in pairs and linked together by colonnades. The triglyphs, the column bases and caps are of Coade stone—made from a secret formula which died with Elizabeth Coade and is said to be composed of Roman cement, glass from Lambeth Glass Works and other constituents. It seems to be quite unaffected by time and weather.

The Paragon, photographed by A. F. Kersting.

So many words have been written about Mr. Bernard Brown's conversion of the Paragon that almost everybody must know of it. Paragon Preservation Ltd. has been offering many different kinds of flats and nearly all are small and manageable. There are eighty-five of them and only one has reception rooms so large that they might be difficult to warm. Incidentally, there is no central heating.

Fine Windows

Paragon Preservation Ltd. has sold top flats with fine semi-circular windows, bedroom, sitting-room, tiny balcony, bathroom and kitchen on an eighty-one-year lease for £3,000. Another type of flat consists of a sitting-room, dining-room, spare bedroom, plenty of cupboards, and a sort of minstrel-gallery-cum-master-bedroom for about £4,350 for the same lease. It is easy to arrange a mortgage, and although there is no full-time housing manager, there is the Long Lease Committee which deals with domestic problems of the estate. There is also Dyer Son & Creasy, the agents, who cope with more technical matters.

Tranquil-vale, S.E.3—this is the first street name you see as you come out of the station. Tranquil it says and tranquil it is—and all within twelve minutes by train from the centre of London. Then there is the Heath, the cultural societies for music, poetry and the theatre, the antiques, the rural atmosphere. It is not for nothing that Blackheath is still known affectionately as The Village.

Hilary Maugham

8. The Paragon: Observer August 1958

BLACKHEATH'S SUPERB PARAGON. IT TOOK A SEVEN-YEAR STRUGGLE AND £250,000 TO KEEP IT THAT WAY.

PERILS OF A PARAGON

Blackheath is threatened by a monster road scheme ... Their answer is – a TUNNEL

by J. **WENTWORTH**

BLACKHEATH, t h e proud outpost village of London, high on its hill above the Thames, is a place of ancient pride and present elegance. An aristocratic village.

Its unique charm and achitectural grace was born of noblemen and gentlemen who owned it, planned it and built it with an eye for space and beauty in the Age of Elegance. The Earls of Dartmouth. St. Germans and Chesterfield have left their mark on Blackheath.

Here, only five miles from the heart of the City is a village and a heath unique in beauty, history and good houses. A compact, self-contained little community.

Most of it was developed in Georgian times by responsible landlords—Dartmouth and St. Germans, and the Cator Estate.

Between them they owned most of the land in a horse-shoe surrounding the Heath, with the open end running into

followed The Blackheath Football Club formed in 1857, played rugger on the heath until 1877, when the match with Richmond ended in a free-for-all.

pany appealed and the ter's ruling is awaited

" We supported the an inquiry concerning row in 1961, opposing opment by 'Span' contemporary style. W Paragon. Paragon Hou Colonnade House as bours on this Heath f the LCC favoured rebui a more traditional styl Minister (Mr. Brooke) support us. He appro 'Span' scheme of fla maisonettes. The res

9. Evening News June 1963

HOUSES

By Arthur
Bowers

A touch of snobbery

Overlooking Blackheath is this Georgian crescent called The Paragon, which was completely restored some years ago when flats of various sizes were created. They sell for up to about £30,000 for a three-bedroom style. One-bedroom units make about £18,000. Ground rents are £25 a year.

PARKS and open spaces, which are desirable amenities in their own right, also help to fix values for homes which happen to adjoin or overlook them.

Obviously the more extensive these areas are the greater the number of properties affected. There appears to be little resistance by purchasers to paying extra for the privilege of unrestricted views with the practical guarantee that interference from further building is unlikely.

Among the best-known protected public areas are the commons of London. As may be discerned from the ages of many of the homes fringing them, they have always had an attraction residentially.

In South-East London, for example, there are many fine Georgian properties on the edge of Blackheath, which, with the Royal Park of Greenwich adjoining, contrasts with the streets of densely-packed homes in nearby Lewisham, Deptford and parts of Greenwich itself, mainly the eastern half of the borough.

Great strides have been made to rehabilitate and restore West Greenwich. In streets alongside and just off the park in the vicinity of the impressive Naval buildings and Maritime Museum, are houses dating mainly from the 18th century. With others built later, generally 1830 to 1850, these period properties find sympathetic buyers.

There has developed a sort of inverted snobbery about living in Greenwich, a mixed neighbourhood with typical Thames-side workingmen's pubs and now sporting a most successful local theatre among tourist attractions, which

range from the famous Painted Hall to the Cutty Sark and Greenwich Meridian.

As a result, prices for period homes in West Greenwich broadly match those around Blackheath itself, which has always considered itself to be catering for a more genteel—for want of a better word—class of buyer.

"Those who buy in Blackheath' would not spend the money 'down the hill' in Greenwich," I was told. "The same is true, in reverse, of the Greenwich purchaser. They are two distinct types."

Time has forced changes, so today more people than ever are able to enjoy living on the edge of Blackheath or overlooking the park. Big family houses, many having 30 or more rooms, have been converted into flats; other buildings have been divided vertically to make more than one home.

War-time bombing destroyed many properties, the sites of which have been redeveloped, usually with blocks of flats. These, apart from the occasional small scheme to replace perhaps a

few terrace houses which were knocked out, are the only modern buildings around.

What this has all meant is that prices, for the area, are high. For example, a Victorian three-bedroom house, modernised to the extent of having a bathroom—which in Blackheath or in most fashionable streets of West Greenwich will sell for £17,000 — would scarcely rate more than £12,000 in Lewisham. Anything costing £9,500 or under will tend to be on the Lewisham side of Blackheath, or in East Greenwich.

Some of the West Greenwich houses now enjoying enhanced reputations were in fact built as railwaymen's cottages. Others were previously homes of seafarers.

Victorian developers also produced terraces of two- to four-storey houses—the latter lending themselves to conversions — and developments of distinctive detached and semi-detached types.

Cottage-style homes — two up and two down—are available for £10,500 in Greenwich, and if modernised really well will make £12,000. Flats in conversions start at just below £10,000 for one-bedroom styles. In a purpose-built block a similar unit would be close to £12,000.

Among the early Victoriana are spacious family properties, invariably containing eight or 10 main rooms, which command £25,000 to £38,000, and what can only be described as enormous semis, which usually fetch more than £30,000.

Many buyers of the tall Victorian houses—four storeys with two or three rooms per floor—acquired them specifically to break up into flats. Recently these people

have sought such properties for use as single houses, and there are cases where previously converted places have been restored again to full use as a family home. Such properties can usually be bought for about £25,000.

The Edwardians who found the area attractive filled in the land between Greenwich and Blackheath with a great variety of housing, much of it of outstanding quality. These homes today make £22,000 to £50,000.

Modern builders have had to look farther out for sites—apart from a few here and there on which they have managed a few terrace "town houses" now making £18,000 to £20,000. The person seeking a typical three-bedroom semi will usually have to look towards Kidbrooke and be ready to pay £15,500 to £16,500.

Ranking with heathside homes are those on the private Cator estate known as Blackheath Park. Building has proceeded over the years and there are also one or two recently-constructed properties along with a post-war contemporary development nearby.

A pre-war or post-war built three- or four-bedroom detached house in Blackheath Park, with large garden, could well be £35,000 to £40,000. To be found, too, are styles dating from about 1800.

On the more densely-developed site just off the park, contemporary homes make about £17,500 to £21,000. They have three/four bedrooms. Larger four-bedroom types fetch up to £30,000.

★

Overseas currency premium: gross, 112 per cent.; payable, 65 per cent.

Exploring Blackheath

and

Greenwich

With

W. H. Ower

left: The Paragon, Blackheath. This handsome Georgian Crescent built in 17? by a Greenwich surveyor was skilfull restored after being damaged in the last war. Photo: Pace.

ONE OF LONDON'S finest and most historic open spaces is the combined expanse of Blackheath and Greenwich Park. Divided only by the Old Dover Road and the park wall, it stretches for nearly two miles, from Blackheath village almost to the Thames waterfront.

Although the perimeter of the heath is densely built up, and the existing two hundred and seventy acres are but a fragment of its original area, most of the high and healthy common remains as wild as ever.

Blackheath village, on the south side, preserves something of its rural character, although nowadays the narrow, hilly streets are sorely congested with traffic. But the streets broaden out as they climb from the valley of shops straight on to the open heathland, reaching about one hundred and fifty feet above sea-level.

The Roman highway from Dover (Watling Street), and its close proximity to London – and the former royal palaces at Eltham and Greenwich – account for Blackheath's long and eventful history.

On the heath where local people now stroll

expedition to Britain, looked down on the site of Londinium beside the winding Thames.

In 1012, Danes mustered near the Point to burn and sack London; and later, in turn, Wat Tyler and Jack Cade encamped with their followers before marching on the city. But when Lord Audley with the Cornish rebels arrived in 1497, they were routed by Henry VII's soldiers after a fierce battle – the only one to have been fought on Blackheath.

ONE of the most splendid royal occasions on the heath was the homecoming of Henry V after his victory at Agincourt. He was greeted with lavish ceremony by the Lord Mayor, sheriffs and noblemen of London, all mounted on horses, followed by 'a great multitude of the citizenry on foot.'

Henry's brother, Duke Humphrey of Gloucester, built a manor house in Greenwich village by the Thames, making the first important heath enclosure for its grounds. The Duke's riverside retreat grew into the Tudor palace of Placentia ('the pleasant place'), where Henry VIII and his daughters, Elizabeth and Mary, were born.

coaches and relieve the often wea passengers of their gold and jewels.

The villains, when caught, were hanged the spot, and Pepys records the grues sight of one lately gibbeted, 'his flesh shrur his bones'.

AT THE south-east corner of the heath sta Morden College, a handsome W building set around a cloistered quadrang extensive grounds. It was designed by great architect for Sir John Morden, Lor merchant and member of the Tur Company, who, in 1695, founded his co as a pensionary, or almshouse, for poor aged merchants 'whose fortunes had I ruined by the perils of the sea'.

The college still serves its charit purpose, but on a broader scale. In additic the resident members, who are bachelor widowers, elderly couples and widows housed in self-contained flats in the loca

During the eighteenth century, Blackhe: bracing air and rural charm attra increasing numbers of new residents 1 London

1. Paragon 1864

2. Nos 3 to 8 The Paragon in the 1870s

3. No 1 The Paragon and lodges c1903

South Place, Blackheath.

4. South Row 1903

5a. Paragon 1904

5b. Paragon 1905

6. Paragon c1910

7. Paragon 1920s

8. Paragon c 1938

9. Paragon 1939 Edgar Pitt

10. Paragon 1950

11. Paragon sketch 1939 Gerard Baker

12. Paragon 1950s

13 Paragon 1950s

14. Paragon sketch Graham (Barry) Clilverd (1883-1959)

15. Paragon c1960 (Judges)

16. Paragon 1960s

17. Paragon notelet 1960s

18. Paragon sketch 1984. Bernard Driscoll

19. Blackheath Society Annual Report 1992

20. Paragon 1995 as though in 1875 by D A Wayte

21. Paragon & geese in winter.
Fiona Bell Currie

22. Paragon postcard
Mark Titman.

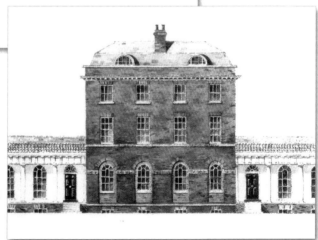

Section L: *Some of the people some of the time*

1. Gwyn & Sioned Bath
No 7 The Paragon

4. Charles Bernard Brown

7. John Cator (1926-1999)

2. Henry Bath
No 7 The Paragon

5. Mrs Margaret Bryan and her
daughters No 2 South Row

8. John Cator (1743-1806)

3. Bath & Crespigny families
outside No 7 The Paragon

6. Lt Col
Henry John Cator MC

9. Robert Curling
Paragon House, South Row

10. William Robert Davidge

13. Jane Dolphin
No 8 The Paragon

16. Mr & Mrs James Dolphin
No 8 The Paragon

11. James Dolphin snr
(1842-1931) No 8 The Paragon

14. James Dolphin jnr

17. Sir John Eamer (No 19)
No 8 The Paragon

12. Jane Dolphin
No 8 The Paragon

15. Dolphin + Soames
wedding at No 8 The Paragon

18. Sir Alexander Grierson.
Paragon House, South Row

21. Grierson family
at Paragon House

19. Fanny, Lady Grierson
Paragon House, South Row

22. John Grigg & John Cator
outside No 14 The Paragon

24. Hailstone family and
friends at No 2 The Paragon

20. Grierson family
at Paragon House

23. Bernard Hailstone
No 2 The Paragon

25 Hailstone family and
friends at No 2 The Paragon

26. Robert Hepple
No 2 The Paragon

29. John Scott Lidgett OM
of No 8 The Paragon

32. Marjorie Mansbridge
Paragon House

27.The Kendalls
of No 1 The Paragon

30. Mrs Maria Lidgett
No 8 The Paragon

28. Joseph Laurence
No 5 The Paragon

31. Albert Mansbridge
Paragon House South Row

33. Martin A R

34. Lady Ellen McDougall
No 13 The Paragon

37. George William Petter
No 4 The Paragon

40. Charles Robertson VIII
Paragon House 1 South Row

35. Harry Obbard
No 3 The Paragon

38. Edward Provis
No 9 The Paragon

41. Lt Col Colin Robertson
(on right) Paragon House
1 South Row

36. Robert Obbard
No 3 The Paragon

39. Mr & Mrs Edward Provis
No 9 The Paragon

42. Elizabeth Robertson
of No 3 The Paragon

43. Rev James Sherman
No 12 Paragon

46. Arthur Watson
No 3 The Paragon

44. Sir John Simon
No 10 The Paragon

47. Richard Wheen Colonnade
House No 7 South Row

45. Nicholas Wanostrocht (Felix) [7 from left]
No 4 South Row

48. Maj-Gen
Orde Charles Wingate
No 11 The Paragon

1817-1831
James Cousens (1782-1861): tea merchant. Later at No 8 The Paragon (q.v. for details)

In October 1819 there was an insurance policy on this house with the Sun Insurance Company, in the name of James Cousens and James Kemp, of 25 Coleman Street, tea dealers. Kemp (1788-1844) lived close by, at No 45 Blackheath Park, from 1827, until his death. James married Caroline Stanfield, at St Paul's, Deptford, on 21 May 1814.

22 June 1826, *The Times:* Death of Mary Anne, after a short illness, infant daughter of James Cousens.

23 March 1829, *The Times:* Birth of daughter to Caroline, wife of James Cousens.

1832-1843
Boswell Hensman (*fl.*1776-1843): solicitor

Hensman's chambers were at No 3 Bond Court, Walbrook, and later at No 9 Queen Street Place, Upper Thames Street. His sister-in-law, Rebecca, lived at No 1 The Paragon during this time. There were many men named Hensman in the law at this period and the records are confused.

Nevertheless, one event is certain: the marriage at St Margaret's, Lee, of George Hensman, son of Boswell and Mary Emily (née Lingham), on 1 September 1840. George Hensman (1811-1874), solicitor, lived at No 11 Shooters Hill Road from 1841 to1860, and subsequently at No 3. Residing at No 12 The Paragon in 1841 were Boswell Hensman, then aged 65; daughters Sarah and Louisa; and a son, Alfred, aged 25.

1845
Peter Bruce Turner (1804-1846): solicitor

Turner was in partnership with George Hensman, at No 8 Basing Lane, Bread Street, and may have been his brother-in-law. Although the Post Office Directory for Kent provides the only discovered evidence of Turner living at the Paragon, the London pages indicate that he was practising as early as 1828 on his own account and joined Hensman in the 1830s. He was living at Cheshunt, Hertfordshire, in the early 1830s; he and his family, including his wife, Olive, and their strangely named daughter, Victory, were resident at Basing Lane in 1841. The partnership with George Hensman may have been dissolved during the 1840s because one Nicholson was in partnership with Hensman by the 1850s.

After the brief time at the Paragon, the Turners moved to No 10 College Street, Islington, where, alas, Peter died aged but 42 years old. His will described him as a 'gentleman'.

1845-1852
John Turner Thurgar (1807-1864): schoolmaster

John Thurgar was born in Norwich. His name (sometimes written Thurgan) does not appear in the alumni lists of Oxford and Cambridge University colleges. He lived at No 47 Blackheath Park from 1842 to 1844 and before that had lived in Algiers. During his time at the Paragon he took in boarders: the 1851 census records the presence of Robert A. Smyth, aged 10, born in Calcutta, and Peter J. Q. King, also 10 but from Surrey. Thurgar's wife was London-born Sarah, and in 1851 they had one daughter, also Sarah, born in about 1846. Although schoolmasters were usually poorly paid, it did not prevent the family from renting a Paragon house and even employing a footman, albeit one aged only 17.

1854-1862
Revd James Weston Sherman (1796-1862): Congregational minister

Sherman was a dissenting divine whose power as a preacher led to his appointment as the first minister of the Congregational Church at Blackheath, erected in the Village in 1853 (see Volume I of this series for more details). James Sherman was the son of an officer of the East India Company. Although educated for the Church, he spent three years as an apprentice to an ivory

turner. But in 1815 he enrolled in the Countess of Huntingdon's training college for ministers at Cheshunt and was ordained in 1818. His career blossomed and he preached in Bath and Bristol at Huntingdon Connexion chapels. In 1836 he was appointed Congregational minister at Blackfriars, a post he held with considerable success until failing health led to his retirement.

Notwithstanding, he was tempted to Blackheath to open the new 1,000-seat chapel [in 1854]. His patrons were rich and influential but the power of his oratory was such that the church was filled more often than not. Continuing ill-health meant that services had to be conducted by his assistant, Joseph Beazley (see below). The death of his 22-year-old daughter, Martha Rose, in March 1860, would not have helped. After a visit to Egypt, Sherman returned to No 12 The Paragon, where he died on 18 February 1862. He was married twice and widowed twice. One unhappy episode in his life came in April 1856 when he was prosecuted for owning two houses in Greenwich that lacked privies, so that the sewage was disposed of in the street. James Sherman enjoys a short entry in the *Dictionary of National Biography*.

1861-1862
Revd Joseph Beazley (1812-1899): Congregational minister

Beazley assisted Sherman at the Blackheath Congregational Church during the latter's illnesses and conducted the services when Sherman was absent on his travels. On Sherman's death, Beazley was appointed minister. He moved to No 19 Shooters Hill Road but took No 13 The Paragon (q.v. for biographical details) in 1871. Beazley was a widower while resident at No 12. 12 July 1862: 19-year unexpired lease for sale.

1866-1868
Revd John Hoole (1805-1868): clergyman

Hoole, who was educated at Wadham College, Oxford, was the son of Revd Samuel Hoole, Rector of Poplar and grandson of the distinguished author and classical translator, John Hoole (1727-1803), who was unflatteringly described by John Lockhart as '… a noble transmuter of gold into lead'. The family dominated Poplar church and John was curate there in the years 1827 to 1833. He lived for a period in Camberwell, and in 1847 was in Walthamstow where his youngest son, Arnold Hankinson Hoole, was born.

1868-1874
Mrs Mary Anne Hoole (1812-1905): widow of the above

Mary Anne Hoole (née Green) was born in Limehouse, the daughter of the owner of Green's Shipping Services. With her at the Paragon were two of the Hooles' four children: John Waineford and Arnold Hankinson (often miswritten, and sometimes as Dickenson). Another son, Stanley Hoole, became an insurance underwriter and lived at Eltham; the daughter, Evelyn, married John Philip Lawrence, of No 95 Belmont Hill. Mrs Hoole and the two older boys moved to No 1 Vanbrugh Terrace in 1874, remaining there until 1888 when they all moved to No 45 The Avenue, Beckenham. They were still in residence there in the summer of 1905 when Mrs Hoole died, aged 93.

1874-1890
William Stobart (1795-1890): coal, shipping, and insurance broker

Stobart's initial career was as a Russia broker as early as 1828, with offices at the Baltic Coffee House. His company initially specialised in coal but by 1843 it was trading as Fenwick, Laroche & Stobart, coal, shipping and insurance brokers, with offices in Abchurch Street until at least 1878. Stobart had lived at Cheshunt, Hertfordshire, in the 1840s to1860s, but had moved to No 7 Belmont Park by1869, by which time he was a magistrate and Justice of the Peace [for Hertford]. He died at the Paragon at the great age of 95 and 10 months in the summer of 1890, and his widow (see below) matched his longevity. William left an estate valued at £54,000, to be divided between his four children, Elizabeth, William James, Louis Walker and Mrs Fanny Elizabeth Bellamy, their church and many charities.

1890-1898
Mrs Elizabeth Stobart (1811-1906): widow of the above

During her widowhood Mrs Stobart shared the house with her widowed sister, Amelia Deslanges. Elizabeth died at Weymouth on 20 November 1906, aged 95. The only child known to have lived at No 12 The Paragon was Louis Walker Stobart who, at the age of 50, married Harriet (27 years his junior), daughter of Alfred Haycraft (1846-1910), of No 57 Lewisham Hill, in January 1897. The junior Stobarts went to live in Yeovil, Somerset.

1899 Empty

1900-1911
Charles Edward Bretherton (1840-1911): barrister

Bretherton (sometimes miswritten Brotherton) was a Liverpool-born barrister, a member of the Middle Temple. Charles Bretherton and his family (wife Elizabeth and children Dorothea E. and Cyril H) were frequently away from this address. Nevertheless, he was a member of the (Royal) Blackheath Golf Club in the years 1900 to 1903. The 1908 municipal rate book notes the property as empty that year. The reason for this was that Bretherton was mostly based in the United States where he was a practising attorney at the New York Bar. He died at Santa Monica, California, on 8 January 1911, aged 71.

1911 enumerated census return:
Robert Woods, widower, aged 72, gardener, born Sutton, near Woodbridge, Suffolk; **Julia Ann Woods**, daughter, single, 46, housekeeper, born Old Kent Road.

1912
Mrs Elizabeth Bretherton (1848-1913): widow of the above

Mrs Bretherton died at Tonbridge, Kent, in 1913, aged 68.

1913 Empty

1914
Ernest Harvey Dunn (1851-1916)

Dunn lived previously at No 4 The Paragon. He died at No 3 Belmont Grove in September 1916. His father-in-law, Revd John Ormond, MA (Oxon), died at No 12 The Paragon in December 1914. Ormond had been Vicar of Kimble, near Wendover, from 1857 to 1872; and Rector of Horsenden from 1886 to 1898. Ernest Dunn was one of the seven children of Mrs Elizabeth Jane Dunn (1815-1895) of Nos 20-22 St John's Park, which Mrs Dunn, widow of, ran as a boarding school: Shirley House. With eight in the family, eight servants and 35 boarders, the overcrowding must have been frightful. Ernest's brother, William (1866-1948), moved to No 4 The Paragon in 1909 and remained there until 1946 (q.v. for details).

1914-1916
William Pellew-Harvey (1864-1954): mining engineer

Pellew-Harvey, a Cornishman, served an apprenticeship in mine engineering at Swansea. After a spell in Redruth, where he married Elizabeth Hichens (1863-1954), his employer's daughter, he emigrated to British Columbia to work in the gold-mining industry. Having set up the Assay Office in Vancouver, he returned to London in 1901 to establish it as the Dominion Assay Office for the whole of Canada. It was at this time, while living at No 10 Eliot Place, that he inserted the hyphen between his surnames. For the following 40 years he conducted a mining consultancy, travelling all over the world.

He was frequently in Russia and was caught in Siberia during the months of the Russian Revolution of 1917. In 1931 he became President of the Institution of Mining and Metallurgy. Pellew-Harvey continued to conduct his firm in the heart of London through the Blitz of the 1939-45 war, retiring to Hove in 1942 at the age of 78. William and Elizabeth died within three days of each other in 1954.

The oldest son, Claughton (1890-1966) was a professional artist. He studied at the Slade School, dropped the Harvey from his surname. Claughton converted to Roman Catholicism, and his subsequent work reflecting much religious symbolism. Perhaps most dramatically, he refused conscription when his call-up papers arrived in 1916. As a result he was imprisoned for technical desertion, latterly in HM Prison, Broadmoor. The experience marked his psyche for ever, resulting in what the artist John Nash described as 'a sense of permanent isolation from which Claughton never recovered'. On his release he settled in north Norfolk where he remained reclusive for the rest of his life, with his wife, fellow artist Emma ('Ketchie') Tennent (1888-1968), the daughter of Charles Stanhope Tennent (1855-1943) of Eliot Vale. Pellew's reputation as a wood engraver was considerable in his lifetime and there has been a late (post-1990s) re-evaluation and appreciation of his undoubted talent in other mediums.

The Pellew-Harvey daughter, Dorothy (1893-1962), married Lieut. Geoffrey Oliver Hempson, MD, RAMC (1889-1945), in January 1916. A brief childhood memoir by the youngest son, Edward (1906-1994), was published in the *Blackheath Gazette*, September 1986.

1917-1919 Major Guy Owen: two of his daughters were born here, in June 1917 and 1919.

1917-1921 Major C. B. Owen

1922 and 1926
Mrs Melita E. Hall (1876-1955): boarding house
(still a lessee in 1926)

Residents included:

1922 J. G. Smeaton

1924 Lionel John Peters (1879-1962): at No 5 Meadway from 1929.

Henry Whittacker [sp?]

1926 Frank Day

1929-1940
Revd Joseph James Cooksey (1872-1940)

Cooksey was a Baptist missionary in Tunis for 30 years and became an authority on Arab and Abyssinian affairs. For some years he was a Times leader writer on Abyssinia and North Africa. Joseph Cooksey died in November 1940, aged 68. His son, Howard, became headmaster of the George Dixon Grammar School, Birmingham.

1940-1942
Mrs Mary Ann Cooksey (1869-1942): widow of the above

House restored and converted into flats by the autumn of 1952.

No 13 The Paragon

Bonwitt was certain that Nos 12 and 14 The Paragon were completed by 1795. There is no proof for this, only the circumstantial evidence of the Deed of Assignment of April 1796 when Searles compounded with his creditors. The author finds it difficult to accept that No 13, one half of a semi-detached pair of houses, would remain unfinished for so long – nearly five years – after the completion of No 14 where Searles himself may have lived. Nevertheless, Searles may have 'camped out' in the house from time to time and not spent time or money on fitting it up, beyond satisfying his own comfort. The Lewisham records indicate a Mr Burnside in the immediate vicinity in 1798 and it would be reasonable to place him at No 13. Fortunately, there is hard evidence for Mr Browne's time here.

1798-1799
Andrew Burnside (died by 1801)

Burnside enjoyed a pew at St Mary's parish church, Lewisham, in October 1799, and a family vault in 1801. Nothing further reliable about him has been discovered although the name was frequent in the records of the time. An Andrew Burnside married Mary Susanna Ross, in February 1793, at St Clement Danes Church in the Strand. Three children, at least, were born to them, including Andrew William (1794-1863) who matriculated at Trinity, Cambridge, in December 1812, aged 18, and took his MA in 1821. He was to become Rector of Farningham parish church in Kent in the 1830s and remained there until his death in the summer of 1863; William in 1794, and Francis in 1796. The best-known local family of this name was that of William Burnside (1806-1872), a bookseller, who traded from the bookshop now replaced by the newsagent and confectioners at No 20 Tranquil Vale (*see Volume I of the author's series*) which has enjoyed a bewildering variety of names in recent years.

1800-1801
Robert Browne, merchant

26 November 1801: *The Times* advertisement:

Country House, Paragon, Blackheath. By Peter Coxe, Burrell & Foster, on the premises on Monday, 7th December, at 11 o'clock by order of the assignees. The valuable lease of that newly-erected family dwelling finished in a neat and superb style, abounding in rich and extensive views, situate No 13, The Paragon, Blackheath, the residence of Mr Robert Browne, merchant; the premises contain eight family bedchambers, a dressing room, a commodious dining room, a well proportioned drawing room and breakfast parlour, a gentleman's room and boudoir, a store room and water closet, an excellent entrance hall and light staircase. The basement contains a roomy kitchen, housekeeper's room, servants' hall, wash house, pantries and good wine- and other cellars with pleasant gardens. The premises are well-supplied with fine water, are held for a term of 14 years from Midsummer last at the low rental of £60 per annum and form an admirable residence for a person of fortune. May be viewed by tickets 10 days preceding the sale when particulars may be had of Messrs Palmer & Tomlinson, solicitors, Warnford Court, Throgmorton Street; and of Messrs Peter Coxe, Burrell & Foster.

26 November 1801: *The Times* advertisement:

Peter Coxe, Burrell & Foster sell by auction on 7 December and following days the contents of Mr Robert Browne's Paragon premises. The lease of the house will be sold before the furniture is offered for sale.

1801-1825
Godfrey Feise (fl.1765-1824)
(sometimes written Feize, Freize or Freise)

Feise was a merchant with an office at Baker's Coffee House in 1794. He later moved his counting house to No 129 Upper Thames Street; then to Suffolk Lane. From 1812 until 1824 he was in Laurence Pountney Hill, Cannon Street. His elder daughter, Rebeccca Dorothea, married James Woone at St Mary's, Lewisham parish church, on 12 May 1814. Alas, she died at Danzig in August 1832 aged only 44.

Feise enjoyed a pew at Lewisham, in 1818. In 1824 the Lee parish registers note the death of Caroline Feise, aged 24 – perhaps a daughter. A Mrs Eve Maria Freese (sic), of the Circus, Greenwich (now Gloucester Circus), died in September 1837, aged 63. Godfrey may have died in 1824/5 because his name disappears from both the Paragon and the City commercial records after 1824.

1826-1828
John Noble: insurance broker and merchant

At these dates Noble conducted his business from offices at Dunster Court, Throgmorton Street, and was still there as late as 1835.

1829-1831
C. Smith: Nothing has been discovered about Mr Smith.

1832-1838
John Caleb Lowell (1791-1838): orange and fruit merchant

His middle name was sometimes written Capel or Cabel. In partnership with Samuel Lowell (father or brother) by 1822 at No 6 George Lane, Botolph Lane, and until 1835; thereafter in business in his own name. The company was trading as Lowell & Co. until 1840. Lowell died on 16 April 1838, a little before this time because Mrs Lowell is the householder named for No 13 The Paragon in a commercial directory of 1839. His eldest son, also John, died aged only 59 in 1882, and the notice in *The Times* (31 December 1882) refers to him as being the son of John Cabel (sic) Lowell, 'late of The Paragon', despite it being more than 40 years after Lowell senior's death.

1839
Mrs Margaret Lowell (1801-1871)

The widow of the above. She died in April 1871, aged 70.

1841-1864
Samuel Lawford (1778-1864): banker

Lawford is described as 'independent' on the 1841 census return, but as a retired banker on the 1851 and 1861 returns, and his age is given as 63, 70, and 83 respectively. His wife, Margaretta, resided with him until his death. Some of the children listed in the 1841 census are aged only 7 (Margaret), 4 (Alfred) and 1 (Emily): these may be his grandchildren. The family previously lived in Peckham. A number of Samuel's boys were educated at the Blackheath Proprietary School, including Edward H.A. and R.C. Lawford. Other children included Louisa; Thomas A., who was a wine merchant in 1841 but a member of the London Stock Exchange by 1847; Margaret; and Henry Lawford, who had retired as a Lieutenant-Colonel and was a widower by 1861. Lawford was in the habit of letting his house during the summer holidays: in 1860 it was let to a Mr J. Wilson, of Tunbridge Wells, for four weeks at £6.6.0; and in 1861 to one J. H. Latham, but for nine weeks at the same rate (although 9/- [45p] was added for the gas consumed). Mr Latham's butler approved the inventory on this occasion.

Samuel Lawford may have been a relative (father or uncle) of John Lawford (1811-1875), Chief Cashier of the Glynn, Mills Bank, who lived at No 7 Morden Road from 1858 to 1875.

1864-1866
Mrs Margaretta Lawford (1782-1869): widow of the above

Mrs Lawford died in Greenwich – not, so far as can be established, at this address – in the winter of 1869, aged 87.

1868-1870 Empty

1871-1899
Revd Joseph Beazley (1812-1899): Congregational minister

Beazley, a widower, was appointed assistant to Revd James Sherman, at the Blackheath Congregational Church, in 1860, when the latter's health prevented him from taking divine service from time to time. On Sherman's death in 1862, Beazley was promoted to take full charge of the Blackheath church. He had lived with Sherman at No 12 The Paragon for a year or two but moved to No 19 Shooters Hill Road on his appointment. He returned to the Paragon (this time No 14) with a second wife, Louisa, in 1871. Beazley, who was born in Ickford, Buckinghamshire, trained at the Barnet Congregational College and emigrated to the Antipodes, where he was successively a pastor in both Tasmania and on the Australian mainland. He served the Blackheath congregation until ill-health forced his retirement in 1874. He took no ministerial appointments thereafter but spent some time in Switzerland.

There were two sons, one at least of whom achieved distinction: Sir Charles Raymond Beazley (1868-1955), Fellow of Merton College, Oxford, and Professor of History at the University of Birmingham from 1909 to 1933.

1899-1904
Mrs Louisa Beazley (1828-1904), widow of the above

1905-1913 No mention in commercial directories

1911 enumerated census return: William Henley, widower, 71, handyman; **Elizabeth**, his wife, a cook, aged 63, born Greenwich. The couple had been married three years.

1914-1921
Miss Emily Sarah Stone (1854-1931)
Miss Elizabeth Susannah Stone (1848-1922)

The Stone sisters were the daughters of Thomas Stone (1813-1893) and his wife Susannah (1820-1901). Their brothers were Sir Charles Stone, JP (1850-1931), solicitor and Mayor of Greenwich eight times, and John Morris Stone (1857-1930), also a solicitor. The Stone sisters had lived independently at No 37 Blackheath Park from 1903. When they left the Paragon in 1921 they moved to No 28 Kidbrooke Park Road to live with brother Charles and the third Stone sister, Cecilia.

1922-1928
Lady Ellen Mary McDougall (1858-1952)

Daughter of George Lidgett, JP (1832-1907), of Blackheath, and born at No 13 Shooters Hill Road. Second wife, and widow, of Sir John McDougall (1844-1917) of the flour family; he was Chairman of the London County Council in 1902, for which service he was awarded a knighthood. The family had lived previously at Clifton House, Crooms Hill, and on Sir John's death Lady McDougall moved to No 12 Lee Road. She spent the last 23 years of her long life at the family house at Appleton le Moors, Yorkshire. (See also No 8 The Paragon)

1928-1930 Nothing found

1931-1932
Charles Frederick Pickering

George A. Aitken (address was No 13a The Paragon)

1933-1941
Mrs Annie Harrison: boarding house

House restored and converted into flats at the end of 1947. The first occupants of the house (and, indeed, any other in the Paragon after Brown's restoration) were Mr and Mrs Arthur N. Hollis (in Flat 1). Although they had long moved away, they attended the reception to mark the Paragon's 200th anniversary in 1994. Arthur Hollis was the grandson of the astronomer Henry Park Hollis (1858-1939), who lived at No 65 Tranquil Vale.

No 14 The Paragon

1795-1796
Michael Searles (1751-1813): architect

Bonwitt was of the view that Michael Searles lived in this house, and that it was the first to be finished and occupied, because the Deed of Assignment of 1796 refers to the architect as 'late of the Paragon'. He may have done from time to time – builders and developers often live for a short period in their own properties pending a purchaser. The theory is confirmed by the advertisement which appeared in *The Times* on 15 April 1795 and was repeated on 20 and 27 April:

LEASEHOLDS, PARAGON, BLACKHEATH

By Messrs Griffith & Co. At Garraway's Coffee-house, Change-alley, Cornhill, on Monday 27th inst. [April 1795] at 12 o'clock, in two lots, A VALUABLE LEASEHOLD BRICK DWELLING-HOUSE, truly eligibly situated in the Paragon, a short distance from Morden College, on Blackheath, numbered 14. The premises contain a Drawing-room, a Dining-room, Breakfast Parlour, 4 good Rooms on the principal floor, and 8 Bed-rooms on the upper stories [sic]; a good Kitchen and every necessary domestic office on the basement; detached, is a double Coach-house, Stabling for 6 Horses, and a good Garden, in the occupation of Mr Searles; the annual value £100.

Also, a HOUSE in the said Paragon, No 12, built nearly to the same plan, but with the addition of a circular bow at back front; at present unfinished, but to be completed in the like manner as No 14; are held for a long term of years, and subject to very low ground rents. May be viewed and particulars had on the Premises; at the Green Man, Blackheath; the Tyger's Head, Lee Green; the Bull, Shooters Hill; the Greyhound, Greenwich; at Garraway's; and of Messrs Griffith & Co., Blackman-street, Southwark. – N.B. Grass land may be had near the Premises, if required

1797-1799
Joshua Kirby Trimmer (1767-1829): brick and tile merchant

A Joshua Trimmer appears in the rate and tax records for a house close to this vicinity in 1798 and 1799. It is known that Joshua Kirby (sometimes written Kirkby) Trimmer lived at North Cray, Kent, in 1795, and that there was a firm called Joshua & William Trimmer, lime merchants, of Whitefriars Wharf, in 1798. This may indicate a building-materials manufacturer to whom Searles owed money. Even so, Trimmer's name does not appear in the Deed of 1796. The Trimmer family moved to Brentford, Middlesex, in 1799 or 1800. Joshua's son, also Joshua (1795-1857), was to become a distinguished geologist and earn a place in the *Dictionary of National Biography*. In 1809 and 1810 the commercial directories list Joshua, William and Joseph Trimmer, trading as brick and tile merchants, at Kew Bridge. *The Times* notes, for 15 July 1829, the death of Percival, seventh son of Joshua Kirby Trimmer, of Kew Bridge, and the death on 27 September that year of Joshua Kirby himself, aged 62, at his house at Strand-on-the-Green, Chiswick – undoubtedly our man.

1800-1825
Charles Rivington Broughton: solicitor

A man of exactly the same name was a senior clerk in the Foreign Secretary's Office by 1809 and until at least 1814, but whether they are one and same person has not been established.

Certainly someone of this name was a member of the Blackheath Society of Golfers in 1802. The Lewisham parish records note the death of Amelia-Ann Broughton, of the Paragon, in March 1825, but her age is not given. All was not well, as the following notice, in *The Times*, of May 1825, makes clear:

Paragon, Blackheath.—Elegant Residence, with Coachhouse, Stabling, Pleasure Grounds, Garden, and Offices; Household Furniture, Plate, China, Books, Wines, &c.—By Mr. PULLEN, on the Premises, on Wednesday, May 11, at 11, under a Writ of Extent issued against Charles Rivington Broughton, esq.

A Valuable Leasehold Estate, held for 55 years, at a ground rent of 16l. 7s. 6d. per annum (very desirable for occupation or investment); comprising a capital and substantially built residence, with coachhouse, stabling for 5 horses, extensive garden, lawn, shrubberies, cold bath, and excellent attached and detached offices, delightfully situate,—No. 14, Paragon, Blackheath. On the same and following day will be sold all the household furniture, 400 ounces of plate, fine old china, glass, scarce prints, library of books, 160 dozen of port and madeira wines, and miscellaneous articles of value. The house may be viewed 6 days and the effects on Monday and Tuesday preceding the sale. Particulars of the estate had on the premises; also of H. Legatt, esq, solicitor for the Affairs of Taxes, Adelphi-terrace; and Mr. Pullen, 80, Fore-street, Cripplegate; catalogues of the effects to be had on the premises at 6d. each, and of the auctioneer.

PARAGON. Blackheath. Elegant residence , with Coachhouse, Stabling, Pleasure Grounds, Garden and Offices; Household Furniture, Plate, China, Books, Wines, &c. - by Mr Pullen, on the premises, on Wednesday May 11, at 11, under a Writ of Extent issued against Charles Rivington Broughton, esq.

A Valuable Leasehold Estate, held for 55 years, at a ground rent of £61.7s.6d. per annum (very desirable for occupation or investment); comprising a capital and substantially built residence, with coach house, stabling for 5 horses, extensive garden, lawn shrubberies, cold bath, and excellent attached and detached offices, delightfully situate, No 14 Paragon, Black-heath. On the same and following day will be sold all the household furniture, 400 ounces of plate, fine old china, glass, scarce prints, library of books, 160 dozen of port and madeira wines, and miscellaneous articles of value. The house may be viewed 6 days and the effects on Monday and Tuesday preceding the sale. Particulars of the estate had on the premises and Mr Pullen, 80 Fore Street, Cripplegate; catalogue of the effects to be had on the premises at 6d. each, and of the auctioneer.

1826
Captain John Drew (? d.1829)

John Drew is difficult to pin down: his name appears in the Lewisham and Blackheath pages of the commercial directories (*Pigot*) for 1826, 1828 and 1832 as Captain J. Drew, The Paragon, but whether this was a military or naval rank is not known – it may have been a courtesy title for a member of a volunteer brigade. Also, no house number is given and his residence here is guess-work. The 1828 directory is identical to that for 1826 in any event. Long before 1832 the resident of No 14 was John Meadows White (see below). Nevertheless, other records indicate by default that this house is the most likely candidate for Drew's occupation.

A Mr Drew was living in Clifton, Bristol, when his daughter, Sophia, married Augustus Applegath (1788-1871), the printer and inventor, in 1813; the couple were later, in 1825, to live at No 5 St Germans Place (see *Dictionary of National Biography*). The author of the DNB entry has assumed that Sophia's father was Captain J. Drew of the Blackheath Paragon – but the indications are that this is unlikely. The death of J. Drew Jnr, at Clifton, aged 44, occurred in October 1829, '… deeply regretted by his numerous relatives'. Perhaps he was Sophia's brother.

The Times noted in November 1829 the marriage, at St Mary Cray, of Edmund Neal Wilford Esq., RA, to Jane, daughter of the late John Drew.

Drew (or his executors) must have let the Blackheath house because the occupants of No 14 from 1829 to 1838 without doubt were as below. From at least 1839, the name James Drew was listed (see below), almost certainly John's son. When Mrs Mary Ann Drew's death was noted in the press in May 1857, she was described '... the relict of the late John Drew of the Kent Road and mother of James Drew, of the Paragon'.

1 November 1827, *The Times:* No 14 The Paragon to be let. Details from No 14 or Mr Stevens at the Lodge (next door).

1829-1835
John Meadows White (1799-1863): solicitor

White was famous in Blackheath for his pioneering work in establishing two important schools for boys in the area: the Blackheath Proprietary School and the Blackheath New Proprietary School. He was the son of Robert Gostling White (d1831), of Halesworth. J. M. White followed his father's profession and practised as a solicitor (with T. Borrett, at Great St Helens), specialising as a parliamentary draughtsman, in which field he became eminent. He prepared many social, legal and ecclesiastical reform documents, including the Poor Law Amendment Act (1834), and acted as parliamentary draughtsman and solicitor to the Ecclesiastical Commission from1842 until his death. He was an authority on tithes and must have been kept very busy during the period of the Tithe Commutation Act of 1836, which converted the payment of tithes due to the rector of a parish into an annual rent. During the period 1838 to 1854, all English and Welsh parishes were accurately mapped, in some cases for the first time, as a result of this reform.

White was also interested in education, especially for his own children. Along with many other parents, he was dissatisfied with the local schools. There were a number of these but none was on a par with the great institutions, and some parents had no wish to send their children to boarding schools. In January 1830 a meeting was convened at White's house to discuss the foundation of a day school for boys. Out of that meeting grew the arrangements for the establishment of a public school: the Blackheath Proprietary School – an institution owned by proprietors, whose shareholding entitled them to send a boy to the school. White was appointed Secretary and the process began. By January 1831 a building had been erected on the corner of Blackheath Village and Lee Terrace.

The school grew to become one of the most distinguished in the land but declined in the 1890s when its smallness of size left it unable to compete with the growing number of large, well-endowed schools established later in the century. It closed in 1907 (*see Volume I of this series*).

As it happened, White's connection with the school was severed quite early on. There was disagreement among committee members over policy and White and others left to establish a New Blackheath Proprietary School in 1835, operating on the same principles. It was established in purpose-built premises in Lee Terrace but did not survive beyond 1852. Its buildings remained in private school use until demolition in 1869-70 when the site was developed for No 42 Lee Terrace (now the Blackheath Hospital). White, meantime, had moved to No 48 Lee Terrace where he remained until 1855. He died at Weymouth in 1863.

Although 17 years his senior, White was a close friend of Sir John Simon (of No 10 The Paragon) who, in turn, was a great friend of White's children. His second son, Frederick Meadows White, QC (1829-1898), followed his father into the law, but as a barrister, and became a recorder and a judge.

1835-1839
Colonel (Sir) Thomas Gore Brown, KCMG, CB (1807-1887)
(sometimes written Gowar Browne)

It is likely that Brown rented the property from the Drew family. In April 1839, the contents of his house were sold for a total of just over £382. He contributed £2 to the Distressed Irish Clergy Fund appeal in January 1836. He enjoyed a distinguished career, eventually becoming Governor of New Zealand in 1856 and Minister of Native Affairs in Australia in 1869.

1839-1861
James Drew (*fl.*1800-1861): wholesale druggist

The son of Captain John Drew (see above). Previously living at Highbury. Drew's company was established by the 1820s when, as James Drew & Co., it operated from Cannon Street. The origins may have dated back to 1809 when a Walter Drew was in business as an apothecary in Gower Street. By 1835 Drew had been joined by a partner, one Heyward, and in 1849 the company was Drew, Heyward & Barron, based at No 7 Great Bride Lane. After Drew's death (at the end of 1861) the company continued in business, eventually trading as Drew, Beriah & Co. at No 91 Blackman Street, as late as 1882.

The Drews sent their two sons (1844-1914) Charles Edward and Frederick Adolphus (1846-1925), to the Blackheath Proprietary School. Charles, who was ordained, was to become the Rector of Wymington, Bedfordshire; Frederick became a wine merchant. There were six daughters: Clara Howard Drew (1850 1930) married architect Edward Drury (1842-1919) in November 1870. The other children were Edith Rosalie; Emma Mary (married Henry Francis Smith, of Clapham, in August 1851); Adah Jane (married David Satow, of Clapton and Idol Lane); Frances Elizabeth (married Frederick Hayter, of Upper Clapton, in August 1856); Jane and Marion. By 1913, the *Blackheath Local Guide and District Advertiser* reported that the Drew clan had reached 21 grandchildren and 23 great-grandchildren. The youngest boy, Frederick Adolphus Drew, died in Queensland, Australia, in July 1925, aged 79.

One curious incident involving James Drew was reported in the *Kentish Mercury*, in August 1856. The garden of No 14 The Paragon was (and still is) very small. The 19th-century lessees rented additional land to the south, some of which bordered the round pond. Drew was 'very tenacious' towards his rights to the pond and fired a gun at two boys playing with a model boat.

The shots missed both the boys and a carriage party which had stopped by the pond to watch the boys. Unfortunately, a goose belonging to William Scudds, the fly proprietor whose stables stood on the far (west) side of the round pond, was killed. The newspaper reported that the magistrate had decided to wait on the police to bring a formal complaint.

1861-1878
Mrs Mary Prockter [sometimes written Proctor] **Drew** (1806-1878) (sometimes written Prochter): widow of the above; daughter of Thomas Ling, of Launceston, Cornwall.

1879
Mrs Frances Elizabeth Hayter (1835-1882)

Widow of Frederick Hayter (d.1878) and daughter of James and Mary Drew. Mrs Hayter, previously of Camberwell Terrace, moved to No 24 Rochester Way in 1878 after the death of her husband, a shipping agent and woollen merchant. Mrs Hayter died when only 47 at Poole, in Dorset, during the winter of 1882.

1880-1888
James Meikle (1844-1893): wholesale tea dealer

There were tea dealers trading as Meikle, Meacher & Co., at No 4 Savage Gardens, in the commercial lists of 1866, which may have been James starting young or a family business. By the 1870s, the company was simply James Meikle & Co. and established at No 14 Philpot Lane. Each year there seemed to be a new partner: in 1876 the firm's name was Meikle, Marshall & Co., and by 1878 Meikle & Godlee; in 1882 and until the mid-1890s it was Meikle & Passmore, at No 94-96 Southwark Street. James Meikle's brother, William, was an East India merchant, and also lived in Blackheath – at No 57 Lee Terrace. James and his wife, Jennie, who enjoyed a large family, had previously lived at No 37 Granville Park. Living with them at No 14 The Paragon were Florence M., Edith C., James, Robert M., William P., Isabel B., Annie M., Henry K. and Frederick A., and four resident servants.

It was no wonder that Mrs Meikle advertised in January 1884 for a nurse to look after four of the younger children. The new nanny was required to be between 15 and 30, of good temperament and an early riser; a *sine qua non* was the qualification that she be 'fond of children'. Of the boys, only James was educated, briefly in 1883, at the Blackheath Proprietary School; Edith Meikle was one of the first pupils to be enrolled in 1880 at the then newly opened Blackheath High School for Girls.

The Meikles moved from the Paragon to Denmark Terrace, Brighton, where James died in 1893 aged 49. Jennie Meikle died three years later at Steyning, Sussex, in her 51st year.

1889 Empty

1890-1907
Henry Fletcher (1854-1907): Cape of Good Hope merchant

Fletcher left £13,326, which included £10,000 to his clerk, George Elmy. The family, all of whom were born in South Africa, were unmarried and clearly of substantial means. They included a sister, Ethel, and a brother, William. Henry was away on the night of the census of 1891 and Ethel, at 28, was described as head of the household. There were five servants to attend the family's needs. Fletcher was an early, and substantial, shareholder in the Blackheath Concert Hall Company. He died on 28 December 1907, aged 53.

4 February 1908: Contents for sale

1908-1913: No names given in commercial directories.

1914-1917
Miss H. M. Richards

In March 1914 there was a meeting of the Penal Reform League at this house.

1918-1920
Mrs M. K. (Percy) Dale: matron

No 14 was recognised as the official boarding house for the Blackheath High School for Girls until April 1920.

1921-1925
Southlands: boarding and day school for junior boys and girls
Principals: Misses F. M. Barnes and E. Stevens

1926-1941
Blackheath High School for Girls: Preparatory (Junior) Department

The growth and development of the High School in Wemyss Road led to the decision in 1925 to move the kindergarten out of the overcrowded main school building. The council of the school's governing body (the Girls' Public Day Schools Trust) took No 14 The Paragon on a long lease, which may have been because the building had been in educational use and had once enjoyed a connection with the High School. Whether true or not, the Trust eventually decided that it was suitable for educational use and converted the drawing rooms and bedrooms into classrooms and cloakrooms. Further, the school laid down two hard and one grass tennis courts on the additional land to the south; the garden ground was a generous and attractive playground for young children.

Blackheath High School occupied this house from 1926 and remained in occupation even after the outbreak of war, in September 1939. Initially, the house had not been used, but by autumn 1940 the pupils returned. This was largely for the benefit of those girls who could not join the evacuation to Tunbridge Wells – a number reduced to 30 at the height of the 1940 Blitz. Also, when the Royal Army Pay Corps took over most of the Wemyss Road building, No 14 The Paragon became the principal London centre for the Blackheath High School, even admitting a few small boys.

Although the building was not seriously affected in March 1941 – when a bomb virtually destroyed nearby Bryan House – it was sufficiently damaged to be declared unsafe, not to be occupied again until the restoration by Brown in 1947. The High School took No 20 Montpelier Row for its boarding house in 1944. After the war, the Preparatory Department was reinstated at Wemyss Road.

This department moved, in March 1948, to No 13 Morden Road where it stayed until Christmas 1994, at which time it re-formed at the old Wemyss Road site. The senior school meanwhile evacuated its original premises (designed for it in 1880 by Paragon resident, Edward Robert Robson: see No 2 The Paragon, above) to No 27 Vanbrugh Park, the erstwhile Wilson Carlile College of Evangelism, belonging to the Church Army.

1941-1946 Empty, following slight bomb damage

House restored and converted into flats, 1947-8, and first occupied in 1949.

1950-1956
James Lansdale Hodson (1891-1956): Author and journalist, novelist and playwright. Probably best known for Grey Dawn – Red Night.

Mrs [Enid] Olga Stokes (1901-1989): Lived in Flat 1 from 1975 until her death.

No 15 The Paragon (the Porter's Lodge)

Searles designed the porter's lodge at the west end of the Paragon for that purpose. But who paid the porter and carried the cost of keeping his little house in repair and rated is not known. For the first ten years, when many of the Paragon houses were hardly built and certainly not fitted up and occupied, this would have been difficult. It is likely that the porter's employer was the Cator family, using the tenant for various odd jobs around their estate. By the 1830s other lodges had appeared on the estate, including one next to the round pond to the south of Nos 10 to 14 The Paragon. The task of the Paragon porter was to take in parcels, help around the estate generally, fetch and carry and, most important, keep out undesirables such as itinerant vendors and professional mendicants.

Before the days of the universal postal delivery system (after 1840) the porter probably collected the letters from the Village post office. No doubt, some of the Paragon porters were fiercely protective of the residents and, as a result, were duly rewarded at Christmas by grateful householders.

In 1793 and 1795 there are references in the parish registers to births and deaths in the family of Thomas Harvey, of 'Mr Cator's lodge'. The exact location of this lodge cannot easily be determined but it may have been in the vicinity of what was to become Colonnade House or the Princess of Wales public house, to judge by its position in the Land Tax returns. Harvey was to borrow £200 on mortgage from solicitor Charles Rivington Broughton (of No 14 The Paragon) in December 1802, towards the cost of building what was known as the High House – next to the Princess of Wales and now the site of its car park. Harvey was later declared bankrupt. Also, throughout the lists of early 19th-century recipients of Hatcliffe's and other charities administered by St Mary's parish church, Lewisham, were a number of entries for people living in 'Paragon Mews'. This was later to be gentrified as Paragon Place.

By 1805, there is evidence in the Highway Surveyors' book for a Mr Walton in the Paragon lodge.

1805-1807
Mr Walton

Probably the Thomas Walton who, by 1808, was described as a painter, living near the Paragon, Blackheath, when Bryan House was advertised for sale in October 1808. He could be applied to for particulars. In December 1806 there was the registration of the burial of a William Walton, aged three years, from the Paragon.

1812
John and Elizabeth Cornell: 'Mr Cator's Lodge'

1816-1843
Jacob Stevens: porter

According to the 1841 enumerated census return, Jacob was 70 and his wife, Marriet (sic) was 50. Their daughters, Mary and Elizabeth, were laundresses, and their son George, then aged 12, was described as a male servant.

Marriet (Harriet or Maria, perhaps) was living in Camden Row by the late 1840s, and a George Stevens was in charge of Cator's lodge at the south-west end of Blackheath Park (demolished in 1895). The church charities supported one 'Stevens (watchman) Paragon' throughout the period 1816 to 1830.

1849-1851
William Beale: porter

Beale was aged 39, and was born in Windsor according to the 1851 census details. His wife, Augusta, had been born in Barbados, and was a dressmaker. Their two children were James, aged 6, and Ann, only one year old on the census of 1851. Before moving to the Paragon, William lived in the cottage attached to The George public house (since demolished) on Maze Hill.

1855
Samuel Hawer

1861-1874
Thomas Gibbs: Chelsea pensioner, porter

Gibbs was born in Brasted, Kent, in about 1813. His wife, Elizabeth, was born in Blackheath c.1812. No children are mentioned on the 1861 or 1871 census returns.

1875-1900
Henry Sancto (1837-1909): porter

Sancto, who came from Maidstone, served the Paragon residents for 26 years. He was an ex-soldier (in retirement a Chelsea pensioner) and had served in the Indian Mutiny campaigns as a Royal Artillery wagon driver. During his service he had been present at the Relief of Lucknow. In 1879 he had saved the life of a road mender who had severed an artery. Sancto's prompt action was possible because he had attended the life-saving classes held at St John's church hall. He was a registered voter in 1891. His wife, Elizabeth, had been born in Sevenoaks in 1842. In 1881 the Sancto lodge also gave shelter to a boarder, George Stanbridge, a young grocer's assistant, who was to become manager and, eventually, the owner of Goater's, the grocery shop at No 26 Montpelier Vale (*see Volume I in this series*)

It was possibly in Sancto's time that the Paragon porter first wore a livery that in later years – up to about 1928 – consisted of black trousers, a three-quarter-length frock coat cut square back and front, and a gold-braided black top hat. He was often seen in Blackheath Village, pushing a dark-green-painted wheelbarrow to and from the station with luggage belonging to the residents. The barrow had a slatted flat base with a rounded front and a slatted barrier all round to prevent the luggage from sliding off.

1901-1912
Henry Richmond: porter

The 1901 and 1911 census returns note that Richmond was born in St Pancras. His occupation is given as: 'Porter to the Paragon'; his wife Mary Jane, born 1844, was a native of Plymouth. By 1911 Henry is acknowledged as an army pensioner.

1913-1928
Charles Marchant (1857-1928)

Charles Marchant may have been the last of the 'official' Paragon porters.

1929-1936
Mrs Alice Marchant: widow of the above

1937-1939
Thomas Courtenay and **Mabel Hall**

1945-1952
Arthur J. and John L. Sextone (listed as at 14a The Paragon in 1949)

It is unlikely that the Sextones were porters or nightwatchmen (official or otherwise) to the Paragon during this period.

Restored and reorganised internally as a separate dwelling, No 15 The Paragon, by Charles Bernard Brown, and occupied by 1953.

Beyond the lodge, to the south-west and before Paragon House (No 1 South Row – see below), was a collection of stable and store buildings, usually attached to No 14 The Paragon and No 1 South Row (Paragon House). A resident sometimes occupied these: in 1901 it was William Cripps, a domestic coachman. When the whole Paragon complex was restored by Brown, he rebuilt and partly re-faced what had become broken-down garages, adding the arms of the ground landlord, the Cator family. He named the small, quality dwellings he had created Paragon Close, Cator Manor and Cator Lodge (*see illustrations*).

Paragon Place (west side) in 1938. The entrance to the Colonnade House stables on the extreme left. B Soc

The Keep Span Estate & The Paragon c1965. B Soc.

SOUTH ROW REGISTERS

**Being a schedule of all those residents
discovered living in the South Row houses
from the beginning to about 1940**

Below and opposite:

South Row on the 1866-1867 Ordnance Survey (published 1869)
and the 1893-1894 map (published in 1897)

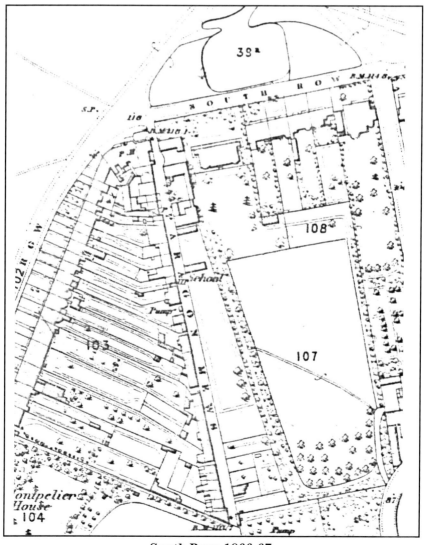

South Row: 1866-67

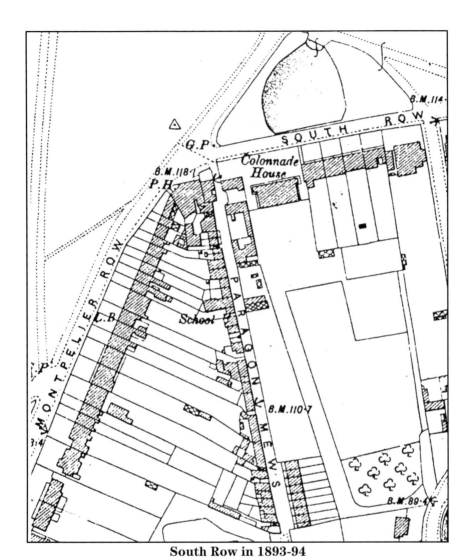

South Row in 1893-94

No 1 South Row (Paragon House)

This house (and Bryan House: No 2 South Row) were designed as a pair and the carcases must have been finished by 1791. The Deed of Assignment [of 14 April 1796] indicates two houses at the entrance to the Park (Sir Gregory Page's Park, although owned by John Cator since 1783) and refers to any interest Searles may have had in them.

The earliest surviving documentation touches on a wider development lease of 90 years' term for two pieces of land, commencing in midsummer 1789, at £12.12.0 per annum after a year at a peppercorn ground rent. The Paragon House site was 85 ft wide and 200 ft in depth. The lease states that no building erected could be used by soap boilers, sugar bakers, dyers or distillers, and so on. In addition Searles (or whomsoever) was obliged to pay Cator 5/- for every cart of sand, clay, loam or gravel removed from the site for brick- or tile-making. Whether the spoil was used for bricks, either for Paragon and Bryan Houses or for sale to others, is not hinted at. The cost of building was not to be less than £1,000 and Cator agreed to grant a lease on each house to a nominee by the head lessees.

An advertisement in *The Times* of 25 May 1791 described the two new houses in some detail so that, without exact addresses, they are unequivocally Paragon House and Bryan House:

> ## BLACK-HEATH, KENT.
> ### By THOMAS GRIFFITH,
> At Garraway's Coffee-house, 'Change-alley, Cornhill, on
> Monday the 6th of June, at Twelve o'Clock,
>
> TWO Capital well-built LEASEHOLD Brick DWELLING HOUSES, delightfully fituated on that much admired fpot, the entrance of the late Sir Gregory Page's Park. The Premifes comprife on the Attic Story four exceeding good Bed-chambers, with Clofets; on the Chamber Floor are four very excellent Rooms, and a Water-clofet; on the Parlour Floor is a Dining and Breakfaft Parlour, and a capital Drawing-room 30 feet by 20, and a neat Hall; on the Bafement Story is a good Kitchen, a Houfe-keeper's-Room, a Pantry, Store-room, Butler's Pantry and Powder-ing-room; detached is a Laundry, a four-ftall Stable with Lofts, and double Coach-houfe, a paved Yard, and fpacious Garden inclofed. The Rooms are of large dimenfions, are finifhed in a very neat and elegant ftile, and poffefs every neceffary requifite for a refpectable Family; are held for a term of ninety years, fubject to the fmall Ground-rent of Twelve Guineas per ann. each
>
> May be viewed, and Particulars had on the Premifes; at the Green Man, Black-heath; at Garraway's, and of Mr. Griffith, No. 92, Blackman-ftreet, Southwark.

The Times 1791.

Searles was not alone in developing Paragon House: the Deed of 1 May 1790 engages the interest of John Cator as landlord, and then Michael Searles, of the Paragon, Southwark, surveyor; John Searjeant (*sic*), of Dockhead, Rotherhithe, bricklayer; Samuel Barnard of Greenwich, carpenter; and Alexander Doull of Greenwich, painter. They acknowledged that they had received from Cator funds amounting to £2,749 (plus £251 interest) – a total of £3,000, to pay for the building. The houses were to be the security Cator needed so that, once buyers had been found, he would be repaid. After Cator's death in February 1806 his interest passed to a trustee, William Cator. The repayment was made but it took a while.

The Land Tax notes that Robert Stuart was resident here by 1798 and, because of his marriage in Lewisham in November 1796 and his membership of the Blackheath Society of Goffers by 1797, it is likely that he was living in Paragon House by those dates. There are no discovered earlier official or parish records for this property which give the name of a resident in the years 1792 to 1796. A later deed (simply a recital of an earlier document) does mention Lady Stuart as having lived here but without a specific date.

1796-1803
General Sir Robert Stuart (c.1745-1819)

Also of Fitzroy Square and Brighton. Stuart (sometimes written Stewart) is a man of some mystery in that Bonwitt was unable to establish the credentials for his title. But it was common in the 18th century for people to adopt, somewhat informally, ranks which were rarely questioned. It has been suggested that his title was conferred when he served abroad. He was born in Clackmannanshire, commissioned in 1761 and joined the 77th Regiment of Foot in 1770, rising to become its Lieutenant-Colonel.

During this period Stuart was caught up in the mutiny of 1783 when conscripts from the Highlands, promised demobilisation after the American War of Independence, were tricked into boarding boats bound for the East Indies. Stuart supported the men and was rewarded by a verse or two of a song written by the successful mutineers:

Our Major like a soldier bold / He said: 'My lads, you shan't be sold / for of your hands I'll take a hold / and bring you off this morning.'
Sir Robert Stewart of birth and fame / and long may he maintain the same / to be an honour to the name / may all that's good come o'er him.

Stuart was gazetted Major-General in 1796. In 1797 and 1798 he was Commander of the Loyal British Fencible Infantry (a sort of territorial army and strong in Greenwich). It was this appointment that may have brought him to south-east London, in that the Heath was frequently used as a display ground for the Fencibles. While here he was, briefly, a member of the Blackheath Society of Golfers. He was married (possibly for a second time) in Lewisham parish church in November 1796, Elizabeth, 'of the West Indies', the wealthy widow of Alexander McLachlan, of Jamaica. This relationship would have brought him into contact with a number of local residents with connections to the West India trade, sugar merchants, and plantation owners.

Sir Robert and his lady were part of the social set which gathered around HRH Caroline of Brunswick, the Princess of Wales (1768-1821), then living at Montague House, on the south-west corner of Greenwich Park. The Stuarts remained in Blackheath until about 1803 and then moved to Brighton. But not before, in April 1802, Sir Robert gave 10 guineas to help wounded men and the families of those who fell in the Fleet under Admiral Hyde Parker, at Copenhagen.

In March 1804 Lady Stuart advertised her intended disposal of the lease of the Blackheath house: 77_ years unexpired. The elegant drawing room measured 30 ft by 20 ft. Elizabeth died at Brighton in 1811. Two years later Sir Robert was promoted to full General, probably on his formal retirement from the Army. He died in 1819, possibly also in Brighton. Lady Stuart's will – she left £800 a year to her husband – mentions property in Jamaica and '... negroes, slaves, cattle and other utensils'. There seem to have been no children.

1804-1806 and 1807-1811
Nathaniel Edward Kindersley (1763-1831): proctor and Commissioner of Land Tax

Lease dated 1 September 1805 between John Cator, of Beckenham, and Nathaniel Edward Kindersley esquire, of Blackheath, for a parcel of land on ground, field or paddock behind [to the south of] a house in occupation of Kindersley. It was 80 feet wide and 100 feet deep. To the east was ground in occupation of Charles Rivington Broughton [No 14 The Paragon] and on the west was the road, now Pond Road, once the driveway to Wricklemarsh House. Kindersley paid Cator a consideration of £1,600.

It is the lease to Kindersley that reveals quite a lot about Searles' development of this plot and the subsequent complications of the assignment of his properties and goods to his creditors. Each time a new document had to be prepared it needed to recite all the details from previous indentures, and that meant repeating the Deed of Assignment involving Michael Searles, John Cator and half a dozen or so tradesmen with a pecuniary interest or obligation. The interests (if any) of those who died had to be represented by their executors or assigns.

Kindersley was in service abroad with the Hon. East India Company before he came to Blackheath because at least one of his sons (Richard) was born in Madras in 1792. In May 1794 there was an advertisement for Kindersley's book, Specimens of Hindoo Literature, published when he was with the Madras Establishment.

When back in the UK, the family continued to have connections with both the law and India. The Kindersleys left Blackheath in 1807 (their pew at St Mary's, Lewisham, is marked as empty in September of that year) and moved to Sunninghill, Berkshire. The family were generous to charities, particularly for the Irish poor and for London down-and-outs, and Kindersley's name appears quite often in the published list of donations. Even after his death, his sons gave to the Mendicity Society from his estate.

Most of the sons seem to have done well. Nathaniel William (1794-1844) rose high in the Madras Civil Service, although he lost his young wife, aged but 25, in June 1831. Richard (later Sir Richard) Torin Kindersley, PC (1792-1879), was destined for India but, instead, was called to the Bar. He finished his career as a Master in Chancery, later Vice-Chancellor, and was knighted on

that appointment in 1851. He retired from the Bench in 1866 with a pension of £3,500 p.a. – a massive sum in those days. A third son, Edward, was born as late as 1819, at Sunninghill, and also entered the law.

On 6 June 1806 Nathaniel transferred his interest in the house, field and paddock to Jemima Kindersley, possibly his mother, for a consideration of £2,400. By 1811 it was back in the ownership of Nathaniel.

The lease was assigned by Kindersley to William Curling (see below) on 11 April 1811.

1811-1821
William Curling (*fl*.1776-1842): shipbuilder and broker; whaling underwriter

William was the son of Robert Curling, a ship and insurance broker, of Torrington Street, Ratcliff Highway, who was also a director of the London Dock Company. The firm, trading as Curling & Domet, had moved to Castle Court, Birch Lane, by 1809 – the same year [1811 above] that William had moved into Paragon House, possibly indicating that his circumstances had improved because he had taken over the firm's direction at about that time. From 1812 to 1819, there was also a company designated Curling, Cox & Co. but only Curling & Domet remained by the 1820s. The firm pursued a considerable variety of shipping interests over the years, principally as insurance brokers and merchants but also as shipbuilders, with yards at Limehouse and Duke Shore Dock, and with offices at St George's Yard, Lombard Street. The company, trading as Curling & Young by 1826, flourished until the mid-1840s. It specialised in building ships for the East India Company and, in 1835, constructed steamships as well. William was a trustee of the New Cross Turnpike). He and his wife Elizabeth (who died in October 1850), moved to Itchen Abbas, Hertfordshire, but eventually returned to Blackheath, to reside at No 14 West Grove where they spent the years from 1831 to 1842. In December 1824 they lost their son, Daniel, a Secretary of Customs at Trinity Square, 'who had been for some time in a state of decline'.

The 1811 edition of Holden's Annual London County Directory lists a Mr J. Arnold, at Paragon House. Also, a Mrs Arnold with addresses in Argyll Street, Halstead (Essex) and Blackheath (Kent). Nothing else confirms an Arnold residency in Paragon House. Nevertheless, a George Arnould (sic) lived at Hyde Cliff, a large house on the south-west corner of Crooms Hill, from 1804 to 1808; and a Mrs Arnould (probably his widow) was there from 1808 to 1810. J Arnould was a bookseller in Piccadilly in partnership, until March 1818, with one J. Bradford.

[*See also No 1 The Paragon, for details under Edward Spencer Curling.*]

Curling retained the head lease and granted a 27-year-term under-lease to Samuel Prior on 5 September 1821. Attached to the lease was a schedule of fittings within the house, listed room by room and far too long to repeat here. The items were mostly bells, cranks and wires, canvas window blinds, hat pegs, and Romford stoves – a patent wood-burning stove fashionable since the late18th century. By then there was an ice house, probably built many years earlier but not thought worthy of mention on earlier schedules. The rooms and spaces described were, from the top to the bottom of the house:

Attic storey: nursery; bow bedroom; store closet; Right hand front room; Left hand front room; on the Landing was a linen press and a hatch gate at the staircase; First storey bow bedroom; a bedroom adjoining; a Right hand front bedroom; Dressing room; on the next Landing down was a water closet; then the Principal Storey and hall with a mahogany sideboard and a bell pull; Bow room with a cast iron register stove and three green venetian sun shades; Dining room; Drawing room; Basement Kitchen: with wind-up range with drop bar, oven and boiler, swing trivet, etc. etc., a wood cistern lined in lead; Scullery, with an ironing board on iron legs; Butler's room; Butler's pantry; Larder; Store room; Servants room; Passage to kitchen with coffee mill shelf and pepper ditto; Servants hall with small range and an ironing board; Stable yard – three tier bottle rack; Wash house; Stables – the fittings of three stalls; Harness room – three rows of harness pegs and a saddle tree, corn shoot from loft. Loft – a deal closure for corn room. Garden – the erection of a Greenhouse with glass etc. …

1821-1858
Samuel Prior (1788-1859): merchant

There was an Edward Prior, merchant, at No 16 Great St Helens in 1814 who may have been Samuel's father. In 1819, Prior, Turner & Co. was trading from No 88 Cheapside, and afterwards at chambers in the Commercial Sale Rooms, Mincing Lane. The company stayed at that address even after management passed to Samuel's son, Samuel Turner Prior (1820-1876). While in Blackheath, Samuel senior entered into the social life of the area: he contributed £5 to the Distressed Irish Clergy Fund in 1836; subscribed to shares in the Blackheath Proprietary School in 1831; and worshipped at St Margaret's, Lee, although he lived in Lewisham parish. Charles Henry (1823-1868) was the only one of his sons to be educated at the Proprietary School. Other members of the family included Alexander, Harriott and Elizabeth.

His first wife, Harriott, died in June 1845 aged 53 and was buried at Lee. Samuel married again shortly afterwards but in February 1858 the family home was sold and Samuel and his new wife, Elizabeth, moved to Brighton. He died less than a year afterwards, in January 1859, aged 71. His son, Samuel Turner Prior, continued the business, specialising in the Mediterranean region and, in due course, became Manager of the Commercial Sale Rooms. Samuel junior married, in April 1842, the daughter of Samuel Lawford, who lived next door at No 13 The Paragon. The young couple made their home at No 57 Shooters Hill Road from 1847 until Samuel junior's death. Their son – stockbroker Frederick William Prior (1847-1912) – was a distinguished cricketer and one of the founders of the present Blackheath Cricket Club.

On 25 March 1859 William Curling Jnr (by then of Maesmawyr, Montgomeryshire) granted a new under-lease to the lawyer John Hollams. The term was for 20_ years from 1859 (i.e. expiring in 1879-80). The rent started at £120 and rose, by June 1863, to £200 a year. The attached schedule of fittings – room by room – was almost identical to that on the Samuel Prior lease.

Advertisements by Prior to dispose of the lease appeared as early as June 1853 and again in April and June 1856. The later sale was conducted by agents Norton, Hoggart & Trist whose advertisement spoke of eight bedrooms and dressing rooms, a drawing room of 32 ft by 19 ft and a dining room of 25 ft by 17 ft. The lease to Prior ran until 1863 at an 'inadequate rental' of £120 p.a. The ground rent for the unexpired lease was still Cator's £14 p.a.

The house contents were sold in March 1859 at an auction conducted by local estate agent Benjamin Octavius Engleheart. The items included all of the furniture and 1,000 ounces of silver plate.

1860-1876
Sir John Baptist Hollams, Kt, JP (1820-1910): solicitor
Member of Council and later President of the Law Society, 1878-79

Hollams was already a senior member of his profession when he came to live in Paragon House. Previously, he had lived at No 4 Cresswell Park (from 1846-51) and then at No 6 The Glebe. He was the son of John Hollams, curate of Loose, Kent, and grandson of Sir John Hollams, five times Mayor of Deal. He was articled to a solicitor in Maidstone and was admitted in 1844. He came to London in 1846 to join the practice of Brown, Marten & Thomas, the year after he married Rice (1814-1891), daughter of the Revd Edward Allfree, Rector of Strood, Kent.

In due course Hollams was taken into partnership and there followed a long period when he and his senior partner, Griffith Thomas (living at No 6 The Paragon from 1851 to 1860), conducted one of the most successful practices in London. They specialised in banking and Hollams so enjoyed his work that he refused better offers even when still comparatively young. He served on the Council of the Law Society in 1866 and was appointed President for the session in 1878-79. Other honours followed and he was appointed a Deputy Lieutenant for the City of London in 1882 and was a JP for the County of Kent

Despite achieving much distinction in his profession, Hollams did not accept a knighthood until 1902, when in his early eighties. Having been a partner of his practice since 1844 and senior partner from 1873, he retired to his London home at Eaton Square and a magnificent country

seat, Dene Park, near Tonbridge. He died there in 1910, leaving an estate valued at £601,587 – the equivalent, it has been calculated, of between £15-20 million in 1994 values.

John Hollams' sons were educated at the Blackheath Proprietary School before university (Trinity, Cambridge, for John and Percy, and Trinity, Oxford, for Frederick) and the former two joined the company. John junior (1846-1926) eventually became senior partner of the practice. Frederick William (1848-1941) was called to the Bar and became Counsel to the Law Society. Hollams & Thomas eventually became, with new partners, Hollams Son, Coward & Hawksley and, in due course, Coward Chance. In 1987 the company merged with Clifford Turner to create one of the largest firms of solicitors in the world.

1877-1879
Joseph Kitchin (1824-1905): Sicilian merchant

Previously of Naughton Villa, Sydenham. Suffolk-born Joseph Kitchin moved to No 5 Morden Road in 1880 and stayed there until 1888; he then lived at No 5 Glenluce Road from 1889 until his death. Joseph's wife, Ellen Mintz Kitchin, and their daughters, Ellen, Emma and Isabella, all survived him. There were at least eight children – six girls and two boys – the youngest of which, Joseph, attended the Blackheath Proprietary School from 1880 to 1884.

1880-1881
Charles Robertson VIII of Kindeace and Glencalvie, Ross-shire (1831-1905): merchant and landowner

Previously with homes in Rutland Gate and Southend, Essex. Robertson, whose stay at Paragon House was brief before a move to No 26 and then to No 2 Vanbrugh Park, found it necessary to earn his living and was described on the 1881 census as a merchant. He had married well, taking for his wife, in 1869, Helena Emma (1837-1891), youngest daughter of Sir John Maryon Wilson (1803-1874), Lord of the Manor of Charlton. It was this connection that, later, may have helped his son, Lieut.-Col. Colin John Trevelyan Robertson, OBE, MC, MA (1877-1957), in his subsequent career as a schoolmaster. In 1903, Colin Robertson became a partner of Harry Townsend Simmons Storrs, MA, in the ownership of Shirley House School, at Cherry Orchard, on the south side of Charlton Road – enjoying a lease from the Maryon Wilson family. The partnership was amicably dissolved in October 1921 when Robertson took over the equity and became sole proprietor. The school closed in 1934 and the land it occupied was developed by the municipality.

The Robertson children who lived at Paragon House included: Gilbert (1873-1922) and Dudley Maryon, both of whom were educated at the Blackheath Proprietary School; Arthur William Gerard, Spencer Duncan Charles and Lionel Montague (1881-1948). The girls were saddled with extraordinary and lengthy names: Helena Kindeace Perceval Charlton Cruikshank Robertson (1869-1969), who married Admiral John Bridges Eustace (1861-1947); and Amy Orkney Stracatheo Robertson, who married George Bankes, of Winstanley Hall, Lancashire, and Balconie Castle, near Invergordon.

1883-1890
Franz Briessmann: timber merchant

Briessmann, who was born in Germany in about 1843, suffered from the inability of the clerks who kept the local records to spell his name properly. His first name was sometimes anglicised to Frank. The form used here is probably correct. Before moving to Paragon House, Briessmann and his wife Sophia lived at No 57 Blackheath Park from 1873 to 1875, and then at No 55 Kidbrooke Park Road until 1882.

1891 enumerated census return: house empty

1892-1893
Mrs Joanna Ballard (1834-1920)

Mrs Ballard, who was born in Dalkeith, Scotland, was the widow of Maj.-Gen. John Archibald Ballard (1829-1880), of No 49 Shooters Hill Road, where she was still living in 1885. By 1901 she was residing at No 11 Cheyne Walk, Chelsea, with her brother, Sir Colin Campbell Scott-Moncrieff, KCSI (1836-1916), then the Under-Secretary of State for Scotland. Joanna ended her days at No 17 Waldegrave, Twickenham, where she lived with her daughter (one of seven children), also Joanna. Mrs Ballard died in the summer of 1920, aged 86.

1894-1910
Sir Alexander Davidson Grierson, 9th Bt, JP (1858-1912)
Paragon House was Grierson's London residence and his home was at Rockhall, in his native shire of Dumfries where he was a JP. The estate was substantial but, as with the Robertsons', was gradually whittled away and the family house is now a hotel. Grierson was a career soldier, serving in the 3rd Battalion of the King's Own Scottish Borderers as Major and, later, as an honorary Lieutenant-Colonel. He served in the South Africa War, being mentioned in despatches. In 1882 he had married Fanny (sometimes written Fannie) (d. c.1940), daughter of Major George White, RMLI (1825-1902), of No 100 St John's Park. There were three sons: Robert G. W., Alexander and Frederick (d.1919). Once the boys were packed off to Uppingham School, Lady Grierson, in May 1896, was sufficiently impressed with their governess to recommend her to local families seeking such assistance. Grierson's family claimed ancient aristocratic lineage, with descent from Gilbert, second son of Malcolm, 11th Lord of MacGregor, who died in 1374. This Gilbert took the name of Grierson by a charter of 1400. The family was granted the Baronetcy of Nova Scotia in 1685. Sir Alexander Grierson's entry in Who's Who (as customary, written by himself) was brief.

The line descended eventually through the second son because Robert Gilbert White (1883-1957), 10th Bt, had only one son: Richard Douglas (1912-1987), 11th Bt, who died unmarried. .. The most recent holder of the title Sir Michael John Bewes Grierson, 12th bart, inherited the title (but none of the estates) from his cousin in 1987. Michael (b 1921) died in March 2008 and with him the barony became extinct. Michael's father, Lieut.-Col. Alexander George William Grierson (1884-1951), a career soldier with the Royal Marines and, later, with Admiralty Intelligence, was the second son of Sir Alexander and spent much of his boyhood at Paragon House.

1911-1924
Lawrence Clark (1862-1925): stockbroker

Clark was the son of Alexander Clark, of Forest Hill. After education at the Mercers' School, he started work in the City, eventually becoming senior partner with McAnally, Inglis & Littlejohn, stockbrokers. He was much engaged in local charity work, especially with the West Greenwich Working Lads' Institute. Clark, who had lived previously at The Nook, No 95 Belmont Hill, and then at No 4 Church Terrace, was married to Annie Belton (d.1965).

After Lawrence Clark's death, Mrs Clark lived, briefly, at No 2 The Paragon (q.v.) and then at No 116 Westcombe Park Road. Their daughter, Kathleen, died three months after her father, on 26 March 1925, aged only 20.

1926
Miss Burke

1926-1928
William Richard Williams (No 1a): hotelier

Mrs Alice Mary Colley, widow of P. Colley (No 1b)

1926 lease: Mrs Annie Harrison, owner and tenant

1928-1940 *Paragon Hotel*
Proprietors: **William, and Annie Harrison** (manageress)
Also of Nos 9 and 10 The Paragon (*Leven's Private Hotel*)

In January 1938 Mr and Mrs Harrison added No 109 Blackheath Park to their boarding-house business. It was a useful addition, in that Paragon House and Nos 9 and 10 The Paragon were rendered useless in 1941 as a result of enemy action. During its time as the Paragon Hotel, the building was much used for private parties and wedding receptions. Also, the Harrisons

encouraged its use as a social centre, with bridge and tennis clubs (the Arcadia Club of 1931). Its bar was an attractive resort for those who felt that public houses were not quite part of their social interest.

March 1941 Severely damaged

1946-1947: *Restored and converted into flats.*
Among the first residents after the conversion were the artist John Mansbridge (1901-1981) and his wife, Marjorie (1900-1994). Mansbridge, who taught at Goldsmiths College, earned a reputation as one of the artists working on posters for London Transport, especially the London Underground.

Another early flat occupier in the restored house was Sir George Rostrevor-Hamilton, who was here from 1952 to 1959 and then moved to Flat 5, No 8 The Paragon.

No 2 South Row – Bryan House

This house and Paragon House had been built by May 1791 when both were offered on the open market as carcases ready for fitting. The house was substantial, supposedly 25 rooms, and had a huge garden and substantial stable block. Until modern times it was believed that the property had once matched Paragon House and had been extended during the 19th century. The recent identification of an early 19th-century unattributed contemporary watercolour (reproduced in this book) shows that not to have been the case.

A drawing by Michael Searles of a house that was the mirror image of Paragon House (labelled 'for Mr Delight') may indicate that the original intention was for a pair of matching houses, standing like sentinels over the carriageway to the derelict mansion and overgrown park of the late Sir Gregory Page. This has romantic appeal but it is unlikely that either Cator or Searles would have indulged in romantic fantasies. The carriageway – a useful facility – was to be retained and eventually named, firstly, Church Road, and then Pond Road.

The Land Tax and Lewisham parish Highway Surveyors' record book note a Mr John Wells in a substantial house in the close vicinity for the year 1798 but his name does not appear again, and the Land Tax record notes William Wells (sic). If the first-mentioned Mr Wells is the shipbuilder of the period, then he could have afforded the property. John Wells (1761-1818) was the son of William Wells (1729-1805), shipbuilder of Deptford, Rotherhithe and Blackwall. The company's origins stretched back to the mid-17th century and it built a large number of substantial ships for the Royal Navy and the East India Company. The business was inherited by John and his brother William (1768-1847) and flourished until the end of the 17th century. For many years the family lived at the Manor House, Crooms Hill.

As it happened, the first known occupant of No 2 South Row was Mrs Margaret Bryan and her name was attached to the house until its virtual destruction in March 1941.

1799-1807 or 1808
Mrs Margaret Bryan (*fl.*1765-1815): author and schoolmistress

Mrs Bryan is probably one of the most interesting and unusual people to have lived in South Row. Little is known about her background and social life – there is an inadequate entry in the *Dictionary of National Biography* – but something can be gleaned from her teaching activities and from the remarkable textbooks she wrote. Mrs Bryan – her husband's name is not known (but see below) – came to attention with the publication, in 1797, of a book on astronomy, which was based on the lectures she delivered at her seminary for young women. One of the delights of the book – well subscribed and much praised by her supporters – was the frontispiece depicting the extremely attractive Mrs Bryan and two of her teenage daughters. She seems to have enjoyed connections with Margate as well as Blackheath but whether the seminary was in South Row by 1797 cannot be established. By 1799 it was here and remained until about 1807 or 1808. Mrs Bryan's enthusiasm for mathematics and astronomy not only led to more books (in 1806 and 1815) but the erection of a wooden-framed observatory on top of the Blackheath house. Mrs Bryan is known to have left the parish by 1810 but evidence points to a departure a little earlier.

There are two credible hypotheses on the life and times of Mrs Bryan. The first, plausible, is that Ann Waller (born at St John's, Margate, in 1748) married Michael Bryan at St Pancras Old Church in 1773. This could mean that Margaret Bryan was related through marriage to Ann Waller/Bryan. Some, however, have suggested that Margaret may have been the wife/widow of John Nesbit Bryan, who died in an accident in his carriage in 1799, but at the time he was living at No 2 Lloyds Place, Blackheath. It seems unlikely that he was residing in one house and his wife (as she still was in1798) in the mansion on South Row.

It is also of interest to note that the Revd Sir Charles Townshend Waller, Bt (1771-1830), resident at No 5 South Row from 1805 to 1808, was a subscriber to one of Mrs Bryan's textbooks. He was the son of Sir Robert Waller, of Co. Tipperary. Charles Waller was a graduate of Trinity College, Dublin. On his death the barony was extinguished.

The Times notes in June 1830: 'On the road to France' the marriage at St George's Church, Hanover Square, of Mr T Bickerdike, of Burrage House, near Woolwich, to Mrs Bryan, widow of the late John Bryan, of Park Place, Kennington.

Margaret was a subscriber to Thomas Noble's collection of poems: Blackheath: *A Didactic and Descriptive Poem in Five Cantos'*, in 1808 Mrs Bryan's subscription for two copies may have been influenced by Noble's inclusion of two verses dedicated to her, her achievements, and her beauty. Comparing her to one of the muses, Noble wrote:

On earth, in human form, she now is seen: / in form expressive of her race above: / All Science knows her, and reveres its queen, / Learns Nature's laws, and how the planets move. / This [Blackheath] she selects her seat in Britain's isle: / Here on the softer sex bestows her care. / Hence Science shall be armed with Beauty's smile, / And Love shall all his spoils with Knowledge share.

Another verse moves even closer to revealing Noble's fixation on Margaret Bryan:

Presumptuous Pen, that durst essay to write / The name of her, who rules the orbs of Light! / Dost thou not see thy feeble letters fade, / Awed by the word their blending form had made: / Sinking, all conscious of deserved disgrace, / While a bright constellation takes their place? / In Stars she deigns to date the rolling year, / With Stars she writes the volume of the sphere / By which the Sun preserves his endless way, / Leads the bright seasons and directs the day. / Cease then, thou foolish Pen, thy fruitless aim: / Stars are the rightful symbols of her name.

Bryan House, Blackheath, was put on the market in 1807 (and further advertised in 1808), by which time Mrs Bryan seems to have moved or concentrated her resources on her new educational boarding establishment at No 27 Lower Cadogan Place, near Hyde Park Corner.According to the *Dictionary of National Biography* she moved to Margate and it is suggested that she may have died there about 1815. But there is no trace of her name in the Margate parish records from 1810 to 1820. She may have remarried but, if so, not in that town within those dates.

The subscription lists for her books of lectures and essays, often illustrated by her own hand, show not only considerable support from her neighbours in the Paragon and South Row, but also the names of some of her pupils. The Misses Atkins, Bailey, E. Grant, Harvey, Mann, Newport, Radley, Read and Robertson all bought copies of the Lectures on Natural Philosophy. Her final known work was *The Comprehensive Astronomical and Geographical Class Book*, which was being advertised in November 1815.

26 June 1807: *The Times* advertisement:

Capital residence with an early possession. By Messrs Skinner, Dyke & Co, at Garraway's, on Tuesday July 16th, at 12 o'clock. A valuable leasehold estate near The Paragon, a most desirable part of Blackheath, bordering on the late Sir Gregory Page's park and opposite the Royal Park, comprising an excellent commodious dwelling house, offices, garden and paddock, in the occupation of Mrs Bryan. The premises are erected, fitted up and finished in a superior manner, containing a capital hall, a music room 50 feet by 20 feet, a drawing room

31 feet by 20, a sitting room and a study, ten principal bedchambers and dressing rooms, servants' chambers and every convenient domestic office, double coach house, four stall stable, court yard, pleasure garden and paddock, the whole forming a most respectable residence. Held for 72 years at a ground rent of £15.12.0 [£15.60]. To be viewed 14 days preceding the sale by tickets which may be had, with particulars, of Messrs Skinner, Dyke & Co., Aldersgate Street; particulars may also be had at the Green Man, Blackheath; and at the place of sale.

21 October 1808: *The Times* advertisement:

Blackheath, 5 miles from town, Family residence with pleasure grounds and paddock. By Mr Bates, at Garraway's on Tuesday, November 1st, at 12 o'clock. A valuable leasehold residence containing a dining parlour 31 feet by 16, drawing room 30 feet by 20 feet, a ballroom or music room 50 feet by 20, sitting room and study, ten principal bed chambers, servants' apartments and every domestic office, laundry, double coach house, 4-stall stable, courtyard, pleasure ground and field. The house is erected in a most substantial manner, judiciously planned, fitted up and finished in a superior style, abounding with every convenience requisite to the accommodation and comfort of a large establishment, situate near The Paragon, in that much admired part of Blackheath, commanding delightful varied views of Shooters Hill and the rich fertile counties of Kent, Surrey and Essex; and the proximity to the metropolis renders it equally desirable for a banker, merchant etc. whose attention is often required in town, blending in one establishment the benefits of a town and country residence. The estate is leasehold, held for a long term at a low ground rent. To be viewed by tickets to be had of Mr Bates, 5 Welbeck Street, Cavendish Square.
2 January 1809: *The Times* advertisement:

Seminaries (sic), to be sold by private contract at Blackheath, Kent. A most valuable lease-hold estate, consisting of a commodious dwelling house containing three rooms of very large dimensions and two smaller ones on the ground floor, sleeping rooms for 10 to 100 pupils. The situation remarkably healthy and the accommodation peculiarly adapted to a large and residential seminary. Proximity to the metropolis renders this estate equally eligible to a Banker's or a merchant's family, uniting the advantages of a town and country residence. For particulars, enquire of Mr Walton [the lodge keeper] near The Paragon, Blackheath.

1809-1811
Captain (later Rear-Admiral) John Hardy Godby, RN (d.1856)

The naval career of Godby was not spectacular but indicated a gentle climb over 20 years, from June 1794 when he entered the service to his elevation from Lieutenant to Captain. The rank of Rear-Admiral may have been a retirement bonus to ensure a better pension. He served on *The Experiment* in September 1800, soon after his commission as a Lieutenant.

Godby's command followed when he took over the *HMS Bolla* in March 1808. He seems to have ended his active service on *HMS Prospero*, on which he served from November 1809 to August 1814. His captaincy came in June 1814.

He was married, firstly, to Mrs Mary Ann (née Palmer?) (1785-1830). Their children included John Palmer Godby (1809-1854) and twins Hesther and Maryanne born in 1811. (Hesther died in July 1812.) A distressing number died in early childhood. The parish registers record the death of Eleanor Andrews, aged 28, of Bryan House, in January 1816, which may indicate that some of the Godbys were still living here at that date. Eleanor was the sister of Catherine Andrews who became, on 24 April 1832, the second wife of Captain Godby. However, the rate books note Mrs Palmer, Mary Ann Godby's sister, as the householder in 1817.

The Greenwich parish rate books show that Godby was the owner of No 32 Gloucester Circus in the years 1811 to 1820. He died in the winter of 1856, at Kingston, Surrey.

1811-1819
Mrs Hesther Palmer (1766-1853)

Mrs Palmer's name is given in the 1811/12 edition of Holden's *Directory of London* as well as in the Lewisham parish rating records of 1817 and 1818. It seems likely that she shared Bryan

House with relatives – the property was large enough – as well as continuing to use it as a school. The Godby family would have suffered the lack of a father for many months, if not years, so the arrangement would have been sensible. The parish records note the death here of Fanny Mary Deborah Davies, aged 15, in December 1818. She would have been a pupil if, as is likely, the building was in school use at the time. Hesther Palmer moved to No 115 Maze Hill, where she lived from 1820 until her death in 1853.

1820-1841
Miss Rebecca Truman Nightingale (1791-1850): ***Boarding School for Girls***

Miss Nightingale's school had been established here by 1821 because the parish records of that year note that there was a pew reserved for the pupils at St Mary's parish church. She almost certainly took over the business established by Mrs Palmer (see above) and sometimes Miss Nightingale's school is listed as at the Paragon. Clearly, this was a form of easy identification – there is no evidence that she ever occupied a Paragon house per se. Rebecca joined a number of local causes: she was a member of the Lewisham and Blackheath Benevolent Society in 1826, which was set up '... to afford relief and nourishment in all cases of sickness, and particularly to poor married women during their confinement ...' No doubt Rebecca's pupils took calves'-foot jelly and other nourishing foods to 'the ... industrious sick and aged poor'. Such charity did not prevent Miss Nightingale being robbed, in March 1835, by her ex-footman.

It is fortunate that the school was still in business at Bryan House in April 1841 because the 1841 census return indicates the size of the establishment: as well as Rebecca, who was in her fifties, there were Mary and Rebecca Nightingale, both 15 and possibly her nieces, as well as 22 other female pupils aged between nine and 15, and six female servants.

After 1841 there is no trace locally of Miss Nightingale and the school had certainly left Bryan House. In fact, Rebecca retired from business and moved to No 16 Clapham Park Terrace where she stayed until her death in the winter of 1850. She died a spinster and was generous and even-handed in her will, leaving her estate in equal proportions to her brothers and two nieces, Rebecca and Amelia, who lived with her. She also left £100 in consuls (Government stock) 'to my kind friend' Hesther Palmer, of Maze Hill (see above).

1843-1861
Edward Willoughby (1797-1873): solicitor

Willoughby was qualified as a solicitor and his practice was principally to act as lawyers to the Duchy of Lancaster. He was also a High Bailiff of the Authority and Liberty of Westminster. These duties were probably ceremonial but his official activities did not prevent Willoughby from taking part in local concerns. He was a member of the Blackheath Improvement Association and the volunteer superintendent on the east side of the Heath concerned with matters like clearing litter, dredging junk out of the ponds and ensuring that encroachers did not steal the gravel, turf and sand. In April 1861, the whole Willoughby family (which was considerable) took temporary accommodation with Edward's brother, Henry, at Lydia House in Dartmouth Grove. This was prior to their removal to No 3 Lancaster Place, near Waterloo Bridge – no doubt a more convenient address for Willoughby's professional concerns. The family finally settled at No 24 Warwick Square, near Victoria, where Edward was, by then, described as a landowner.

Four of the boys were educated at the Blackheath Proprietary School, enrolling even after the move to Waterloo Bridge. The children living at Bryan House with Edward and Lucy Willoughby were: Edward J.; William A.; Emily; Charles C.; Arthur Henry; Agnes J.; Robert F. Also living there in 1851 were Mrs Willoughby's mother, Mary Williams, aged 81, a widow of a Sergeant-at-Law, and Lucy Williams, a niece of 15, born at the Cape of Good Hope. Six servants, including a footman, were in residence to attend to the family's needs. Edward Willoughby died at Truro, Cornwall, in the spring of 1873, aged 77. His widow, Lucy, died in July 1882 at the London home.

1861 enumerated census return: William Brooker, bricklayer. Resident caretaker while the house was empty.

1862-1869
Thomas Stirling Begbie (1822-1899): merchant

Thomas Begbie, the son of Thomas Begbie (1782-1872) and Mary, née Hamilton, first appears in the London commercial directories as an engineer with premises at No 4 Mansion House Place, Cannon Street. By 1861 he was also trading as an iron merchant and by the 1870s was advertising himself as a shipowner and merchant. By 1874 he had moved his offices to No 36 Walbrook. His stay at Bryan House was not lengthy and he seems to have left the district during 1870.

Begbie reappears at No 15 St Germans Place in 1876 where he and his wife, Gertrude, née du Verner (1821-1893), and their two daughters – Gertrude and Emily – were to live until 1883 when they moved to Kensal Green. The business remained at No 36 Walbrook until at least 1878.

1870-1881
George Russell (1822-1898): shipbroker

Russell and his wife, Justina, lived most of their lives in the vicinity. He was the son of Samuel Russell, a poulterer of Stockwell Street. By profession he was a ship and steamship insurance broker and maintained his offices in Fenchurch Street until 1876. From 1882 until 1888 he may have lived at No 2 Brandram Road (a George Russell is listed in the directories for that address).

Tragedy struck twice while George Russell was living at Bryan House: his wife, Justina, died before 1880; and their only son, Frank Gordon Russell, had committed suicide at the age of 22 in December 1877. The daughters at Bryan House were Jessie, Louise, Annie, and Amy. George Russell died in November 1898 at Southfields. His sister, Henrietta Maria (1819-1872), married Charles Hart (1811-1863), licensee of the Trafalgar Tavern, Greenwich. Hart's time there made him a rich man and after his death Henrietta was able to afford a substantial mansion: Newfield, (No 9) Pond Road.

1882-1895
Job Ashton (1830-1897): commissioning merchant

Ashton was the son of Job Ashton, a corn and salt dealer in business in City Road and Caledonian Road from the mid-1830s until 1860. When Job junior (a graduate of St Edmund Hall, Oxford) started his business is not known but it seems likely to have been in the 1860s when he was working for Edwards, Eastty & Co., at 19 Old Broad Street, and was a member of the Baltic Exchange. By the 1870s the company was Edwards, Ashton & Eldrige; it is likely that Ashton had retired by 1882, on his move to Bryan House. His son, Walter Stanley, was educated at the Blackheath Proprietary School; his daughter, Rosina Mary ('Cissie'), was one of the first pupils at the Blackheath Conservatoire of Music when it opened in 1881. Ashton moved to No 5 Shooters Hill Road in 1895 and died there in January 1897. His widow, Ann Rosina, continued to live at this address for a year. Members of the family remained in Blackheath until the late 1930s. The family were away on the night of the census of 1891.

1896 Empty

1898-1907
John Allen Bowron (1843-? 1920)
Sidney Bowron (1863-c.1940)

The Bowron brothers were leather merchants, importing sheepskins from New Zealand, with substantial works at Bermondsey and Crayford. The company went bankrupt in September 1915 – something not easy to do in their business during the Great War. Creditors were paid 2.5d (1p) in £1 out of assets judged to be only £2,000. By then the Bowrons had moved to Falsgrave House, No 19 Morden Road. After John's death, at Croydon, Sidney (the younger brother) moved to No 55 Blackheath Park. He was still alive (living in Christchurch, New Zealand) in October 1940 when his wife, Fanny (1864-1940), died at No 51 Lee Terrace.

The Bowron story is remarkable because the brothers managed to live in two of the largest houses in Blackheath, on the Cator Estate. Despite this, they ran up colossal debts for the company. This led to John Allen – by then in his seventies – receiving an 18-month prison sentence for criminal fraud in 1912. Sidney was found not guilty on a technicality but the whole drama must have been wounding for their families. The local press said not a word but *The Times*, in particular, printed a detailed record of the formal court hearings.

1908-1913 Empty: no names given in the commercial directories

1914-1919 No rates paid for this period, probably because the house was in use for approved war work.

The Khaki Club
A social and rest club for soldiers training in the Blackheath area or in transit, opened on 21 November 1914. It was founded and run by Miss Dulcie Ommaney (see below). More details of the Khaki Club will be found in Chapter 5. When the Khaki Club closed, on 25 October 1919, Miss Ommaney said that she hoped to reopen the building as a residential club for ex-service-men. This did not happen but Miss Ommaney remained at Bryan House after the Club closed.

1919-1923
Miss Dulcie Mildred Ommaney (1875-1925)

Fourth daughter of Lieut.-Col. Edward Lacon Ommaney, CSI (1834-1914). Miss Ommaney died in January 1925 after a fall from a window. Her last surviving sister, Elizabeth Capel Ommaney, died at Wimbledon in January 1947.

It was during this time that Bryan House drifted into use as a boarding-house/hotel – more than half a dozen of those eligible to vote are listed here in 1922-23. Mrs Clough (see below) was a resident in 1919 but not, perhaps, the proprietor until 1924. Dulcie Ommaney's brother – Hugh Travers Ommaney – was resident here in 1923.

1919-1925
1925-1931
Mrs Norah Farrar (ex Clough) (1881-1970)

Daughter of Frank Ironmonger (1849-1926) and widow of patent agent Charles Eric Clough (1887-1915), a Major in the London Army Service Corps who was killed in action. Norah Clough was a friend of Dulcie Ommaney and worked as her assistant at the Khaki Club. Mrs Clough married Walter Frederick Farrar in October 1925. She died in 1970 in Eastbourne at the good age of 90.

1925-1931
Walter Frederick (Nick) Farrar, MC (1894-1934)

Organising Secretary of the Legion of Frontiersmen. Farrar (who died in June 1934, aged 40) served in the (Royal) Tank Corps during the Great War. He was the son of the Rt Revd Walter Farrar (1865-1916), Bishop of British Honduras. During Farrar junior's time at Bryan House, it passed into use as a private hotel.

In June 1927 a bazaar for the benefit of All Saints' Church was held in the garden and was due to be opened by Lilian Baylis (1874-1937), founder of the Old Vic Theatre and the Sadler's Wells Opera Company. Unfortunately, she failed to arrive because she was unwell.

Among the 'permanent' residents at the Bryan House Hotel were R. Macdonald Wilson, AMICE (1868-1929), an explosives expert; and Major Philip Montague, MC, RA, Honorary Secretary of the Blackheath Lawn Tennis Club.

1931-1940
Mrs Margaret Spence: Bryan House Private Hotel

During the 1920s and 1930s the number of residents at Bryan House grew. The voters' lists in

October 1937 give 17 names and, additionally, there would have been some residents not eligible to vote. Some were married couples; a few remained residents for many years, others stayed briefly.

In 1940, Miss (*sic*) J. M. Spence moved to Glebe Lodge, No 11 Lee Terrace.

March 1941: *Badly damaged by enemy action. Declared uninhabitable by April 1941. Ruins demolished later that year. Site developed with prefabricated houses during 1946 and 1947. In August 1948 Lewisham Borough Council acquired 293 ft of the back garden by compulsory purchase for the erection of municipal flats (see Chapter 9).*

No 3 South Row

A semi-detached house with No 4. The premises were sometimes held as one. The early records for these buildings (until 1837) are very sparse and no early leases have been found.

1801-1804
Mrs Cope (or 'occupier' according to Land Tax records)

1805-1806
Thomas Millington (d.1808): fanlight manufacturer of Bishopsgate

Thomas died on 14 November 1808, a little before the marriage of his daughter, at Bishopsgate. A Thomas Millington was a named as a visitor to the Blackheath Golf Club in 1821 and this man could have been the son: a Thomas Millington, merchant, is listed in commercial directories with offices at New City Chambers, Bishopsgate, in 1809 and 1810. In 1821 a public notice from the High Court sought claimants against the will of Jane Millington, widow, who died in August 1812.

1806
John Serjeant: bricklayer

Possibly one of Michael Searles' creditors, Mr Serjeant, of Dockhead, Bermondsey, may have taken the lease on this house as a security for his investment.

1808
Dr Rogers

1815-1818
James Burgess (d.1833)

James Burgess, a corn lighterman and granary keeper, was in business at Horsleydown Lane, Southwark, from at least 1804 until the 1830s. He traded with his brother, William Burgess. James, while living in the Paragon, and enjoyed a pew at the parish church of St Mary's, Lewisham, from October 1815

1825
William Hunter: possibly the solicitor, of Bedford Row

The reference to Hunter at this address appears in the Land Tax returns in 1825.

1829-1833
Samuel Granger (1781-1855): master lighterman

The son of Benjamin Granger, lighterman. Samuel moved to No 6 Eliot Place in 1833, sharing the house with East India Company Captain Peter Cameron (1777-1843), where he remained until 1844, the year his wife, Elizabeth Penelope, died. Granger was an enthusiastic member of the Blackheath Golf Club and was its Captain in 1838. He married Miss Jane Lewis, 30 years his junior, in February 1846. She survived him by 45 years, not departing until June 1900.

1835-1837
Alexander Dobie (1796-1876): solicitor

A parliamentary and Scottish agent, Dobie, whose professional career was very long, was in chambers at 5 Palsgreave Place (gone), Temple Bar, in the 1830s. He moved his home from Blackheath to No 4 Hyde Park Terrace, Kensington Gore, in 1837 and, in the early 1850s, to No 2 Lancaster Place, Strand, where he was still in business (in name at least) as late as 1875. Alexander Dobie, like his predecessor in the house, was an enthusiastic golfer and a member of Blackheath Golf Club from 1825. During his Blackheath years he was the club's Captain in 1830 when he won its spring medal; he also won the summer medal in 1831 and 1836. During his membership, Dobie was affectionately known as the 'Attorney-General'.

Professionally, Dobie seemed ageless, his name appearing from time to time attached to property sales as late as 1875 when he was entering his ninth decade. One notable local disposal was the Beehive Brewery, in Greenwich South Street, in July 1870. Dobie was also an active freemason, helping to lead the festivities at a massive Masonic festival in April 1869.

Dobie and his wife produced a number of children between 1826 and 1838. Daughter Elizabeth Mary married solicitor John Eyre Furiss, of Endcliffe, Sheffield, in April 1861 and spent the rest of her life with him, near York. During this time she not only managed to reduce her age by 10 years, but to alter her birthplace in the records from St Clement Danes on the Strand, in London, to 'Yorkshire'. All very curious.

1839-1859
John Bowen (1785-1859): flax and linen merchant

Bowen was an importer of linen and flax, with offices at No 3 Budge Row and a warehouse at No 5 Barge Yard, Bucklersbury. Born in Pembroke, Bowen may have retired after 1845 when his name ceases to appear in the commercial section of the London directories. He lived previously at No 20 Dartmouth Row and in his early business life was a corn chandler, with offices at Whitechapel. While at South Row he was a member of the Blackheath Improvement Association. John died at the Marina, St Leonard's-on-Sea, Sussex, on 1 November 1859.

1859-1871
Mrs Elizabeth Stubbs Bowen (1792-1873): widow of the above

There were only two children living with the Bowens, at Blackheath: James Hill Bowen, who became Chief Clerk in the Civil Service Design Office and lived at No 10 Eliot Place from1856 to 1866; and Caroline Sophia. Caroline married Edward Lawes (1817-1852), a barrister who was Chairman of the Metropolitan Commission for Sewers. On his premature death, at the present No 48 Kirkdale, in Sydenham, Caroline moved back to live with her parents at No 3 South Row. Their son, Edward Brown Lawes, after education at the Blackheath Proprietary School, also entered the law, but as a solicitor. Mrs Elizabeth Stubbs Bowen, the daughter of Dr Thomas Forbes Leith (1746-1819), of Crooms Hill and Whitehaugh, Aberdeen, died here on 25 March 1873, aged 81.

1874-1878
Mark Shattock (1838-1886): tutor

Shattock, the son of Mark Shattock of Hatcham, New Cross, was educated at Christ's Hospital school and Pembroke College, Cambridge, achieving a BA in 1860. From 1869 to 1872 he was an assistant master at the Blackheath Proprietary School (where his sons were educated) and he lived at No 21 Glenton Road. Thereafter he set up as a private tutor. Clearly, his business did not flourish and he was declared bankrupt in June 1878. The contents of the house had to be sold in May 1878 to meet his debts.

1879 Empty

1880-1882
William Edwards (1812-1885): accountant

Edwards, a public accountant and liquidator, and a Fellow of the Accountants' Institute, who was born in Bristol, worked first in Birmingham before establishing himself at Gresham Street in 1850. His offices remained in the City until the 1880s and his home for much of that time was in Camberwell and then at Copers Cope House, in Beckenham. His wife was Susan (sometimes written Sarah) of Walworth, and they had at least one son (also William) and six daughters: Maria (born Birmingham), Mary Ann, Florence, Maud, Louise and Alice Ruskin.

Edwards may have moved to No 3 South Row on his retirement but nothing further of great significance has been discovered about him, either socially or professionally. Some of the family, at least, moved to Oakbank, Speldhurst, Tunbridge Wells, where William senior died in the winter of 1885, and William junior married Dolly La Lacheur, in October 1891. Alice Ruskin Edwards married Walter James Cousins, of No 83 Shooters Hill Road. Cousins, an Oxford graduate and destined for the teaching profession, was the son of Stephen Cousins (d.1885)

1884-1903
Mrs Catherine E. Borrett (1824-1912)
(sometimes written as Barrett)

Catherine Borrett was the widow of Thomas Borrett, of Great Yarmouth, Norfolk. Their children included (Major-General) Herbert Charles Borrett, CB (1841-1919), Annie L. S. and Frank Collingwood Hall Borrett, who became a solicitor. The family lived at No 4 Cresswell Park from 1877 to 1884. Annie and Frank were living at No 3 South Row in 1891 and 1901. At some time the entire family moved to Wyesham House, in Monmouth, where they were all still living in 1911. Catherine Borrett died at Monmouth in the winter of 1912, aged 88.

1904-1907 No names given in the street directories
1908-1913
George Wedgbury Fawkes (1874-1956): tobacco manufacturer's clerk

Mrs Charlotte (Lottie) Fawkes (1872-1949): boarding-house keeper

George and Lottie moved to Brighton where they lived until the end of their days. Their son, Cyril Wedgbury Fawkes, died in March 1926, aged but 29 years.

Residents included:
1908-1909
Mrs Sarah E. Hicks (1857-1909)

The wife of George Mitchinson Hicks (see below); previously at No 5 South Row

1909-1911
George Mitchinson Hicks, MA (1852-1935): tutor and crammer

Hicks had conducted a private cramming establishment in the locality, at a number of addresses. He started in Blackheath at No 4 South Row (q.v.), from where he operated from 1880 to 1883, and then moved to Lee High Road. Eventually, he returned to Blackheath and set up his plate at No 3 Belmont Grove, in partnership with C. II. Martin, MA, from 1897 to 1906. A brief spell at Granville House, Granville Park (probably too large for the volume of business he attracted) dictated a move back to South Row, this time to No 3 as a tenant of George Fawkes. Hicks was still living in this house (along with many other boarders) until at least 1911, when he moved to Hastings. He turns up again as a resident of No 4 South Row from at least 1922 until 1924.

1914-1921
Mrs Jemima Porter (1851-1933).

Later at No 43 Blackheath Park. Mrs Porter, who was born in Australia, was the widow of Revd John Robinson Porter (1839-1914), of No 10 Vanbrugh Park. For many years Porter was the Vicar of Wartling, Sussex.

1921-1932
Edward Baker (1888-1932): of Lever Bros
(see also No 4 South Row)

1932-1940
Mrs Winifred M. Baker (née Shingles): board residence

Mrs Baker also kept a house at Worthing. After 1945 she lived at No 4 Pond Road. Among the many residents who came and went, the following are of interest:

1921-1938 Edward and Margaret Franklin Corner

1922-1930 George Clarrise Dobson (1879-1930)
Parliamentary draughtsman; son of Captain Charles Meadows Dobson (1843-1909), of No 70 St John's Park.

1938 N. R. M. Janvrin
Honorary Treasurer of Air Defence Cadet Corps

Bombed March 1941. House demolished April 1941.

No 4 South Row

Alfred House (1836) or Homeleigh (by 1890)

1801-1807
Mrs Weatherall.

She may have been the lady of this name who lived at No 33 Tranquil Vale in the years 1798 to 1800.

1808-1811
Colonel James Viney:? Major-General by July 1830

Viney distinguished himself in Spain during the Peninsular War campaigns of 1808-14.

1814-1819
George William Young, Jnr (fl.1792-1822): broker

The son of George Young (1761-1823), of No 4 Grotes Buildings, Blackheath. He was probably the sibling of Adam Young (d.1846), of Vanbrugh's Field at Westcombe Park, and of Letitia, Ann Bryan and Frances Bentley Young. The brothers were in business together as merchants at No 3 Mildred's Court, Piccadilly. By 1822 George was trading on his own account at No 2 Pope's Head Alley, Cornhill. Young, who was a trustee of the New Cross Turnpike, married Mary Ann, daughter of John Bax, of Great Baddow, Essex, in December 1815. Confusingly, there were a number of men in the district at this period called Adam, George and John Young, making identification difficult from records which give only Blackheath as an address. Nevertheless, some fragments can be relied upon: for example, George's sister, Frances Bentley Young, married Charles Parr Burney, of the Manor House, Crooms Hill, in 1810, and Ann Bryan Young married Simeon Warner, of neighbouring Colonnade House, in 1811. Letitia married at Lewisham, in November 1818, the brewery magnate Charles Samuel Goodwyn. She survived until 1878, living for many years at No 62 Hyde Vale.

1825
Mr Knowles

1826-1835
Richard Humber (fl.1789-c.1851): merchant
(sometimes written as Robert Hunter)

Humber was born in Queenborough, on the Isle of Sheppey, Kent, whence his wife, Mary, came

and where three of his children were born. The third and fourth children were born at the Blackheath house: Henry, in 1831, and Charles in 1833.

The family enjoyed a pew at the parish church of St Mary, Lewisham, in September 1833, and Richard was qualified to vote in 1835.

Richard had previously lived at Alfred Place, Bedford Square. Humber's daughter, Adeline Pennal, married Joseph Henry Dart (1817-1887) of No 11 The Paragon (q.v.) in September 1842. In June 1835 Humber joined with Joseph Warter, of No 6 South Row, in a policy with the Sun Insurance Company. By 1841 the family were at Burton Street, Marylebone, and by 1851, by which time Humber was a widower, they lived at Upper Gower Street, Bloomsbury, close to his former home at Bedford Square. There is no trace of any family members after that and it may be that the Humbers emigrated.

1836-1843
Nicholas Wanostrocht (Felix) (1804-1876): cricketer and schoolmaster

It was Nicholas Wanostrocht who, allegedly (but see Humber, above), named this building Alfred House, after the school of the same name that had been established by his grandfather, also Nicholas (1745-1812), in Camberwell. Wanostrocht senior was of Belgian origins and a remarkable linguist. His school flourished but on the death of his son, Vincent, in January 1824, the enterprise passed to his grandson, the 20-year-old Nicholas. Unfortunately, the boy was by then embarked on the passionate interest that was to bring him down: cricket. He had studied the game under Harry Hampton, at Camberwell, and was to develop as a powerful left-hand batsman and a slow underarm left-hand bowler. He was playing at Lord's by 1828, and in the Gentlemen v. Players matches from 1831 to 1852

There can be little doubt that Nicholas Wanostrocht was one of England's most distinguished cricketers but one of nature's hopeless businessmen. He moved the school to Blackheath because, it was claimed, he needed a residential qualification to allow him to play for Kent. He was already appearing for the Blackheath Dartmouth Cricket Club in 1834, then the best local side. Because Felix (as he styled himself) was away so often playing cricket, the running of the school was usually left to his long-suffering wife, Elizabeth (née Heale; 1806-63) and her assistants.

Felix was not averse to giving the boy's holidays to watch important matches or cancelling lessons for cricket practice. The parents grew increasingly exasperated by his behaviour and the school roll dwindled, although the enumerated census return for 6/7 June 1841 indicates that there were 20 boys, between the ages of nine and 15, along with three teachers and four servants, at No 4 South Row. Wanostrocht was forced to close the school in 1843 and he moved to Heath Cottage, on Blackheath Hill, where he was adjudged bankrupt in October 1844.

An attempt to start another school, at Mayfield House at the south-east end of Maze Hill, did not succeed and, despite his efforts to establish himself as a portrait painter, Felix was in desperate circumstances. A scheme to improve his finances came with the publication of his monograph on cricket, *Felix on the Bat*, which he published in 1845, illustrated by himself. Although it ran to a number of editions, it did not make the money he expected. He was an inveterate inventor: the *catapulta* (for fielding practice), and tubular India-rubber gloves were his idea.

There are countless match reports in the local and sporting press through the 1830s and 1840s, from which it would seem that Felix would turn out for almost any team which cared to invite him. It is likely that he was paid appearance-money by some of the richer teams from time to time although – like Dr W. G. Grace – it was not unknown for him to be quickly dismissed or fail to take the number of wickets expected of him.

Eventually, he moved to Brighton where he remarried, after Elizabeth's death, at Peckham, in April 1863; he died at Wimborne, Dorset, in September 1876. Despite his extraordinary approach to life, Wanostrocht's family managed to survive without him. A son, Nicholas Gibbs Wanostrocht (1833-1895), became an insurance agent and lived at No 37 Vanbrugh Park until the mid-1850s. His daughter, Mary, in partnership with her aunt Agnes and cousin Elizabeth Heale, conducted various schools for girls in Blackheath until the 1880s. Felix's sister, Anne (1808-

1878), married the rich corn merchant Hayter Thornton Read (1800-1881) and lived firstly at No 8 West Grove and then at No 11 Granville Park.

1845-1860
Revd William Gambier Hawtayne, MA (Oxon) (1814-1884): clergyman without cure of souls, and schoolmaster

Wanostrocht's failure did not deter the next lessee of No 4 South Row from running a school. Hawtayne, born in Berkshire, was educated at Eton College and was a classics scholar of Balliol and Magdalen Hall, Oxford, taking his MA in 1842. In Blackheath he combined the task of educating boys with assisting at the Dartmouth Row chapel from time to time. In 1851 there were 10 lads in residence at South Row, many from the colonies or foreign parts: Rio de Janeiro, Cape of Good Hope, and so on – no doubt the sons of men away on business.

Hawtayne was assisted by Thomas Kimber, a BA of the relatively new University of London, to teach mathematics. William and his wife Caroline (née Martin) had only one child while at South Row, also called Caroline. Kimber (1818-1891) later opened his own academy at No 115 Lee Road where he was most successful in the teaching of mathematics and sciences.

Towards the end of the 1850s Hawtayne moved to Boulogne and the house was let: in 1857 to a Mr Ryssmans (for £54.12.0 [£54.60] for three months); and, in 1858 and 1859, to a Mr Nelson. In November 1860 the remainder of the lease (14 years) was offered for sale: the notices described the house as having 10 bedrooms, a large dining room and downstairs offices, as well as a good garden. The estate was in 'the most cheerful part of the Heath'. The number of bedrooms would indicate subdivision, perhaps made by Wanostrocht for the school. The taker is not known but the next resident was a retired army officer.

Hawtayne was appointed Acting Chaplain to the Military School of Music at Kneller Hall, Twickenham in 1862 and was to remain in service there until his retirement in 1880. He died on 26 May 1884.

1860-1861
Colonel Tudor Lavie (1807-1877)

A retired artillery officer in the East India Service, Lavie, who had served in the Madras station, stayed only briefly at South Row before moving eventually to No 32 Lee Park. One son – C. A. B. Lavie – was enrolled at the Blackheath Proprietary School by 1859; another, the much older William (1839-1891), was already a clerk in the Madras Civil Service. Lavie, and his wife, Emma Maria (née Wade), eventually moved to Queen Square, near Southampton Row, and afterwards to Colville Square, Westbourne Park, where he was living in 1877. While there were few men called Tudor Lavie at this time, a number served in the Indian Army and Civil Service and it is difficult to pin down who was who.

There is every reason to believe that our Tudor Lavie was the son of a similarly named army officer serving with the East India Company and/or Indian regiments.

1862-1866
John Charles Rees (1827-1903): solicitor and parliamentary agent

His offices were in Lincoln's Inn Fields, where he served a client base which included the South East Railway Company. He later set up as a parliamentary agent, in partnership as Dorington, Rees, Seager & Norton. Their offices were in Great George Street, close to the Houses of Parliament. Rees, his wife Sarah Ann (née Day) and their niece Emily Barnes, from Australia, moved to Addison Road, Kensington, where they were still living when Sarah died in 1884. Rees married again in the summer of 1886 and he and his new wife, Ellen Elizabeth Roberts, moved to Eliot Lodge, Sydenham Hill Road, where a daughter, Elaine, was born. It took five resident female servants to attend to the Rees family's needs. Eventually, they moved to No 36 Albemarle Road, Beckenham. Rees died in Eastbourne in the summer of 1903. Mrs Ellen Rees and her daughter Elaine then moved to Blakesley Avenue, Ealing.

1868-1869 and 1874-1878
George Barber: merchant (*fl.*1826-1881) *(sometimes written Baker or Barker)*

Barber, a member of the London Stock Exchange, lived at No 4 South Row for two brief periods: 1868-9 and 1874-8. The house was let in the interim. He had lived at Walton-on-Thames before coming to Blackheath, where he moved, firstly, to No 8 Grotes Place and then to No 3 Eliot Place. In the gap between his time at No 4 South Row the family – George, his wife Harriet W. and their five children – lived at Leamington Road Villas, in Paddington.

1869-1871
Thomas Paton (*fl.*1803-1876+)

Paton, by profession a bank manager, resided in Canada for some years, where all four of his sons were born, and may have returned to the UK on his retirement. His interest in the Blackheath area was sufficient to encourage him to buy three shares in the Proprietary School (in September 1869) and three of his sons were educated there: Arthur Blakesley, Charles James, and Henry John. All had left by July 1873, by which time the family was living at No 4 Brandram Road, where they remained until 1876. The eldest son, also called Thomas, set up as a landscape painter, and when married moved to No 8 Cambridge Villas, in Lewisham. He was not to enjoy much success at the easel, it seems, because by 1891 Thomas Paton Jnr was living in Richmond, Surrey, and working as an accountant, specialising in international investment.

1872-1873
John Walkden (1806-1876)

A skin, flannel, and drugget wholesaler, Walkden was the son of John Walkden of Lawrence Lane, Cheapside, who was in business by the 1830s as a flannel and baize supplier. This branch of the Walkden family had lived at Haverstock Hill, Hampstead, before moving briefly to South Row. They lived at No 99 Shooters Hill Road in the years 1874 and 1875.

Walkden died in September 1876, at No 6 Grotes Buildings. Perhaps because of his father's death, John junior joined Richard Witherby, of No 107 Morden Hill, in the latter's dried-fruit broking business. John was related to Samuel Walkden (1817-1878) of No 80 Shooters Hill Road, who was in a similar business.

1874-1878
George Barber (see above)

During this time he enrolled his boys, Basil Cadogan and George Sison Barber, at the Blackheath Proprietary School but both left at the end of 1874.

17 May 1879 Contents for sale

1880-1882
George Mitchinson Hicks (1852-1935): tutor

Hicks was to conduct a private cramming establishment at a number of addresses in the locality. He started in Blackheath at this address (combined with No 4) in 1880 but stayed only a couple of years before moving to the less stylish Lee High Road. While at No 4 he was assisted by his wife, Sarah (1857-1909), and three servants including a 17-year-old boots boy. There were only three resident students but some others may have attended during the day. Eventually, Hicks returned to Blackheath (more or less) and set up his plate at No 3 Belmont Grove, in partnership with C. H. Martin MA from 1897 to 1906.

A brief spell at Granville House, Granville Park (probably too large for the volume of business he attracted), dictated a move back to South Row, this time to No 3, as a tenant of Fawkes.

Hicks was still living in this house (along with many other boarders) until at least 1911, when he moved to Hastings. He later returned to Blackheath where he was again a resident at No 4 South Row from at least 1922 to 1924.
(See also No 3 South Row.)

1883-1888
William Edward Westrup (1834-1909)

Westrup was a miller, baker and flour factor, previously resident at No 20 Dartmouth Terrace (later styled No 1 Lewisham Hill). He moved to No 19 Glenton Road and then, in 1891, to No 27 Shooters Hill Road where he remained until at he died. The Westrup family were prominent in the farinaceous business: the company, trading in Lambeth as early as 1851 as Edward & Frederick Westrup, millers, was being managed by George Westrup (probably William's father) in the mid-1850s. They moved the business to Whitechapel where there were various companies with the Westrup name involved in baking and milling, including Henry & Joseph Westrup who were ship's biscuit brokers. By 1876 the company's office was at Millbank Street, Westminster. William, who was an Honorary Colonel in the Volunteer Brigade of the Royal West Kent Regiment, based at Holly Hedge House, left over £97,000 and the management of the company to his son, Charles J. Westrup.

1890-1903
Herbert Ford, FRIBA (1834-1903): architect

Ford's outstanding achievement as an architect was the design of over 400 office blocks and warehouses, through a time of great commercial expansion in London during the period 1870 to 1900. His offices were at No 21 Aldermanbury and his practice hugely successful (he left over £22,500). Among other schemes from his office were those for Nos 5-23 St Paul's Churchyard (1898). He warranted obituaries in The Builder and the *Journal of the Royal Institute of British Architects* when he died in 1903. The family previously lived in Erith. Mrs Susannah Jane Ford died in January 1893, aged 57. Herbert's son, Herbert Lloyd Ford (1869-1902), entered the profession and lived, briefly, in Ulundi Road, but predeceased his father. The last surviving member of the immediate family, Ada Susannah, died in 1950 aged 84. Other children living at South Row were Florine Henrietta, May and Violet, and Walter Cook Ford (1872-1916), a surveyor, who died in Canada.

One of the important social occasions in Blackheath in 1892 was the marriage, in July, of Florine Ford to Harold Blurton Norris, of Erith, a silk salesman. Harold was living at South Row in 1891.

A very pretty wedding took place on Thursday, 14th inst., at All Saints' Church, Blackheath, the bridegroom being Harold Blurton, son of Mr William Blurton Norris, of Trevethan, Erith, and the bride Florine Henrietta, third daughter of Mr Herbert Ford, of 'Homeleigh', South Row, Blackheath. The officiating clergy were Revd F. Gribbell, vicar of Ringmer, Lewes, and the Revd H. W. Snell, vicar of All Saints', Blackheath.

The bride, who was given away by her father, was attired in rich white Duchesse satin, the bodice arranged with lace; real orange blossom in the hair, and a lace veil. Her shower bouquet was the gifts of the bridegroom.

The four bridesmaids – the Misses May and Violet Ford (sisters of the bride) and the Misses Ethel and Winifred Norris (sisters of the bridegroom) – wore dresses of white surah, trimmed with white lace, white chip hats with white feathers and lace, and carried posies of white roses. They each wore a pearl brooch, the gift of the bridegroom. Mr J. Stephens acted as best man. After the ceremony a reception was held at 'Homeleigh', about 100 guests being present, when most delightful music was performed by the Misses Eisler, on the piano, harp and violin. Later in the afternoon Mr & Mrs Blurton Norris drove to London, en route for North Wales. The bride's travelling dress was of blue-grey cloth, trimmed with faile francaise and passementerie to match, black hat, with tips and black guipure lace over blue-grey ribbon. The refreshments and wedding cake were supplied by Messrs Buszard, of Oxford Street; and the costumes by Mrs Pearce, 2 South Vale-terrace, Blackheath. The presents, which were ninety in number, included a pearl bangle from the bridegroom to the bride; gold sleeve-links and a Gladstone bag from the bride to the bridegroom; a Collard pianoforte, Wheeler-Wilson sewing machine, and cheque from the parents of the bride; and a dining-room suite, cheque, case of dessert knives and forks, pearl and coral ring from the parents of the bridegroom.

The young couple settled at No 60 Coleraine Road where they remained until 1914 when they moved to Dartford Heath. Mrs Norris busied herself with helping to raise comfort funds during the South Africa War (1899-1902) but the family suffered a tragedy in the loss of their son, Harold Aubrey, who was killed in action in July 1917.

1904-1905
Miss Ada Susannah Ford (1866-1950)

Last surviving child of Herbert and Susannah Ford, later resident at No 39 St John's Park.

1906-1907
George A. Johnston

1908-1909
Revd William Harrison Rigg, MA (1850-1932)

Vicar of Anson, Sheffield, 1881 to 1906. He settled in Blackheath on retirement but, after a couple of years at South Row, moved to No 48 Blackheath Park, where he lived until 1931. He died at Hove, Sussex, in March 1932. His son, also William Harrison Rigg (1877-1966), was Vicar of Christ Church, East Greenwich, from 1913 to 1921, and Vicar at Beverley Minster from 1921 to 1936. He completed his career as Archdeacon of Bodmin and Canon of Truro.

1910-1932
George Frederick and Elizabeth Shingles (1865-1942): board residence

George Shingles' daughter, Winifred Marsden Shingles, married Edward Baker, of Birkenhead, in January 1920. The couple took No 3 South Row (next door) and Mrs Baker (who was widowed in 1932) was to live there until 1940. George (who was affectionately known as 'Gong-Gong') moved in with his daughter, Winifred, and both relocated to No 11 Lawn Terrace, Blackheath Village, when South Row was largely destroyed.

1925-1928 Henry Kelloch and **Bertha Mackay**

1932-1936
Mrs Irene Fergusson: board residence

1937-1941
Mrs Olga Fedrovna Madill (1894-1966): board residence
(sometimes written Modill)

In 1937 Mrs Madill provided creature comforts to at least 10 paying guests. After the bomb damage, the business was transferred to No 46 Lee Terrace, where it remained until at least 1951.

House badly damaged in enemy action in March 1941. Demolished April 1941.

No 5 South Row: Albany House

Nos 5 and 6 were the final pair of houses to be built in South Row as part of the original development. In subsequent years Nos 5 and 6 were often linked by use and lessee.

1805-1808
Revd [Sir] Charles Townshend Waller, Bt (1771-1830)

His name appears in the parish records as the Revd Mr Waller and he was a subscriber to one of Mrs Bryan's textbooks (*see No 2 South Row: Bryan House*). The son of Sir Robert Waller, of Co. Tipperary, Charles Waller was a graduate of Trinity College, Dublin. On his death the barony was extinguished.

1808-1813
Mr Rea

This could be John (d1814) or Thomas Rea (d1822), gun makers, of No 91 The Minories. Three generations of the Rea family provided guns to both the Ordnance Office and the East India Company from the 1770s until 1829: John senior (d1804), his sons, John and Thomas, and their children. A George Rea married Mary Williams at St Luke's, Charlton, in March 1804. She died in May 1842 and is buried in the graveyard of the old church of St Margaret's, Lee.

1813-1818
Mrs Elizabeth Katencamp (née Crewe) (d.1820)

Widow of Hermann Katencamp, of Bath, one-time His Majesty's Consul-General in Spain. Mrs Katencamp's niece was married from here to Thomas John Culliford, of Great Winchester Street, in December 1813. Elizabeth died at her house in Worthing in 1820.

1823-1826
John Armstrong

Armstrong's wife, Elizabeth, died at this house on 22 September 1823, aged only 28.

1831-1836
Revd Henry Worsley, MA, DCL (1783-1860)

Worsley was born at Newport, Isle of Wight. He combined the roles of teacher and boarding master at the then newly established Blackheath Proprietary School, with the incumbency of the private chapel in St Germans Place. He was one of the shareholders who shifted his support to the *New* Blackheath Proprietary School in 1836. Worsley had previously lived at No 3 Cresswell Park, but later moved to No 50 Lee Terrace where he managed a boarding house for the new school. In due course he was appointed incumbent of St Lawrence Church, Isle of Wight.

By 1850 Henry was living with his son, also the Revd Henry Worsley, the youthful Rector of Easton, Plomesgate, Suffolk. Henry junior (1820-1893) wrote 'a standard life' of Martin Luther.

1837-1847
Thomas Watson Parker (1806-1879): solicitor

Parker was a member of a three-generation practice of local solicitors. He was the son of another Thomas Watson Parker (1772-1861), of Lewisham House, 224 Lewisham High Street. All the sons did well and Thomas junior entered the family company along with his brother George Parker (1804-1889). The practice was one of the most important in the area: the Parkers were much involved in property matters, handling convincing and arranging mortgages and finance for private and business purchasers. During his time at South Row, Parker was a member of the Blackheath Golf Club. He was to return to Blackheath in the 1860s, living at No 16 Montpelier Row until his death in November 1879. He shared the house with his son, also Thomas, and also a solicitor, but the boy lived little more than a year longer than his father, dying in 1880 at the early age of 45.

Parker and his wife, Caroline, had at least seven children living with them at South Row, including Thomas, Henry, Frederick, Emily, William, Marianne and Elizabeth. Thomas Parker's brother, George, became Private Secretary to the Governor of New South Wales, and married Emmeline Mascarthur in that colony in 1843.

1847-1849
Revd Sanderson Tennant, MA (1802-1872)
(sometimes written Tenant)

Tennant was appointed the first headmaster of the Blackheath Proprietary School, 1831-46, by the committee led by Revd Joseph Fenn. The son of James Tennant, of Liverpool, he was educated at Leeds Grammar School, and was a scholar of Trinity College, Cambridge (as was

Fenn). He took a BA in 1823 (12th 'wrangler') and his MA in 1827. Tennant initially took holy orders and served as Chaplain at Trinity College from 1827 to 1838. The Blackheath School took a risk in his appointment at the relatively early age of 29. He was stay for over 15 years, seeing the school roll rise from 25 to 121 and establishing it as a day school of quality. Unfortunately, he was also in charge when the school went through a decline in the mid-1840s. Despite his loyalty and hard work he was a victim of the slump and when all the masters were put on formal notice, his was not rescinded.

For most of the time that Tennant was headmaster at the Prop he lived at No 27 Blackheath Park but when he moved to the larger No 5 South Row he tried to convince the school governors that he should be allowed to take in boarders to supplement his income. They refused, suggesting instead a per capita reward for each new pupil enrolled. As it happened, the pupil numbers fell to 53 and Tennant left Blackheath clearly a disappointed and unhappy man. His life was also touched with tragedy at this time: his wife, Charlotte (daughter of Robert Ogden, of Leeds), whom he had married in January 1838, at Scarborough, died in 1845, leaving him to bring up three sons: Thomas, Robert and Sanderson junior, then aged only three.

 He was eventually appointed a curate at St Paul's, Bedford, where he served until at least 1861. Tennant died in February 1872 at his home in South Kensington.

Sanderson Tennant Jnr was also a Trinity man but entered the law and became a member of the Inner Temple in 1861. He was called to the Bar in 1865. Unfortunately, he died in 1880 aged only 38. The Trinity records say that he was educated at the Proprietary School, but there is nothing in the BPS alumni lists to support this claim.

1849-1866
Andrew Babb Brandram (1815-1877)

Brandram was a colour merchant with an abiding passion for the militia cause and he held the honorary rank of Lieutenant-Colonel in the 5th Kent artillery volunteers. The son of the Revd Andrew Brandram (1790-1850), his was the third generation of Brandrams to live in Blackheath. His grandfather, Samuel Brandram (1742-1808), a vitriol manufacturer, lived at The Cedars, Belmont Hill, to be succeeded by the eldest son, Thomas (1778-1855), Andrew's uncle. Andrew Babb Brandram (his middle name was his mother's maiden name [Elizabeth Brandram (1784-1855)]) was born in Wiltshire, and entered the family business, by then trading in white lead and other ingredients for paint and colouring materials. He married Maria (the second daughter of Edmund Read, also of Blackheath) and their early married life was spent in Finsbury. They returned to Blackheath in 1848, initially to live in Montpelier Row but, by 1849, at No 5 South Row.

Brandram was one of the first to enrol in the local company: the 5th Kent artillery volunteers, which were based from the 1860s in the disused proprietary chapel on Dartmouth Hill. He was eventually to become Colonel of the battalion. In due course, the artillerymen and rifle brigades merged to become part of the Royal West Kent Regiment. Brandram's sons, Andrew (1850-1916), Henry Mackay, and Samuel Thomas Brandram (who took holy orders), were educated at the Proprietary School, of which Andrew was a shareholder. This was where his younger brothers were initially educated, being among the first to enrol. There was one daughter, Maria J.

The family moved to No 10 Eliot Place in 1866, where it remained until Andrew Brandram's death in 1877. Maria Brandram predeceased her husband in 1872.

1868-1879
Revd Edmund Augustus Claydon, MA (1827-1886)

A schoolmaster and clergyman without cure of souls, Claydon conducted what was known as a cramming establishment – that is, he coached boys who had failed to shine at school for entrance to the Army and the universities. The son of Charles Claydon, butler to Trinity College, Cambridge, Edmund was a graduate of St John's College, Cambridge, and had achieved his MA in 1854. His first job was as Chaplain and Senior Master at the Ordnance School, Carshalton. He came to Blackheath in 1859 and established himself at No 4 Church Terrace, adding No 3 two years later. He moved to South Row in 1868 and was successful enough to take extra premises at Bennett Park in the 1870s. His pupils – mostly aged 16 to 18 – were sufficient in number and skill to take on the football and cricket teams of the Proprietary School from time to time.

In 1871 there were 12 boys at South Row, aged between 16 and 18, many born abroad, including the Hon. Frederick George Wynn (1853-1932), son of Baron Newborough. Among Claydon's assistant masters was German-born Henry Wolffram (1831-1915), later one of the most distinguished army tutor/crammers of his day, with his own establishment at the Manor House, Old Road, Lee.

In 1875 he was appointed to the Rectory of Luton, an ecclesiastical district near Chatham, Kent, but did not sever his Blackheath connections until 1880, the year his wife, Annie (née Walker), died at the young age of 48. Claydon remained Rector at Luton until his death in May 1886.

1882-1885
George Mitchinson Hicks, MA (1852-1935): tutor

Hicks was born in Cornwall and his wife, Sarah (1857-1909), came from Barnstaple. He may have purchased the lease and goodwill of Claydon's business because he advertised his services as a tutor once he had moved to South Row. He had started his career as an assistant with Wolffram, at the Manor House (see above), but left after only a short time. Perhaps because of his age and limited experience, the business did not flourish here and by 1887 he had moved to a less fashionable, and no doubt cheaper, address: No 166 Lee High Road. He moved again twice: to No 3 Belmont Grove (from 1897 to 1906) and then to Granville House, Granville Park, where he lived from 1907 to 1909. At Belmont Grove the business was a partnership: Hicks and Clifford H. Martin, MA, tutors and crammers. Hicks was on his own again at Granville House which soon proved too large for his needs. He therefore moved back to South Row, this time to No 3, as a tenant of George Fawkes, where he remained until at least 1911 when he moved to St Leonard's, Hastings. He later turns up as a resident of No 5, where he lived from at least 1922 to 1924. He was 'very ill' during the last six years of his life and died in 1935, aged 83.

March 1888: Alterations and additions were made to Nos 5 and 6 South Row, for the freeholder, Albemarle Cator, under the supervision of R. W. Collier, architect. It is likely that the head lease had expired and the houses needed refurbishment pending the grant of a new lease.

1890-1903
William Oliver Smith (1856-1942): electrical engineer

Smith was eventually to become Chairman and Managing Director of Elliot Bros, leaders in his field, with whom he achieved sixty years' continuous employment until 1933. Smith moved to No 4 St John's Park in 1904 and was to remain there until his death. His wife, Evelyn, died in 1929, aged 71, after nearly 50 years of married life. All the Smith boys married into well-known and respectable Blackheath families: the Brocklebanks, the Wisslers and the Monktons.

Two of the boys were educated at the Blackheath Proprietary School: Lawrence Willoughby Smith (1880-1959), and Douglas Donovan Smith (1889-1970) who was still at his desk when the school finally closed in 1907. Douglas remained in Blackheath until his death, in 1970, at The Lawns, an active member of the Old Boys' Association to the end.

1905-1908
Vice-Admiral Frederick Ross Boardman, CB, RN (1843-1927)

Boardman's brief stay at Blackheath was connected with his professional duties. The eldest son of Frederick Boardman, of Liverpool, Boardman was Commander of the *HMS Salamis* during the Egyptian War of 1882, and was Captain Commander of the Nile flotilla for the Gordon Relief Expedition of 1884-5, for which service he was specially commended in despatches. He died at Lewes, Sussex, in September 1927.

1909 Empty

1910-1916
Samuel Stagoll Higham (1860-1936): solicitor

Faversham-born Samuel Higham was living in Kensington when he married Lilian Mary Davies (b.1875) in September 1899. They had three children, including the curiously named daughter Vuadine Agassiz. Higham's office was at No 36 Berners Street, in London's West End.

1918-1925
George and Melita Ethel Hall (1876-1955): *Albany House Hotel*
(combined with No 6 in 1921).

Their son, Frank Hall, married from here in September 1925. (See also Nos 11 and 12 The Paragon). At Christmas that year the hotel threw a party for 'old guests'. Forty were present to witness Mrs Hall dressing up as 'Mrs Christmas'.

1926
Mrs Florence Maud Morrell

10 April 1926, advertisement: Reopened as 'a 1st class private hotel'.

1927-1936
Mrs Lilian Emery

1937-1940
Mrs F. M. Morrell

As Mrs Morrell's name appears for these premises in the rate books for 1926, she may have let the property to Mrs Emery and returned later.

Bombed March 1941. Demolished April 1941.

No 6 South Row

Albany House (when linked with No 5)

1808-1809
Lieut.-Col. (later Major-General) William Mudge (1762-1820)

Lieutenant-Governor, Royal Military Academy, Woolwich. After an initial career as an artillery officer, Mudge's skill in mathematics led to his appointment to the Board of Ordnance with the task of undertaking a trigonometrical survey of England, in 1791. He became its director in 1798. This was the origin of the Ordnance Survey agency which survives to this day. Pioneered by Lieut.-Col. William Roy (1726-1790), Mudge can be regarded as one of its founding fathers. Although Mudge's career embraced other aspects of army life, including the training of cadets, his enthusiasm for surveying continued, leading to the publication of the various volumes of ordnance surveys from 1797 to 1811.

His son, Lieut.-Col. Richard Zachariah Mudge, RE (1790-1854), who was educated at a Blackheath school (probably George Walpole's, at No 17 Montpelier Row), succeeded William Mudge in much of the surveying work. William, who had lived at No 97 Blackheath Hill from 1799 to 1803, eventually (c.1813) purchased a house in Holles Street, which remained his home until his death. Mudge may have held a lease on No 6 South Row until 1813 but there is no record to prove this.

1811-1830
Robert Sowerby (1737-1830)

Sowerby was in business as a wine and brandy merchant, at No 34 Bread Street, on the corner of Trinity Lane, Cheapside, from at least 1804. The Joseph Sowerby, insurance broker, of Hatton Garden, in 1798, may have been a relative; so might the Robert Sowerby living in Charlton at the end of the 18th century. Whether or not this was the case, Robert seems to have moved to Blackheath on retirement, some time before 1811. He retained City interests, including acting as mortgagee of a house at No 1 Half Moon Passage, Leadenhall Street, valued by the Sun Life Insurance Company at £1,000 in 1820.

Meanwhile, the business at Bread Street was in the name of William Sowerby – perhaps a son? – from 1814 onwards. Robert died at 'his house on Blackheath' on 27 May 1830 at the great age of 93, if his death notice in *The Times* is to be believed. A Robert Sowerby, perhaps another son or even a grandson, was living at No 58 Blackheath Park in 1829. And The Times has a notice of the death, in the winter of 1838, of Elizabeth Ann, widow of Robert, aged 68. If this is also correct, she was Robert's junior by 33 years.

1833-1834
Joshua Andrews (d.1834): stockbroker

Andrews, whose business was based at No 23 Threadneedle Street, was living at No 11 St Germans Place when, in January 1831, he was one of the first to take a share in the newly established Blackheath Proprietary School. His son, Henry Wych Andrews (1822-1866), was in the first batch of pupils and stayed at the school until Christmas 1836. Henry was a distinguished amateur cricketer, playing for Blackheath teams and for Kent.

He followed his father into the Stock Exchange. In May 1832 Joshua's daughter, Anne Emily (1816-1866), married the young stockbroker Lawford Richardson (1802-1870), of No 3 The Paragon, and son of bookseller James Malcott Richardson (1770-1854) of No 97 Blackheath Park. The principal family home was at Bartley Manor, near Southampton, in the New Forest.

1835-1841
Joseph Henry Warter, Jnr (1800-1852): cheesemonger

The Warters' family business was wholesale cheesemongery, certainly in Aldgate High Street by 1824, and later in Borough High Street, Southwark. It remained there for many years, although by 1846 was trading as Warter & Fitch. The company flourished mightily and, although not part of this story, it is worth noting that it has survived as part of the wholesale provision merchants, Fitch, Lovell. The family kept the same first name for over three generations and Joseph Henry was probably the son of Joseph Warter (1766-1839) of High Street, Southwark, who died in January 1839. Joseph junior lived at No 11 The Paragon, on the New Kent Road, before moving to Blackheath in 1835.

Joseph junior's son, also Joseph, joined the company by 1839 (after leaving the Blackheath Proprietary School where he had been educated since 1835). The original firm disappears from the commercial directories after 1852 although the youngest Joseph returns as a wine merchant, at No 50 Mark Lane, specialising in Xeres and other wines from Portugal, in a company were trading as Wisdon & Warter. Living with Joseph Henry and his wife Elizabeth at South Row, in 1841, were their daughters Elizabeth and Maria.

Joseph junior died on 28 August 1852, at the family home of No 27 Finsbury Square. He had been active in various ways, being a member of the Committee of the Cheesemongers' Benevolent Institution and serving as a director of the United Mercantile and Travellers' Association (an insurance company). To judge by the listed names many other Blackheath men were involved in the management of that company. After Joseph's death the family moved, eventually, to Bedford Place, Brighton, and then to Hastings.

By the 1880s, there were four companies registered with Warter in the name, all active in the wine and sherry business; one such was Webb, Warter & Co., of Lower East Smithfield, running bonded warehouses. Henry and William Henry Warter, partners in these companies, may have been the grandsons of Joseph Warter, of No 6 South Row.

1843-1847
James Shelton Newbon (1806-1863): solicitor
(sometimes written Newborn)

James Newbon was admitted a solicitor in 1829 and was eventually in a practice known as Newbon & Evans, at No 1 Wardrobe Place, Doctor's Commons. He had lived previously at No 29 Shooters Hill Road, having married Ann Brocklebank, daughter of Thomas Brocklebank (1774-1843), the steamship owner, of Westcombe House, Blackheath, in January 1831.

Three of their eight sons, Thomas, H. G. T. and J. T. B. Newbon, were educated at the Blackheath Proprietary School. Another son was born here in August 1843. There was one daughter, Annie, who died as an infant.

James's business partner, John Llewellyn Evans, was living at 120 Westbourne Terrace in the 1850s. By 1855 the Newbons were resident at Elm House, High Road, Hammersmith, and this was where James died in February 1863. Ann died in 1866.

James Newbon's brother Robert Algar Newbon (1823-1891), was an auctioneer. He left huge amounts of money to the (Royal) National Lifeboat Institution on condition that it named five boats after members of his family, including their mother Ann, and sisters Betsy and Nancy, and his "late" wife, Lucy White Newbon [1821-1880]. More money was left to his church and to hospitals in Bethnal Green and Islington.

1849-1886
Dr John Elliot Pasley Robertson, DCL (1804-1886)
Advocate of Doctor's Commons. Chancellor of the Diocese of Rochester 1856-1886

Robertson (whose middle name was sometimes written as Paisley) was the son of Dr Robert Robertson, MD, FRS (1742-1829), the physician at the Greenwich Hospital for Seamen. Dr Robertson had lived for some years at Orchard House in Blackheath, but was resident in Greenwich Hospital when his son John was born. John Robertson was educated in Greenwich and at Exeter College, Oxford, although he was granted a doctorate of common law by Magdalen Hall in 1835. He established himself at Doctor's Commons (the colloquial name for the College of Advocates and Doctors of Law, near St Paul's Cathedral: abolished in 1859) where he was stewart (sic), librarian and, eventually, Treasurer. In 1856 he was appointed Chancellor of the Diocese of Rochester, a position he held until his death in February 1886. He also held a similar role with the Diocese of St Albans from 1877. Inevitably, his speciality was ecclesiastical law and he edited a number of volumes of reports on cases in the ecclesiastical courts.

When he married Louisa, from Pershore, Worcester, she was nearly 30 years his junior. They were blessed with at least five children: Murray, Louisa E., Susan Ann, Edward George (who became a solicitor) and Margaret Jane.

April 1886: The contents of the house, amalgamated with those of No 4 Montpelier Row for convenience, were sold by auction.

1887-1888 Empty

March 1888: The house was altered and repaired along with No 5 South Row (q.v.).

1889-1920
Charles Willis Troughton (1856-1920)

Troughton, a stockbroker, who came from Stockport, Lancashire, was living at No 1 Handen Road in Lee by 1882. He and his wife, Caroline E., originally from Chatham, had three children living with them at the time of the 1891 census: sons Charles V. and Harold Willis, and a daughter, Kate M. Troughton. The boys were educated at the Blackheath Proprietary School. Lieut. Harold Willis Troughton, RNVR, was killed in action in October 1916; Charles was a captain on the Special List and survived the war.

Charles Troughton Snr was an enthusiastic golfer, a member of the Royal Blackheath Golf Club and its Captain in 1910, as well as a frequent winner of its medals and trophies. His estate was valued at £20,589.

1921 to 1941
Albany House Hotel
For details, see No 5 South Row.

No 7 South Row

Colonnade House

Colonnade House was built in 1802-3 by William Dyer for Robert Parry (d. 1804), on the authority of a head lease from John Cator. The lease was for a term of 73 years from Michael-mas 1803. On 21 May 1804, a further under-lease, from William Dyer, was granted to Alice Parry and William Parry the younger for land contiguous to this property.

William and Thomas Parry were merchants, of Aldermanbury, in the City of London. They were well established by 1798 and Thomas was a director of the East India Company, which indicates some considerable wealth. It is likely that the Robert mentioned in the Times adver-tisement of 13 June 1804 (see below) was their father. He may have commissioned the house directly from Searles or made arrangements for its construction with local developer William Dyer (d.1833). Dyer, who would have known Searles, may have encouraged the architect to supply a suitable scheme for the remaining plot on the original Searles/Cator agreement of 1790). But Robert Parry's plans were upset by his premature death. For some reason the Parry sons did not wish to move to the new house, or were prevented from so doing by the terms of Robert's estate.

Whatever, both William and Thomas continued in business, at Aldermanbury, and were still trading together until at least 1812. From 1814 to 1826 William junior prospered independently, eventually becoming a member of Lloyd's.

1804
Mrs Alice Parry

Widow of Robert Parry; the lessor, even if not in residence.

13 June 1804: *The Times* advertisement:

Blackheath. Singularly elegant and newly erected villa with garden, paddock and offices. By Peter Coxe, Burrell & Foster, at Garraway's, on Wednesday, June 20th, at 12 o'clock, by order of the executors of Robert Parry, Esq, deceased. An uncommonly elegant and beautifully constructed villa with extensive Portland stone colonnade, delightfully situate at Blackheath opposite Greenwich Park, commands in the back front the grounds belonging to the late Sir Gregory Page, bart, with rich views into Kent and Surrey, finished and fitted up, painted and papered for the immediate reception of the genteelest family in a complete style of architec-tural taste and comfortable accommodation, containing a drawing room and dining parlour, each 30 feet by 18' 6", with statuary enriched chimney pieces, windows to the floor with plate glass, breakfast parlour, gentleman's room, entrance hall, arched passage and capital staircase, a ladies boudoir painted and embellished with trelliage and rural scenery, three principal bed chambers, large closet, dressing room, water closet etc. with 5 handsome bedchambers on the upper floor, a most complete range of domestic offices including house-keeper's room compose the basement [with rooms] uncommonly numerous and convenient in every circumstance and admirable cellary with extraordinary commodious outdoor offices, detached, a double coach house, suitable stabling, a wash house, brew house, farm yard etc. Iron railings with double gates, stone plinth and piers, separate the mansion from the Heath, with lawn, shrubberies and plantations, a capital kitchen garden with lofty fruit-wall richly clothed, planted with dwarf trees well cropped with adjoining paddock. These valuable premises have been constructed with every possible attention, no expense whatever spared and are held for a long term of 76 years at the rent of £40.15.8 per annum. May be viewed by tickets only 8 days preceding the sale upon application to Messrs Peter Coxe, Burrell & Foster and at Lloyd's and Garraway's.

20 June 1804: *The Times* advertisement:
As above, but with the addition 'Sale today', and still offering viewing eight days preceding!

1 June 1805: *The Times* advertisement:

Excellent residence, Blackheath, by Mr Smith. At Garraway's on Friday, 14 June, 12 noon, unless an acceptable offer is made in the meantime by private contract. A spacious elegant leasehold residence, delightfully situate opposite the Park, near The Paragon, Blackheath, forming a handsome elevation with a colonnade, stone pillars and pilasters in front. The house contains eight airy bed chambers, marble chimney pieces, principal and second staircases, dressing room and water closet, a morning room elegantly finished in landscape panels opening on a cheerful balcony, lofty, elegant dining room 30 feet by 18'6" and drawing room of the same proportions with enriched cornices and statuary marble chimney pieces, opening to a tasteful lawn and rich, diversified prospects of the Heath and surrounding country; a breakfast parlour, gentleman's room, lofty hall, handsome approach, stone piers, iron gates and rails, lawn and flower gardens in front, excellent offices of every description, standing for two carriages, stabling for four horses, productive kitchen garden, lofty fruit walls and a selection of prime fruit trees with a plot of ground for a paddock adjoining, containing together about six acres, amply supplied with fine water. To be viewed six days previous to the sale.

22 June 1805: *The Times* advertisement:

As above, but notes that the sale has been postponed until 28 June 1805.

There is no mention of a resident in Colonnade House before Randall (see below) in any official or other record discovered

1807-1822
William Randall (1766-1825)

Shipbuilder and dock owner. His company was trading as Randall & Brent by the time he took Colonnade House. His business partner was John Brent (1729-1812), of Heathfield House, Eliot Place. The shipyard was at Rotherhithe. Randall also lived at The Retreat, Battersea, and in Lambeth at various times; his memorial stone, at St Mary's parish church, Lewisham, mentions both these places, as well as Blackheath. John Brent's presence at Eliot Place may have encouraged Randall to settle in Blackheath, a district he would have known from visits to his partner. The company was substantial and had started in the 1750s as John Randall (later as Randall & Co.), eventually in partnership with Brent. Its future, after William's retirement or death, lay with the Brent family and, from about 1817 onwards, John's son Daniel guided the firm, eventually taking it into the days of the steamship. The company built over 65 ships, including 33 warships of 30 guns or more, between 1756 and 1821.

By 1807 William Randall had taken over the Dyer/Parry lease of 1804 on the South Row property, negotiated another for land at the south-west end of Pond Road (now the site of St Michael's Church and Nos 1-9b Pond Road) and, in 1822, a further agreement for land at the rear of the house. In the end, the property consisted of nearly four acres, which included meadows and pleasure grounds. The stable block was substantial but was separated from the house by the 1830s. William was a trustee of the New Cross Turnpike.

Colonnade House cannot always have been a happy home for the Randalls. Three sons died there: William aged 14, in 1810; Henry, in 1816, aged only 9; and Nathaniel, who was 22 when he died in March 1822. Sarah Randall, who was born in 1764, outlived her husband by 20 years and died in 1846.

1823-1852
Simeon Warner (1786-1866)

Landowner and coal merchant, and an early member of the Coal Exchange (established in law in 1807). He was the son of Isaac Warner (1744-1822), of No 7 The Paragon. The family were in substantial business, particularly in coal and land. Simeon married Anne Bryan Young (1789-

1869), daughter of George Young of No 4 South Row, in March 1811. The Warners eventually moved to Brighton where Simeon died in 1866, and Anne in October 1869.

Family members living at Colonnade House from time to time were Algernon (a solicitor), Frederick (a stockbroker), and Laura; Mary (daughter) and her husband Arthur Rasch; and in 1861 Caroline (daughter) and her husband Leonard Shuter, a cooper and the son of Thomas Allen Shuter (of Dacre House, Brandram Road, from 1835 to 1842). They needed six resident servants, including a butler, to run their household

1853-1863
Richard Wheen (1808-1885): soap manufacturer

Wheen was probably one of the most successful Blackheath businessmen of his time. Not only was he was closely involved in the manufacturing process of his factory in Deptford, but also philanthropic and able to accommodate a large family in this relatively prosperous and rural suburb. Nevertheless, he rode to work on his horse each day. Also, the sons entered the family business and learned the technology and marketing systems, which ensured that the company remained profitable. It flourished in Deptford from 1849 until 1955.

Wheen had been in partnership with his brother, John Frith Wheen (1816-1903), from the 1830s, with a soap factory in Ratcliff Highway, Finsbury. The factory, which had been founded in 1769, was eventually owned by Joseph Moate, Richard Wheen's uncle. The boy married Moate's daughter (also his cousin), Anna Maria, eventually siring 13 children. He encouraged brother, John, to join the business. By 1837 the firm was manufacturing 645 tons of soap a year. In 1838 the figure had risen to 715 tons, then worth over £10,000. After a few years, however, the brothers decided that the business was not profitable enough to support two families so they parted company, but without rancour. Richard moved to Creek Road, Deptford, taking over a pin factory on the water's edge and once the Ravensbourne Wood Mill. He pioneered a number of techniques in soap manufacture, including the first use of soap coppers boiled by steam and not direct heat.

Before taking Colonnade House, Richard Wheen had lived at York Terrace, Regent's Park. The move was clearly necessary: over the ten years that the Wheens lived in Blackheath, 11 of their children were born. Richard and Maria employed no fewer than 11 resident servants, including a butler, a footman and a coachman – the largest number in any house in the district, even Rangers House, then occupied by HRH Prince Arthur (later Duke of Connaught). In 1863 the Wheens moved to Hayes Place, Keston, then to Lancaster Gate. Richard's retirement was spent enjoying sporting activities, with shooting in Scotland. Mr and Mrs Wheen finally retired to Courtlands, at Tunbridge Wells, where Richard died in November 1885. He left £50,000 as well as property and a thriving business. Maria Wheen had died in 1881, aged 63.

The business passed to the control of three of their sons: Richard (1838-1910), Francis (1850-1925) and Charles Wheen (1860-1935). It was floated as a public company in 1898 but remained with the Wheen descendants until competition from the big names led to an agreement with Lever Bros and its closure. From the early Deptford days, and until recently, the company and family had turned for legal advice to solicitor Griffith Thomas and his descendant partners in the practice now known as Clifford Chance. Thomas was resident at No 6 The Paragon (q.v.) from 1851 to 1860.

During his time at Blackheath, Richard Wheen had been an active member of the Blackheath Improvement Association; his eldest son, Richard, was educated at the Blackheath Proprietary School from 1852 to 1854. Children at Colonnade House were: Richard, Maria, Diana, Helen, Anne, Francis, Mary, Emma, Louisa, Edward, and Charles. In 1861 Wheen extended and altered the house, perhaps to the form that it retained until 1941. The works were substantial, costing nearly £1,500, and requiring the services of architect Francis Freeman Thorne (1829-1885, then at No 101 Dacre Park.

1865-1869
Charles Richardson (1818-1886): brewer

Richardson, born in St Marylebone, was a master brewer and eventually Managing Director of the City of London Brewery Co. Ltd. By 1861 he was married to Emily Frances and with a growing family, living in Bushey Hill Road, Camberwell. Three of the children (at least) were born in the City, where Charles was based initially. But the move from Camberwell to the grandeur of Colonnade House was not to last long. By 1871 they had all settled at Foxwood, Princes Road, in Wandsworth, where the occupants consisted of Mr and Mrs Richardson, seven children (three born in Blackheath), a resident governess, a coachman and four female servants. A household of this size would have fitted Colonnade House admirably but perhaps the daily journey from Blackheath to Richardson's place of work became too much for him.

Emily died, alas, in the early summer of 1877, aged but 43. Three of the girls were sent to board-ing schools: two to Brunswick Square, Brighton/Hove, and one to Chelsea. Richardson was a shareholder of the Blackheath Proprietary School, where his son, Charles Norman, was educated from 1865 to 1871. During his tenancy at Colonnade House, Richardson's gardener, John Hilton, stole lead from a house in Blackheath Vale and hid it in the garden of Mill House, Talbot Place.

The City of London Brewery Company was, at some stage, the owner of the Princess of Wales public house (almost next door to Colonnade House) but not – so far as the author is aware – in Charles Richardson's time.

1870-1876
John Paterson (1813-1876): silk merchant and warehouseman

The Paterson family lived previously at Clapham, then at No 22 Belmont Hill (from 1849) and No 7 Vanbrugh Terrace. John Paterson, who was born at Berwick-on-Tweed, was a businessman active in the politics of the City. He was a member for the Aldersgate ward for many years, on the Court of Common Council, and was appointed alderman in due course. He did not achieve his ambition to be Lord Mayor but he did take up the office of Junior Sheriff in the year before he died.

His great moment came on 6 November 1869. As Chairman of the Bridge House Estate com-mittee, he was chosen to deliver the loyal address to HM Queen Victoria when she formally opened both Blackfriars Bridge and Holborn Viaduct – on the same day. Joseph Cubitt (1811-1872) had designed the bridge and he and Paterson were presented to the monarch. The only disappointment came with the failure to meet the target date for the occasion: the 100th anniversary of the original Blackfriars Bridge and the 50th birthday of the Queen. For this, Cubitt blamed everyone other than his own company and contractors.

With a family of at least ten children, it probably became necessary for the Patersons to take a property the size of Colonnade House. There were eight servants, three less than required by the Wheens, not counting the gardener in his own lodge house. The children resident in 1871 were: Elizabeth Ann, Esther, Margaret Jane, John, Robert, Edith, George Morton (who died young, at Colombo, Sri Lanka, in September 1879), Bella, Sidney and Walter. The boys were ed-ucated at the Proprietary School. Of them all, probably John achieved the most distinction, as a barrister of the Inner Temple. After John Paterson's death in 1876 his widow, Elizabeth, and members of the family remained at Colonnade House for the next 32 years.

1878-1904
Mrs Elizabeth Paterson (1821-1904)

Widow of the above. During some of this time Mrs Paterson's sister, Mrs Rebecca Oliver, a widow, shared the house. In 1890, during the Paterson ownership, consent was obtained from the freeholder – Albemarle Cator – to develop part of the south-west garden land, facing what is now Paragon Place on the corner of Wemyss Road. The group of houses built there was called Paterson's Cottages and these are discussed at the end of this section.

1905-1908
Sidney Paterson (1876-1944): son of the above

Sidney and some of his unmarried sisters lived at Colonnade House after their parents' death. Margaret Jane died in 1926, at Camden House Court, Kensington; and Elizabeth Ann, the last surviving child of the family, died in September 1937, aged 92, at No 19 Montpelier Row, which had been her home since 1906. Miss Paterson lived in Blackheath for all but about four years of her long life.

1909 Empty

1910-1911
Jack Palmer
Nothing has been discovered about him. Palmer may have started the process of letting rooms.

1911 enumerated census return:

Frank Shrimpton: police pensioner/caretaker, aged 50, born Amersham. Kate Shrimpton, his wife of 25 years, also aged 50, born Deptford.

1912 Empty

1913
Miss Florence Gadesden MA (1852-1934)

Headmistress of the Blackheath High School for Girls, Wemyss Road, from 1886 to 1914.

Miss E. Colson FRHS (Dip.)
Blackheath School of Gardening

1914
Charles Welbourne Piper, ARIBA (1864-1919): architect, previously at No 46 Shooters Hill Road.

1914-1941
Edward William Japp (1864-1944): 'architect'

Japp, who was born in Montrose, Scotland, was living at No 14 Granville Park from 1908, and is described (in his own hand) on the 1911 enumerated census return as a 'house decorator'. Mrs Japp is Jane Ann, and they had been married for two years. On the move to Colonnade House, Mrs Japp becomes Jeannie and her three children by her first husband (see below), Leslie, Helen and Sheila, must have been quite excited to move to the probably crumbling, but magnificent, Colonnade House from the comparatively dull villa in Granville Park.

1914-1941
Mrs Jane Ann (Jeannie) Japp (1873-1948): boarding-house keeper
[Widow of Dr W. T. Scott, MA MB, before her marriage to Edward Japp]

Although Edward Japp is listed as the householder in the rating records from 1914, increasingly through the years Mrs Japp's name figures in the official record. Colonnade House was one of the first properties in South Row to convert to a boarding house or private hotel, with advertisements appearing as early as 1920. Nevertheless, the house was the centre for family occasions, and announcements of the engagement or marriage of Mrs Japp's children by her first husband (Dr W. T. Scott, MA, MB) would always mention Colonnade House. There was plenty of room for receptions and parties to celebrate these events. In January 1923 a party was held for Sheila Scott, younger daughter of Mrs Japp, when she married John Hugo Goolden, whose parents were resident at Colonnade House at the time. Leslie Scott married from here in March 1927; and the youngest daughter, Helen, in May 1928

Wedding of Lieut Comm C A L Mansergh DSC RN to Miss H R Scott

The Parish Church of St Margaret, Lee, presented a beautiful and interesting spectacle. On Saturday last, the 5th inst, when Lieut Commander Cecil Aubrey Lawson Mansergh DSC RN, youngest son of Mr Ernest Mansergh, of Woking, was united in marriage to Miss Helen Rayner Scott, elder daughter of the late Dr W T Scott and Mrs Japp, of Colonnade House, Blackheath.

The ceremony was performed by the Rector of Lee (the Rev F H Gillingham) and Mr Frederic Leeds BMus FRCO, organist and director of the choir was at the organ. During the service the hymns "The voice that breathed oe'r Eden" and "O, perfect Love", were sung. Psalm lxvii ("God be merciful unto us") was sung to a chant setting (Leeds in D) and the organ music prior to the ceremony included Minuet in G by Borowski and the Bridal Music from Wagner's "Lohengrin"

During the signing of the register the choir gave a lovely rendering of the Anthem: "True Love's the gift that God has given" (Charles Wood) and the Melodie from "Salomé, and Mendelssohn's Wedding March was played as the party and guests left the church.

The bride, who was given away by her stepfather Mr E W Japp, wore a charming picture dress of ivory tulle with closely fitted bodice and sleeves of ivory satin. Her tulle veil was arranged with a wreath and clusters of orange blossom, and she carried a bouquet of lilies-of-the-valley and pale pink roses. There were four bridesmaids – Miss Irene Butler, Miss Joyce Beauchamp, Miss Paula Jennings-Bramly and Miss Lesley Mansergh, who were attired in very pretty dresses of pink tulle over pink satin with wreathes of forget-me-nots and pink roses tied with blue and silver ciré ribbon.

Lieut Commander R Mansergh RN (brother of the bridegroom) acted as best man. Reception was subsequently held at Colonnade House, and later Lieut-Commander and Mrs Mansergh left for their honeymoon, which is being spent in Paris. The bride travelled in a Lido blue suit with cape and an oyster satin jumper in blue. She had a felt hat to match, trimmed with oyster-shell flowers.

From the *Blackheath Local Guide & District Advertiser:* Saturday May 12 1928

Many people lived at Colonnade House, with stays of a few weeks to many years, during the time when it was a boarding house. In the later 1930s, the house was so full of paying guests that, according to reliable testimony, Mr and Mrs Japp retreated to live in a wooden cottage/shed in the garden known as The Bungalow.

Edward Japp died in the spring of 1944, aged 82; Mrs Jeannie Japp died on 31 January 1948, aged 75.

Among the many Colonnade House residents for whom some details survive were:

1920 -1928 Albert, Evelyn & Gertrude Hessey

1920 Charles Stuart Meers

Herbert Laurence Wethered

1922-1925 J. Robert Kennedy

1928-1929
Geoffrey (George) Murton Gill: previously of Foyle Road, Shooters Hill Road and No 30a Kidbrooke Park Road.

Bruce Burrell, who married Nansi (*sic*) Roberts, of Cardiff from here in September 1929.

1928-1932 Mrs Mary Kate Adkin (1857-1932): widow of Henry John Adkin.

1930-1939
Dr John Webb Waghorn, RN (retd) (1849-1940): founder of the Blackheath Bridge Club. His wife, Amy Gertrude (née Sply), whom he married in 1885, died at Eltham on 22 December 1939, aged 79.

1939
William James Ladeveze Davies: previously at No 104 Westcombe Park Road. Moved to Newlyn, Cornwall, in December 1939.

March 1941: *Colonnade House badly damaged in bombing: house looted and vandalised.*
1947-1948: *Restored by Charles Bernard Brown. Converted into seven self-contained flats.*
The bulk of the garden ground taken, by compulsory purchase orders, for municipal housing
(fronting Paragon Place and Pond Road) in 1952.

Colonnade House stables

Although Colonnade House was blessed, at the outset, with a substantial stable block and carriage houses, these were not to remain with the property for long. The house kept a basic stable adjacent to the property (eventually used as a garage) until the 1930s, but it was so badly altered and damaged during the war that there was no protest when it was demolished – it can be seen in part in one of the illustrations in this book showing the damaged Colonnade House. It was replaced in 1955 with the present No 41 South Row, built to the design of architect Derek Acton Stow. A further house, No 32 Paragon Place, was erected at the rear of No 41, in 1958, because Stow's client decided to sell part of his plot. The result was No 32 Paragon Place, designed in 1958 by architects Hildebrand & Glicker, of London Wall. In 1966 No 32 was extended by a scheme designed by architects Colin Roach-Bowler.

The original stable blocks, on the east side of Paragon Mews [now Paragon Place] were in commercial use by 1831 when a section, with a brick house and standing for four vans, was offered for sale by Samuel Towner, a carrier. He was offering 31 year lease at a ground rent of £26.12.0 pa. The taker was probably Robert Vice, stable keeper, job and post master who, when he sold out in March 1840. His advertisements speak of stalls for 14 horses, and the stock included one landau, flies, coaches, saddles, bridles, etc. The business was acquired by the Greenwich-based carrier, George Reeve, trading as Reeve & Price. Reeve's name was attached to the premises until at least 1866. The dwelling sections of the block took the name Colonnade Cottages. In July 1864 it suffered a bad fire, which excited comment in the local press, lamenting the absence of a fire brigade in Blackheath. Appliances had to be summoned from as far away as Tooley Street, Morden College, and possibly the Penn works at the bottom of Blackheath Hill, not from John Penn's house on Belmont Hill. The stables survived and passed through a number of cab and carriage owners.

In 1890 the Paterson family obtained development rights and granted an under-lease for the south-west end of the Colonnade House plot to local builder George William Gorrum (1825-1904). He built a row of eight houses (Paterson's Cottages, later numbered 24 to 31 Paragon Place) and lived in one of these until his death in 1904. Although the Gorrum lease was not to expire until 1978, Lewisham Borough Council acquired the plot in October 1950. The buildings were then demolished, to be replaced by a block of flats with frontages to both Paragon Place and Ryculf Square.

The stables, meanwhile, were converted to motor engineering in the early years of this century and were in use as the Paragon Motor Works. From 1903, the company was in the ownership of S. T. Norfolk, a most enterprising and far-sighted man since there was precious few cars in the district at the time and those were mostly owned by enthusiasts capable of undertaking their own repairs. By 1910 the proprietor was William Henry Nurton (1863-1935), automobile engineer, of No 29 Montpelier Vale. Although Nurton retained ownership, the business was acquired in the 1920s by Messrs Newman & Williams (also working from Nos 15 and 16 Paragon Place). After Nurton's death, the premises passed to Thomas William Croft, of Vanbrugh Park. However, the whole enterprise disappeared only a few years afterwards through war damage and the subsequent redevelopment of the ground by the local authority (Lewisham).

> ** **
> PARAGON MEWS, BLACKHEATH.—The Blackheath and Lewisham Committee of the Lewisham District Board of Works have considered a letter from residents in and near the Paragon-mews, Blackheath, complaining of nuisances committed there, particularly on Saturday afternoons and Sunday evenings, and the Committee recommend that a letter be written to the police requesting them to prevent the nuisance complained of ; and that a letter be also written to the landlord of the Princess of Wales public-house there, requesting him to provide and maintain sufficient urinal accommodation for the persons frequenting his premises.

Blackheath Local Guide, August 1889.

Appendices

Appendix I

The Kendall family at No 1 The Paragon

See end of this Appendix for the footnotes

1881
The Kendall family arrive in England from Australia, 'the Gov' to take up his managerial appointment in P&O Head Office. After the family's sojourn in icy-cold Bournemouth (home of the Kendall grandmother) they take rooms in Notting Hill.

(*March*) The family move into No 1 The Paragon on Lady Day (25 March). Nicholas, 'Nix' (13), and Frank (11) start at the 'Prop' (Blackheath Proprietary School) [A]; Ed (rising 10) at 'Vipans' (Mrs Mackinnon's school [B]. The other children are Mary (5) and Charles, 3.

The Robsons [C] (Leon[ard], Ethel, Philip, Maurice) live next door at No 2.

The Barray-Jupps [D] also live in Blackheath: Bertram or Bertie ('the Inev'), Daisy, Ernie, Maggie.

(*6 June*) Birth of the Twins, Fred and Herbert..

1882
(*July*) The Kendall family spend the summer holidays at Southsea, Miss Boyd also being in attendance as 'governess'(the incident of Miss B accosting the Australian cricketer Spofforth).

1883
The family holiday in Southend.

1884
Nix (16) and Frank (14) still at the 'Prop'; Ed (13) joining them there from Miss Vipans'. Mary at Blackheath High School [E]. Charles (6) at Miss Birch's Kindergarten [F]. Fred and Herbert have their third birthday in June.

The elder brothers pay a 'memorable visit' to Notton, the home of their Awdry relatives, 'learning a variety of new songs'.

Their cousin Rosina Kay, from Australia, comes to stay and has measles.

Another cousin, Harry Kendall, has been staying with the family for about two years. He is of an age with Ed and goes to school at 'Vipans' with him. Harry later joins his parents [as well as Uncle Edward and Aunt Alice in Southsea.

For the family holidays, the children split up – Nix and Frank go to Ramsgate, Charles and Fred to Bournemouth, Mary and Herbert to Clifton.

Relations between Nix and his brothers become strained at about this time, resulting in the beginnings of the 'Paragon Club' by the institution of the HOL (House of Lords) in the harness room of the Coach House – a refuge for Frank and Ed from Nix, who is in a state of war with the others.

A Terrible Secret (FKK: 'a thoroughly rotten piece') is performed in the Xmas holidays.

Bertie Barray-Jupp ('the Inev') probably leaves for abroad, first as Assistant Purser with P&O, then Australia, then South Africa.

1885
'Uncle Mike' (friend of the Gov) probably at No 1 for the first time.

Charles and the Twins holiday at Bournemouth.

Ed (14) at the 'Prop' (1885-8). Frank (15) after leaving school goes to 'Jerrards' for architectural training (until Aug 1887).

At about this time an armistice is declared between Nix and his younger brothers and he is allowed to associate with the 'HOL' and help transform it into the Paragon Club.

St George and the Dragon put on in Xmas holidays (or possibly at Xmas '84, '83, or '82?).

1886
The Kendall theatre performance of *A Charming Pair*.

Ed (15) and Charles (8) visit the Awdrys at Notton (? Easter) and dislike 'Jack'. The Gov writes his first introspective treatise on his failure and inability to have made money since his posting with P&O in Australia.

Nix (18) leaves the 'Prop' and studies at Burton's dispensary before going on to 'Mr Cross'. He goes on the Norfolk Broads as a pioneer with Leon Robson and [Edward Alexander] Whichcord. The Twins (5) go to Clifton for their holiday and Charles to Bournemouth with Ed. On leaving school, Nix starts his 'Social Evenings'.

Charles starts at 'Possy's' (Vipans) [**B**].

At Christmas-time Charles is compelled by Nix to dance the hornpipe at the 'Christy Minstrels' Show'.

1887
Done on Both Sides is performed at No 1 [The Paragon].

(*June, Diamond Jubilee Year*) Charles (9) catches measles and mumps and is glad to miss school at Possy's.

The last year in which the family spend the summer holidays at 'Granny's' in Bournemouth. The elder brothers holiday on the Broads.

Frank (17) leaves Jerrards for one year at King's College.

1888
The Bear with a Sore Head and Boots at the Swan performed in the Xmas holidays – Charles in bed with earache.

The Twins (7) go to Possy's, joining Charles (10) there.

The Gov writes a further treatise on his financial misfortunes and misgivings.

Nix (20) takes Charles to Malta on HMS Shannon with Prince George (later HM George V) on board. They return on the *Clyde*.

The first of the family excursions, with the younger children, to the seaside – Boscombe – but apparently it is rather a failure. Charles remembers it for lunch at the Great White Horse Inn (Pickwick's Pub) on the Orwell (sic) and being allowed to drink cider. They eventually visit Pendre, Bournemouth (Granny's), again.

Frank (18), on leaving King's College, is articled to Roger Smith for three years. Ed (17) attends the Metropolitan School of Shorthand (Sept. '88–March '89). The Gov starts an 8-9 month tour of the East on behalf of P&O (?).

German measles at Possy's.

'The Inev' [Bertie Barray-Jupp] is in South Africa getting a job with the Standard Bank.

1889
Uncle performed at No 1 in the Xmas holidays.

After finishing his shorthand course Ed (18) joins the Australian Mortgage Land and Finance Co. in London.

Charles (11) goes in for the 'OPB' Scholarship at the Prop (candidates being described by a master as 'a poor lot') and wins the £10 award. He makes himself so sick smoking a pipe that he does not resume the practice until he is 17.

The family holiday at Sandgate on the Kent coast, going on to Boulogne *en famille*. Afterwards, Charles goes on to Ostend with the Gov.

Charles enters the Prop in the IXth [sic] form (Henderson's class). [This was Form II.]

1890
C. L. Money (a friend of the Gov) presents a clock to the Paragon Club and receives a letter of thanks from Archer Legg (Secretary, No 90 Burnt Ash Road), Ed Kendall (Treasurer) and members Leon Robson (No 2 The Paragon), Edward Henderson (No 16 Belmont Park), Frank Kendall (No 1 The Paragon), Gilbert

Appendices

Tunks (No 7 Vanbrugh Park Road), Nix Kendall (No 1 The Paragon) and Shirley Aspinall (No 39 Bennett Park).

The family holiday at Sandgate, and on the way home spend a week at Staplehurst in Kent, on the Simons' farm. For Charles (12) this is the 'last and greatest' visit there, but with the Simonses away, but Daisy Day present, the Twins (9) have difficulty rowing on the river.

The Gov goes out to India on P&O business.

Turn Him Out and *Ici on Parle Français* performed (Nov).

1891
Charles (13) goes with 'Uncle Mike' to Ticehurst (Feb?).

After the 'Great Fire' at No 1 (suspected of being caused by Herbert), Herbert has scarlet fever, followed by a mystery complaint over his knee.

Mixed hockey (girls as well as boys including Mary – 16 in August) and cricket played on Blackheath.

During this period (? work on the Coach House?) the Club is briefly resuscitated in a room off the McDougalls' stables (or '92 ?) [G].

The family holiday in lodgings at Deal – 'a dull holiday, full of rain'– but they discover Parson Parker and the Rectory, which is booked for the following year.

1892
Robert Macaire performed at No 1 during the holidays.

(*30 April*) Silver Wedding anniversary for the Gov and DOM (Dear Old Mater). Paragon garden cricket begins to flourish (1892-5) with 'hot sausage' in the winter.

The older boys holiday on the Broads while the parents and younger children stay in the Rectory at Deal; they entertain several friends and relations and have an unsuccessful tennis party.

Final improvements made to the Paragon Club which has long been extended from the 'HOL' (House of Lords).

The Twins, Fred and Herbert (11), join Charles (14) at the Prop (1892-8).

? '*Robert Macaire*' performed again, at St Mildred's

1893
Away with Melancholy and Fitzsmythe of Fitzsmythe Hall performed at St Stephen's School Room, Lewisham.

A year of 'great development' for Charles (15) who goes on holiday to Devon with Ed (22) and falls in love with the area.

On return to the Prop, Charles is in the VIth form and is made a Monitor. He plays in the 1st Rugger XV.

1894
Frank (24) passes his ARIBA exams and goes to Emersons [architectural practice?] '94–'95.

Ed (23) and Charles (16) go to Chertsey. Charles has German measles and later starts smoking seriously.

A wet summer in which Charles develops into a cricketer, scoring 81in the 2nd X1; he also develops an interest in Beethoven (sister Mary plays the Sonatas) and 'discovers' Kipling.

'Living Whist' at St Stephen's Bazaar in Penn's grounds [**H**].

The parents take Mary (19) to Switzerland, Charles accompanying them as far as Antwerp. Charles and Ed go for their August holiday to Devon again; the Twins go to Lympstone. Nix and Frank with 'Pi' and 'JAD' to the Broads.

Charles is well-established in the Prop VIth form, and in the 1st Rugger XV. Nix (26) starts working for P&O as a ship's doctor. For the past two years he has had appointments at NW London Hospital and Woolwich.

Christmas at No 1 The Paragon is the last time all six brothers celebrate together.

210

Appendices

1895
Nix sails for Calcutta on the *Himalaya.*

Charles (17) unexpectedly wins two VIth form prizes and starts smoking again.

Charles gets his cricket colours and makes his first century.

The Gov rents St Stephen's Rectory in Cornwall from Kendall Rashleigh. Charles subsequently meets Ed (24) ('a most fearful dog, with unlimited wealth') at Newton Abbot; they go to Thurlston and Lustleigh, liking the latter so much that they repeat the visit the following year.

Nix on a voyage to Bombay on the *Khedive.*

1896
Frank (26) leaves England for South Africa, his engagement to Annie Izard before sailing having been disallowed by old Mr Izard [**J**]. [*Marginal note: possibly this was in 1900.*] He [Frank] is seen off by the Gov, his sister Mary, and Pip Durnford who gives him a pipe of notable longevity.

At about this time the Twins (15) have to have extra tuition in mathematics, and 'Rinking Parties' start up. They also, with Gren[ville] [Granville] Orde Browne, establish the 'Kenorde Club' leading to pranks, though not so dire as those conducted previously under the leadership of Bertie McDougall.

Charles (18) leaves the Prop in great glory, having won a scholarship to Wadham College, Oxford. In the summer holidays he is in Devon again with Ed, 'Pip' and Cam Watson.

Charles, his parents and Ed stay at the Mitre in Oxford, to secure rooms on his going up to university.

Ed (25) leaves for Australia in his employment with the Australian Mortgage Land & Finance Co. With Charles going up to Oxford, the family has broken up, never to reunite.

Nix (P&O doctor) and Ed (AML & F Co.) spend Christmas together in Sydney.

1897
Charles home from Oxford for Xmas. – 'a very small party this year, no Nix, no Frank and no Ed – no hot sausage'.

Nix returns from his voyage to Sydney, and Fred gets whooping cough.

Charles returns to his digs at Oxford and is associated with the revival of the 'Pagan Club' (the Old Blackheathen Oxford club): 'Its chief charm is that there are no subscriptions, Lamb President and Hone Secretary.' Other fellow Blackheathens are Harry Banning, de Havilland and Smyth.

On his return to Oxford after the Easter vacation, Charles moves into college. Mary is keen on cycling 'but I suspect that she will soon get sick of it'.

Charles fails to get home for the [Diamond] Jubilee (*22 June 1897*) as celebrated in Blackheath, but manages the Naval Review (*2-11 July 1897*).

Nix joins Mary, Charles and the Twins on summer holiday in Cornwall.

On his return to Oxford, Charles, as Secretary of the Pagan Club, has to organise the Annual Dinner – 'a great anxiety' but it turns out a great success. Marchant coming over from Cambridge as Hone's guest.

Charles is back in Blackheath for the Xmas vacation; Nix also at home, with the prospect of starting practice in Chiddingfold, Surrey.

1898
Frank in South Africa and Ed in Australia send frequent letters home which are circulated among the family.

Charles, home for the Xmas vacation, plays in the Blackheath Golf Tournament with 'Ethel' [? Robson], Edith Tate and Mrs Spurling. Mary spends time at Alverstoke, Portsmouth.

Nix starts practice at Chiddingfold, and is visited there by Charles during the Easter vacation. Back in Oxford, Charles is elected future President of the Pagan Club. As Secretary of the cricket and rugger clubs he arranges to take a cricket team to Chiddingfold. He also keeps up with the Prop's sporting activities in which the Twins, Fred and Herbert, participate.

Fred and Herbert (17) leave the Prop and Fred achieves a £40 p.a. appointment as bank clerk. Charles spends part of his vacation in Devon again.

After a successful autumn term at Oxford, Charles joins Nix in attending a fancy-dress dance given by Conan Doyle, taking two Oxford friends, before spending Xmas at Blackheath.

1899
Frank and Ed continue life in Cape Town and Sydney respectively, while Nix is developing his medical career in Chiddingfold.

Charles moves from his rooms in college to digs with friends.

Fred gets an appointment with P&O and is invited to a party in Oxford where he wins 15/- [75p] at vingt-et-un, to the alarm of his parents. Charles takes his 'Greats' (June) and goes home to Blackheath afterwards.

Fred has to work from 6.00 to 9.00 each evening at his bank job.

Ed (28) becomes engaged to Minna Gibson in Australia.

1900
Frank returns from Cape Town (*Feb*).

Charles is still at Oxford and goes to stay with 'Uncle Mike' at Wolverhampton in the autumn, just before the latter's fall and criminal conviction.

Mary (25) pays a visit to Ed in Australia but, unknown to the rest of the family, has become seriously ill.

1901
Ed, in Australia, marries Minna Gibson (*Feb*).

Herbert, in his P&O appointment, is posted to Suez where he meets Mary on her way back from Australia; he travels with her on the *Himalaya* as far as Port Said and later moves on to Bombay.

Cousin Harry Kendall returns from leave from the East and is a given a drink by Charles at the Paragon while the latter is working for the ICS [Indian Civil Service] exam.

Nix marries Kathleen ('Kaf') Izard (*May*).

After passing the ICS exam and having taken a 'good 2nd in Mods and Greats', Charles is in Devon again, walking on Dartmoor.

Frank takes possession of his house in Kenilworth [a suburb of Cape Town] named 'Penlyn' in honour of the family's traditional home in Cornwall.

1902
The Gov is asked to become a trustee for the Kendall home of Penlyn in Cornwall but turns this down.

Nichol is born to Nix and Kathleen.

Death of Mary (*17 June*).

Charles leaves for India (Nov) on the Egypt on his appointment in the ICS, accompanied by the Gov as far as Marseilles. On reaching Bombay he stays with Herbert, still posted there by P&O.

1903
Fred leaves England (26 Feb) for his appointment with the Hong Kong & Shanghai Bank. He is posted (Aug) to Shanghai for three months and then goes on to Tientsin where he gets rheumatic fever.

By writing his 'contribbber' in a notebook, Nix initiates the start of the 'Round Robins' between the six brothers, in place of letters which have been passed around the family.

Nix, with 'Kai and Jo', spends Xmas with the Gov and DOM at the Paragon.

1904
Fred, in Tientsin, is recovering from rheumatic fever. Charles is stationed in Gonda in the United Provinces, Herbert in Bombay.

Frank, in the architectural firm of Baker, Massey & Kendall, is transferred from Cape Town to Bloemfontein (*March*) but he is struck down (*May*) with a mild attack of enteric. Ed is still in the Sydney office of AML & F Co.

Charles is called in from Gonda to do duty in the Secretariat at Allahabad (*Oct*). Nix moves house in Chiddingfold (*Dec*) but spends Xmas at Blackheath.

Appendices

1905
Herbert is transferred from Bombay to Hong Kong with P&O.

Charles (*April to June*) and Ed and Min (May to Sept) on leave in England and spend time at the Paragon.

Charles, on return to India, is posted to Aligarth and then Hamirpur. Fred, in the HK & S Bank, is transferred from Tientsin to Hong Kong, joining his twin brother Herbert there (Aug).

Frank arrives home on leave from South Africa, coinciding briefly with Ed and Min. He accompanies them on their voyage back to Australia as far as Marseilles.

Charles, in Hamirpur, starts a long period in camp (*Nov*) on famine relief work.

1906
At the end of his leave Frank becomes formally engaged to Annie Izard (*Jan*) who comes out to Cape Town to stay with Strubens before marrying Frank (*May*).

A dinner is given at the Great Eastern Hotel [Liverpool Street], to celebrate the Gov's 50 years' service with P&O (*20 Feb*). He retires from his position as Chief General Manager in August.

Betty is born to Nix and Kathleen.

1907
Herbert, on leave from Hong Kong, goes to Melbourne (*April*), where Ed has been transferred with AML & F Co., to visit Ed and Min before travelling to England.

Nick is born to Frank and Annie in Cape Town.

The death of the Gov (*23 Dec*) brings about the break-up of the family home at No 1 the Paragon.

Notes on the people mentioned above
The children of Franklin Richardson Kendall and his wife, Frances Margaret (née Kay), were as below. Home for them all from 1881 to 1907 was No 1 The Paragon. Although a number of them wandered off to their various professional postings within those dates, the house remained the Kendall family base until the tragic death of Franklin Kendall in December 1907.

The boys kept in touch throughout their remaining lives and generated a remarkable correspondence (which survives in an archive in Cornwall) covering their professional and private lives and travels. This correspondence mostly spans the years from 1908 to the end of their days, as time unfolded, and does not touch to any degree on the Paragon except in occasional reminiscences.

Bryan Kendall, of the third generation, compiled a checklist of their activities and schooling from the letter books, when they were boys in the Paragon and afterwards. With kind permission of Ric hard Kendall, of the present generation, this is reproduced here. Coupled with these notes are the floor plans of the house drawn from memory by Frank Kendall in 1915 and the sale catalogue of 1908 when the contents of the house were sold. It is the only record we have of the everyday life of a Paragon family until the wartime notebooks kept by some of the paying guests in the crescent in the early 1940s (*see Chapter 6*).

The Kendall boys were:

Nicholas Fletcher Kendall, 'Nix' (1869-1929). 4/81-7/85

Franklin K. Kendall (1870-1949). 4/81-7/85

Edward William Allan Kendall (1872-1952). 4/85-7/88

Sir Charles Henry Bayley Kendall (1878-1935). Easter 86-6/96.
Entry in *Who's Who*.

Herbert M. Kendall (1880-1964). 12/91-Easter 98

Frederick C. Kendall (1880-1944). 12/91-10/97

They had one sister: Mary Ann (who died aged only 26 on 17 June 1902).

Cousin Harry lived with the Kendall family some of the time before joining his parents at Southsea, Hants. He had returned to Blackheath by 1891 when he was boarding at No 39 Bennett Park.

The dates on the right indicate the time that the boys were at the Blackheath Proprietary School (see Chapter 4).

Notes

A – Blackheath Proprietary School: a modest public day school for boys which stood on the corner of Lee Terrace and Blackheath Village from 1831 to 1907. Although small, it achieved astonishing success, with a large number of the boys finding distinction in their professions, largely in the Church, the law and the Army (see Chapter 4).

B – 'Vipans' was the nickname of the small preparatory school which was housed at No 20 St John's Park and was conducted successively by Mrs Mackinnon, Mr and Mrs Vipan, and Thomas Postlethwaite, during whose time the boys called the school 'Possy's'.

It functioned as a school from 1865 to 1901. In the Kendalls' time it was run by Mrs Elizabeth Mackinnon; then by Edward and Frances Alice Vipan, who called the enterprise Shirley House School; and then by Thomas Norman Postlethwaite, aided by Revd Frederick William Stamp Le Lièvre until 1895.

C – The Robsons: architect Edward Robert Robson (1835–1917) and his family lived at No 2 The Paragon for the entire period that the Kendalls occupied No 1, and the families became close friends.

D – The Barray-Jupps: Edward Barray-Jupp and his family lived at No 76 St John's Park. The Kendall boys were particularly friendly with Bertie Barray-Jupp (known to them as 'the Inev' ('the Inevitable'?). He subsequently worked for P&O.

E – Blackheath High School for Girls: established in 1880 in Wemyss Road in a splendid building designed by architect Edward Robert Robson, the Kendalls' next-door neighbour.

F – Miss Birch's Kindergarten: a small nursery school at No 41 St John's Park, conducted by the Misses Elizabeth and Elsie Birch. In January 1891 it advertised itself as 'a High-Class Preparatory School for Girls', but closed soon afterwards, perhaps for lack of takers.

G – The McDougalls (flour millers) lived at Dunnolly, now No 4 Morden Road – then the Kendalls' nearest neighbour to the south.

H – Living Whist, Living Draughts and Living Chess were great favourites at garden parties and charity bazaars. Mrs Penn's house – The Cedars on Belmont Hill – enjoyed enormous grounds and she lent them willingly for charitable events. Children would dress up as the appropriate token, piece or suit and move about according to the instructions of the players. Whist was more difficult in that it was hard to hide all one's hand from the opponents at the beginning of a game.

J – Walter George Izard (1840–1918), civil and railway engineer, lived at No 10 The Paragon from 1880 to 1917. Two of his daughters married Kendall boys.

K – Mods and Greats: in full, Moderations and Greats. Moderations was the first public examination in certain faculties for the BA degree at Oxford University. Greats: the Oxford University final examination for an honours course, especially in classics and philosophy.

By Order of the Executors of the late F. R. KENDALL, Esq.]   [No. 1755.

1 THE PARAGON,

BLACKHEATH.

(Within 10 minutes' walk of Blackheath Station).

A CATALOGUE

OF THE SUPERIOR

FURNITURE

Comprising Brass French Bedsteads,

WALNUT BEDROOM SUITE,

Mahogany Duchesse Tables, Dressing Chests and Washstands, and
the usual Bedchamber Appendages,

DRAWING ROOM APPOINTMENTS

Occasional Armchairs upholstered in Tapestry,

A GRAND PIANOFORTE

By JOHN BRINSMEAD & SONS, in Rosewood Case, a Set of Lac Japan Coffee
Tables, Set of Fancy Rush Seat Chairs, Ebonized and Gilt Mirrors,

INLAID WALNUT CABINET,

With Ormolu Mount,

DINING ROOM FURNITURE

Principally in Oak, comprising Extending Tables, Pedestal Sideboards,
Two Dinner Wagons,

SUITE UPHOLSTERED IN GREEN MOROCCO

Mahogany Pedestal Writing Tables, Six Chairs in Saddlebags, Walnut Hat
and Umbrella Stand, Oak Hall Chairs,

500 VOLUMES OF BOOKS,

AXMINSTER AND BRUSSELS CARPETS,

A few items of China, Glass, and Ornamental Effects,

WHICH WILL BE SOLD BY AUCTION BY MESSRS.

DYER, SON & HILTON

On the Premises, as above,

On THURSDAY, JANUARY 30th, 1908,

AT ONE O'CLOCK PUNCTUALLY.

May be viewed the Day prior and Morning of Sale, and Catalogues had of
the Auctioneers,

30 Budge Row, Cannon Street, E.C., and Blackheath, S.E.

Telephones—5792 Bank and 19 Lee Green.

CHARLES NORTH, THE BLACKHEATH PRESS, S.E.

CONDITIONS OF SALE.

I.—The highest bidder shall be the purchaser. If any dispute arise between the bidders, the lot to be put up again at the bidding immediately preceding dispute, or the auctioneer may declare the purchaser.

II.—The advance in the biddings to be regulated by the auctioneer, who is to be the sole arbiter in any matter of dispute. He also reserves to himself the right to refuse any bidding, to withdraw, consolidate or divide any lot or lots, or to submit the lots in any order, without regard to the position of the same in catalogue, as may be deemed advisable.

III.—The purchasers to pay (if required) a deposit of five shillings in the pound as part payment, such deposit to be a general deposit on the whole or any of the lots of such buyers. Every purchaser to give his name and place of abode.

IV.—Each and every lot shall at the fall of the hammer be considered as delivered, and no lot or lots can be removed until the whole amount of the purchaser's account shall be paid in full, and payment is to be made to the person appointed to deliver. No warranty is given, or to be implied by the description in the catalogue.

V.—The lots **must be paid for and cleared away from the premises**, with all faults, imperfections, and errors of description, **before 4 p.m. on the day after the sale**, and no allowance whatever shall be made for misdescription or errors of whatsoever nature. *Any damage caused by removal, or otherwise, must be made good by the person committing the same; principals being considered responsible for the acts of their servants.*

VI.—The auctioneer reserves the right of making an allowance for the whole or any portion of a lot not delivered from any cause whatsoever—at the same rate at which such lot was purchased; and inasmuch as Dyer, Son & Hilton act only as agents for the vendors, they shall not be considered personally responsible for any default on the part of either vendor or purchaser. The vendor reserves the right to bid by himself, themselves, or their agents, or his agent.

VII.—Any lots uncleared by the appointed time, agreeably with the conditions, will be forfeited, and may be re-sold or warehoused at the expense of the purchaser; any deficiency arising from re-sale, together with warehouse charges and all attendant expenses, including sale foreman's charge of 5s. per day, shall be made good by the purchaser.

Lastly.—On failure of complying with the above conditions, or non-performance of all or any part of them, the defaulters will lose their deposits, and the auctioneer or clerk of sale shall be at liberty to take such steps as may be deemed necessary to bring the transaction to a close; and if a re-sale be effected, either by public auction or private contract, all loss and expenses shall devolve upon the defaulter at this sale.

No lots will be transferred,

The nett total I should estimate to me about £112 — I was not there at the beginning or end of the sales, & missed the prices of some of the lots.

Hutles

30. 1. 08

CATALOGUE.

On Thursday, January 30th, 1908,

At ONE o'clock punctually.

Upper Floor—Cistern Room.

Lot

1 A strip of Brussels carpet, a 4-fold screen, a wicker linen basket and a lamp stove

2 - A 2ft. 6in. iron bedstead, a pair of palliasses, a wool mattress, a feather bolster and 2 pillows

3 A 3ft. grained chest of 3 long and 2 short drawers

Front Room.

4 A 3ft. iron bedstead, a pair of palliasses, a wool overlay, a hair mattress, a feather bolster and a pillow

5 A 2ft. 6in. grained dressing table fitted drawer, a 2ft. painted washstand, 6 pieces blue floral pattern toilet ware and a white slop vase and cover

5

Lot

21 A mahogany swing frame toilet glass (plate 16in. by 12in.), and a 2ft. 6in. iron fender and a scoop

22

23

Second Floor—Left Front Room.

24 The blue ground Brussels carpet as planned to room about 18 yards and 1 cork mat

25 A pair of tapestry curtains, a pair of short muslin ditto and a worked table cover, a linen basket and a small hanging bookshelf

26 A 3ft. 6in. walnut .dressing table fitted 2 drawers with swing frame mirror over (plate 22in. by 16in.)

27 The companion 3ft. 6in. washstand fitted 2 drawers with marble top and tiled back

28 A set of white and gilt toilet ware (8 pieces), a white ware slop vase and cover, a ditto foot bath, a water bottle and tumbler and an odd chamber

29 A *4ft. superior walnut chest* of 3 long and 2 short drawers *3/-*

30 A ditto pedestal cupboard, 2 cane-seat chairs and a 5-rail towel airer

31 A 2ft. 10in. Italian walnut Sutherland table with oval top on turned supports and castors *25/-*

32 A mahogany frame easy chair spring and hair stuffed and upholstered in cretonne with extra loose cover *22/-*

33

34

35

36

Bath Room.

Lot

37 The linoleum as laid, a cork bath mat

38 A 3ft. 6in. white enamelled washstand with shelf under

39 A mahogany circular washstand and 5 pieces of blue and white toilet ware

40 A floral pattern basin, a small white and gilt ditto, 2 chambers, 4 pieces of odd toilet fittings and a water bottle

41 A patent magnetic filter, a japanned footbath, a ditto pail and 9 hot-water cans

42

43

Back Room.

44 A 2ft. grained dressing table, a green canvas cover, 4 casement curtains, an ottoman box-covered cloth, a japanned hip bath, a pair of tongs, a shovel and 5 opal gas globes

45 A cane-seat and back folding chair and an ebonized frame ditto

46 A fancy wicker chair and 2 oak frame rush seat chairs

47 A mahogany commode fitted liner and cover

48 A *3ft. well-made walnut hanging wardrobe* enclosed by bevelled mirror panel door with drawer under

49 A 3ft. 4in. ditto chest of 3 long and 2 short drawers

50 Two 3-tier hanging bookshelves and a corner bracket

51

52

53

7

· First Floor—Front Room.

Lot

54 A 3ft. 8in. iron fender, a railed fire-guard and a japanned coal hod and scoop

15/-

55 Two pairs of marone repp curtains and 4 short muslin ditto

£3. 3.,

56 A *5ft. brass French bedstead*, a wire spring mattress, a hair ditto, a feather bolster and 2 ditto pillows

£1, 1.,

57 A 3ft. 9in. birch chest of 3 long and 2 short drawers

£1. 14.,

58 A 3ft. 9in. well-made birch Duchesse dressing table fitted 3 drawers with swing frame mirror over (plate 30in. by 20in.)

16/-

59 The companion 3ft. 9in. washstand with marble top and tiled back fitted drawer

60 A 4-rail ditto towel airer, a pedestal cupboard and 3 cane-seat chairs

61 A set of pink and gilt decorated toilet ware 9 pieces, a white ware slop vase and cover, a water bottle and tumbler and a japanned hip bath

62 A wicker lounge chair, a folding mahogany table and a corner bracket

63 Four white opal gas globes, 2 plaster figures, 2 ditto placques, a tobacco jar and cover, a metal dragon inkpot, 2 lac japan vases and 3 small ornaments

4/-

64 An oleograph in oak frame, a ditto in gilt frame, a small oil painting "Seascape," 3 photographs and a text

65 A trunk stand, 3 pottery vases, a fur rug and a hassock

10/-

66 A finely embroidered panel in ebonized frame

Back Room.

Lot

67 Two pairs brown serge curtains

£3. 68 A *5ft. brass French bedstead*, a wire spring mattress, a hair mattress, a feather bolster and 2 feather pillows

8/. 69 A 3-fold Japanese screen and a large glazed case

70 An *exceptionally well-made walnut and gilt bedroom suite* comprising:—

> A 6ft. 6in. wardrobe fitted sliding trays drawers and hanging pegs, enclosed by 2 panel and centre mirror door

£13. - 13. > A 4ft. 6in. ditto dressing table fitted 6 drawers with swing-frame mirror over (plate 28in. by 20in.)

> The companion 4ft. 6in. washstand fitted 2 drawers with marble top and tiled back

> A pedestal cupboard

> A 5-rail towel airer

> Three cane-seat chairs

71 A set of green band and gilt toilet ware (13 pieces), a white ware slop vase and cover and a water bottle and tumbler

72

73 An engraving in Oxford frame, "Jesus at the Well," and a mahogany hanging bookshelf

3/- 74 A plate glass showcase (3ft. 8in. by 2ft. 2in. by 1ft. 6in.)

75

76

10

Study.

	Lot	
3/-	97	A 3ft. steel top fender, a set of brass mounted implements and a hearth brush
2/-	98	A pair of damask curtains and a pair of casement ditto
4/-	99	A 24in. oak oval top table on folding frame
13/-	100	A ball frame armchair and cushions upholstered in saddle-bags and velvet
18/-	101	A 24in. mahogany revolving bookstand
£1 4	102	Six oak frame chairs seats and backs upholstered in saddlebags
	103	An etching in oak frame and a print in oak frame
10/-	104	
18/-	105	*Harewood flower stand*
2/-		*gas brackets in Charlie's & smoking roo*

Drawing Room.

2. 4	106	The green-ground floral pattern bordered pile carpet as planned to room (about 80yds.)
8/-	107	A 5ft. brass-rail fender and a set of fire brasses
5/-	108	A 4ft. 6in. brass-rail curb fender
5. 9/-	109	*Four pairs of heavy tapestry curtains with twill linings*
	110	Two Oriental tapestry portiere curtains and 4 pairs of casement curtains
5/-	111	A 4-fold panel screen
15/-	112	Six birch frame chairs with fancy rush seats and a child's ditto
17/-	113	An ebonized frame rush seat corner chair, 3 ditto railed back occasional chairs and a settee
5/-	114	A corner seat upholstered in figured damask and a ditto window seat

II

Lot

18/- 115 Three walnut-frame occasional easy chairs spring stuffed
and upholstered in tapestry

£1. 116 A marqueterie inlaid stained frame armchair and 2 small
ditto

12/- 117 An ebonized ball frame rush seat corner chair and a burr
walnut Sutherland table on turned supports and castors

£10. 118 A *fine toned 7-octave grand pianoforte* in rosewood case
by *John Broadwood & Sons*

119 A carved oak music stand, a folding bamboo stand for
dumb waiter and a painted stool

12/- 120 A set of 4 lac-japan coffee tables

£3.3. 121 A *5ft. inlaid walnut cabinet* with ormolu mounts enclosed
by glazed side and centre panel doors

1-5. 122 A mirror in oval gilt rope pattern frame (plate 50in. by
40in.)

15/- 123 A 4-fold carved and inlaid panel screen and a folding card
table

£1.11. 124 An 8-day timepiece in black marble case

£1.6. 125 A 4ft. 6in. ebonized and gilt overmantel (centre plate 50in.
by 40in.) with shelves at sides

10/- 126 A silvered plaque in plush frame and 6 Indian clay figures

8/- 127 An ebonized corner hanging bracket enclosed by glazed
door

8/- 128 A pair of 12in. painted and gilt ewers

7/- 129 A ware figure of cat and ball, a plaster group under glass
shade and 3 ware ornaments

17/- 130 A valuable Chinese painting on long scroll (12ft. by 4ft.)

6/- 131 A wrought-iron and brass-mounted extending floor lamp

7/- 132 Six ornaments various

12/- 2 Gaseliers.

223

Dining Room.

Lot

5/- 133 The linoleum as planned to surround, a 4ft. 6in. brass rail kerb fender, a set of brass-mounted implements and a hearth brush

8/- 134 An inlaid mahogany coal purdonium fitted liner and scoop

£1.— 135 Two pairs of lined blue-ground tapestry curtains and holders

£2.17.6. 136 A 4ft. 3in. oak extending dining table on turned supports and castors fitted 5 extra leaves (opening to 11ft.)

13. 137 A 4ft. 6in. ditto side table on turned supports

£8. 138 *A well-made oak dining-room suite hair stuffed and upholstered in green morocco, comprising :—*

Couch

Two easy chairs

Ten small chairs

13/- 139 A 3ft. 9in. oak 3-tier dinner wagon

13/- 140 A 3ft. 6in. carved ditto

141 A 7ft. oak pedestal sideboard fitted shelves and cellarette enclosed by panel doors with 4 drawers in frieze and mirror back

£3.3. 142 A 4ft. superior mahogany pedestal writing table fitted 9 drawers with lined leather top

6/- 143 A pair of blue felt bordered curtains and a felt table cover

16/- 144 A carved ebony box and an inlaid ivory ditto

8/- 145 A pair of pottery bottles, a brass bell, a cigar box and a plated cup

3/- 146 Two ware jardinieres, 3 cigar boxes and sundries

5/- 147 A copper and wrought iron footman and a 3-fold screen with silk panels

148 Three etchings in black reeded frames, an engraving in maple frame and 2 engravings in oak frames, "Ancient Greece"

10/- 149 A mahogany hanging medicine cupboard

10/- **3/-** 150 *gaselier*

Entrance Hall.

Lot

13/- 151 A 4ft. oak hall table fitted 2 drawers

11/- 152 Two oak hall chairs with tile panel backs

£1.2. 153 A 2ft. 6in. walnut hat and umbrella stand with mirror panel back and brass pegs

15/- 154 A ware umbrella drainer and 4 pairs of antlers

9/- 155 *A pair of heavy tapestry curtains*

11/- 156 An engraving in gilt frame, "A Day Dream"

7/- 157 An oleograph in gilt frame, "Steamship," an engraving in oak frame, "Malta," a photograph, "Niagara" and 3 others

3/- 158 A small brass gong and beater on oak stand, a brass match holder and a calendar frame

14/- 159 4 ornaments in drawing room

11/- 160 2 lamps.

———

Basement—Schoolroom.

6/- 161 The linoleum as laid to surround and a bordered Brussels carpet (4ft. by 4ft.)

5/- 162 A 3ft. 6in. brass rail fender, a wire spark guard and a pair of serge curtains

£1.1. 163 A 3ft. 6in. oak extending table on turned supports and castors with 2 extra leaves

£1-16 164 A 4ft. oak enclosed pedestal sideboard fitted shelves and cellarette with drawer in frieze

3/- 165 A wicker armchair and a mahogany-frame cane-seat folding lounge chair

2/- 166 An ebonized bentwood cane-seat chair, a rush-seat ditto and a stained-frame ditto

14

Lot

2/- 167 A mahogany-frame invalid's chair and ~~3 canvas lounge chairs~~

10/- 168 A model of ship in glazed case and a case of butterflies

3/- 169 A 3-tier hanging bookshelf, a timepiece in fret-carved case and 15 small ornaments (various)

5/- 170 A small water-colour in gilt frame and 11 photographs (various)

3/- 171 A jack plane, a set square, a leather tool wallet and sundries as lotted

9/- 172 An Arctic rifle in case and another

4/4 173 A carved bookslide and sundry curios

4/- 174 A writing desk in leather case

7/- 175 *revolver and pillows*

10/- 176 *scioptican*

———

Books.

Vols.

6/- 177 Beaconsfield's Works 3, Lytton's Works 2, and 15 novels (various) — 20

5/- 178 Family Physician 1, Graham's Domestic Medicine 1, Every Man's Lawyer 1, Victorian Year Book 2, The Sailor's Handbook 1, and 40 others — 46

2/- 179 Our First Century 1, Paley's Works 4, Polar Regions by Richardson 1, and 50 others — 56

12/- 180 History of Merchant Shipping 4, Thearle's Modern Shipbuilding 2, Australian Handbook 2, and 30 others — 38

9/- 181 Oriental Races 1, Flowers from an Indian Garden 1, Dalmatia Illustrated 1, and 20 others — 23

6/- 182 Robinson Crusoe 1, Every Boy's Annual 1, Grimms' Fairy Tales 1, and 30 others — 33

15

Lot

2/- 183 100 volumes various

1/- 184 A similar lot

185 A similar lot

8/- 186 Fifty volumes various and a quantity of unbound
magazines and reviews

£1. 2. 187 A large number of unbound copies of Punch

13/- 188 A ditto lot of Vanity Fair with cartoons

189

190

191

———— —

Front Room.

6/- 192 The linoleum as laid, a large bordered Oriental rug, a
length of bordered Axminster carpet and a length of
Brussels carpet

3/- 193 A 4ft. slide bar kitchen fender and a japanned and brass
mounted coal purdonium and scoop

3/- 194 A 4ft. 6in. by 2ft. 6in. deal kitchen table and a Windsor
chair

7/- 195 A 3ft. grained chest of 3 long and 2 short drawers, 2
bentwood-frame chairs and a cane-seat ditto (faulty)

6/- 196 A deal top Pembroke table, a cane seat and back folding
chair and a canvas ditto

197 An oil painting in gilt frame, "Portrait"

14/- 198 A printed damask table cover, a crumb cloth and a serge
table cover

199

200

18

Larder.

Lot

237 Two brown ware pans, a cover, a ditto sugar jar and cover, a ditto cooker, a butter jar and cover, a pestle and mortar and 2 moulds

238 A set of scales and weights, 8 store canisters and 2 zinc baths

239 Four copper stewpans and covers

240 A deal meat safe, a flour tub, a knife board and a beer stollage

241 A 3ft. painted washstand, a deal chair (faulty) and 3 iron coal hods

242

———

Basement Passage.

243 A deal napkin press on stand, a turk's head broom, a hair broom and sundry brushes and a mirror in mahogany frame

244
245
246

END OF SALE.

Appendix II

Miss Eliza Robertson and Miss Charlotte Sharpe
of No 3 The Paragon

by Bill [William] Bonwitt

(gently revised 2011 by Neil Rhind and Jane Birkett)

The two women whose names head this chapter were the first occupiers of No 3 The Paragon, and they were a far cry from the solid, well-established and comfortably-off middle-class residents for whom John Cator's terrace was built.

Miss Robertson, the leading character of this tragicomedy, wrote her own story and as there are few independent reports left, this biographical note is, of necessity, based on her own writings. Her account has been accepted where self-justification was unnecessary but everything else had to be weighed carefully against known facts and probabilities. No other account of the early days in the Paragon can be found and, therefore, her recollections are of particular interest.

Eliza Frances Robertson was born on 5 February 1771, in Bermondsey. Her father was an oilman, resident in the Horsleydown district. He was a shiftless character and of his wife Miss Robertson says that she had no affection for either her husband or her children. In fact, she calls her mother 'her most inveterate and cruel enemy', yet claims to have supported her in later years.

Eliza must have had a reasonably good education for, in 1787, she became a teacher in a school run by a lady in Richmond. She alleges that she became that lady's partner within a few months. That seems remarkable at the age of 16 but she had a forceful character capable of subjecting other people to her will. In any case, the partnership did not last long. In 1788, her father took a house in Sloane Street, Chelsea, where he wanted Eliza to educate his other daughters and 'yet be all mistresses'.

How far she managed to prepare her sisters for their putative profession is unknown. She says that apart from them, she had 19 of the most respectable children in the neighbourhood as her pupils. But, once more, this venture ended soon. In mid-1789 her father 'again' had all his effects seized for non-payment of excise duty and be-came a bankrupt.

Miss Robertson appears to have been fairly astute and quick to take advantage of a favourable situation but matters of business were not her strong suit. Consequently, she always appears as the dupe. Following her father's bankruptcy, a draper sued on a bill for £50 '... though he would have settled for £25', and tried to arrest her. He failed to do so as she was still a minor. Proba-bly her father induced her to sign the bill because his own name was unacceptable in view of his previous record. Later in the same year her father again persuaded her to endorse one of his bills to enable him to avoid arrest. She obliged because she thought that she was succeeding with her school and was in '... expectations of a fortune from her maternal grandfather'.

This was the first of many flights of fancy which led to her ultimate destruction. Her maternal grandfather's name was Earle, who was a prosperous woollen draper and who resided for some time in Lee and Lewisham.

After the death of Eliza's grandmother he married, in 1775, his servant. It is unlikely that he would have left any money to Eliza as the relationship between him and her parents was bad and he did not ap-prove of his son-in-law. There is no evidence that he left Eliza any money at any time.

She writes that over a period she managed to pay off her father's debts (of up to £200 and attendant costs) by running a seminary of her own in Chelsea. A seminary is unlikely to have generated sufficient profits to discharge such a considerable debt because, in November 1789, her school failed. This was hardly surprising considering her lack of experience. The responsi-bilities she claims to have undertaken at the age of 18 were considerable and, in any case, far too many incidents are crammed into so few months that this part of her story is not credible.

Being of presentable appearance she did not lack suitors and one man, a Mr J. Flowerdew – the father of one of her pupils – offered her £200 a year and a house if she would consent to be his mistress. This offer she claims to have declined although there is a suggestion in her story that she used the occasion to try a little genteel blackmail. Miss Robertson left London in 1790 because she had once more signed one of her father's bills, in favour of a Mr Larkin. He must have been an unrelenting creditor and may have tried to have her arrested, for the memory of Larkin and his bond haunted her for the rest of her life. Her memoirs contain the following account of her absence from London from 1790 to1795.

First she obtained employment in Scotland as governess to the daughters of the 'Honourable Mrs Cunningham'. The son of the house, Colonel Robert Cunningham, fell in love with her and proposed marriage but his father did not approve. It is much more likely that the son attempted and perhaps succeeded in seducing her.

Mrs Cunningham, however, took a liking to Eliza. As her own maiden name was also Robertson and as she imagined facial similarities between Eliza and herself, she tried to establish a family relationship. Eliza claims that a real friendship developed between her and her employer which, given the social gap between them and the short time Eliza stayed there, is highly unlikely. In fact the whole story sounds rather far-fetched but it forms the basis of the swindles in which Eliza Robertson engaged later in her life.

She stayed with the Cunninghams for five months but her relationship with Robert Cunningham made the position untenable. She then took another job in Scotland, near the Cunninghams, at a seminary at Tottenham Cross, where her suitor, the Colonel, used to call on her almost daily. The ladies in charge of the seminary took an unfavour-able view of this and Eliza was soon dismissed. She journeyed south and found an-other position, this time in Cheshire, where she remained for about four-and-a-half years.

This explanation of her years away from London is highly suspect. She says that the Cunninghams lived in Donoghadee, Scotland. There seems to be no such place in Scotland but in Ireland are several villages, seats and a small town of that name on the Irish Channel, 20 miles east of Belfast. Later in her story she mentions Mrs Cunningham's son-in–law, Sir W. H. Pagett, of Summer Hill.

Such a place written as two words exists in England, and as a single word can be found in Ireland and in Aberdeenshire. None of these places, whether in England or Scotland, have any discovered connection with a family called Pagett.

Further, the fam-ilies of Sir W. H. Pagett and of the Hon. Mrs Cunningham have not been traced in any of the standard reference books covering the period. As for Tottenham Cross – there is no such place anywhere in Scotland of that name listed in the authoritative reference gazetteers.

The inference is that she fled from London on account of either her father's or her own debts, and spent varying periods of time in Ireland, Scotland and Cheshire.

Her acti-vities during these five years cannot have been entirely to her credit or honour inasmuch as she is always careful to describe only those events in her life which were in her favour. Anything to her disadvantage is glossed over. Nevertheless, whatever she did must be judged in the context of the times. Life for a young woman, entirely alone with neither family connections nor money, must have been difficult and yet Eliza Robertson seems to have escaped relatively unharmed from whatever difficulties she met. In fact she obtained an excellent reference from the teaching job which she held in Cheshire.

In February 1795, now aged 24, Eliza was back in London, teaching at a school at No 66 Crooms Hill, owned and conducted by Miss Charlotte Sharpe. Charlotte Sharpe had started her school around Christmas 1791 at No 1 [now No 21] Gloucester Circus, Greenwich, of which house she was the first formal tenant. But by Christmas 1794 she had left The Circus and had moved to Crooms Hill where her school continued until 1801. It would be interesting to know why she moved from a brand new to an old house. Although the lease had only five years to run, it was a larger property and, perhaps, the school was successful.

Little is known about Charlotte Sharpe. She wrote no books and there are no refer-ences in Miss Robertson's memoirs to her age, background or education. Dr Thomas Forbes Leith, a Greenwich physician, described her as 'a woman of respectability'. But she remains an enig-matic figure who seems to have played a somewhat equivocal role in Eliza Robertson's life.

The two women became attached to each other and, after two or three years, Eliza may have become Charlotte Sharpe's business partner. The Greenwich parish rate books for 1799 and 1800 show them to have been jointly responsible for the rates, so her claim was possibly true. Their intimacy, however, did not please a Mrs Neal, a boarder in Charlotte Sharpe's house for a period who had known her since about 1786 or 1787. According to Eliza, Mrs Neal became querulous and troublesome and, to judge by character, it would have pleased Eliza to see her gone.

The partnership continued until at least 1799 when the lease of the Crooms Hill property was about to expire. During these five years, both women seem to have behaved themselves with propriety and their financial affairs were conducted honourably. But to-wards the end of 1799 Eliza received some news which set her imagination aflame.

When in Scotland, Eliza claimed to have taken a liking to the Hon. Mrs Cunningham and, as indicated above, she claims that the affection was reciprocated. Eliza looked upon Mrs Cunningham as her second mother, but was unwise enough to claim later, when in Greenwich, that Mrs Cunningham was her real mother.

The train of events which culminated in 1799 had begun shortly after she had left the Cun-ninghams. Colonel Robert had married, probably with the blessing of his father who had died in August 1795.

In December 1795 Robert Cunningham's wife died and he was then free 'to renew his suit' of Eliza Robertson. Next (according to Eliza's memoirs) Mrs Cunningham married, in 1799, a Mr Hill of Lungergreen. This was another location which has proved impossible to identify. Once again, the marriage was of short duration because Mrs Cunningham died later in the same year.

Shortly after Mrs Cunningham-Hill's death, Colonel Robert and Lady W. H. Pagett remitted her £100 for family mourning, as instructed in their mother's will. She alleges that they also told her the old lady had expressed hopes that she would marry her widowed son and that she had bequeathed to Eliza the estate of Faskally near Blair, Perthshire, in a vale beyond the Pass of Killiecrankie.

The administration of the will was entrusted to the Hon. Mrs Cunningham's brother, a Mr Robertson, an attorney of Dalkeith, near Edinburgh. He was 'to use his endeavours for the recovery of considerable unclaimed property' and Eliza claims to have executed a power of attorney in his favour. Later, she accused Mr Robertson of having swindled her, an accusation which she levelled against almost everybody with whom she had any business dealings.

Possibly Mr Robertson had sent her some money and she would have signed a receipt. But having received something, and very likely having seen the Faskally estate during her wanderings between 1790 and 1795, her imagination went to work. As far as she was concerned she was an heiress, soon to come into considerable money.

The seat of Faskally exists; it lies at the confluence of the rivers Tummel and Garry, two miles north-west of Pitlochry. But it did not belong to the 'Hon Mrs Cunning-ham' and she could not have left it to Eliza Robertson.

It is easy to see why Eliza claimed to be the heir to Faskally rather than any other estate she might have seen. Faskally had belonged to a certain George Robertson who, on 19 October 1764, 'because of the present state of my private affairs, the extent of my debts and the nature of other obligations', executed a trust disposition and settlement by which, on his death, the whole land and barony of Faskally were to be disposed to Trustees for them to sell and dispone the lands and with the money pay off his debts and thereafter certain annuities.

George Robertson may well have been an ancestor or relative of Eliza Robertson and of her father, whose private affairs and extent of debts matched those of George Robertson. He, although married, had no children, only four sisters who were his heirs after his wife. He died in 1776 or 1777 and on 28 November 1777 the surviving Trustee sold the lands and the barony of Faskally to Henry Butter of Pitloch-ry, in whose family they remained until the beginning of the twentieth century.

It is possible that Eliza had heard of George Robertson and his connection with Faskally when she passed through Scotland. Deprived of a carefree, loving childhood and having worked for her living from the age of 16 onwards, Eliza longed for better things. She had a good training in devious dealings from her father and so must have decided to use a tenuous or even non-existent family connection as the foundation of a large-scale swindle.

On learning of Mrs Cunningham-Hill's death, Eliza staged a high drama to show her grief. According to Mrs Neal, she was bathed in tears and in utmost distress but managed to let it slip out that she would soon receive a fortune of $10,000.

Her 'mother' was to be brought to town and she consulted an apothecary as to the propriety of prostrating herself at the feet of her deceased mother, who was to lie in state at the home of the famous Dr Lettsom. Many mourning rings were distributed, one of which went to Mrs Creasy, a friend of Charlotte Sharpe's, and another to Mrs Neal. After this wonderful show of affection she borrowed $500 from the latter and had visiting cards printed: 'Miss Robertson, of Faskally and Blackheath'.

Mrs Neal described Eliza as a very amiable, sensible woman who was most attentive to the duties of religion. Eliza, on the other hand, did not show a charitable and Christian disposition towards Mrs Neal and calls her grasping and scandal-mongering. Probably Mrs Neal wanted her $500 returned.

The forthcoming expiration of the lease made it necessary for the school to be moved from Crooms Hill. Having received, at best, a small amount of money but believing herself to be the heir-ess to a fortune, Miss Robertson writes: 'I wished by all means Miss Sharpe should have a very genteel and comfortable establishment. After looking at several she fixed on one in The Paragon, for which we agreed with Mr Searles, surveyor, who had been concerned in the build-ing of it. The one we agreed for (No 3, The Paragon) was about to fall into the hands of Mr Cator, the landowner, in consequence of a mortgage. We had his agreement signed to make our title clear, in case we chose to purchase it within 3 years, or else we were to have a lease of 28 years. Mr Searles was so sanguine in the business that he set the men to work several days before the agreement was executed. No further representation of property was made to him than I meant to expend £400 on it and he promised it should be ready in July 1800. This house was taken in the joint names of Miss Charlotte Sharpe and Miss Eliza Robertson and no one knew but we intended carrying on the school jointly as we continued to do at Crooms Hill till the young people left us for the vacation.'

The remark about the 'mortgage' has been explained earlier and as to carrying on a school, the restrictive covenant in the lease would have prevented her from doing so. Miss Robertson had little knowledge of such matters. She was a skilful confidence trickster and it sufficed her to have induced Mr Cator or Michael Searles (or both) into assigning her a lease without a penny 'representation of property'. However, as she needed money to pay the workmen, she mortgaged the premises for £850 to Mr Cator, who took the title deeds as security.

Her fantasies did not only embrace an entitlement to a landed estate. Whilst matters regarding the will were supposedly being sorted out – and she hints that the family of Colonel Cunningham's first wife were unhappy about it and took legal advice – she met her Colonel on various occasions.

She claims they became engaged to be married and intended to move into The Paragon after the wedding. Although she volubly denies having communicated her expectations and forthcoming marriage to anybody, she seems to have known how to drop a few confidences here and a few hints there and to make allusions to certain matters to a few people upon whose indiscretion she could rely.

If everything regarding the will and the considerable property was above board, there would have been no need to hide the facts. But, she says, the Colonel himself asked her to keep the contents of the will sub rosa. It becomes more and more difficult to believe in either the will or the engagement.

Moreover, it was not only the engagement and the purported inheritance which she spread around, but she again let it be known that she was in possession of considerable property following the death of her maternal grandfather.

From the end of April 1800 onwards, Eliza Robertson began to incur enormous debts. The ironmonger's goods alone, which she bespoke for her house in The Paragon, came to £485.9.4. At the same time, her lies grew in proportion to her debts. She was related to the Secretary for War, Mr Dundass; her father had been received by General Washington at Mount Vernon because he was related to him; some of her brothers and sisters were born at Mount Vernon; one of her sisters was widowed and thereafter married an eminent KC. Another widowed sister married again, this time to Lord Paget, son of the Earl of Uxbridge. She bought a wax doll in London over which she shed bitter tears because the doll resembled her sister Lady Paget's dead baby girl. A res-pectable lawyer was called in to execute a power of attorney to enter and take possession of the Faskally estate and to prepare a bond for the steward of the estate to execute and to remit her £10,000.

It is difficult to decide whether to marvel more at the extent of her fantasies or the gullibility of her victims.

In 1800, builders differed little from their successors in the early 21st century when it comes to promises. The Paragon house was not ready in July 1800 and, as the Crooms Hill property had been vacated, Miss Robertson and Miss Sharpe took lodgings in Montpelier Row. From there, Miss Robertson went on a holiday to Margate with Mr and Mrs Creasy, whose children had attended their school. Miss Robertson paid the Creasy's expenses and when they returned she stayed with them at their house in Greenwich. During her stay there she bought a coach that had once belonged to the Earl of Exeter but she did not exert herself to remove the coronets from the doors. The two women were frequently seen about in that carriage.

From the Creasys' house the two friends went to Brighton where they received several anonymous letters, the contents of which Eliza does not disclose but they clearly worried her.

In one curious statement she says that she positively wished some settlement to be made for Miss Sharpe and that this desire delayed her marriage to the Colonel.

The two women moved into No 3 The Paragon some time in October 1800. The house was still unfinished and scaffolding obstructed the front door. Hence, for a while they both lived in a small room in the basement. At that time, No 3 The Paragon appears for the first time in the parish rate books with a rateable value of £72 and quarterly rate payments of £5.8.0. These were duly paid for the first two quarters. This was quite a step up from a house of half the rateable value and with no funds to support such a venture. The installation of the two women in The Paragon marked the high point of a tremendous spending spree and a series of confidence tricks which, in the course of ten months, swindled the local tradesmen out of some £15,000-£20,000, a large sum even at today's values, a fortune at that time.

Although the house had been taken in their joint names, it was Eliza Robertson who ordered the goods and services. Whether she did so of her own free will, or whether Charlotte Sharpe induced her to do so and was sharp enough to keep out of the way when it came to signing orders, is not known. Consequently, Miss Robertson again became the dupe. She ordered extensive alterations and refurbishing to be carried out, paid small amounts on account and was soon plunged into heavy debts.

The extravagance of the two women and their constant association set tongues wagging even before their affairs had become utterly hopeless. Mrs Neal accused Eliza of being a kept woman, the inhabitants of Blackheath regarded both of them as swindlers, and some called Eliza 'Creasy's whore'. Her own mother accused her of being mad and a swindler. But the most serious allegation was that they were lesbians. Not that such a word was ever uttered. Society in George III's time was far from prudish, and heterosexual and even male homosexual adventures were known and tolerated. But lesbianism was a different matter altogether.

Various people asserted that Eliza walked around in men's clothes. About this accusation she wrote sarcastically: 'These opinions were strictly corroborated by my masculine appearance, strong limbs, robust make, coarse manners and manly voice.'

The satirical tone is justified, for her portrait shows her to be quite pretty and feminine, well proportioned and with a twinkle in her eyes. She had a sense of humour which found expression in her Poetical Epistle (see below).

In the local Congregational Chapel the minister, inappropriately called Good or Goode, preached delicately on this unmentionable subject and the accusation was carried far and wide, even reaching Dublin. It is hardly conceivable that Dublin news-papers would print such a story if Eliza Robertson had not been there during her wanderings in 1790-1795 and become well known. At this distance in time it is, of course, impossible to determine whether there was any truth in the allegation of lesbianism. It seems quite possible that it was true. The above-quoted sentence about the delay in her marriage sounds strange. Further, Charlotte Sharpe was very much opposed to her forthcoming marriage, yet it would have been of considerable advantage to her friend. Another remark of Eliza in her memoirs has a suspicious ring: 'Ours has been an attachment for many years cemented by disappointment yet doubly cemented by a most flattering renewal.' In this day and age, the sexual inclinations of the two women hardly matter but in 1801 public opinion did not tolerate such aberration.

From about Christmas 1800 onwards the monetary troubles of Eliza Robertson and Charlotte Sharpe started in earnest. By that time the tradesmen had become extremely suspicious and were certainly pursuing Eliza Robertson, although not, it seems, Charlotte Sharpe. By February 1801, Eliza admits that even her Colonel realised what was happening and she suspected him of not 'acting uprightly'.

In February, Jones, a bricklayer, sued her for £821.12.8 and a half after he had received £100 on account. Monk, a house painter and glazier, sued for £567.15.11, having previously received £130 on account. She also owed £1,000 to Oakley, a bedstead and mattress maker. Martyr, the carpenter, tried to have her arrested for non-payment of £1,193.15.3. As befitted her station – heiress to an estate and betrothed to a Colonel – she had commissioned the carpenter to build an aviary, a swing and seats for the garden, in addition to the cupboards and wardrobes in the house. She displayed a large quantity of silver plate, obtained on credit, of course. In addition, there were gardeners' bills and at least four other tradesmen presented their accounts after the two women had moved into The Paragon. Their servants had to be paid but Eliza does not say how many they kept. She mentions a footman in her Memoirs but it is known that she also employed a coachman.

All the above-mentioned traders were local suppliers. But Eliza also owed £208 to Mr Crighton of King Street, Soho. The total comes to £4,276.13.2 and a half, excluding the sums paid on account but including the ironmongery.

Yet that was not the entire story. She had her bills checked by a surveyor, including those from the plasterer and the chimney-piece manufacturer, and subsequently paid £2,000, although she admits to a total debt of £15,000. However, she thought that only £5,000 was due. The sums of £15,000 and £20,000 appear in The Gentleman's Magazine and The Monthly Visitor but how that total was reached cannot be ascertained in detail. We know that in addition to the bills mentioned there were dresses and the furniture to be paid for. A report in one of the papers has this to say about the auction of the two ladies' personal effects which took place later in 1801:

Some of their gowns were so rich and elegant as to sell, at second hand, at £30 a piece; and the looking glasses alone, which they obtained upon the credit of their appearance, were worth upwards of £1,500. They constantly rode about in their fashionable carriage and lived in every respect in a most extravagant style.

Explicit as her books are, there is never any mention of how Miss Robertson or Miss Sharpe earned, possessed or obtained sufficient money to make payments on account, pay for food, ground rent, rates, wages, let alone those suppliers not listed among her creditors. The profits from running a school cannot have been sufficient to enable 'the two artful, fair ones', as one newspaper described them, to live in such a style. The answer is that Eliza Robertson resorted to large scale-borrowing and signed a number of bills, mainly at the instigation of Mr Creasy.

Thomas Creasy was a currier by trade and a man of considerable fortune. He lent her money without security, or obtaining a bill or even an IOU. By February 1801 she owed him £4,000. Creasy had swallowed all the tales which Eliza had spread about and, as no man likes to be duped, it is not surprising that their initial friendship developed into a deep hatred and Creasy became her chief persecutor. Only on the day before Eliza fled did Creasy manage to obtain her signature on a bill and a power of attorney authorising him to dispose of her belongings.

Creasy's constant attendance on the two women earned him a great deal of unpopularity and deep suspicion among his fellow tradesmen. He had been at all times in and out of The Paragon to supervise the work being done and, whilst there, met other tradesmen either in the company of Eliza or alone, acting on her behalf. The tradesmen disliked him so much that he found it necessary to insert the following piece into a local newspaper:

Mr Creasy of Greenwich has contradicted the report that he had introduced the Swindlers of Blackheath to any trades men.

This was a blatant lie. He not only induced Joseph Haycraft, ironmonger, to supply them with goods on credit, but actually came to Haycraft's shop with the two women and introduced them to Haycraft. Moreover, when Haycraft sued Creasy for misrepresentation, Creasy's counsel pleaded that judgement adverse to his client would lead 'to a multitude of other actions which would be brought on similar grounds'.

The lawsuit Haycraft v Creasy took place on 14 July 1801 before Lord Kenyon, CJ, and a special jury at the Guildhall. It transpired that Haycraft and his son had asked Creasy several times most meticulously whether Eliza Robertson was credit-worthy, as the order was very large.

Haycraft remained doubtful but Creasy repeatedly assured him of her trustworthiness, that she was the owner of a Scottish estate, had exhibited plans thereof and had appointed a respectable man of business as her agent to receive rents, etc.

Creasy's assurances culminated in this statement: 'I can positively assure you of my own knowledge that you may credit Miss Robertson to any amount with perfect safety.'

During this lawsuit, in which John Cator, Michael Searles and many other people mentioned above appeared as witnesses, there occurred some examples of courtroom 'wit' which deserve resurrection. When the Reverend Good stated that he was a Dissenting Minister at Greenwich, he was asked by Counsel for the plaintiff, Mr Erskine, whether, if Miss Robertson had asked him to lend her £1,000, he would have been a Dissenter. Mr Good answered in the affirmative. John Cator testified that he had lent her £850 on the security of her lease, without which, he said, he would not have lent her 800 farthings. The remark that he did not gape and let others steal the teeth out of his mouth was made by Counsel at this trial.

A Mr Webster related that he had dined at the Creasys' house where the company partook of some venison. During the meal both Miss Robertson and Miss Sharpe held forth about Eliza's estate, whereupon he was asked by Mr Erskine whether he swallowed all these stories as he had swallowed the venison. There were other examples in the same vein. The jury found for the plaintiff but Creasy went to appeal, where the judgement was reversed.

At the beginning of 1801 the two women's affairs had become so complex that they thought it prudent to get Miss Robertson away. She went to London on 4 February and stayed with a Mr Hardy, whilst Charlotte Sharpe packed a few things, covered up the furniture and left her brother's wife as caretaker in charge of the house. Hardly had Miss Sharpe left when her brother betrayed his sister's and her friend's confidence and arranged for an auction of all their belongings left at The Paragon. In short, Miss Robertson claims, everybody turned against them and their affairs went from bad to worse. She had signed bills, borrowed from Peter to pay Paul, bought goods on credit and cheated everyone with whom she came into contact.

On 26 February 1801 Eliza went to Enfield, returned shortly afterwards to London where she stayed with Charlotte's brother and then departed again, this time for Ipswich.

Meanwhile, some of their belongings were seized by minor creditors. Eliza returned once more to London but the hue and cry was up and both women decamped for Ware, Hertfordshire, by which time they were almost penniless. But Ware, too, was no haven as Martyr, the carpenter, pursued them relentlessly. They decided to leave and finally arrived in Huntingdon towards the end of March. There they lodged under the name of the Misses Cunningham!

But Martyr, acting on his own and on behalf of the other Greenwich tradesmen, caught up with them. His son, an attorney, had prepared the legal formalities against Eliza, the local sheriff arrested her and she was taken to the house of Mr Drage, the keeper of the county gaol. There she was kept in two small rooms. In a small place like Huntingdon the arrest of a middle-class young woman created a sensation. She was literally 'exhibited as the most extraordinary creature' to all and sundry, provided, of course, that all had the sundry with which to grease Mr Drage's palms. Among those who went to see her was the Marquis of Salisbury, together with some of the officers of his regiment.

She describes her situation wryly: 'It was quite a sufficient licence and precedent to all travellers afterwards and it would have been an impeachment of anyone's love of natural curiosities not to go to see this miraculous creature if they came within a stage of Huntingdon.'

Though she proposed to pay for her rooms in advance, as was then the custom in debtors' prisons, the sheriff decided to put her into the county gaol, ostensibly because her debts were so large. The more likely reason was her inability to pay Mr Drage and that her promissory notes were unacceptable.

The gaol was a 'horrid, dirty, small place underground' with a filthy kitchen and passageways. She was fortunate to be the sole inmate of the room in which women felons were normally kept, but describes it as being less well fitted than a rabbit hutch or a pigsty.

Miss Robertson spent seven months in Huntingdon gaol during which time she continued to be 'exhibited' by her gaoler, Drage, who found her stay most lucrative. But she was allowed to take occasional walks and visited nearby Hinchingbrooke House, the seat of the Earl of Sandwich, who, she says, waited upon her twice.

Charlotte Sharpe stayed at Huntingdon whilst Eliza was there and visited her friend as often as possible. Visits were allowed during daytime. The inhabitants of Huntingdon gradually warmed towards these two unfortunate women, helped them with fruit and vegetables and also gave them some needlework to pass the time.

Whilst in gaol, Eliza wrote a book, *Who are The Swindlers?*, to counter a pamphlet called Chronological Tablets in which she was called a notorious female swindler. That book was published and sold by Vernon & Hood, Ridgway, Crosby, Hurst & Badcock; whereas Eliza's book was printed by J. W. Dewicke, Aldersgate Street, London, for the author, and sold by J. S. Jordan, Ludgate Street, and Mr Row, Huntingdon, price 1/6. *Who are The Swindlers?* contains an account of the conduct of Oakley, Creasy, Searle (an attorney of the Inner Temple, not the surveyor), Hardy and Charlotte Sharpe's brother, all of whom she accuses of swindling both women out of whatever they had left.

The first edition appeared on 24 August 1801. A second edition was needed which was ready on 9 September, showing the speed with which printers and booksellers worked in those days.

Miss Robertson obtained £52.10.0 for the copyright and 400 copies of the second edition and she says she made about £120 out of the book. In addition, both women managed to obtain a little money from the sale of some of their former belongings. This enabled Eliza to keep a servant in gaol. Her name was Patty Frisk whom she calls 'her little domestic animal'. She even managed to buy new coats and dresses. As Eliza had not been made a bankrupt, which proceedings would have cost her creditors a lot of extra money, and she was en-titled to keep any money which she earned and to sell any of her belongings.

Later, Miss Robertson wrote a pamphlet entitled *Dividends of Immense Value: To which is added a Poetical Epistle*, also printed in 1801. The Dividends are a defence against the charge of lesbianism and consist of innumerable biblical quotations concerning the innocent friendships of Naomi and Ruth, David and Jonathan, etc. It is a dreary booklet but the Poetical Epistle has charm and humour. It describes her life in Huntingdon gaol and the ministrations of her guardian angel, Charlotte Sharpe, in easy flowing, pleasant verse.

In October 1801 Eliza arranged for her removal to the debtors' prison in London, the Fleet. She wrote to an acquaintance to procure the best furnished apartment for herself and her servant, to have the rooms aired and to bring in coal. If one had money, life in a debtors' prison must have been quite comfortable and Eliza appears to have earned reasonable sums of money from her oks.

'I must say this place is well constructed for the convenience of prisoners, it is very large. The rooms are a good size ... Those who have the management of it are [not] respectful, civil and obliging, nor do they attempt to interfere with the privileges of the prisoners, some of whom have very good and lucrative employment and are, I believe, perfectly satisfied with their situation.'.

Alas, she does not say how much these privileges cost her. The payment of garnish to the prison keepers was a well-known practice. Poor debtors who paid little or no garnish were not treated respectfully, civilly and obligingly, but were kept in the most degrading, insanitary and unhealthy conditions.

Soon after her arrival at the Fleet, Miss Robertson tried to arrange an accommodation with her creditors through her attorney, Mr Searle, probably William Searle of 3 Child's Place, Temple Bar. In the London Gazette for the period 29 December 1800 to 2 January 1801 we find this advertisement:

Meeting of Creditors: *Miss Robertson's, of Blackheath, intend to meet on Wednesday, 6th January 1801, at the London Coffee House, Ludgate Hill, at 3 o'clock.*

As usual, everybody with whom she came into contact, except Charlotte Sharpe, 'swindled and defamed' her, including her attorney, and the meeting with her creditors was abortive. She suggested that the creditors should recover her interest in the Paragon house and sell it. But as the lease had been mortgaged to Mr Cator, the creditors cannot be blamed for taking little notice of such a proposal.

Writing and visits by Charlotte Sharpe consoled Eliza Robertson during her years in prison. From the Fleet she published *An Address to the Public*, price 6d; *Siste Viator*, price 2/-; *A Country Gaoler*, price 2d; *Miss Sharpe's Letter to the Congregation Meeting at the White Row*, Spitalfield, price 6d; *Story of an Eel-Pye*, price 2d; and finally she wrote *The Life and Memoirs of Miss Robertson of Blackheath*, which has provided much of the basic material for this chapter. The book was prin-ted by 'W. Burton for C. Sharpe and may be had of the author in The Fleet. Sold also by the Printers, 82 Fetter Lane. Price 4/-. Entered at Stationers' Hall.'

The Annual Register of 1805 carried the following notice in its *Deaths* column:
June 7. In the Fleet Prison where she had been confined about 4 years for debts contracted in fitting up an elegant house at Blackheath, in Kent, aged 32, Miss Elizabeth Robinson (or Robertson) of swindling notoriety. Her remains were deposited in St Bride's churchyard

❦

Appendices

Appendix III

No 4 The Paragon

Inventory: 8 October 1833

Inventory of Fixtures, Furniture, China, Glass etc. the property of Mrs Neale on the premises No 4 Paragon Blackheath, taken October 8th 1833. Corrected for Mr Hart 16th December 1834.

This extraordinary collection of household furniture, odds and ends and bric-a-brac seems to indicate that the house had once been used as a boarding establishment or a school. The huge quantity of glasses, plates, china, dishes and so on – much of it damaged – indicates an owner with the inability to throw anything away, however useless. No trace has been found of a sale of house contents and Mrs Neale stayed on at No 4 until at least 1837, perhaps adding to her store.

Much of the spelling is eccentric and the author has amended only where necessary, for example, the word palliasse. But many others I have left alone. Some of the patent items I have been unable to trace, not only for a correct spelling but also to discover what they may have been.

Those items followed by an asterisk are crossed out of the Inventory.

Kitchen

The range with oven and boiler. C... spit racks,
2 swing trivets a return iron fender with sliding bar
a brass jack rack as fixed
a smoke jack and chain
an oven on side of fireplace
a deal table
a deal ironing board with iron supports
a mesh screen, lined with tin, wanting handles
6 wood chairs
a mahogany stool
a piece of oil cloth
2 pieces of ditto to windows

Iron
1 spit
1 cinder shovel
1 large poker
1 urn hook
1 meat fork
1 toasting fork
an oven rake
a sugar nipper
a coffee mill
2 flat irons, one stand handle wanting
1 Italian iron and 2 heaters
1 box iron and 2 heaters
a balance weight
a holdfast
a chopper
a fire basket
a winder to range
1 pot and cover
1 ditto and tin cover
5 saucepans and 4 covers
1 trivet – damaged
a footman
2 frying pans
1 gridiron
a meat stand
a saw
a charcoal burner

Tin
a circular meat screen, damaged
dripping pan complete

5 oval meat covers, one damaged
a dripping pan and stand, ladle, skimmer and a slice, damaged
a fish kettle drainer and cover, and a small drainer, damaged
a Dutch oven complete
1 saucepan steamer and cover
5 saucepans and covers
3 coffee pots and a chocolate pot and mill
3 tea kettles
1 round dish
1 funnel
1 jelly mould
2 boxes of paste cutters complete
a flower [sic] dredger, handle off
a nutmeg grater, handle off
a spice box
a small Dutch oven, defective
2 tart dishes
a Yorkshire pudding pan
26 patty pans
a water can
2 dish candlesticks
2 cake moulds

Copper
2 coal scuttles and 1 scoop
a warming pan
a preserving pan
a jelly mould
a boiler

Brass
2 high candlesticks
a bottle wasting [sic] jack complete
a chamber candlestick

blue and white dinner service Swiss pattern
15 meat dishes – one cracked
1 fish plate
11 soup plates
40 meat plates
17 pudding ditto
13 cheese ditto
1 salad bowl

239

4 vegetable dishes and covers
1 flask ditto in three pieces
1 ditto imperfect
2 tart dishes, one cracked
1 tureen imperfect
4 sauce tureens, cover, stands and 2 ladles

a sandwich tray in six pieces, 1 cracked
24 plates to match

Dessert set blue and gold china *
2 round dishes and 2 square ditto
2 sugar pots, covers and stands
1 centre piece – 17 plates

green dessert set – 4 leaves and 12 plates
2 blue and white gruel cups with saucers, handles and covers
tea set pink and white
a tea pot cover and stand – the pot cracked
a milk jug
a cream ditto
2 sugar pots and covers
1 slop basin
2 bread and butter plates
6 meat plates
10 cups and 12 saucers
4 coffee cups and saucers

1 large brown jar
1 ditto and cover – cover broken
2 sugar jars and covers
2 ditto without – ditto 1 broken
1 large ditto with shells – handle off
a small ditto without ditto
2 white ditto with covers
1 jar and cover broken
a Japan tin sugar canister
a bed pan – handle broken
a brown glazed tea pot spout chipped
a ditto hot water pot
a ditto coffee pot
a ditto sugar basin and cover – basin chipped
2 Wedgwood chamber candlesticks, cracked
2 night lamps complete
1 cut quart water jug *
1 ditto trifle dish and stand
2 ditto butter glasses, cover and stand with drawer *
a ditto sugar glass and cover
3 ditto pickle glasses
2 ditto pickle leaves
4 ditto quart decanters and stoppers – odd and chipped
4 ditto pint ditto and ditto
19 ditto champagne glasses – not all one size
24 ditto wines
12 plain ditto
16 half pint tumblers, cracked
a funnel
5 ditto salts chipped
1 ditto butter glass cover and stand – cover and stand chipped
7 water crofts [sic], 3 chipped
10 ditto custard cups and handles
4 plain ditto
15 purple finger glasses
4 green and 42 white glasses
a plated dinner stand with five cut glasses *
a mustard spoon

1 glass, no cover to the mustard *
2 ditto fish stand ?
4 glass and spoon *
1 toast rack *

1 pair candlesticks
1 ditto snuffer tray and steel snuffers
2 chamber candlesticks, extinguishers steel snuffers *

tea set blue and white embossed
a tea pot and cover
2 cream jugs and a milk ditto
1 slop and 1 sugar basin
4 bread and butter plates
12 meat plates, cracked
9 tea cups and 13 saucers, two cracked
7 coffee cups, 2 cracked, and 6 saucers
1 buff embossed tea pot chipped
4 blue and white breakfast cups and saucers, 2 cups cracked
3 tea cups and 4 saucers – 1 cup cracked
3 coffee ditto
3 meat plates
a slop basin
a milk jug
a blue and white egg stand
2 two-quart blue and white jugs – 1 chipped
1 quart ditto
2 buff jugs and covers, 1 cover odd
1 green spig half pint jug
1 pink ditto
1 buff ditto
1 half pint embossed ditto
3 painted china *

Blue and white ware various

1 large well dish, cracked
2 ditto meat dishes and 8 smaller dishes, 2 cracked
4 pie dishes
2 cheese stands
1 soup tureen cover and stand cover, cracked
a hash dish in three pieces
2 vegetable dishes, drainers and covers
2 ditto and covers, both cracked
1 salad bowl
2 sauce tureens and covers, 1 tureen and cover, cracked
14 soup plates
1 mustard and cover
18 meat plates
1 salt
2 fish plates, both cracked
2 half pint mugs *
1 two quart white jug
1 quart ditto
8 cups and saucers, 1 saucer cracked
Kitchen set red and white
2 black tea pots, 1 chipped
3 basins
6 white jars
1 cracked pane in kitchen window

Scullery
The range as fixed
an iron fender
the copper with cover damaged
a plate rack

4 shutters
a door and sundry pieces of wood
a 2 leaf clothes horse
2 washing tubs
1 brewing ditto
a piggin
2 dish tubs
a house pail
a   ... fork *
1 glass tub *
4 sieves (withdrawn)
a deal table
a towel roller
2 tin cinder pails and covers
a plate basket lined with tin
a knife tray
a piece of oil cloth *
a rope mat
a wood bar to window
an iron bar ditto to door
windows perfect

Larder
a green drag venetian blind complete
a chimney board
1 chopper
2 bath stoves, 1 unfixed
a chopping board
a ditto knife
a balance scale
an iron spoon
1 paste board and roller
2 wood spoons and a paste brush
a salt box
1 four quart and 1 two quart white jug
2 lip basins, both cracked *
1 quart ditto broken
5 pudding basins
3 white cups *
1 large brown pan *
1 ditto and cover, broken
1 ditto pickling pan
1 ditto milk ditto
1 ditto cheese pan *
2 ditto jars *
a two gallon kitchen jar, broken
lock and key to inner door
glass in window perfect
Butler's pantry
The swing dresser with wood supports
a painted press bedstead
1 feather bed
a bolster
a pillow
3 blankets
a coverlet
a horsehair cushion
a bell on carriage
a deal washing stool white ... & blue *
blue chamber, handle off
jug, broken *
2 tea urns and a coffee ditto – 1 urn damaged
3 Japan tin tea boards – 8 waiters
a knife tray
a bread basket
2 light shades
3 ditto with wells complete
1 pierced hand lantern
2 wire hand lanterns

1 glazed lantern, 1 glass out
3 Japan tin flat candlesticks, much damaged
two extras and 2 snuffers
six Save-alls
a ditto plate warmer
a ditto snuffer tray and steel snuffers
an oil can and a ditto filler
a wood stool
a glass tub *
a mahogany knife box
12 table mats
a ditto butler's tray and stand
4 pieces of carpet
a loose bar to window shutter
a cork screw and a bottle brush *
key to door *
two cracked panes
Kitchen passage

9 spring bells on carriages
3 candle boxes
a deal slip and three keys
a Turk's head broom
a shower bath complete
a sedan and two poles
a beer stand
a set of high folding steps
2 mallets
3 leaves to table in stand *
3 rope mats

Schoolroom
a Rumford stove as fixed
a green wire fender and brass frame
a wire fire guard
a cottage piano forte, lock and key *
a mahogany washing stand
a white soap dish *
a mahogany stool
a wood stool, broken
3 yellow rush green chairs
2 cane ditto
1 Astley Cooper chair
2 round wainscot tables
3 pieces of oil cloth, carpet and hearth rug
a clothes basket *
an iron bar
two thumb screws
3 bells to window [*sic*]
1 cracked pane

Knife house
a corner wash stand
a knife board and knife brush
sundry pieces of wood and matting

Wine cellar
sundry tubs, bath, baskets and a hamper of wine
key to the door complete

No 1 Front attic
1 bath stove and a chimney board
a stained four post bedstead Dity furniture and base
a wool mattress and feather bolster and pillow
4 blankets and cotton quilt
a stained stump bedstead footboard and shaped head piece and base
a wool mattress in Holland case

2 feather beds
1 bolster and 1 pillow, 3 blankets and a white quilt
a wainscot chest of drawers, one handle off
a japanned chest of drawers
a ditto dressing table with a drawer
4 rush seat chairs
an oval wash stand
a white basin
a blue ewer, broken
a slop pot drain and cover
1 white saucer
a white chamber, chipped
1 blue and white chamber, handle off *
a corner wash shelf as fixed
a white ...

1 ewer
1 tumbler *
2 mahogany frame dressing glasses – knobs of one wanting
(above amended to 1 glass)
5 pieces of carpet much worn
2 d...ty curtains to window
windows perfect

No 2 attic
a skeleton stove as fixed
a green pierced fender with brass top
3 green blinds to window
bell pull cranks and wires ...
a stained four post bedstead and d...ty furniture
1 wool mattress in Holland case
1 feather bed
1 bolster and 1 pillow
3 blankets and white quilt
a japanned chest of 5 drawers and 1 key complete
a ditto high back wash stove
1 blue and white basin
1 ditto ewer
1 blue and white soap pot and cover
1 ditto brush and ch... tray
1 buff half pint mug
a plain water bottle
half pint tumbler
a dressing table with drawer and handle off (last time crossed out)
an arm chair white fr... d...ty case
horsehair cushion and c...pt
1 rush and 1 cane seat chair
a deal 3 rail airing horse
a mahogany frame dressing glass, 1 knob off
a black book shelf
3 pieces of carpet
window perfect

a piece of carpet on landing

No 3 bedroom
a bath stove as fixed
a green fender with brass frame and a fire guard
a set of fire irons
2 green drag venetian blinds
2 dimity val... on deal laths, iron rods
2 dimity curtains and 2 curtain pins
2 bell pulls & complete and night bolt pin
2 mahogany and tent bedsteads with d...ty furniture
2 wool mattresses in Holland cases
1 ditto in stripe case
2 feather beds – 2 bolsters – & 4 pillows

8 blankets and 2 counterpanes
2 mahogany chests of 5 drawers, 2 knobs missing and front chipped
1 mahogany dressing glass, 3 drawers
1 mahogany dressing glass, no drawer
1 mahogany folding airing horse
2 japanned wash stands
2 blue and white basins, 2 ewers both broken
2 soap pots, drainers and 2 covers
1 brush tray
1 pint mug
2 ditto chipped
chambers
1 water bottle
3 small oil mats
3 japanned cane seat chairs, 2 bottoms out
a ditto ... table and drawer
a ditto child's chair
5 pieces of carpet
a painted card rack
3 worsted baskets
keys to closet doors
ditto to room doors
1 cracked pane

No 4 bedroom
a bath stove not fixed
a green ... in brass frame
a set of fire irons
a green diag Venetian blind complete
a deal lath & wood rod m... valeurs
2 ditto curtains and 2 curtain pins to window
2 bell pulls complete and a night bolt ditto
a carved mahogany 4 post bed stead with dimity furniture and frieze
1 folding straw palliasse – 1 wool mattress
1 bordered feather bed, 1bolster
2 pillows in fustian cases
4 blankets and cotton counterpane
a mahogany chest of 5 drawers, front chipped
a ditto wash stand with bidet & white pan complete
1 ditto ewer, 1 ditto soap pot & cover
1 blue and white brush tray
1 ditto washing stool and cover
1 ditto night convenience pan, broken
1 ditto folding airing horse

Water closet complete and a muslin curtain

2 spring bells complete
a white roller blind complete
a Dutch clock
4 pieces of stair carpeting and 22 rods and eyes complete

In closet
a white foot bath (?) cracked
1 glazed water pitcher a ditto frame swing dressing glass
a ditto frame hand glass
a ditto three tier tray bookshelf
a japanned wash stand
1 blue and white basin
1 ditto chamber
1 plain water bottle
& pint tumbler
4 ditto rush seat chairs
a ditto dressing table

a Kidderminster carpet and a piece of ditto
and a hearth rug
key to closet door complete
ditto to room ditto
2 cracked panes

a house pail
1 rush light stand
a water can
1 blue and white chamber, cracked
glass in window perfect

No 5 front bedroom
1 Rumford stove as fixed
a green fender and brass frame
a ditto fire guard
a set of fire irons
2 green venetian blinds and 2 stout brass rods
4 dimity curtains and 4 brass pins to windows
1 bell pull, cranks and wires and a night bolt
a carved mahogany 4 post bedstead, japanned cornice, full dimity furniture and frieze
1 straw palliasse, 1 wool mattress in Holland case
1 feather bed, 1 bolster, 2 pillows in fustian cases, 4 blankets, a white counterpane
a mahogany chest of 5 drawers, no key
a ditto chest of 4 drawers, no key
2 ditto frame dressing glasses
a ditto table with a drawer and carved feet
ditto small ditto
a ditto folding airing horse, damaged
a japanned dressing table with a drawer
5 ditto no. cane seat chairs
a ditto arm ditto with white pan cushion etc., dimity cover complete
a ditto double wash stand with a drawer
2 black and white basins
2 ditto ewers
1 ditto quart jug
2 brush trays and covers
2 tumblers, 1 broken
2 soap pots covers and drainers, 2 cut
water bottle and 2 ditto tumblers
5 oil cloth mats
a black handle hearth brush
a flower basket and cover
a carpet and hearth rug
a mahogany chamber cupboard
key to closet door complete
glass perfect

No 6 bedroom
a Rumford stove as fixed
a green wire fender and brass frame
a ditto fire guard
a set of fire irons
4 bell pulls, cranks and wires and a night bolt
a circular lath and brass rod drab M...
valins and frieze, 2 ditto curtains, 2 gilt curtain pins and 3 green venetian blinds
3 outside ditto shades
a carved mahogany 4 post bedstead, furniture as window
1 folding straw palliasse
1 wool mattress in Holland case and 1 feather bed
1 bolster and 2 pillows
4 blankets and a white counterpane
a mahogany wardrobe, 5 sliding trays, 4 drawers, lock and key complete

a ditto claw table
a ditto folding and rail airing horse
a ditto frame dressing glass, 1 knob off
a ditto handle hearth brush
a bedside easy chair with loose cushion & Stormont cotton case
a couch with 1 wool and 1 horsehair mattress, 1 bolster and dimity covering
a stained trunk stand
a japanned dressing table with 2 drawers
a ditto with 1 ditto
4 ditto cane seat chairs
a ditto wash stand
blue and white china basin
a ditto ewer
a brush tray and cover
a soap dish drainer and cover
2 white chambers and covers, 1 cover chipped
1 plain water bottle and a tumbler
a worsted rug
a pair of bellows
2 card racks
2 hand screens
1 card watch pocket
a piece of sea weed
Brussell's carpet to room
a large hand bell
a hearth rug
key to room door
1 cracked pane
The mahogany slab on landing
a sheep skin rug
2 pieces of Brussell's carpet and 22 brass rods
a venetian blind to landing window
3 cracked panes

Entrance hall
The oil cloth as planned to floor and down kitchen stairs
4 mahogany hall chairs
a ditto side board on brackets
an 8 day clock in mahogany case
a mahogany hat stand
a barometer in mahogany case
a mahogany bracket
The lamp with brass frame, chain and fully complete
1 rope and 3 sheepskin mats
key, bell pull etc. to front door complete

Dining room
a Register stove as fixed
a polished steel fender and a set of fire irons
a lever bell pull, cranks and wires complete
2 deal laths and wood rods
2 gilt cornices
2 valens and spring, 4 centre tassels
4 curtains ... 4 curtain arms
2 spring roller blinds and 2 wire ditto in mahogany frames
a mahogany dining table in 5 pieces and 8 brass fastenings
a rod cover
a ditto sideboard with oil cloth cover lined with baize
8 ditto chairs, haircloth seats
an inlaid rosewood tea caddy with
2 cut glass boxes lined with lead, lock and key *
in cabinet drawer a plaid table cover
4 papier de c... stands, rings defective

a worsted rug
2 painted China jars on xxx, damaged handle
a pair of hand screens
a hearth brush
a Brussell's carpet & hearth rug
a piece of drugget
windows perfect

Drawing room
a Register stove
a polished steel fender & a set of fire irons
a lever bell pull, cranks & wires complete
a circular deal lath and iron rod
a ditto gilt cornice, blue valence & frieze, 2 tassels,
2 curtains bound with gimp
2 gilt curtain arms
3 venetian blinds to window
a mahogany sofa table & 1 key
a ditto card table
a work ditto & blue silk
8 ditto chairs, cane seats, horsehair (1 chair
damaged)
curtains, chintz covers & Holland cases
2 elbows to match
2 wooden pole fire screens & painted velvet and
loose Holland cases
a ditto sofa squab, 2 bolsters figured chintz cover &
Holland cases
a wooden Astley Cooper chair
a chiffonier with blue silk panels
a stool carpet
a carpet ottoman
a Teliscope hearth brush
an urn & glass cover – cover crack'd
2 cut lustres with drops complete
2 painted hand screens
a painting in gilt frame
3 drawings framed and glazed
the carpet planned to room
a piece of drugget and a hearth rug
2 crack'd panes

Library
a Gothic front Register stove as fixed
a wire fender, brass frame – paws and stands
a set of cut steel fire irons
a lever bell pull, cranks and wires complete
2m poles, 2 damask valeurs and 4 ditto curtains &
bands
2 sprung roller blinds, cords & pulleys
2 wood dwarf blinds, flush bolts
Damage to windows
mahogany writing table, 4 drawers, key complete and
a printed oil cloth coverlet
ditto side table on plinth and castors
ditto What Not with a drawer
ditto couch, horsehair squab and bolster
ditto chairs & sofa
ditto foot stool
ditto glazed front bookcase, locked. Perfect
Brussell's carpet & a hearth rug
a hearth brush
5 maps affixed on spring rollers, cords and tassels
a portrait framed and glazed
a stuffed Bird on Branch
2 black marble candlesticks, ditto vase
2 glass cases
a taper stick
a Chinese card tray

2 painted scenes & 2 M....sted bookends on
mantelpiece
1 rosewood & glass ink stand
3 finger plates to outer door
1 crack'd pane

Schoolroom
an Eliptic Rumford stove
a green fender, brass top and paws
a set of fire irons
4 green iron fire guard
4 xxx of book shelves
a carpet planned to room
a mahogany Pembroke table
a ditto ? ditto
a ditto writing table on castors
6 imitation Rosewood cane seat chairs
a glazed case of stuffed birds
2 shell card racks
key to door
a crack'd pane

Anti room [*sic*]
2 nests (?) of painted book shelves as fixed, with
10 shelves
a mahogany folding top wash stand
white plug, basin, soap dish & covers
a carpet in room
a set of folding ?? carpet tops
2 japanned cane seat chairs
2 finger plates on door to hall
window perfect

Water closet complete

Garden
an iron scraper
a rope mat to back xxxx
key shutter & ??? screen
an iron roller
3 watering pots
rakes, trowels and a shovell

Binding xxx in cellar

Picture credits

The images reproduced in this book have been obtained from a wide variety of sources. Most come from the collection held by the Blackheath Society and its permission has been granted for their use. Some of the more dramatic images of the ruined and then repaired sections of the Paragon were taken for Charles Bernard Brown by a number of distinguished architectural photographers, mostly by Sidney W Newbery (1894-1985) and many of the interiors of the restored units by Anthony F Keating (1916-2008). All those identifiable are marked in the acknowledgements below. A third seriously professional photographer who figures strongly in the Brown archive was Ms Lucilla Sherrard, but no trace has been found of her or of her subsequent career.

Many of these extraordinary pictures were entrusted by Charles Brown to the safe keeping of Mr Frank Boswell, his agent and executor. When he attended the unveiling ceremony of the 200th anniversary plaque, on No 14 The Paragon, in June 1994, he handed these files to the Blackheath Society into its permanent safe keeping.

The pictures here are divided into a number of timeline categories and credit is given to each image used where such credit can be established. Some picture owners are untraceable and the author hopes that they may be identified in due course and due credit can be given in subsequent editions. Whatever, there is no intention of breaching copyrights and he hopes that this process will prove acceptable. The abbreviations used are as follows:

B Soc = Blackheath Society; BLG = Blackheath Local Guide; NBR = The author; NMR = National Monuments Record; RBG = Royal Borough of Greenwich

Index to plates

Section A: In the beginning
1: B Soc; 2: Morden College; 3-9: B Soc; 10: B Soc – NBR; 11: B Soc – A R Martin; 12; Cator trustees; 13-15: B Soc; 16: B Soc – NBR; 17: B Soc – A R Martin; 18-22: City London; London, Metropolitan Archives; 23-25: British Architectural Library – RIBA; 26-27: Ramsey & Harvey *Small Georgian Houses*: 1923 & 1977; 28, 31 & 32: RBG Heritage Centre; 29, 33-35: B Soc - NBR

Section B: 19th century
1: *The Times*; 2: Late Bill Bonwitt; 3: *Bengalee* – British Library; 4: B Soc – NBR; 5-7: B Soc; 8-11: Maps from Royal Borough of Greenwich Heritage Centre. 12: B Soc – A R Martin; 13: B Soc; 14: English Heritage; 15: The late D A Wayte; 16: B Soc – NBR; 17: B Soc. *BLG*. 18: B Soc – NBR; 19: Tithe schedule 1839 for Charlton parish- RBG Heritage Centre; 20: Tithe schedule 1843 (part) for the Parish of Lewisham – Lewisham Borough Council Local History Centre

Section C: 1900-1939
1-8: Floor plans of No 1 The Paragon - Richard Kendall; 9: English Heritage - NMR; 10: Small Georgian Houses – Ramsey & Harvey, 1923; 11 & 12: English Heritage – NMR; 13: Royal Borough of Greenwich Heritage Centre; 14: B Soc; 15. *BLG* – B Soc; 16 & 17: *BLG* – B Soc; 18: *Country Life*; 19: the late Amory Leggatt; 20: *BLG* – B Soc; 21 & 22: Donovan Hailstone;

Section D: Damage & Decay 1939-1947
1: Bernard Hailstone - W Leadlay; 2-5, 9-10, 12-16, 19, 30-39: Sydney W Newbery; 6 & 8: Donovan Hailstone; 11, 25, 40, 42: Miss Lawson – Crown Copyright; 17, 18, 21, 22, 27, 28, 46: Lucilla Sherrard; 24: C B Brown (?); 26: Derek Cooper; 29: B Soc; 43-45: Crown Copyright; 47: *Illustrated London News* – Capt Bryan de Grineau; 48: B Soc.

Section E: Restored: 1949-1958
1: Aerofilms Ltd; 2: Ordnance Survey 1963; 3, 8, 17, 30, 31, 36: B Soc; 4: Warwick Leadlay; 5, 6: Odhams Photographic Ltd; 7, 19-24, 32: Sydney W Newbery; 11-13, 33: C B Brown; 10, 14: Anthony Blake; 15, 26-29: Lucilla Sherrard; 35: *Manchester Guardian* – Geoffrey Fletcher, November 1951; 37: *The Times*, June 1958

Section F: Modern: 1960s to the present day
1-10: B Soc – NBR: B Soc 11-13: J Stocks; 17-21: B Soc – Stephen Moreton Prichard; 19 & 22: Richard Klose; 25-27: Mary Harman; 28-31: D Ann Wayte; 32-35: John Harman; 36 & 37· Allsops Ltd; 38. Messrs John Payne

Section G: The Cator Lodges – Nos 15-18 the Paragon
There was some confusion by Charles Brown when he named and numbered the four bijou dwellings he created in the old workshop and Paragon House stable building. At one time he numbered them from the corner lodge of the Paragon proper as Nos15 and then run on with 16, 17 and 18. But then he adopted names: Cator Lodge, Cator Manor, etc, not always correctly captioned on the work-in-progress photographs.

Picture credits and Index to plates

The author has had to use his guesswork and judgement as to nomenclature. Brown at some stage also named the new dwelling next to No 1The Paragon as Cator Lodge, which didn't help.

1: Miss Lawson – National Monument Record; 2, 3, 15: Charles Bernard Brown; 4, 6, 9, 11-14, 17: Sydney W Newbery; 7-8: Odhams Photographic Ltd; 10, 24, 36: B Soc - NBR; 16: Watercolour by John Harvey; 18-32, 37: Anthony F Keating

Section H 1: South Row – historic
1, 2, 3, 5-11, 21, 22, 25-27: B Soc; 28, 29, 31,-33, 35, 36, 37, 41,44: B Soc – A R Martin; 12, 13: London Metropolitan Archive; 14-17, 19, 20, 42, 43, 50-57: Sydney W Newbery; 23, 30, 34: British Architectural Library [RIBA]; 24: Gideon Franklin; 38: *Illustrated London News* – Capt Bryan de Grineau; 39: Prefabs in 1944 – Maureen Black; 40: *Small Georgian Houses* – Ramsey & Harvey, 1923; 47, 58-63: *Country Life*; 48 & 49: Charles Bernard Brown; 64: Watercolour - Francis Dodd

Section H 2: South Row – modern
1: B Soc. Mrs Tanya House; 2. Span Developments Ltd; 3, 5, 6, 7, 10: John Donat; 4: B Soc; 8, 9, 11, 12: B Soc – NBR

Section I: Paragon Place and its neighbours
1, 2, 5 & 18: *BLG*; 3, 4 & 7: B Soc - A R Martin; 6, 9, 10-14, 20, 21: B Soc – NBR; 8: Lionel Lewis; 15-17: B Soc. Sydney W Newbery; 18: *BLG* – M H Forward; 19: *Manchester Guardian* - Adolf Morath.

Section J: Press clippings
1: *BLG*; 2: *Kentish Mercury*; 3 & 4: *Manchester Guardian* – Adolf Morath; 5: *Sphere Magazine*; 6 & 7: *The Times*; 8: *The Observer*; 9: *Evening News*; 10. *Sunday Telegraph*; 11: *The Lady*

Section K: Postcards and notelets
All these come from the Blackheath Society images collection. Special credit must go to the following: 9: Edgar Pitt; 10: Gerard Baker; 14: Graham Clilverd; 18: Bernard Driscoll; 20: D A Wayte; 21: Fiona Bell Currie; 22: Mark Titman

Section L: Some of the people some of the time
These are just some of the people who lived in The Paragon and South Row or were connected with them in some way. Alas, the one face which is missing is the architect himself: Michael Searles - no image of him has yet been discovered.

1-3: de Crespigny family; 4, 5, 10, 17, 22 (Stephen Moreton Prichard), 33 (Wayland), 6-8, Cator trustees; 11-16 Dolphin family; 18-21, 40: Sir Alexander Grierson; 23-25 Donovan Hailstone; 26: *The Times*; 37: Richard Kendall; 29-30: Lidgett/MacDougall family; 35 & 36 Guy Obbard; 38-39: Anthony Warrick; 42: RBG Heritage Centre; 45: Gerald Brodribb; 46: David Kent-Lemon; 47: Wheen family

Illustrations elsewhere:
Front cover:
The Paragon in about 1875. Blackheath Society collection

Inside front cover:
The Paragon from the air. Aerofilms Ltd. 1959

Inside back cover:
The Paragon from the air. Blackheath Society collection. Photograph by kind permission of Michael Sullivan.

Back cover:
The author. Photograph by Iain Rhind

Page ii:
Modern photograph by kind permission of Mr Alec Wylie
Postcard of South Row in about 1902 from Blackheath Society images collection

Page 4:
South Row in about 1966: Blackheath Society collection

Appendix II:
Portrait of Elizabeth Robertson from the Charles Kadwell Collection, RBG Heritage Centre

Pictures at the end of chapters
page 14
Samuel Travers' Survey of the Royal Manor of East Greenwich, 1695-96. B Soc.

page 14
Drivers Brothers survey of the boundary of the ancient Royal Manor of East Greenwich, 1808. B Soc

page 36
Pigot's Commercial Directory, 1832. B Soc

page 53
Cricket on what was the home ground of the Paragon Cricket Club. Drawing by John Gilbert, May 1832. Royal Borough of Greenwich Heritage Centre

Page 54
Blackheath War Hospital Supply depot – August 1916. *BLG*

Page 62
Last advertisements for hotels and boarding houses, December 1939, before the onset of War. *BLG*

Page 73
Exhibitors at the Royal Academy Summer Exhibition. May 1940. *BLG*

Page 74
The Village in 1935. B Soc

Page 74
The Village in March 1945. B Soc

Page 83
Pond Road housing. Prof Richardson appointed July 1950. *BLG*

Page 84
Details of the London Development Plan. *BLG*.

Page 93
John Gower's Panorama of the Paragon and South Row, Society of Architectural Historians of Great Britain, 1987

Page 94
Advertisement for Messrs Wookey, estate agent, 1962. *BLG*

Page 104
The Paragon (1-8) in about 2003. B Soc.

Page 171
Paragon Place (west side) in 1938. The entrance to the Colonnade House stables on the extreme left. B Soc

The Keep Span Estate & The Paragon c1965. B Soc

Page 207
Blackheath Local Guide, August 1889

Bibliography & principal sources

Periodicals

Blackheath Gazette: 1986-1993

Blackheath Local Guide & District Reporter: 1889-1957

Blackheath Reporter: 1959-1966

The Guide: 1970-2000

Gentleman's Magazine: 1790-1850

Greenwich, Woolwich & Deptford Gazette: 1833-1839; later the Kentish Mercury and variant titles from 1840 to 1990

Kentish Independent: 1843-1990

The Times: 1785-2011

Times Digital: 1785-1985

West Kent Courier and variant titles from 1880-1889

Directories

Samuel Bagshaw: History, Gazetteer and Directory of the County of Kent, 1847

Clayton's Court Guide. London, 1830

Flashman & Daw: the Greenwich Directory 1859-1860. Greenwich. 1859

Green's Court Guide & Commercial Directory of Kent. 1867

Holden's Triennial Directories of London and 10 mile radius: 1799, 1802, 1805, 1808, 1811

Kelly's ("Buff Book") Directories of Blackheath, Lee, Greenwich & Lewisham: 1881, 1883-1937

Mason's Greenwich & Blackheath Shilling Directory and Handbook. Greenwich, 1852

Melville's Directory & Gazetteer of Kent. W & H Collingridge. London. 1858

J H Muzzall: Greenwich, Eltham, Lee, Blackheath & Lewisham Directory: 1869 & 1870. J H Muzzall & Co, Brighton

Pigot & Co's National London & Provincial Commercial Directory: editions 1823-1840.

Post Office Directory of Kent: editions 1845-1891

Post Office Directory of London & Suburbs: editions 1850-1980

William Robson: Commercial Directory of London & Six Home Counties. 1838

Underhill's London Directory: 1817 & 1822

Wilmshurst's Blackheath, Lee & Lewisham Directory of 1878-1879. Ebenezer Wilmshurst. Blackheath. 1879

Official and unpublished records

Transcripts of the registers of St Mary's Parish Church, Lewisham: 1751 to 1830

Electoral registers for the Parliamentary Borough of Greenwich: 1892-1982

Enumerated census returns for every tenth year: 1841 to 1911

Rate books:

    for the Parish (later Borough) of Greenwich: 1790-1930

    and churchwardens' accounts for the Parish of Charlton: 1790-1900

    for the Parish of Lewisham: 1817-1818; 1837; 1849; 1855; 1916-1930

Lewisham: Account book for the Highway Surveyor for the Parish of Lewisham: 1798-1812

Land Tax returns for the Parish of Lewisham: 1780-1832

Poll books for the County of Kent: various until 1869

Tithe schedules for the parishes of Charlton (1839), Greenwich (1844), Lee (1839) and Lewisham (1843)

Minute books of the Trustees of the New Cross Turnpike: 1797-1803

Drainage records for Greenwich & Lewisham Boards of Works then borough councils: 1856-1960

Parish registers of St Alfege, Greenwich: 1799-1815

Books, pamphlets etc

Aslet: Clive – The story of Greenwich. Fourth Estate. London. 1999

Baker Collection: L A J Baker material (various). Lewisham Council Heritage Library

Banbury: Philip: Shipbuilders of the Thames & Medway. David & Charles, Newton Abbot. 1971

Barker: Felix & Aldous: Tony – Guardians of the Heath. Blackheath Society. London. 2009

Bingham: Frederic – The "Borough" Pocket Guide to Blackheath. Edward J Burrow. Cheltenham, 1909

Birchenough: Edwyn & Josephine – A record made in 1967 of the memorial inscriptions on tombstones in

Bibliography

St Margaret's, Lee, Old Churchyard. Privately printed by the authors. London. 1982

Birchenough; Josephine & Blackmore: T A – Transcriptions of the Parish Registers of St Margaret's, Lee: 1755-1850. North West Kent Family History Society. 1979-1980

Blackheath Society: Annual Report and other publications 1937-2010

Blake: Lewis – Red Alert - South London 1939-1945. Published by the author. London. 1982

Boase: Frederick – Modern English Biography (and supplement) 1851-1910. Reprint edition by Frank Cass & Co. London. 1965

Bold: John – Greenwich. Yale University Press & English Heritage. New Haven & London. 2001

Bonwitt: W [illiam] – A History of the Paragon & Paragon House. Bookshop Blackheath. London. 1976

Bonwitt: W [illiam] – Michael Searles – a Georgian architect & surveyor. Architectural History Monograph No 3. Society of Architectural Historians of Great Britain. 1987

Brown: Charles Bernard - The conversion of old buildings into new homes for occupation and investment. B T Batsford. London. 1955

Colvin: Howard Montagu – A Biographical Dictionary of British Architects 1600-1840. Yale University Press. New Haven & London. Revised edition 2008

Coulter: John – Lewisham. Alan Sutton Publishing Ltd. Stroud. 1994.

Curl: James Stevens. Encyclopaedia of Architectural Terms. Donhead. London. 1993

Dictionary of National Biography. 2011. Oxford University Press.

Duncan: Leland Lewis & Kirby: Herbert Charles – Monumental inscriptions in the Church & Churchyard, St Mary's Parish Church, Lewisham. Charles North. Lee. 1889

Foster: Joseph – *Alumni Oxonienses* – members of the University of Oxford 1715-1886. Park & Company. Oxford. 1888

Glencross: Alan – The Buildings of Greenwich. London Borough of Greenwich. London. 1974

Greenwich Antiquarian Society: Transactions. 1905-1914

Greenwich & Lewisham Antiquarian Society – Transactions. 1920-1983

Greenwich: London Borough of – Greenwich & Blackheath Conservation Area. 1970

Hasted: Edward – History of Kent – Volume I: The Hundred of Blackheath. Edited by Henry Holman Drake. Mitchell & Hughes. London. 1886

Joyce: Patrick – Patronage & poverty in merchant society. A history of Morden College, 1695 to the present. Gresham Books and the Trustees of Morden College. Henley-on-Thames. 1982

Kendall: Franklin - Dearest Mother: Letters of Franklin Richardson Kendall (edited by Brian MacDonald). Lloyd's of London Press Ltd. 1988

Lansdell: Henry – Princess Aelfrida's Charity (a history of the charity of Sir John Morden). Burnside. Blackheath. 1916

Lewisham Antiquarian Society – Transactions 1887-1912

London County Council: Names of streets and places in the Administrative County of London. 1955 and various editions

Lewisham Local History Society: Transactions 1963-to date

Martin Collection: – Material (various) from the A R Martin Collection, Royal Borough of Greenwich Heritage Centre

May: Leonard Morgan – Copies of inscriptions in the old Charlton parish church (St Luke's) and the churchyard. Blackheath Press. London. 1908

Ramsey: Stanley & Harvey: J D M – Small Georgian houses and their details 1750-1820. Architectural Press. 1923. Revised edition 1977.

Rhind: Neil – Blackheath Village & Environs, Volume I (revised edition 1993); & Volume II (1983). Bookshop Blackheath Ltd. London.

Rhind: Neil – The Heath, a companion volume to Blackheath Village & Environs. Bookshop Blackheath Ltd. & Warwick Leadlay Gallery, London. 2002 (revised edition)

Simms: Barbara (editor) – Eric Lyons & Span. RIBA Publishing. London. 2006

Summerson: John – Georgian London. Pleiades Books (1945) & Pelican Books. London. (1969 edition)

Venn: John & Venn: J A – *Alumni Cantabrigiensis* – a biographical list of all known students, graduates etc .... of the University of Cambridge from earliest time to 1900. Cambridge. 1922

Ward: Frances (editor) - Parish registers of St Luke's Charlton, 1653-1850. Transcribed by Frances Ward and published by John G Smith. Charlton, London, 1977

Weinreb: Ben; Hibbert, Christopher; Keay, Julia; & Keay, John – The London Encyclopaedia. Macmillan. London. 3rd edition 2008

Who's Who? & Who Was Who? 1897-2010. A & C Black since 1897 and now available (including on-line) from Oxford University Press.

Index

Index

Wallinger: John Arnold (1797-1860), Sergeant at Law – 42, 153
Wallingford, Berkshire – 9
Walpole: Robert (Sir) (1676-1745) – 8
Walton: Thomas – 169, 170
Walton: William (1805-1889), solicitor – 42, 50, 153
Wanostrocht: Mrs Elizabeth (nee Heale) – 190
Wanostrocht: Nicholas (1745-1812), school proprietor – 190
Wanostrocht: Nicholas (1804-1876), cricketer (aka Felix) – 43, 50, 52, 190
Wanostrocht: Nicholas Gibbs (1833-1895), insurance agent – 190
War Damage Commission – 79
Warner: Simeon – 41
Warner: Isaac (1744-1822) – 41, 135, 202
Warner: Mrs Mary (1756-1842) – 135
Warner: Simeon (1786-1866), coal merchant – 44, 135, 189, 202
Warrick: Anthony – 69
Warrick: Anthony B – 65
Warrick: Mrs Evelyn Blanche
Warrick: Walter – 67
Warter jnr: Joseph Henry (1800-1852), cheesemonger – 44, 199
Warter snr: Joseph (1766-1839), cheesemonger – 199
Warter: Joseph – 190
Watson: Arthur (1873-1927), antique dealer – 45, 121
Wayne: Philip Arthur (1889-1963), schoolmaster – 76
Weatherall: Mrs – 189
Webber: Mrs – 66
Welby: Arthur Robert (1876-1935), architect – 61,77
Wells: John – 48
Wells: John (1761-1818), shipbuilder – 48, 180
Wells: William (1729-1805), ship builder – 180
Wells: William (1768-1847) – 180
Wemyss Road – 10, 59, 168
Wendt: Ernst Emile (1818-1892) – 133
Wesleyan Methodist Church, Blackheath Grove, 1863 – 142
West Greenwich Working Lads Institute – 179
West Grove – 11, 37, 39, 42, 48, 51, 77; No 8 – 191; No 14 – 176; Cambridge House – 13, 117; 17 (Manna Mead) – 19, 51, 119; Point House – 131
West India Dock Company – 139
West Kent Volunteer Militia – 196
West: Benjamin (1738-1820), artist – 27
Westcombe House, Westcombe Park – 135, 200
Westcombe Park – 147, 200
Westcombe Park Road: Nos 3-9 – 135; No 104 – 206; 116 – 117;
Westminster Abbey – 28
Weston's Academy, Greenwich – 48
Westrup: George – 193
Westrup: William Edward (1834-1909): miller and flour factor – 193
Wethered: Herbert Laurence – 206
Wheen: Charles (1860-1935) – 203
Wheen: Francis (1850-1925) – 203
Wheen: John – 203
Wheen: Richard (1808-1885), soap maker – 44, 50, 82, 203
White: John Meadows (1799-1863), solicitor – 43, 49, 166
White: Major George (1825-1902) – 179
White: William George (1837-1895), marble mason – 147
Whittaker: Henry – 160
Wickham: Evelyn Marjorie, hotelier – 134
Wilcoxon: Arthur (1839-1920), plate glass mfr – 135
Wilcoxon: Mrs Lucretia – 145
Wilcoxon: Robert (1801-1866) plate glass manufacturer – 41, 135
Wilkie & Soames Ltd , soap makers – 144
Wilkins: Miss D M – 155
Williams: William Richard, hotelier – 43, 179
Williams: William Robert – 58
Willoughby: Edward (1797-1873), solicitor – 50, 183
Wilson Carlile College, Vanbrugh Park – 168
Wilson: J – 162
Wilson: James Edward (1861-1931) – 130
Wilson: John Walter/s (1836/37-1912), wine merchant (Spain) – 121, 136
Wilson: R Macdonald (1868-1929) – 185
Wilson: Rev Thomas – 124
Wilson: Sir John Maryon (1803-1874) – 178
Wilson: Sir Thomas Maryon (1773-1821) – 34, 42, 48, 138
Winchester House, Independent Road – 55
Wingate: Maj-Gen Orde Charles (1903-1944), soldier – 154
Winter Golf Club (Blackheath) – 51
Wintoun Place, Blackheath Road – 111
Wissler: Frederick (1855-1924), sugar merchant – 147
Witenemers – 5
Witherby: Richard – 192
Wolffram: Henry (1831-1915), crammer – 197
Woodbastwick Hall, Norfolk – 103
Woodlands, Mycenae Road – 56, 147
Woods: Robert, gardener – 159
Wookey & Wookey, estate agents – 97
Woolwich – 37
Wormwood Scrubs – 87
Worsley jnr: Rev Henry (1820-1893) – 195
Worsley: Rev Henry (1783-1860) – 195
Worthington: Prof Arthur Mason (1852-1916) – 113
Wren: Sir Christopher (1632-1723) – 6
Wricklemarsh & House – 5, 9, 10, 11, 23, 28, 38
Wricklemarsh School for boys and girls – 71, 72, 137
Wright: George Edward (1875-1936), electrical engineer – 148
Wright: Mrs Elizabeth Annette (d1932) – 151
Wyesham House, Monmouth – 188

X-Y-Z

XL Lawn Tennis Club – 148
Yews, Blackheath – 61
Yorke, Rosenberg & Mardell, architects – 96
Young jnr: George William (fl1792-1822), broker – 189
Young snr: George (1761-1823) – 189
Young: Adam (d1846) – 189
Young: George – 48, 203
Young: Miss Anne Bryan (Mrs Warner) – 202
Zeppelin raid, 1916 – 58
Z-rocket batteries – 64

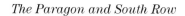

The Paragon and South Row